CliffsNotes®

FTCE Elementary Education K–6

CliffsNotes®

FTCE Elementary Education K–6

2ND EDITION

by
Janet B. Andreasen, Ph.D., Lee-Anne T. Spalding, Ed.D.,
and Enrique Ortiz, Ed.D.

Houghton Mifflin Harcourt
Boston • New York

About the Authors

Janet B. Andreasen, Ph.D., is a lecturer for mathematics education and coordinator of secondary education programs at the University of Central Florida. She is a former Seminole County, Florida, high school teacher. She lives in Winter Springs, Florida, with her husband, Robbie, and two children, Zachary and Sarah.

Lee-Anne T. Spalding, Ed.D., is a former Seminole County, Florida, public school educator and is currently a lecturer at the University of Central Florida. She has previously authored 12 nonfiction library market books for elementary age students. She lives in Oviedo, Florida, with her husband, Brett, and two sons, Graham and Gavin.

Enrique Ortiz, Ed.D., is an associate professor at the College of Education and Human Performance, University of Central Florida. Since 1987, he has been very active in the mathematics education profession. He lives in Oviedo, Florida, with his wife, Diana, and three children, Enrique Gabriel, Samuel, and Natalie.

Dedications

To my husband, Robbie, and children, Zachary and Sarah. —JBA

To the Elementary Education students at the University of Central Florida; to Brett, Graham, and Gavin for allowing me the time to reach new and greater heights in my professional career. —LTS

To my wife, Diana, and sons and daughter, Enrique G., Samuel, and Natalie. —EO

Editorial

Executive Editor: Greg Tubach

Senior Editor: Christina Stambaugh

Copy Editor: Lynn Northrup

Technical Editors: Andrew Beames, Jane Burstein, Jeff Johnson, Tom Page, Scott Ryan, and Mary Jane Sterling

Proofreader: Donna Wright

CliffsNotes® FTCE Elementary Education K–6, 2nd Edition

Copyright © 2015 by Houghton Mifflin Harcourt Publishing Company

All rights reserved.

Cover image © Shutterstock / Mavrick

Library of Congress Control Number: 2014955761
ISBN: 978-0-544-31353-8 (pbk)

Printed in the United States of America
DOO 10 9 8 7 6 5 4   4500587753

For information about permission to reproduce selections from this book, write to trade.permissions@hmhco.com or to Permissions, Houghton Mifflin Harcourt Publishing Company, 3 Park Avenue, 19th Floor, New York, New York 10016.

www.hmhco.com

Table of Contents

Introduction

General Description

The Florida Teacher Certification Examination (FTCE) Elementary Education (K–6) Subject Area Examination (SAE) is designed to assess knowledge about teaching elementary grades including the areas of Language Arts and Reading, Social Science, Science, and Mathematics. The test is comprised of approximately 220 multiple-choice questions divided into four subtests as follows:

- Language Arts and Reading: approximately 60 questions
- Social Science: approximately 55 questions
- Science: approximately 55 questions
- Mathematics: approximately 50 questions

Each multiple-choice question contains four response options—A, B, C, and D. Your score is determined by how many questions you answer correctly. There is no penalty for incorrect answers. You must pass all four subtests to pass the entire examination. You are given a total of 4½ hours to complete the test, broken down by subtest as follows:

- Language Arts and Reading: 65 minutes
- Social Sciences: 65 minutes
- Science: 70 minutes
- Mathematics: 70 minutes

A 15-minute break is given for examinees taking three or more subtests in one sitting.

The Role of the Elementary Education (K–6) Subject Area Examination in Teacher Certification

The Florida Teacher Certification Examinations include three examinations: General Knowledge Test (GKT), Professional Education Examination (PEd), and Subject Area Examinations (SAEs). One part of becoming a certified teacher in the state of Florida is to pass all three examinations. The SAEs determine certification areas. The Elementary Education (K–6) Examination is a Subject Area Examination.

The Elementary Education (K–6) Competencies

The Elementary Education (K–6) test is based on a set of 20 competencies that are meant to ensure a breadth of knowledge of content and pedagogy appropriate for teaching elementary grades in Florida public schools. The Elementary Education (K–6) test is divided into four subtests: Language Arts and Reading, Social Science, Science, and Mathematics. Each subtest is comprised of five competencies. Each competency is further defined by a list of knowledge, skills, and behaviors that demonstrate the competency. As listed in the *Competencies and Skills Required for Teacher Certification in Florida,* 20th Edition (available at www.fldoe.org/asp/ftce/pdf/ftce20edition.pdf), the competencies/skills and their approximate number of questions on the FTCE Elementary Education (K–6) SAE include the following:

Language Arts and Reading

The Language Arts and Reading competencies include five areas: 1) Knowledge of the reading process;
2) Knowledge of literary analysis and genres; 3) Knowledge of language and the writing process; 4) Knowledge

of literacy instruction and assessments; and 5) Knowledge of communication and media literacy. These five competencies encompass approximately **60 questions** of the examination.

Competency 1: Knowledge of the Reading Process (approximately 17 questions)

1. Identify the content of emergent literacy (e.g., oral language development, phonological awareness, alphabet knowledge, decoding, concepts of print, motivation, text structures, written language development).

2. Identify the processes, skills, and stages of word recognition that lead to effective decoding (e.g., pre-alphabetic, partial-alphabetic, full-alphabetic, graphophonemic, morphemic).

3. Select and apply instructional methods for promoting the development of decoding skills (e.g., continuous blending, chunking).

4. Distinguish among the components of reading fluency (e.g., accuracy, automaticity, rate, prosody).

5. Choose and apply instructional methods for developing reading fluency (e.g., practice with high-frequency words, readers theater, repeated readings).

6. Identify and differentiate instructional methods and strategies for increasing vocabulary acquisition across the content areas (e.g., word analysis, author's word choice, context clues, multiple exposures).

7. Identify and evaluate instructional methods and strategies for facilitating students' reading comprehension (e.g., summarizing, self-monitoring, questioning, use of graphic and semantic organizers, think alouds, recognizing story structure).

8. Identify essential comprehension skills (e.g., main idea, supporting details and facts, author's purpose, point of view, inference, conclusion).

9. Determine appropriate uses of multiple representations of information for a variety of purposes (e.g., charts, tables, graphs, pictures, print and nonprint media).

10. Determine and analyze strategies for developing critical-thinking skills such as analysis, synthesis, and evaluation (e.g., making connections and predictions, questioning, summarizing, question generating).

11. Evaluate and select appropriate instructional strategies for teaching a variety of informational and literary text.

Competency 2: Knowledge of Literary Analysis and Genres (approximately 10 questions)

1. Differentiate among characteristics and elements of a variety of literary genres (e.g., realistic fiction, fantasy, poetry, informational texts).

2. Identify and analyze terminology and intentional use of literary devices (e.g., simile, metaphor, personification, onomatopoeia, hyperbole).

3. Evaluate and select appropriate multicultural texts based on purpose, relevance, cultural sensitivity, and developmental appropriateness.

4. Identify and evaluate appropriate techniques for varying student response to texts (e.g., think-pair-share, reading response journals, evidence-based discussion).

Competency 3: Knowledge of Language and the Writing Process (approximately 10 questions)

1. Identify and evaluate the developmental stages of writing (e.g., drawing, dictating, writing).

2. Differentiate stages of the writing process (e.g., prewriting, drafting, revising, editing, publishing).

3. Distinguish among the modes of writing (e.g., narrative, informative/explanatory, argument).

4. Select the appropriate mode of writing for a variety of occasions, purposes, and audiences.

5. Identify and apply instructional methods for writing conventions (e.g., spelling, punctuation, capitalization, syntax, word usage).

6. Apply instructional methods for teaching writer's craft across genres (e.g., precise language, figurative language, linking words, temporal words, dialogue, sentence variety).

Competency 4: Knowledge of Literacy Instruction and Assessments (approximately 13 questions)

1. Distinguish among different types of assessments (e.g., norm-referenced, criterion-referenced, diagnostic, curriculum-based) and their purposes and characteristics.

2. Select and apply oral and written methods for assessing student progress (e.g., informal reading inventories, fluency checks, rubrics, story retelling, portfolios).

3. Analyze assessment data (e.g., screening, progress monitoring, diagnostic) to guide instructional decisions and differentiate instruction.

4. Analyze and interpret students' formal and informal assessment results to inform students and stakeholders.

5. Evaluate the appropriateness of assessment instruments and practices.

6. Select appropriate classroom organizational formats (e.g., literature circles, small groups, individuals, workshops, reading centers, multiage groups) for specific instructional objectives.

7. Evaluate methods for the diagnosis, prevention, and intervention of common emergent literacy difficulties.

Competency 5: Knowledge of Communication and Media Literacy (approximately 10 questions)

1. Identify characteristics of penmanship (e.g., legibility, letter formation, spacing).

2. Distinguish among listening and speaking strategies (e.g., questioning, paraphrasing, eye contact, voice, gestures).

3. Identify and apply instructional methods (e.g., collaborative conversation, collaborative discussion, presentation) for developing listening and speaking skills.

4. Select and evaluate a wide array of resources (e.g., Internet, printed material, artifacts, visual media, primary sources) for research and presentation.

5. Determine and apply the ethical process (e.g., citation, paraphrasing) for collecting and presenting authentic information while avoiding plagiarism.

6. Identify and evaluate current technology available for use in educational settings.

Social Science

Social science is broken down into five competencies: 1) Knowledge of effective instructional practice and assessment of the social sciences; 2) Knowledge of time, continuity, and change (i.e., history); 3) Knowledge of people, places, and environment (i.e., geography); 4) Knowledge of government and the citizen (i.e., government and civics); and 5) Knowledge of production, distribution, and consumption (i.e., economics). These five competencies encompass approximately **55 questions** of the examination.

Competency 1: Knowledge of Effective Instructional Practice and Assessment of the Social Sciences (approximately 10 questions)

1. Select appropriate resources for instructional delivery of social science concepts, including complex informational text.

2. Identify appropriate resources for planning for instruction of social science concepts.

3. Choose appropriate methods for assessing social science concepts.

4. Determine appropriate learning environments for social science lessons.

Competency 2: Knowledge of Time, Continuity, and Change (i.e., History) (approximately 14 questions)

1. Identify and analyze historical events that are related by cause and effect.
2. Analyze the sequential nature of historical events using timelines.
3. Analyze examples of primary and secondary source documents for historical perspective.
4. Analyze the impacts of the cultural contributions and technological developments of Africa; the Americas; Asia, including the Middle East; and Europe.
5. Identify the significant historical leaders and events that have influenced Eastern and Western civilizations.
6. Determine the causes and consequences of exploration, settlement, and growth on various cultures.
7. Interpret the ways that individuals and events have influenced economic, social, and political institutions in the world, nation, or state.
8. Analyze immigration and settlement patterns that have shaped the history of the United States.
9. Identify how various cultures contributed to the unique social, cultural, economic, and political features of Florida.
10. Identify the significant contributions of the early and classical civilizations.

Competency 3: Knowledge of People, Places, and Environment (i.e., Geography) (approximately 10 questions)

1. Identify and apply the six essential elements of geography (i.e., the world in spatial terms, places and regions, physical systems, human systems, environment and society, uses of geography), including the specific terms for each element.
2. Analyze and interpret maps and other graphic representations of physical and human systems.
3. Identify and evaluate tools and technologies (e.g., maps, globe, GPS, satellite imagery) used to acquire, process, and report information from a spatial perspective.
4. Interpret statistics that show how places differ in their human and physical characteristics.
5. Analyze ways in which people adapt to an environment through the production and use of clothing, food, and shelter.
6. Determine the ways tools and technological advances affect the environment.
7. Identify and analyze physical, cultural, economic, and political reasons for the movement of people in the world, nation, or state.
8. Evaluate the impact of transportation and communication networks on the economic development in different regions.
9. Compare and contrast major regions of the world, nation, or state.

Competency 4: Knowledge of Government and the Citizen (i.e., Government and Civics) (approximately 11 questions)

1. Distinguish between the structure, functions, and purposes of federal, state, and local government.
2. Compare and contrast the rights and responsibilities of a citizen in the world, nation, state, and community.
3. Identify and interpret major concepts of the U.S. Constitution and other historical documents.
4. Compare and contrast the ways the legislative, executive, and judicial branches share powers and responsibility.
5. Analyze the U.S. electoral system and the election process.
6. Identify and analyze the relationships between social, economic, and political rights and the historical documents that secure these rights in the United States.
7. Identify and analyze the processes of the U.S. legal system.

Competency 5: Knowledge of Production, Distribution, and Consumption (i.e., Economics) (approximately 10 questions)

1. Determine ways that scarcity affects the choices made by governments and individuals.
2. Compare and contrast the characteristics and importance of currency.
3. Identify and analyze the role of markets from production through distribution to consumption.
4. Identify and analyze factors to consider when making consumer decisions.
5. Analyze the economic interdependence between nations (e.g., trade, finance, movement of labor).
6. Identify human, natural, and capital resources and evaluate how these resources are used in the production of goods and services.

Science

Science includes five competencies: 1) Knowledge of effective science instruction; 2) Knowledge of the nature of science; 3) Knowledge of physical sciences; 4) Knowledge of Earth and space; and 5) Knowledge of life science. These five competencies encompass approximately **55 questions** of the examination.

Competency 1: Knowledge of Effective Science Instruction (approximately 11 questions)

1. Analyze and apply developmentally appropriate research-based strategies for teaching science practices.
2. Select and apply safe and effective instructional strategies to utilize manipulatives, models, scientific equipment, real-world examples, and print and digital representations to support and enhance science instruction.
3. Identify and analyze strategies for formal and informal learning experiences to provide science curriculum that promotes students' innate curiosity and active inquiry (e.g., hands-on experiences, active engagement in the natural world, student interaction).
4. Select and analyze collaborative strategies to help students explain concepts, to introduce and clarify formal science terms, and to identify misconceptions.
5. Identify and apply appropriate reading strategies, mathematical practices, and science-content materials to enhance science instruction for learners at all levels.
6. Apply differentiated strategies in science instruction and assessments based on student needs.
7. Identify and apply ways to organize and manage a classroom for safe, effective science teaching that reflect state safety procedures and restrictions (e.g., procedures, equipment, disposal of chemicals, classroom layout, use of living organisms).
8. Select and apply appropriate technology, science tools and measurement units for students' use in data collection and the pursuit of science.
9. Select and analyze developmentally appropriate diagnostic, formative and summative assessments to evaluate prior knowledge, guide instruction, and evaluate student achievement.
10. Choose scientifically and professionally responsible content and activities that are socially and culturally sensitive.

Competency 2: Knowledge of the Nature of Science (approximately 10 questions)

1. Analyze the dynamic nature of science models, laws, mechanisms, and theories that explain natural phenomena (e.g., durability, tentativeness, replication, reliance on evidence).
2. Identify and apply science and engineering practices through integrated process skills (e.g., observing, classifying, predicting, hypothesizing, designing and carrying out investigations, developing and using models, constructing and communicating explanations).

3. Differentiate between the characteristics of experiments (e.g., multiple trials, control groups, variables) and other types of scientific investigations (e.g., observations, surveys).

4. Identify and analyze attitudes and dispositions underlying scientific thinking (e.g., curiosity, openness to new ideas, appropriate skepticism, cooperation).

5. Identify and select appropriate tools, including digital technologies, and units of measurement for various science tasks.

6. Evaluate and interpret pictorial representations, charts, tables, and graphs of authentic data from scientific investigations to make predictions, construct explanations, and support conclusions.

7. Identify and analyze ways in which science is an interdisciplinary process and interconnected to STEM disciplines (i.e., science, technology, engineering, mathematics).

8. Analyze the interactions of science and technology with society including cultural, ethical, economic, political, and global factors.

Competency 3: Knowledge of Physical Sciences (approximately 11 questions)

1. Identify and differentiate among the physical properties of matter (e.g., mass, volume, texture, hardness, freezing point).

2. Identify and differentiate between physical and chemical changes (e.g., tearing, burning, rusting).

3. Compare the properties of matter during phase changes through addition and/or removal of energy (e.g., boiling, condensation, evaporation).

4. Differentiate between the properties of homogeneous mixtures (i.e., solutions) and heterogeneous mixtures.

5. Identify examples of and relationships among atoms, elements, molecules, and compounds.

6. Identify and compare potential and kinetic energy.

7. Differentiate among forms of energy, transformations of energy, and their real-world applications (e.g., chemical, electrical, mechanical, electromagnetic, heat, light, sound).

8. Distinguish among temperature, heat, and forms of heat transfer (e.g., conduction, convection, radiation).

9. Analyze the functionality of an electrical circuit based on its conductors, insulators, and components.

10. Identify and apply the characteristics of contact forces (e.g., push, pull, friction), at-a-distance forces (e.g., magnetic, gravitational, electrostatic), and their effects on matter (e.g., motion, speed).

Competency 4: Knowledge of Earth and Space (approximately 10 questions)

1. Identify characteristics of geologic formations (e.g., volcanoes, canyons, mountains) and the mechanisms by which they are changed (e.g., physical and chemical weathering, erosion deposition).

2. Identify and distinguish among major groups and properties of rocks and minerals and the processes of their formations.

3. Identify and analyze the characteristics of soil, its components and profile, and the process of soil formation.

4. Identify and analyze processes by which energy from the Sun is transferred (e.g., radiation, conduction, convection) through Earth's systems (e.g., biosphere, hydrosphere, geosphere, atmosphere, cryosphere).

5. Identify and analyze the causes and effects of atmospheric processes and conditions (e.g., water cycle, weather, climate).

6. Identify and analyze various conservation methods and their effectiveness in relation to renewable and nonrenewable natural resources.

7. Analyze the Sun-Earth-Moon system in order to explain repeated patterns such as day and night, phases of the Moon, tides, and seasons.

8. Compare and differentiate the composition and various relationships among the objects of our Solar System (e.g., Sun, planets, moons, asteroids, comets).

9. Identify major events in the history of space exploration and their effects on society.

Competency 5: Knowledge of Life Science (approximately 13 questions)

1. Identify and compare the characteristics of living and nonliving things.

2. Analyze the cell theory as it relates to the functional and structural hierarchy of all living things.

3. Identify and compare the structures and functions of plant and animal cells.

4. Classify living things into major groups (i.e., Linnaean system) and compare according to characteristics (e.g., physical features, behaviors, development).

5. Compare and contrast the structures, functions, and interactions of human and other animal organ systems (e.g., respiration, reproduction, digestion).

6. Distinguish among infectious agents (e.g., viruses, bacteria, fungi, parasites), their transmission, and their effects on the human body.

7. Identify and analyze the processes of heredity and natural selection and the scientific theory of evolution.

8. Analyze the interdependence of living things with each other and with their environment (e.g., food webs, ecosystems, pollution).

9. Identify and analyze plant structures and the processes of photosynthesis, transpiration, and reproduction (i.e., sexual, asexual).

10. Predict the responses of plants to various stimuli (e.g., heat, light, gravity).

11. Identify and compare the life cycles and predictable ways plants and animals change as they grow, develop, and age.

Mathematics

Mathematics includes five competencies. Assessment of the mathematics competencies and skills will use real-world problems when feasible. The competencies for mathematics include: 1) Knowledge of student thinking and instructional practices; 2) Knowledge of operations, algebraic thinking, counting and number in base ten; 3) Knowledge of fractions, ratios, and integers; 4) Knowledge of measurement, data analysis, and statistics; and 5) Knowledge of geometric concepts. The mathematics competencies encompass approximately **50 questions** of the examination.

Competency 1: Knowledge of Student Thinking and Instructional Practices (approximately 13 questions)

1. Analyze and apply appropriate mathematical concepts, procedures, and professional vocabulary (e.g., subitize, transitivity, iteration, tiling) to evaluate student solutions.

2. Analyze and discriminate among various problem structures with unknowns in all positions in order to develop student understanding of operations (e.g., put-together/take-apart, arrays/area).

3. Analyze and evaluate the validity of a student's mathematical model or argument (e.g., inventive strategies, standard algorithms) used for problem solving.

4. Interpret individual student mathematics assessment data (e.g., diagnostic, formative, progress monitoring) to guide instructional decisions and differentiate instruction.

5. Select and analyze structured experiences for small and large groups of students according to the cognitive complexity of the task.

6. Analyze learning progressions to show how students' mathematical knowledge, skills, and understanding develop over time.

7. Distinguish among the components of math fluency (i.e., accuracy, automaticity, rate, flexibility).

Competency 2: Knowledge of Operations, Algebraic Thinking, Counting and Number in Base Ten (approximately 14 questions)

1. Interpret and extend multiple representations of patterns and functional relationships by using tables, graphs, equations, expressions, and verbal descriptions.
2. Select the representation of an algebraic expression, equation, or inequality that models a real-world situation.
3. Analyze and apply the properties of equality and operations in the context of interpreting solutions.
4. Determine whether two algebraic expressions are equivalent by applying properties of operations or equality.
5. Evaluate expressions with parentheses, brackets, and braces.
6. Analyze and apply strategies (e.g., models, estimation, reasonableness) to solve multistep word problems.
7. Apply number theory concepts (e.g., primes, composites, multiples, factors, parity, rules of divisibility).
8. Identify strategies (e.g., compensation, combining tens and ones) based on place value to perform multidigit arithmetic.

Competency 3: Knowledge of Fractions, Ratios, and Integers (approximately 9 questions)

1. Compare fractions, integers, and integers with integer exponents and place them on a number line.
2. Convert among standard measurement units within and between measurement systems (e.g., metric, U.S. customary) in the context of multistep, real-world problems.
3. Solve problems involving addition, subtraction, multiplication, and division of fractions, including mixing whole numbers and fractions, decimals and percents by using visual models and equations to represent the problems and their solutions.
4. Select the representation (e.g., linear, area, set model) that best represents the problem and solution, given a word problem or equation involving fractions.
5. Solve real-world problems involving ratios and proportions.

Competency 4: Knowledge of Measurement, Data Analysis, and Statistics (approximately 8 questions)

1. Calculate and interpret statistics of variability (e.g., range, mean, absolute deviation) and central tendency (e.g., mean, median).
2. Analyze and interpret data through the use of frequency tables and graphs.
3. Select appropriate measurement units to solve problems involving estimates and measurements.
4. Evaluate the choice of measures of center and variability, with respect to the shape of the data distribution and the context in which the data were gathered.
5. Solve problems involving distance, time, liquid volume, mass, and money, which may include units expressed as fractions or decimals.

Competency 5: Knowledge of Geometric Concepts (approximately 6 questions)

1. Apply geometric properties and relationships to solve problems involving perimeter, area, surface area, and volume.
2. Identify and locate ordered pairs in all four quadrants of a rectangular coordinate system.
3. Identify and analyze properties of three-dimensional shapes using formal mathematical terms such as volume, faces, edges, and vertices.
4. Classify two-dimensional figures in a hierarchy based on mathematical properties.

Types of Questions

There are five types of questions included on the Elementary Education (K–6) SAE. All questions are multiple-choice format with four possible choices.

- **Scenario:** Examine a classroom situation or student composition. Then select the response option that best answers a question, recommends a course of action, or gives the appropriate evaluation or teacher comment.
- **Sentence Completion:** Select the response option that best completes the sentence.
- **Direct Question:** Choose the response option that best answers the question.
- **Word Problem:** Apply mathematical principles to solve a real-world problem.
- **Graphics:** Choose the option that best answers a question involving a number line, a geometric figure, graphs of lines or curves, a table, or a chart.

Common Core State Standards

The Common Core State Standards are a set of preK–12 standards, which 43 states have adopted as their state standards. The CCSS were developed by the National Governor's Association Center for Best Practices (NGA Center) and the Council of Chief State School Officers (CCSSO) and describe the knowledge preK–12 students should obtain at each grade level, along with practices in which students should be engaged as they learn. There are two sections of the CCSS: Mathematics and English Language Arts. They are designed to provide a consistent, clear understanding of what students are expected to learn, so teachers and parents know what they need to do to help them. The standards are designed to be robust and relevant to the real world, reflecting the knowledge and skills that our young people need for success in college and careers (www.corestandards.org/). The full standards documents are available at www.corestandards.org/read-the-standards/. Florida has adopted a slightly modified version of the CCSS as their state standards and, as such, teachers in Florida are required to teach them in schools. The competencies for certification are in alignment with the knowledge expected of teachers and students in K–6 environments with the CCSS in place.

Registering for the Test

You must register for the FTCE: Elementary Education (K–6) Subject Area Examination prior to taking it. The exam is administered as a computer-based exam.

Time slots are filled on a first-come, first-served basis. Computer-based testing sites are available throughout Florida, and some out-of-state sites are also available. No registration deadlines exist for computer-based examinations; however, you are encouraged to register as early as possible for choice of time and site.

At the conclusion of the computer-based examination, you will receive an unofficial score report. Official score reports will be mailed within 4 weeks after completion of the examination.

Registration

Registration is completed online at www.fl.nesinc.com/FL_Register.asp. Test fees are paid at the time of registration.

When you register, you will be asked for codes for school districts or colleges and universities to which you wish a copy of your score report be sent. The codes are available on the website. If you are already working in a school district or are a student in an initial teacher preparation program in which the certification examinations are required for graduation, be sure to indicate the appropriate code(s) on your registration form. You will receive an official score report regardless of whether you choose to have additional score reports sent to school districts or colleges and universities. See www.fl.nesinc.com/ for additional information as well as the codes and forms for registration.

Fees for Exams

As of January 1, 2013, the fee to take any Subject Area Examination for the FTCE is $200 for the first attempt (all subtests). If you don't pass a particular subsection, the retake fees are as follows:

- Single subtest retake: $150
- Two subtests retake: $200
- Three or more subtests retake: $220

Day of the Test

The following items must be brought with you to the testing site:

- Your admission ticket: This indicates what test you are taking, the test center/site, test date, and appointment time.
- Proper identification:
  - You must bring two valid and unexpired forms of identification that are printed in English.
  - One must be a government-issued identification that must have a clear photograph and your signature, such as a driver's license, state-issued identification card, United States military ID (with visible signature), or passport.
  - One additional form of identification that must have either a photo or a signature. You may use a second item listed above or a supplemental identification such as a Social Security card or a student ID. If you do not have proper identification, you will not be permitted to test. If you are refused admission, you will not receive a refund or transfer of fees.
- Your photograph will be taken, and you will be given the forms entitled "Important Testing Information and Agreement to the Testing Rules" and "Important Information About Cheating Behaviors and Test Score Invalidations." (These forms are also available at www.fl.nesinc.com/FL_bulletinforms.asp.) You will also be asked to sign the test center log book that indicates you have read the guidelines and understand the procedures, which will be used for computer-based testing.
- The following items are not allowed at any test site:
  - Smoking
  - Visitors
  - Weapons of any kind
- The following items are not allowed in the testing room:
  - Cell phones or any other electronic communication devices, even if it has an on/off switch
  - Scratch paper or written notes of any kind
  - Dictionaries or any other books
  - Audio devices (e.g., MP3, CD)
  - Calculators (one will be provided if allowed for the specific test)
  - Watches of any kind
  - Food or drinks, including water

You should report to the testing site at least 30–45 minutes prior to your scheduled testing time. You will be provided with a secure place to store your belongings while you are taking the exam. You may wish to bring a sweater or jacket. A reference sheet is provided for the mathematics subtest. (A reference sheet similar to the one you will receive at the test center appears in Appendix C of this book, pages 343–344.)

During the test, you may take restroom breaks as needed; however, any time you take for a restroom break is considered part of your allocated test time. You may not leave the testing room except to go to the restroom until you have been officially dismissed by a test administrator. You may not communicate in any way with any other test-takers. The examination may be videotaped.

When you have completed the examination, you can ask to be dismissed from the testing site if the time allotted is not completed yet. Your test materials will be collected and you may not return to the testing site.

How to Use This Book

The following are some tips for you to consider during the preparation period before taking the FTCE Elementary Education (K–6) Subject Area Examination. These ideas should help you analyze and focus your preparation time as you get ready to take the test.

Develop a Focusing Process

The practice tests provided in this book will help you prepare to take the actual FTCE Elementary Education (K–6) Examination. It is a good idea that you read all the background information provided in this book and identify all the areas that the actual test covers: Language Arts and Reading, Social Science, Science, and Mathematics. Begin by taking the diagnostic test that follows this chapter. The diagnostic test will help you to identify potential areas of weakness and strength.

Take a close look at the competency reviews, chapters 2–5. These reviews help you to focus your studies before you take the practice tests and to prepare for taking the actual test. After reviewing these competencies, you should make a list of the competency/skill areas for which you feel you need more background or practice and for which you feel less familiar and confident. The two full-length practice exams also should help you get acquainted with the format of the FTCE Elementary Education (K–6) Subject Area Examination. Check the resources you need to start studying in more detail. Study each of the topics covered in the test, starting with the ones you need more time to study according to your diagnostic test results. Also, take a look at the glossary of important terms in the back of this book. At the end, you should have studied all areas, both those in which you are familiar and less familiar. Do not leave any topic out, and spend sufficient time on each topic.

Setting aside time for your studies before you take the practice tests is very important. You want to have terms, formulas, concepts, and skills fresh in your mind for the practice and actual tests. Select the resources that work best for you to use during this study time. You might also need a tutor, teacher, mentor, advisor, or a study group for support and extra help. However, you should take into account your preferences and study habits as you set a sound study plan.

After carefully studying for the test, find a quiet place (no phone, cell phone, television, radio, stereo, or other forms of electronic entertainment), take the first practice test, and spend 4½ hours broken down by subtest as indicated in the practice test answering the questions. (To mimic a live testing experience, you can take a 15-minute break.)

You should probably use a desk for this and avoid any disruption. This gives you an idea on how to time yourself.

Remember that every person is different in terms of timing. You need to know yourself and the speed that is comfortable for you. For any questions that require computations, you should write your solution process as you work on the questions with as much detail and as clearly as possible. These notes are very helpful when you start evaluating your solutions. Check the answers for the first practice test and see whether you had any problems by competency. Are there any major areas of concern or priority? This gives you another opportunity to narrow down and focus your preparation priorities. We recommend that you go back and study everything a bit more, with an emphasis on the areas of need. Once again, after carefully studying for the test, find a quiet place and take the second practice test. Check the answers for the second practice test and, if you need to, study other competencies before taking the actual test.

After these focusing exercises, you should have a better idea of what the actual FTCE Elementary Education (K–6) Subject Area Examination entails, and if you are ready to take it.

Check the Resources You Need

After you set and focus your preparation priorities, you are ready to find the resources you need. Think about your coursework background and find any college textbooks; web links; class notes; videos; publications from local, state, and national professional organizations; or other material that might help you study for the test. We have included a list of resources in this book that you can use to help with this selection process. You should organize the resources you have in terms of your preparation priorities and use them in that order. Remember to review all the topics—even those you feel you know well.

Refer to the Answer Explanations

Answer explanations are provided at the end of each practice test. Use the answer explanations to help you understand possible solutions and improve your test-taking ability. You should not take more than one practice exam per day. You need some time in between taking the exams to review your answers and possibly readdress your study priorities.

Get R-E-A-D-Y Before the Test!

The following are some ideas to keep in mind before you take the test:

- **R**est and sleep well several days before the test. You will not do as well if you are not rested and feel tired or tense.
- **E**at well. A nutritious and balanced breakfast and lunch (if the test is taken in the afternoon) can go a long way. If you will be taking examinations during both the morning and afternoon testing sessions, you might want to bring along something to eat during the break. Food is not allowed in the testing room.
- **A**ccessories you need for the test:
  - Your admission ticket.
  - Proper identification. Remember, you must bring two valid and unexpired forms of identification that are printed in English. The first identification must be government issued and must have a clear photograph and your signature, such as a driver's license, state-issued identification card, United States military ID (with visible signature), or passport. The second identification, which you may be asked to produce, must have either a photo or a signature, such as a Social Security card or a student ID. If you do not have proper identification, you will not be permitted to test.
- **D**ress comfortably and in layers so you can adapt to the testing room conditions. It is better to wear soft-soled shoes so that you do not disturb others if you need to leave your seat.
- **Y**ou need to relax and get **R-E-A-D-Y.** Leave plenty of time to get to the test session without pressure or anxiety. Remember, you should arrive 30–45 minutes before the testing time. That way, you will be as relaxed as possible and ready to begin the test.

Get Double R-E-A-D-Y During the Test!

The following are some additional ideas to keep in mind during the test:

- **R**ead and review the directions carefully (at least twice). Make sure that you understand and follow the instructions for the test and for each item of the test. This first step is crucial. When answering multiple-choice questions, make sure that you read all of the answer choices before choosing an answer. Remember that you are selecting the best possible answer out of four choices.
- For computational problems: **E**stimate and use common sense before calculating problems; this should give you a rough idea of what the answer should be before you start to work on the problem. You can also use your estimate to check your final answer and calculation errors. Sometimes, with multiple-choice items, you can eliminate one or two of the choices that contain errors or don't make sense and then choose the best

answer out of the remaining choices. You should mark an answer to the multiple-choice items, even if you are not sure of the correct answer. Your score is not reduced because of wrong answers. However, you should attempt to figure out the best answer before guessing.

- **A**lways refer to the original directions and context of the problem, especially when an answer doesn't make sense. You might have missed something about the problem setting. The test contains general directions for the examination as a whole, and specific directions for individual questions and, in some cases, for a group of questions. If you do not understand a specific direction, raise your hand and ask the test administrator.

- **D**ouble-check your answer choice. Don't skip steps. Work carefully and avoid accidental computational or reasoning errors. Check the accuracy of your answers for the multiple-choice items, and make sure that they were marked appropriately. However, don't overdo your checking. Remember to time and pace yourself. Do not rush to finish.

- **Y**ou can do it! You are **R-E-A-D-Y!**

Chapter 1

Diagnostic Test

Answer Sheet

	Language Arts and Reading	Social Science	Science	Mathematics
1	Ⓐ Ⓑ Ⓒ Ⓓ	Ⓐ Ⓑ Ⓒ Ⓓ	Ⓐ Ⓑ Ⓒ Ⓓ	Ⓐ Ⓑ Ⓒ Ⓓ
2	Ⓐ Ⓑ Ⓒ Ⓓ	Ⓐ Ⓑ Ⓒ Ⓓ	Ⓐ Ⓑ Ⓒ Ⓓ	Ⓐ Ⓑ Ⓒ Ⓓ
3	Ⓐ Ⓑ Ⓒ Ⓓ	Ⓐ Ⓑ Ⓒ Ⓓ	Ⓐ Ⓑ Ⓒ Ⓓ	Ⓐ Ⓑ Ⓒ Ⓓ
4	Ⓐ Ⓑ Ⓒ Ⓓ	Ⓐ Ⓑ Ⓒ Ⓓ	Ⓐ Ⓑ Ⓒ Ⓓ	Ⓐ Ⓑ Ⓒ Ⓓ
5	Ⓐ Ⓑ Ⓒ Ⓓ	Ⓐ Ⓑ Ⓒ Ⓓ	Ⓐ Ⓑ Ⓒ Ⓓ	Ⓐ Ⓑ Ⓒ Ⓓ
6	Ⓐ Ⓑ Ⓒ Ⓓ	Ⓐ Ⓑ Ⓒ Ⓓ	Ⓐ Ⓑ Ⓒ Ⓓ	Ⓐ Ⓑ Ⓒ Ⓓ
7	Ⓐ Ⓑ Ⓒ Ⓓ	Ⓐ Ⓑ Ⓒ Ⓓ	Ⓐ Ⓑ Ⓒ Ⓓ	Ⓐ Ⓑ Ⓒ Ⓓ
8	Ⓐ Ⓑ Ⓒ Ⓓ	Ⓐ Ⓑ Ⓒ Ⓓ	Ⓐ Ⓑ Ⓒ Ⓓ	Ⓐ Ⓑ Ⓒ Ⓓ
9	Ⓐ Ⓑ Ⓒ Ⓓ	Ⓐ Ⓑ Ⓒ Ⓓ	Ⓐ Ⓑ Ⓒ Ⓓ	Ⓐ Ⓑ Ⓒ Ⓓ
10	Ⓐ Ⓑ Ⓒ Ⓓ	Ⓐ Ⓑ Ⓒ Ⓓ	Ⓐ Ⓑ Ⓒ Ⓓ	Ⓐ Ⓑ Ⓒ Ⓓ
11	Ⓐ Ⓑ Ⓒ Ⓓ	Ⓐ Ⓑ Ⓒ Ⓓ	Ⓐ Ⓑ Ⓒ Ⓓ	Ⓐ Ⓑ Ⓒ Ⓓ
12	Ⓐ Ⓑ Ⓒ Ⓓ	Ⓐ Ⓑ Ⓒ Ⓓ	Ⓐ Ⓑ Ⓒ Ⓓ	Ⓐ Ⓑ Ⓒ Ⓓ
13	Ⓐ Ⓑ Ⓒ Ⓓ	Ⓐ Ⓑ Ⓒ Ⓓ	Ⓐ Ⓑ Ⓒ Ⓓ	Ⓐ Ⓑ Ⓒ Ⓓ
14	Ⓐ Ⓑ Ⓒ Ⓓ	Ⓐ Ⓑ Ⓒ Ⓓ	Ⓐ Ⓑ Ⓒ Ⓓ	Ⓐ Ⓑ Ⓒ Ⓓ
15	Ⓐ Ⓑ Ⓒ Ⓓ	Ⓐ Ⓑ Ⓒ Ⓓ	Ⓐ Ⓑ Ⓒ Ⓓ	Ⓐ Ⓑ Ⓒ Ⓓ
16	Ⓐ Ⓑ Ⓒ Ⓓ	Ⓐ Ⓑ Ⓒ Ⓓ	Ⓐ Ⓑ Ⓒ Ⓓ	Ⓐ Ⓑ Ⓒ Ⓓ
17	Ⓐ Ⓑ Ⓒ Ⓓ	Ⓐ Ⓑ Ⓒ Ⓓ	Ⓐ Ⓑ Ⓒ Ⓓ	Ⓐ Ⓑ Ⓒ Ⓓ
18	Ⓐ Ⓑ Ⓒ Ⓓ	Ⓐ Ⓑ Ⓒ Ⓓ	Ⓐ Ⓑ Ⓒ Ⓓ	Ⓐ Ⓑ Ⓒ Ⓓ
19	Ⓐ Ⓑ Ⓒ Ⓓ	Ⓐ Ⓑ Ⓒ Ⓓ	Ⓐ Ⓑ Ⓒ Ⓓ	Ⓐ Ⓑ Ⓒ Ⓓ
20	Ⓐ Ⓑ Ⓒ Ⓓ	Ⓐ Ⓑ Ⓒ Ⓓ	Ⓐ Ⓑ Ⓒ Ⓓ	Ⓐ Ⓑ Ⓒ Ⓓ
21	Ⓐ Ⓑ Ⓒ Ⓓ	Ⓐ Ⓑ Ⓒ Ⓓ	Ⓐ Ⓑ Ⓒ Ⓓ	Ⓐ Ⓑ Ⓒ Ⓓ
22	Ⓐ Ⓑ Ⓒ Ⓓ	Ⓐ Ⓑ Ⓒ Ⓓ	Ⓐ Ⓑ Ⓒ Ⓓ	Ⓐ Ⓑ Ⓒ Ⓓ
23	Ⓐ Ⓑ Ⓒ Ⓓ	Ⓐ Ⓑ Ⓒ Ⓓ	Ⓐ Ⓑ Ⓒ Ⓓ	Ⓐ Ⓑ Ⓒ Ⓓ
24	Ⓐ Ⓑ Ⓒ Ⓓ	Ⓐ Ⓑ Ⓒ Ⓓ	Ⓐ Ⓑ Ⓒ Ⓓ	Ⓐ Ⓑ Ⓒ Ⓓ
25	Ⓐ Ⓑ Ⓒ Ⓓ	Ⓐ Ⓑ Ⓒ Ⓓ	Ⓐ Ⓑ Ⓒ Ⓓ	Ⓐ Ⓑ Ⓒ Ⓓ
26	Ⓐ Ⓑ Ⓒ Ⓓ	Ⓐ Ⓑ Ⓒ Ⓓ	Ⓐ Ⓑ Ⓒ Ⓓ	Ⓐ Ⓑ Ⓒ Ⓓ
27	Ⓐ Ⓑ Ⓒ Ⓓ	Ⓐ Ⓑ Ⓒ Ⓓ	Ⓐ Ⓑ Ⓒ Ⓓ	
28	Ⓐ Ⓑ Ⓒ Ⓓ			
29	Ⓐ Ⓑ Ⓒ Ⓓ			
30	Ⓐ Ⓑ Ⓒ Ⓓ			

CUT HERE

Tip: For the Mathematics section, you may consult the Mathematics Reference Sheet in Appendix C (pages 343–344) for common formulas.

Language Arts and Reading

30 Questions

33 Minutes

1. The _____ mode of writing aims to convince the reader.

    A. explanatory
    B. informational
    C. narrative
    D. opinion/argument

2. After analyzing Gavin's developmental reading assessment (DRA), his second-grade teacher notices that while he reads accurately, he is not completely comprehending the text. Which of the following would be considered the most effective course of action to improve Gavin's comprehension?

    A. Gavin should read basal text repeatedly and answer questions after reading.
    B. Gavin should be placed in an ad hoc guided reading group with other students having comprehension difficulties where the teacher facilitates questions and conversation to improve comprehension.
    C. Gavin should read a lot but not discuss his reading with peers.
    D. None of the above

3. Along with professional judgment, the two measures that should be used to evaluate text complexity are

    A. quantitative and qualitative.
    B. easy and hard.
    C. short and long.
    D. inductive and deductive.

4. A hyperbole is an exaggerated statement used for effect and is not meant to be taken literally. Which of the following is a hyperbole?

    A. She must have weighed 1,000 pounds!
    B. The bar of chocolate was humongous!
    C. She was as radiant as the sun.
    D. Her nose was red like a cherry.

5. Where can you easily access a wide array of multicultural literature, free of charge, for use in your elementary classroom?

    A. the school library
    B. the Internet
    C. a book store
    D. A and B only

6. Knowledge of individual words in sentences, syllables, onset-rime segments, and the awareness of individual phonemes in words is known as

    A. phonics.
    B. phonological awareness.
    C. phoneme segmentation.
    D. phoneme manipulation.

GO ON TO THE NEXT PAGE

7. During what stage of the writing process do students typically correct their writing for mechanical and spelling errors?

   A. brainstorm
   B. revision
   C. edit
   D. pre-write

8. Mr. McKay notices that several of his second-grade students are not reading fluently. Knowing that fluency aids comprehension, he should perform which of the following assessment methods to gather data specific to this issue?

   A. informal fluency checks
   B. story retelling
   C. portfolio assessment
   D. worksheets

9. During a star student modeled writing activity, Ms. Miller shares the pen and allows her first-graders to add the appropriate punctuation at the end of each sentence that tells something special about that student. While she is obviously building classroom community, what else is Ms. Miller teaching her students about the writing process?

   A. comprehension
   B. fluency
   C. writing conventions
   D. vocabulary

10. A fable, a category of folklore, is defined as a

    A. story with a moral.
    B. story with historical references.
    C. story that is realistic and could happen.
    D. poem.

11. What question might you ask to assist a student in using the semantic cueing system?

    A. Does that look right?
    B. Does that sound right?
    C. Does that make sense?
    D. What were you thinking?

12. When students attempt to synthesize what has been read, they are

    A. making generalizations.
    B. using old ideas to create new ones.
    C. predicting and drawing conclusions.
    D. All of the above

13. The peak of a story is known as the

    A. resolution.
    B. conclusion.
    C. climax.
    D. plot.

14. In the classic folklore story, *The Three Billy Goats Gruff,* the goats trip-trap, trip-trap over the bridge. What literary device describes the use of the words, *trip-trap*?

  A. irony
  B. metaphor
  C. onomatopoeia
  D. simile

15. The purpose of anecdotal notes is

  A. to make note of everything a student is doing wrong.
  B. to observe students while they work and record the observations for later study.
  C. to make notes of student work and stick strictly to your lesson plan regardless of these notes.
  D. None of the above

16. A rubric is provided prior to students beginning a unit of study in order to

  A. keep them in the dark about what they are supposed to do.
  B. frustrate and overwhelm them prior to explaining the project.
  C. inform the student of the criteria and expectations of their final project.
  D. allow the teacher to evaluate student work based on his or her own personal requirements.

17. A kindergarten teacher is modeling how to frame the word *the* during the shared reading of a big book to show students where the word begins and ends. What is the focus of this lesson?

  A. fluency
  B. concepts of print, word boundaries
  C. the advantages of using quality children's literature
  D. how to use a pointer

18. In order to communicate in writing, penmanship must be legible. Which of the following contributes to legible handwriting?

  A. spacing
  B. letter formation
  C. letter alignment
  D. All of the above

19. What stage of the writing process could be enhanced by six-trait writing lessons?

  A. brainstorm
  B. revision
  C. editing
  D. All of the above

20. Choral poetry is a way of orally rendering a poem together as a group. Which critical reading skill is NOT positively impacted by the use of choral poetry?

  A. fluency
  B. comprehension
  C. vocabulary
  D. inferring

GO ON TO THE NEXT PAGE

21. An example of visual media is

    A. a glog.
    B. a journal.
    C. the newspaper.
    D. an atlas.

22. Questioning and retelling enhance communication skills among students in the classroom. What critical reading skill is most enhanced by these strategies?

    A. fluency
    B. comprehension
    C. word recognition
    D. phonics

23. Which of the following is a web-based activity that could take place in the classroom?

    A. blog
    B. Prezi
    C. Wiki page
    D. All of the above

24. Which of the following are NOT essential comprehension skills?

    A. main idea and supporting details
    B. author's purpose and point of view
    C. pre-alphabetic and partial alphabetic
    D. inference and conclusion

25. Ms. Jomsky notices one of her students exploring a book in the reading corner of her classroom. She notices the student beginning to read from the bottom of the page rather than the top. Which concept of print should she focus on with this particular student?

    A. one-to-one correspondence
    B. directionality
    C. phonemic awareness
    D. word boundaries

26. Differentiating instruction means

    A. following a scripted teacher's manual with fidelity.
    B. teaching the exact same way to all students regardless of their differences.
    C. marginalizing students' prior knowledge.
    D. planning, implementing, and assessing to meet the instructional needs of all students.

27. Mrs. Loubier quickly checks for understanding regarding her second-grade mini-lesson on the narrative elements in literary texts. Students show one to four fingers to present their individual understanding of this topic. Mrs. Loubier notices that five of her students are showing ones or twos, which means their knowledge of this content is shaky. What should she do to help these students better understand this content?

    A.   Pull a small group, set the purpose for listening to identify characters, setting, plot, resolution, etc., read aloud a quality piece of children's literature, and review the narrative elements through small group discussion of the authentic text.

    B.   Give minimal instructions and quickly send them back to their seats to work on their own.

    C.   Continue whole group instruction. The ones that already know can help the other students get up to speed.

    D.   Encourage this small group to work together as a team to figure it out.

28. Readers theater is an instructional method known to aid fluency. While reading aloud to their peers, the students should demonstrate proper communications skills. Which of the following is NOT a proper speaking skill?

    A.   gestures

    B.   voice projection

    C.   eye contact

    D.   questioning the speaker

29. Which of the following is NOT a current technological tool widely used in classrooms?

    A.   interactive whiteboard

    B.   overhead projector

    C.   document camera

    D.   tablet

30. The ACT is an example of what kind of test?

    A.   diagnostic

    B.   norm-referenced

    C.   criterion-referenced

    D.   informal reading inventory

IF YOU FINISH BEFORE TIME IS CALLED, CHECK YOUR WORK ON THIS SECTION ONLY. DO NOT WORK ON ANY OTHER SECTION IN THE TEST.

STOP

Social Science

27 Questions

33 Minutes

1. Which war was an extension of the European Seven Years War and was a struggle over colonial territory and wealth by the French and the English?

   A.   French and Native American War

   B.   French and Indian War

   C.   French and English War

   D.   War of the Roses

2. In Ancient China, which three forms of art were considered the "three perfections"?

   A.   painting, calligraphy, and poetry

   B.   pastels, scratchboard, and oil painting

   C.   sculpture, quilling, and cuneiform

   D.   None of the above

3. How many voyages did Columbus make in an effort to find a route to the East?

   A.   one

   B.   two

   C.   three

   D.   four

4. The Civil War was the conflict that ended slavery in this country. What document ordered that slavery be abolished in Confederate states when it was signed by President Lincoln in 1862?

   A.   Louisiana Purchase

   B.   Magna Carta

   C.   Emancipation Proclamation

   D.   Treaty of Paris

5. The use of what teaching strategy can assist students in synthesizing and summarizing informational text?

   A.   graphic organizers

   B.   fill-in-the-blank tests

   C.   independent worksheets

   D.   silent reading with no group discussion

6. An absolute location is defined as

   A.   a formal location where street names or coordinates are used to describe the locality.

   B.   an informal location.

   C.   a location where local landmarks are used to describe the place.

   D.   a difficult location to access.

7. What is the name of the revolution that is defined as the transition from manual labor to machine?

   A.   American Revolution

   B.   European Revolution

   C.   Colonial Revolution

   D.   Industrial Revolution

8. Human beings tend to live in environments that meet their needs. Which essential element of geography refers to the interaction between people and their surroundings?

   A. human systems
   B. processes that shape the Earth
   C. world in spatial terms
   D. environment and society

9. What historic document was approved by the Second Continental Congress and laid the foundation for a new government in America?

   A. Poor Richard's Almanac
   B. Preamble to the Constitution
   C. Declaration of Independence
   D. Emancipation Proclamation

10. What representation of the Earth is said to be most accurate?

    A. relief map
    B. globe
    C. thematic map
    D. political map

11. The three branches of government in the United States provide for a system of checks and balances. The three branches are

    A. congress, president, and supreme court.
    B. legislative, judicial, and executive.
    C. first, second, and third.
    D. electorate, electoral college, and state representatives.

12. Small representations, usually shapes and pictures, of real things on a map are known as

    A. symbols.
    B. a legend.
    C. cartographers.
    D. keys.

13. When one company or institution has exclusive control of a particular good or service in a market, this is known as

    A. an oligopoly.
    B. a monopoly.
    C. roly-poly.
    D. capitalism.

14. How many electoral votes are required to win the presidency?

    A. 240
    B. 250
    C. 260
    D. 270

GO ON TO THE NEXT PAGE

15. Electors are representatives of the people who actually elect the president and vice president. As of 2009, how many electors are there in the United States of America?

    A. 535

    B. 536

    C. 537

    D. 538

16. Policies that aid in governmental control of the economy are known as

    A. financial policies.

    B. fiscal policies.

    C. inflation policies.

    D. trade policies.

17. A fifth-grade teacher is preparing a review lesson concerning primary sources. Which of the following online resources would be the most credible source to use?

    A. readwritethink.org

    B. theteachingchannel.com

    C. loc.gov

    D. mrsmithsprimarysources.com

18. Trade between three continents or ports is referred to as

    A. triple trade.

    B. triangular trade.

    C. tri-trade.

    D. None of the above

19. Walter the baker bakes a multitude of confections for his pastry shop in town. In economic terms, Walter himself would be considered what kind of resource?

    A. capital

    B. natural

    C. human

    D. personable

20. What financial institution is owned, controlled, and operated by its members?

    A. federal reserve bank

    B. credit union

    C. stock market

    D. Wall Street

21. Consumer decision making has a large effect on the supply and demand of products in this country and all over the world, therefore teaching our youth _____ skills is vital.

    A. fiscal policy

    B. economic reasoning

    C. global responsibility

    D. home economics

22. Which of the following teaching methods does NOT effectively teach social studies content?

   A. role play

   B. simulation

   C. problem based

   D. independent textbook reading

23. Democracy, monarchy, oligarchy, and dictatorship are four types of government structures employed around the world. Which of the following best defines an oligarchy?

   A. government by the few

   B. government by the people

   C. government by one exercising absolute power

   D. government by royalty

24. Patrick Henry was a true patriot. He is known for which of the following famous phrases?

   A. One if by land, and two if by sea.

   B. Yankee Doodle went to town.

   C. Let justice be done though the heavens should fall.

   D. Give me liberty or give me death!

25. Each state in the United States of America has a constitution that lists the rights guaranteed to the citizens of that state. In Florida, this list is called the

   A. Declaration of Independency

   B. Declaration of Rights

   C. Declaration of Responsibilities

   D. Declaration of Indictments

26. What is the most common form of assessment?

   A. paper-and-pencil tests

   B. graphic organizers

   C. t-charts

   D. observation

27. Henry Flagler was an American industrialist who founded what became the _____ Railway, which was responsible for developing the Atlantic coast of Florida.

   A. AMTRAK

   B. Oakland and Berkeley Rapid Transit

   C. Florida East Coast

   D. Harding Express

IF YOU FINISH BEFORE TIME IS CALLED, CHECK YOUR WORK ON THIS SECTION ONLY. DO NOT WORK ON ANY OTHER SECTION IN THE TEST.

Science

27 Questions
35 Minutes

1. Which of the following is an appropriate use of informal learning experiences to promote students' curiosity?

    A. Students help to maintain fish tanks in the classroom.
    B. Students watch a video about the Florida Aquarium.
    C. Students read a chapter in a book about fishing.
    D. Teachers explain how fish interact with their environment.

2. Cells in which a nucleus exists are called

    A. prokaryotic cells.
    B. eukaryotic cells.
    C. nucleolus.
    D. ribosomes.

3. A computer-based application used to facilitate the preparation, manipulation, modification, and arrangement of electronically developed text, tables, and images for reports and documents is called a

    A. social network.
    B. word processor.
    C. spreadsheet.
    D. database.

4. What is Earth's pull of gravity on an object called?

    A. mass
    B. weight
    C. volume
    D. density

5. The _____ is the innermost part of Earth and is solid.

    A. outer core
    B. mantle
    C. crust
    D. inner core

6. Of the following, which is the most specific level of taxonomy?

    A. species
    B. genus
    C. domain
    D. kingdom

7. Which of the following is NOT a good laboratory procedure?

    A. washing hands frequently
    B. eating in the laboratory
    C. disposing of chemicals properly
    D. wearing gloves

8. Who was the first American to be launched into space?

   A. John Glenn
   B. Neil Armstrong
   C. Alan Shepard
   D. Yuri Gagarin

9. What is the most effective method for controlling the spread of viruses?

   A. antibiotics
   B. radiation
   C. balanced diet
   D. vaccination

10. Which of the following is NOT considered a geological formation?

   A. volcano
   B. earthquake
   C. canyon
   D. mountain

11. A sound wave is produced by

   A. sonar.
   B. pitch.
   C. acoustic.
   D. vibration.

12. _____ reproduction requires only one parent.

   A. Asexual
   B. Nonsexual
   C. Conjugation
   D. Sexual

13. A measure related to the average kinetic energy of the molecules of a substance is called

   A. mechanical force.
   B. contact force.
   C. temperature.
   D. heat.

14. Instruments that can be used to measure absorbance spectrum of a liquid are called

   A. pressure sensors.
   B. temperature probes.
   C. spectrometers.
   D. barometers.

15. Which of the following technologies would be appropriate to use to collect temperature data from various sites around a school or community?

   A. spreadsheet
   B. e-mail
   C. Facebook
   D. PowerPoint

GO ON TO THE NEXT PAGE

16. Which type of force requires physical contact and interaction between objects?

- **A.** at-a-distance force
- **B.** contact force
- **C.** electrical force
- **D.** magnetic force

17. _____ are the ways in which scientists answer questions and solve problems systematically.

- **A.** Laboratories
- **B.** Scientific methods
- **C.** Controlled experiments
- **D.** Hypotheses

18. Which of the following occur when two plates intersect and force each other upward?

- **A.** earthquakes
- **B.** canyons
- **C.** mountains
- **D.** volcanoes

19. In an experiment, students are starting to write statements about the relationships among the variables that they intend to study. They are most likely involved with developing their

- **A.** hypotheses.
- **B.** theory.
- **C.** laws.
- **D.** identification of variables.

20. Which of the following forces is NOT considered an at-a-distance force?

- **A.** frictional force
- **B.** gravitational force
- **C.** electrical force
- **D.** nuclear force

21. Regarding the six steps listed below, what is the correct order of methodology for an experiment?

- **1.** Plan a controlled experiment
- **2.** Revisit the hypothesis to answer the question
- **3.** Analyze data and draw conclusions
- **4.** Identify a research question
- **5.** Formulate a hypothesis
- **6.** Collect data

- **A.** 5, 4, 1, 6, 2, 3
- **B.** 4, 5, 1, 6, 2, 3
- **C.** 5, 4, 1, 6, 3, 2
- **D.** 4, 5, 1, 6, 3, 2

22. Animals that live in water and on land in different stages of their lives are called

- **A.** reptiles.
- **B.** birds.
- **C.** amphibians.
- **D.** worms.

23. _____ rock is formed from the cooling of magma.

    A.   Metamorphic

    B.   Sedimentary

    C.   Igneous

    D.   Compressed

24. Which of the following is an appropriate unit of measure for the length of a giraffe's neck?

    A.   Kilometers

    B.   Meters

    C.   Miles

    D.   Millimeters

25. During an exploration related to light absorption and color, the teacher should be doing which of the following?

    A.   gathering data

    B.   grading papers

    C.   monitoring student progress

    D.   talking to the whole class about light absorption

26. Although a crystal is a nonliving thing, which criteria of living things is still present?

    A.   made up of cells

    B.   obtains energy

    C.   adapts to environment

    D.   grows and develops

27. Which conclusion can be drawn from the following chart?

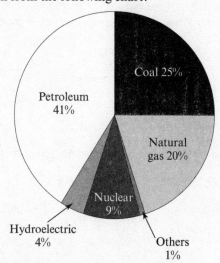

    A.   Petroleum usage is approximately double natural gas usage.

    B.   Nuclear power usage is less than hydroelectric power usage.

    C.   The amount of natural gas consumption should be increased.

    D.   Coal and natural gas provide more than half of the energy usage shown.

IF YOU FINISH BEFORE TIME IS CALLED, CHECK YOUR WORK ON THIS SECTION ONLY. DO NOT WORK ON ANY OTHER SECTION IN THE TEST.

Mathematics

26 Questions

35 Minutes

1. A student used five blocks as part of an activity dealing with numeration. What type of representation model is the student using?

    A. word name
    B. standard numeral
    C. concrete model
    D. pictorial model

2. Find the next term in the pattern 2, 6, 18, 54,...

    A. 58
    B. 72
    C. 108
    D. 162

3. A garden was made in the shape of a triangle, with side lengths of 36 inches, 5 feet, and 2 yards. The gardener added 3 feet to each of the shorter sides of the triangular garden, and 4 feet to the longest side. What is the perimeter of the new garden?

    A. 7.5 feet
    B. 20 feet
    C. 24 feet
    D. 53 feet

4. A bar graph using horizontal rectangular bars to show the frequency of each value and numerals to show the frequency values involves which of the following representation models?

    A. pictorial and abstract
    B. concrete and abstract
    C. pictorial only
    D. abstract only

Use the data set that follows to answer questions 5–8.

The students in a class received the following scores in a test worth 100 points:

80, 23, 55, 58, 45, 32, 40, 55, 50

5. Find the mean of the data set (if necessary, round to the nearest whole number).

    A. 44
    B. 49
    C. 50
    D. 57

6. Find the median of the data set.

    A. 49
    B. 50
    C. 55
    D. 57

7. Find the range of the data set (round to the nearest one).

    A. 49
    B. 50
    C. 55
    D. 57

8. Find the mode of the data set.

    A. 1
    B. 49
    C. 50
    D. 55

9. Which angle in the following figure is complementary to angle *ABD*?

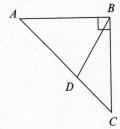

    A. Angle *ABC*
    B. Angle *DAB*
    C. Angle *CBD*
    D. Angle *ACB*

10. The number 3^{-2} is equal to

    A. -9
    B. $\dfrac{1}{9}$
    C. $\dfrac{2}{3}$
    D. 9

11. A farmer sells his crop for \$5 a bushel at the farmer's market. There is a fee of \$50 to have a booth at the market. How much profit will the farmer make if he sells *b* bushels at the market?

    A. $5b$ dollars
    B. $5b - 50$ dollars
    C. $5b + 50$ dollars
    D. 50 dollars

12. Cheyenne is 40 inches tall. She has a shadow that is 36 inches long. A tree in Cheyenne's backyard is 10 feet tall. How long will the tree's shadow be?

    A. 6 feet
    B. 9 feet
    C. 14 feet
    D. 16 feet

GO ON TO THE NEXT PAGE

13. The number 465^0 is equal to

A.   −465

B.   0

C.   1

D.   465

14. The principal of Howard Elementary School, Mr. Taylor, is planning to take a group of students on a field trip. He has 140 students who want to participate in this activity. If he can take 56 students per school bus, then how many buses would he most likely need for their trip?

A.   2

B. $2\frac{1}{2}$

C.   2 R28

D.   3

15. Which one of the following is most appropriate to help students develop classification skills?

A.   Cuisenaire rods

B.   algebra tiles

C.   pattern blocks

D.   fraction tiles

16. Which of the following statements is TRUE?

A.   An acute triangle can be an isosceles triangle.

B.   An obtuse triangle can be an equilateral triangle.

C.   A right triangle can be an obtuse triangle.

D.   An equilateral triangle can be a scalene triangle.

17. What is the value of $2^{-6} \cdot -8$?

A.   −8

B. $-\dfrac{1}{8}$

C. $\dfrac{1}{8}$

D.   8

18. Identify the coordinates of point R in the figure shown.

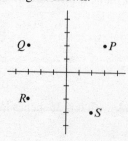

A.   (3, 2)

B.   (2, 3)

C.   (−3, −2)

D.   (−2, −3)

19. Which one of the following is LEAST appropriate to help students develop area ideas?

    A. geoboards
    B. two-color chips
    C. color tiles
    D. pattern blocks

20. Simplify the following expression: $30^2 - 60 \div 12 \cdot \left(\dfrac{1}{5} - 5^{-2} \right) \cdot 15 + 78$

    A. 246
    B. 280
    C. 966
    D. 2,838

21. Which of the following is most likely a principal prerequisite for understanding the process involved in a computation exercise involving 3-digit whole numbers with regrouping (for example, 476 + 258)?

    A. place value
    B. use of a calculator
    C. memorization of basic addition facts
    D. solving computation exercises involving 2-digit whole numbers with and without regrouping (for example, 34 + 59)

22. Solve for x: $3x - 4 + x = x + 8 + 3x - 2x$

    A. $x = 2$
    B. $x = 4$
    C. $x = 6$
    D. $x = 7$

23. Consider the following statement: The expression $2x$ is greater than the expression $2 + x$.

    A. This statement is always true.
    B. This statement is never true.
    C. This statement is sometimes true.
    D. This statement does not provide enough information.

24. A store sells boxes of cookies for $5.00 each, plus a one-time service charge of $0.50. If b represents the number of cookies to be bought and t represents the total cost, which of the following equations could be used to represent this situation?

    A. $t = 0.5(5 - b)$
    B. $t = 0.5 + 5b$
    C. $t = 5 - 0.5b$
    D. $t = 5 + 0.5b$

GO ON TO THE NEXT PAGE

25. It is the beginning of the new school year. Ms. Malone, a sixth-grade teacher, is planning a review session during the first few weeks of school in order to assess whether her students are fluent in their addition computation skills with whole numbers and fractions with like and unlike denominators. Fluency in these areas are benchmarks that students need to have mastered in previous years, and Ms. Malone wants to be sure that students are comfortable with these skills before assessing other basic skills.

Ms. Malone decides to administer a diagnostic assessment to see how well the students are doing in the skills that she will be reviewing. She expected to see at least 85% of questions correct for each student. The following table shows the results of the test.

Ms. Malone's Class Roster			
Name	Whole Numbers: Number correct out of 8 items	Fractions: Number correct out of 4 items	Total Score: Number correct out of 12 items
Tim	8	3	11
Jose	8	4	12
Nicosha	8	0	8
Jennifer	7	4	11
Markeshia	7	4	11
Allan	7	1	8
Nataly	8	4	12
Brady	7	4	11
Daniel	8	1	9
Marcus	8	4	12
Sabrina	7	1	8
Kimberly	8	4	12
Kawain	8	4	12
Damian	7	4	11
T.J.	8	3	11

Which students need intervention and in what area might they need intervention?

A. Jennifer, Markeshia, Allan, Brady, Sabrina, and Damian need intervention in whole number computation.

B. Nicosha, Allan, Daniel, and Sabrina need intervention fraction addition.

C. Jennifer, Markeshia, and Damian need intervention in both whole number computation and fraction addition.

D. Nicosha, Allan, Daniel, and Sabrina need intervention in whole number computation.

26. Which of the following is most likely an example of high complexity level?

A. locating details in a problem solving activity

B. comparing word meanings in a problem solving activity

C. summarizing the major points of a problem solving activity

D. analyzing the use of figurative language in a text in a problem solving activity

IF YOU FINISH BEFORE TIME IS CALLED, CHECK YOUR WORK ON THIS SECTION ONLY. DO NOT WORK ON ANY OTHER SECTION IN THE TEST.

Answer Key

Language Arts and Reading

1. D	9. C	17. B	25. B
2. B	10. A	18. D	26. D
3. A	11. C	19. D	27. A
4. A	12. D	20. D	28. D
5. D	13. C	21. A	29. B
6. B	14. C	22. B	30. C
7. C	15. B	23. D	
8. A	16. C	24. C	

Social Science

1. B	8. D	15. D	22. D
2. A	9. C	16. B	23. A
3. D	10. B	17. C	24. D
4. C	11. B	18. B	25. B
5. A	12. A	19. C	26. D
6. A	13. B	20. B	27. C
7. D	14. D	21. B	

Science

1. A	8. C	15. A	22. C
2. B	9. D	16. B	23. C
3. B	10. B	17. B	24. B
4. B	11. D	18. C	25. C
5. D	12. A	19. A	26. D
6. A	13. C	20. A	27. A
7. B	14. C	21. D	

Mathematics

1. C	8. D	15. C	22. C
2. D	9. C	16. A	23. C
3. C	10. B	17. B	24. B
4. A	11. B	18. C	25. B
5. B	12. B	19. B	26. D
6. B	13. C	20. C	
7. D	14. D	21. A	

Answer Explanations

Language Arts and Reading

1. **D.** Competency 3. The opinion/argument mode of writing aims to convince and share personal opinions with the reader.

2. **B.** Competency 4. Based on analyzing his DRA, Gavin needs time with his teacher and group of peers with similar needs to work on comprehension. The knowledgeable teacher can facilitate the small group using the appropriate questions aimed at gaining meaning from the text.

3. **A.** Competency 2. Quantitative and qualitative measures, along with professional judgment, should be used to evaluate text complexity.

4. **A.** Competency 2. A hyperbole is an exaggerated statement used for effect and is not meant to be taken literally.

5. **D.** Competency 2. School libraries and the Internet contain a wide variety of free and easily accessible multicultural children's literature, nonfiction resources, and various genres.

6. **B.** Competency 1. Knowledge of individual words in sentences, syllables, onset-rime segments, and the awareness of individual phonemes in words is known as phonological awareness.

7. **C.** Competency 3. A teacher, if truly focusing on the content, encourages students to revise and improve upon what they have written during the editing process.

8. **A.** Competency 4. Mr. McKay should perform informal fluency checks to gather data specific to this issue.

9. **C.** Competency 3. Ms. Miller is teaching her students writing conventions, specifically punctuation at the end of a sentence.

10. **A.** Competency 2. A fable is a story with a moral.

11. **C.** Competency 1. The semantic cueing system focuses on meaning (making sense) that is associated with language through prior knowledge and experience.

12. **D.** Competency 1. When students attempt to synthesize what has been read, they are making generalizations, using old ideas to create new ones, and predicting and drawing conclusions.

13. **C.** Competency 2. The climax is the highest point of interest or suspense in a story.

14. **C.** Competency 2. Onomatopoeia is the use of words whose sound is imitative of the sound of the noise and/or action designated.

15. **B.** Competency 4. The purpose of anecdotal notes is to observe students while they work and record the observations for later study.

16. **C.** Competency 4. A rubric is provided prior to students beginning a unit of study in order to provide the criteria and expectations for the final project.

17. **B.** Competency 1. Concepts of print include that print conveys meaning, directionality (left to right and top to bottom progression), concept of a word (word boundaries), one-to-one correspondence, letter knowledge, phonemic awareness, and literacy language (author, illustrations, title, and so on).

18. **D.** Competency 3. Spacing, letter formation, and letter alignment are all factors that impact legible handwriting. Line quality (consistency of pencil strokes) also contributes to legible handwriting.

19. **D.** Competency 3. Six-trait writing lessons can enhance brainstorming, revision, and editing.

20. **D.** Competency 4. Choral poetry enhances vocabulary, comprehension, and fluency. It does NOT enhance one's ability to infer.

21. **A.** Competency 5. Visual media is nonprint media.

22. **B.** Competencies 1 and 5. Comprehension, listening, and speaking skills are all enhanced by questioning and retelling.

23. **D.** Competency 5. Blogs are user-friendly web pages that allow students to post and comment on their work. Prezi is a presentation software and an online storytelling tool. Wiki pages are "mini web pages" that provide collaborative opportunities to post, add, and edit a variety of content related to a specific topic of study or group project.

24. **C.** Competency 1. While each of the other choices are essential comprehension skills, pre-alphabetic and partial alphabetic are not.

25. **B.** Competency 1. Left to right and top to bottom progression refers to the concept of print known as directionality.

26. **D.** Competency 4. Differentiating instruction means planning, implementing, and assessing to meet the instructional needs of all students.

27. **A.** Competency 1. Pulling a small group in order to instruct a group of students who do not understand the content is an effective way to teach many skills, in this case the narrative elements of stories.

28. **D.** Competency 5. While questioning the speaker is a communication skill, it is not one that you as the speaker would employ.

29. **B.** Competency 5. An overhead projector would not be considered a current technological tool.

30. **C.** Competency 4. The ACT is a criterion-referenced test intended to test how well a student has learned a specific body of knowledge and skills.

Social Science

1. **B.** Competency 2. The French and Indian War (1754–1763), which was an extension of the European Seven Years War, was a struggle over colonial territory and wealth by the French and the English. This war resulted in effectively ending French cultural and political influence in North America. In their victory, England gained massive amounts of land but also weakened their rapport with the Native Americans. In sum, although the war strengthened England's hold on the colonies, it worsened their relationship, which inevitably led to the Revolutionary War.

2. **A.** Competency 5. Painting, calligraphy, and poetry were considered the "three perfections."

3. **D.** Competency 2. Columbus made four voyages in an effort to find a route to the East. During his expeditions he discovered the Bahamas, Hispaniola, Cuba, Dominica, Guadeloupe, Jamaica, Central America, and South America. As illustrations and historical accounts depict, he was greeted by Native Americans who had settled the land prior to his arrival. The Vikings had explored these areas as well.

4. **C.** Competency 2. Abraham Lincoln signed the Emancipation Proclamation in 1862. It declared the freedom of enslaved people in the Confederate states.

5. **A.** Competency 1. Using graphic organizers can assist students in synthesizing and summarizing informational text.

6. **A.** Competency 3. An absolute location is defined as a formal location where street names or coordinates are used to describe the locality.

7. **D.** Competency 2. The Industrial Revolution is defined as the transition from manual labor to machine.

8. **D.** Competency 3. Environment and society is the essential element of geography that refers to the interaction between people and their surroundings.

9. **C.** Competency 2. The Declaration of Independence was approved by the Second Continental Congress and laid the foundation for the foundation for a new government in America.

10. **B.** Competency 3. A globe, which is a small-scale model, is said to be the most accurate representation of the Earth.

11. **B.** Competency 4. The three branches of government are legislative, judicial, and executive.

12. **A.** Competency 3. Symbols are small representations, usually shapes and pictures, of real things on a map.

13. **B.** Competency 5. A monopoly is when one company or institution has exclusive control of a particular good or service in a market.

14. **D.** Competency 4. As of 2009, there are 538 total electoral votes. In order for a candidate to receive the majority and win the presidency, they must have 270 electoral votes.

15. **D.** Competency 4. As of 2009, there are 538 total electors. Electors are a body of elected representatives chosen by the voters in each state. While they are human beings who have their own views on whom they would prefer to become the leader of this country, they pledge in advance to vote according to the wishes of the general public.

16. **B.** Competency 5. Fiscal policies aid in governmental control of the economy.

17. **C.** Competency 1. While there are many credible and reliable resources online, there are none more credible than the Library of Congress website (loc.gov). This site provides educators with primary sources and lesson resources for effective use in the classroom.

18. **B.** Competencies 2 and 5. Triangular trade is trade between three continents or ports.

19. **C.** Competency 5. Walter the baker would be considered a human resource.

20. **B.** Competency 5. A credit union is a financial institution that is owned, controlled, and operated by its members.

21. **B.** Competency 5. Economic reasoning is making decisions by comparing costs and benefits. This skill is used daily by American citizens.

22. **D.** Competency 1. Role play, simulation, and problem based lessons all effectively teach social studies content.

23. **A.** Competency 4. An oligarchy is a structure of government by the few.

24. **D.** Competency 2. Patrick Henry is known for having said, "Give me liberty or give me death!"

25. **B.** Competency 4. In Florida, the rights guaranteed all citizens are listed in the Declaration of Rights document.

26. **D.** Competency 1. The most common form of assessment is observation.

27. **C.** Competency 3. Henry Flagler was an American industrialist who founded what became the Florida East Coast Railway, which was responsible for developing the Atlantic coast of Florida.

Science

1. **A.** Competency 1. Students helping to maintain the fish tanks in a classroom provides an informal learning experience that can foster curiosity. Watching a video, reading a book, and a teacher explanation are not examples of informal learning.

2. **B.** Competency 5. Prokaryotic cells have no nucleus. Eukaryotic cells contain a nucleus. Nucleolus is the dark area in which the cell begins to make ribosomes, the smallest of all organelles.

3. **B.** Competency 2. The question stem is describing a word processor. Word processors facilitate the preparation, manipulation, modification, and arrangement of electronically developed text, tables, and images for reports and documents. A social network is an online environment that allows for collaboration and social contact via the Internet. Spreadsheets allow tabulation and performance of simple and complicated calculations, mathematical manipulations, and plots and graphs on various types of data, such as numbers, names, alphabetical information, scientific measurements, statistical information, and budget information. Database software allows easy collection, access, organization, and retrieval of data, such as inventories, experiments, and records.

4. **B.** Competency 4. The measure of Earth's pull of gravity on an object is called weight. It is the force of gravity on objects. Weight is measured in pounds (English or traditional system) or Newtons (SI system). Weight is often confused with mass, the amount of matter contained in an object.

5. **D.** Competency 4. The layers of Earth are the inner core, outer core, mantle, and crust. The innermost part of Earth is the inner core.

6. **A.** Competency 5. The levels of taxonomy are domain, kingdom, phylum, class, order, family, genus, and species. The most specific level of the choices given is species.

7. **B.** Competency 1. Good laboratory procedures include washing hands frequently, disposing of chemicals properly, and wearing gloves. Eating in the laboratory is not a good laboratory procedure.

8. **C.** Competency 4. Alan Shepard was the first American to be launched into space. John Glenn was the first American to orbit Earth. Neil Armstrong was the first American to walk on the Moon. Yuri Gagarin was the first human being in space.

9. **D.** Competency 5. Vaccination is the most effective method for controlling the spread of viruses.

10. **B.** Competency 3. Volcanoes, canyons, and mountains are geological formations. Earthquakes are not geological formations, but rather a release of energy when plates move.

11. **D.** Competency 3. A sound wave is produced by vibration. It is a type of mechanical energy that propagates through matter as a wave. If something vibrates at a reasonably high frequency, then it will make sound. When a vibrating object is large enough and next to air, the air will vibrate as well and produce sound. Sonar is a measuring instrument that is used to send out an acoustic pulse in water and measures distances in terms of the time it takes the echo of the pulse to return. Pitch represents the perceived fundamental frequency of a sound. It is one of the three major auditory attributes of sounds along with loudness and timbre. Acoustic relates to the study of sound, ultrasound, and infrasound (all mechanical waves in gases, liquids, and solids). It refers to the energy in the form of mechanical waves that is transmitted through materials (like plastic or air).

12. **A.** Competency 5. Asexual reproduction requires only one parent. Nonsexual reproduction requires no parents. Conjugation and sexual reproduction require two parents.

13. **C.** Competency 3. Temperature is a measure related to the average kinetic energy of the molecules of a substance. Temperature is one of the physical properties of solids, liquids, and gases. It has to do with how hot or cold an object is with respect to a standard unit of measurement. A mechanical force is a type of contact force. It is the application of force to bend, dent, scratch, compress, or break something. Contact forces require physical contact and interaction between objects (that is, pushes and pulls, and friction). Heat is a measurement of the total energy in a substance. That total energy is made up of the kinetic and the potential energies of the molecules of the substance. Temperature does not tell you anything about the potential energy.

14. **C.** Competency 2. Spectrometers are instruments that can be used to measure absorbance spectrum of a liquid, conduct kinetic studies of absorbance versus time, conduct equilibrium studies of absorbance versus time and/or absorbance versus concentration, measure emissions of gas discharge tubes or other light sources, and other experiments. Tools like spectrometers and sensors facilitate the collection of data, which might also be used with computer software to manage data. A pressure sensor measures pressure of gases or liquids, among others. Temperature probes are used for data collection during temperature-related experiments. Barometers are used for either weather studies or for lab experiments involving pressures close to normal atmospheric pressure.

15. **A.** Competency 1. A spreadsheet is best used to tabulate and analyze numerical data like temperature readings. E-mail and Facebook are communication programs, while PowerPoint is a presentation software.

16. **B.** Competency 3. Contact forces require physical contact and interaction between objects. The two main types of forces are contact force (for example, frictional, tension, air resistant, applied, and mechanical force) and at-a-distance force (for example, magnetic, gravitational, and electrostatic force). At-a-distance forces result even when the interacting objects are not in physical contact, but they exert a push or pull despite their physical separation. Electrical forces and magnetic forces are action-at-a-distance forces.

17. **B.** Competency 2. Scientific methods are the ways scientists answer questions and solve problems systematically. Controlled experiments and hypotheses are parts of the scientific method.

18. **C.** Competency 4. Mountains occur when two plates intersect and force each other upward. Earthquakes occur when two continental plates shift horizontally. Canyons occur when rivers erode soil away. Volcanoes occur when magma erupts above Earth's surface.

19. **A.** Competency 2. The first step in the scientific process is to ask a question. In order to answer the question, observations are needed. Observations may include collecting observed data such as the number of a specific species of frogs in an area. Once the question is formulated and observations are conducted, a hypothesis is created. A hypothesis is a possible answer to the question. Hypotheses are based on what was observed and are testable. Answers to the hypothesis are predicted and an experiment is formulated to test the hypothesis.

20. **A.** Competency 3. At-a-distance forces result even when the interacting objects are not in physical contact, but they exert a push or pull despite their physical separation. Gravitational, magnetic, electrical, and nuclear forces are examples of at-a-distance forces. Frictional forces, however, are a type of contact force.

21. **D.** Competency 2. The correct order of the methodology for an experiment is as follows:

    4. Identify a research question

    5. Formulate a hypothesis

    1. Plan a controlled experiment

    6. Collect data

    3. Analyze data and draw conclusions

    2. Revisit the hypothesis to answer the question

22. **C.** Competency 5. Amphibians are animals that live part of their lives on land and part of their lives in water and have adaptations for living in both places.

23. **C.** Competency 3. Igneous rock is formed when magma cools. Metamorphic rock transforms through change in environment like burial. Sedimentary rock is formed by the accumulation of rocks that fuse together to make a new rock. Compressed rock is formed when forces push the rock toward its center.

24. **B.** Competency 1. A giraffe's neck would be measured in meters. Kilometers and miles are too long. Millimeters are too small.

25. **C.** Competency 1. During an exploration, the students should be working independently or in groups on collecting and analyzing the data. The teacher should be monitoring the students' progress.

26. **D.** Competency 5. A crystal grows and develops, which is a characteristic of a living thing. It is not made up of cells, it does not obtain and use energy, and it does not adapt to the environment; therefore, it is not a living thing.

27. **A.** Competency 2. The chart shows petroleum usage at 41% and natural gas usage at 20%, making petroleum usage almost double that of natural gas. Nuclear power usage is higher than hydroelectric usage. The chart does not provide any indication related to what should or should not be done, so choice C is incorrect. Coal and natural gas together provide for 45% of the usage, which is not more than half of the energy usage shown in the chart.

Mathematics

1. **C.** Competency 1. The use of five blocks as part of an activity dealing with numeration involves the concrete representation model. A word name and standard numeral involve the abstract level. The pictorial model involves pictures or drawings.

2. **D.** Competency 2. Each term is 3 times the term before. The next term is $54 \times 3 = 162$.

3. **C.** Competency 3. First, you should convert to a common standard unit; for example, using feet, we have 36 inches = 3 feet, 5 feet, and 2 yards = 6 feet. We can assume that the legs of the triangular garden are 3 feet and 5 feet (the hypotenuse is the largest side of a right triangle); so, we need to add 3 feet to each one: 3 + 3 = 6 and 5 + 3 = 8. The hypotenuse is now 6 + 4 = 10. Perimeter is the distance around a shape. The perimeter is now 6 + 8 + 10 = 24 feet. Similarly, you could convert to inches instead of feet.

4. **A.** Competency 1. A bar graph using horizontal rectangular bars to show the frequency of each value and numerals to show the frequency values involves the pictorial and abstract representation models. The horizontal rectangular bars are pictorial representations, and the numerals used for the frequency values are abstract representations.

5. **B.** Competency 4. To find the mean of this set of data, find the sum of the scores (out of 100 points), and divide by the number of scores (9 in this case): (80 + 23 + 55 + 58 + 45 + 32 + 40 + 55 + 50) ÷ 9 = 438 ÷ 9 = 48.666… or approximately 49 (rounded to the nearest whole number).

6. **B.** Competency 4. Order data from least to greatest: 23, 32, 40, 45, 50, 55, 55, 58, 80. The median is the middle score in the data. Because we have an odd number of scores (9), the middle of the data is 5th score. Counting from left to right, 50 is the 5th value (counting from right to left, 50 is still the 5th value). The median is 50.

7. **D.** Competency 4. The range is the difference between the greatest score and the least score: 80 − 23 = 57. The range of this data set is 57.

8. **D.** Competency 4. The mode is 55, which is the one with the highest frequency (it appears twice).

9. **C.** Competency 5. Complementary angles add up to 90 degrees. $\angle ABC$ is a right angle. $\angle CBD$ is complementary to $\angle ABD$.

10. **B.** Competency 3. The number 3^{-2} is equal to $\left(\dfrac{1}{3}\right)^2 = \dfrac{1}{9}$

11. **B.** Competency 2. The farmer sells his bushels for $5 each. If he sells b bushels at the market, he would obtain $5b$ dollars. It cost him $50 to have the booth. This should be subtracted from the income of the booth to find the profit. The profit is $5b - 50$.

12. **B.** Competency 3. The shadow and the height are sides of similar triangles. Set up a proportion: $\dfrac{40 \text{ inches}}{36 \text{ inches}} = \dfrac{10 \text{ feet}}{x \text{ feet}}$. Cross multiply, so $40x = 360$. Divide both sides by 40: $x = 9$ feet.

13. **C.** Competency 3. The number 465^0 is equal to 1 because any number with an exponent of zero is equal to 1. It is not negative, zero, or equal to itself.

14. **D.** Competency 2. He needs to have 3 school buses to take the students on the field trip. He can fit 56 students per school bus, and 140 students divided by 56 students per school bus is equal to 2 school buses with a remainder of 28 students. This means that he will need an extra school bus to fit the 28 remaining students. You cannot have one-half of a bus. The choice 2 R28 does not answer the question.

15. **C.** Competency 1. Of the tools listed, the most appropriate to help students develop classification skills are the pattern blocks. Cuisenaire rods are more appropriate for modeling numeration and operation activities, including whole numbers, fractions, decimals, addition, subtraction, multiplication, and division ideas. Algebra tiles are more appropriate for representing equations and functions involving variables. Fraction tiles are more appropriate for modeling fraction concepts and operations.

16. **A.** Competency 5. Consider each choice:

Acute triangles have all angles less than 90 degrees. Isosceles triangles have at least two sides of equal length. A triangle can be acute and isosceles. The statement in choice A is TRUE.

You can stop here or go on to double-check your logic by reviewing choices B, C, and D.

An obtuse triangle has one angle that is greater than 90 degrees. An equilateral triangle has all equal sides. Since all the sides of an equilateral triangle are the same, all the angles will be the same as well. Since the angles of a triangle add to 180 degrees, each angle in an equilateral triangle is 60 degrees. An equilateral triangle cannot be obtuse. The statement in choice B is FALSE.

A right triangle has one angle equal to 90 degrees. The other two angles must be less than 90 degrees for the total of all three angles to be 180 degrees. An obtuse triangle has one angle that is greater than 90 degrees. A right triangle cannot be obtuse. The statement in choice C is FALSE.

An equilateral triangle has all equal sides. A scalene triangle has all different side lengths. A triangle cannot be equilateral and scalene. The statement in choice D is FALSE.

The only choice that is true is A.

17. B. Competency 3. The value of $2^{-6} \cdot -8$ is $\left(\dfrac{1}{2}\right)^{6} \cdot -8 = \dfrac{1}{64} \cdot -8 = \dfrac{-8}{64} = \dfrac{-1}{8}$.

18. C. Competency 5. Point R is three units to the left and two units down from the origin $(0, 0)$. This makes the coordinates of point R $(-3, -2)$.

19. B. Competency 1. Two-color chips are the least appropriate manipulative to help students develop area ideas. Geoboards, color tiles, and pattern blocks are more appropriate for developing area ideas. The two-color chips are more appropriate for working with number combinations, fractions as part of a set, and operations involving whole numbers, fractions or integers.

20. C. Competency 2. Follow the order of operations to simplify the explanation.

$$
\begin{aligned}
30^2 - 60 \div 12 \cdot \left(\dfrac{1}{5} - 5^{-2}\right) \cdot 15 + 78 &= 900 - 60 \div 12 \cdot \left(\dfrac{1}{5} - \dfrac{1}{25}\right) \cdot 15 + 78 \\
&= 900 - 60 \div 12 \cdot \left(\dfrac{5}{25} - \dfrac{1}{25}\right) \cdot 15 + 78 \\
&= 900 - 60 \div 12 \cdot \left(\dfrac{4}{25}\right) \cdot 15 + 78 \\
&= 900 - 5 \cdot \left(\dfrac{4}{25}\right) \cdot 15 + 78 \\
&= 900 - \left(\dfrac{4}{5}\right) \cdot 15 + 78 \\
&= 900 - (4) \cdot 3 + 78 \\
&= 900 - 12 + 78 \\
&= 966
\end{aligned}
$$

21. A. Competency 1. Place value is the principle prerequisite needed for students' solving 3-digit addition computation exercises with understanding because of the decomposition and regrouping processes involved. In this case, the use of a calculator will not help with students' understanding of the computation algorithm. Memorization of basic addition facts could help with students' speed and accuracy, but not necessarily with understanding the problem. Students' prior work with 2-digit whole number computation might help, but will not necessarily help with understanding the computation algorithm involved with 3-digit whole numbers without proper understanding of place value ideas.

22. C. Competency 2.

$$
\begin{aligned}
3x - 4 + x &= x + 8 + 3x - 2x \\
4x - 4 &= 2x + 8 && \text{(Combine like terms.)} \\
2x - 4 &= 8 && \text{(Subract } 2x \text{ from both sides.)} \\
2x &= 12 && \text{(Add 4 to both sides.)} \\
x &= 6 && \text{(Divide both sides by 2.)}
\end{aligned}
$$

23. **C.** Competency 2. The statement "The expression $2x$ is greater than the expression $2 + x$" is sometimes true because it depends on the value assigned to x. If $x = 2$, then both expressions are equal; if $x > 2$, then $2x$ is greater than $2 + x$; and if $x < 2$, then $2 + x$ is greater than $2x$.

24. **B.** Competency 2. The equation $t = 0.5 + 5b$ could be used to represent this situation, where t represents the total cost, 0.5 represents the one-time service charge, and $5b$ represents the cost of 5 boxes of cookies.

25. **B.** Competency 1. A is not the best choice. Getting 7 out of 8 correct meets the criterion of 85% accuracy. These students do not struggle with whole number computation.

B is correct. Generally, all of the students are proficient in problems involving whole number operations. However, these four students seem to be struggling with questions involving fraction addition.

C is not the best choice. None of these three students seem to struggle with whole number computation or fraction addition; they all meet the criterion of 85% accuracy in both skills.

D is not the best choice. Nicosha, Allan, Daniel, and Sabrina do not struggle with whole number computation.

26. **D.** Competency 1. A is not the best choice because locating details in a problem solving activity is a low complexity level activity.

B is not the best choice because comparing word meanings in a problem solving activity is a moderate complexity level activity.

C is not the best choice because summarizing the major points of a problem solving activity is a moderate complexity level activity.

D is the best choice because analyzing the use of figurative language in a text is a high complexity level activity.

Chapter 2

Language Arts and Reading

This chapter provides a general review of Language Arts and Reading competencies with sample questions and explanations at the end of the chapter. Checkpoint exercises are found throughout, giving you an opportunity to practice the skills addressed in this section. The answers to the Checkpoint exercises immediately follow the set of questions. We encourage you to cover the answers as you complete the Checkpoint exercises.

Competency 1: Knowledge of the Reading Process

Competency Description

According to the *Competencies and Skills Required for Teacher Certification in Florida,* 20th Edition (available at www.fldoe.org/asp/ftce/pdf/ftce20edition.pdf), **Competency 1** for the Elementary Education (K–6) Subject Area Examination (SAE) Language Arts and Reading subtest addresses the following key indicators:

1. Identify the content of emergent literacy (e.g., oral language development, phonological awareness, alphabet knowledge, decoding, concepts of print, motivation, text structures, written language development).

2. Identify the processes, skills, and stages of word recognition that lead to effective decoding (e.g., pre-alphabetic, partial-alphabetic, full-alphabetic, graphophonemic, morphemic).

3. Select and apply instructional methods for the development of decoding and encoding skills (e.g., continuous blending, chunking).

4. Distinguish among the components of reading fluency (e.g., accuracy, automaticity, rate, prosody).

5. Choose and apply instructional methods for developing reading fluency (e.g., practice with high-frequency words, readers theater, repeated readings).

6. Identify and differentiate instructional methods and strategies for increasing vocabulary acquisition across the content areas (e.g., word analysis, author's word choice, context clues, multiple exposures).

7. Identify and evaluate instructional methods and strategies for facilitating students' reading comprehension (e.g., summarizing, self-monitoring, questioning, use of graphic and semantic organizers, think alouds, recognizing story structure).

8. Identify essential comprehension skills (e.g., main idea, supporting details and facts, author's purpose, point of view, inference, conclusion).

9. Determine appropriate uses of multiple representations of information for a variety of purposes (e.g., charts, tables, graphs, pictures, print and nonprint media).

10. Determine and analyze strategies for developing critical-thinking skills such as analysis, synthesis, and evaluation (e.g., making connections and predictions, questioning, summarizing, question generating).

11. Evaluate and select appropriate instructional strategies for teaching a variety of informational and literary text.

Overview

Knowledge of the reading process is one of the most important, if not the most important, aspect of elementary education. Approximately **17 questions** address Competency 1. This section addresses the following areas related to **Competency 1** key indicators:

- Emergent Literacy
- The Five Major Components of Reading
  - Word Recognition Skills

- Critical Thinking Strategies
- Reading Fluency
- Reading Comprehension
- Informational and Literary Text Structures

Emergent Literacy

Emergent literacy is defined as the skills, knowledge, and attitudes that are developmental precursors to conventional forms of reading and writing (www.ed.gov/, n.d.). Young children learn that text and pictures provide meaning. They learn to appreciate, explore, and enjoy text. During this phase, children are exposed to the structure or syntax of language and are encouraged to predict what the text may be about. Simply stated, students at this phase are getting to know books and learning about print. The following are terms related to emergent literacy:

- **Oral language development**—In order to enhance a student's oral language or verbal skills, students must be involved in the following on a regular basis: open-ended (whole group, small group, and one-on-one) discussions, read alouds, echo reading, songs, nursery rhymes, storytelling, readers theater, cloze activities, poetry, role play and drama, fingerplays, and so on.

- **Phonics**—Phonics lessons teach readers to associate the letters of the alphabet with their sound values. Knowledge of the letter-sound relationship is vital to beginning readers. For example, digraphs are two consonants that together represent one sound, and a consonant blend is two consonants that together keep their individual sounds.

- **Phonological awareness**—Phonological awareness includes the ability of a student to identify and manipulate large parts of spoken language (words, syllables, onset-rime units) and awareness of other aspects of sound in language like **alliteration,** intonation, and rhyming.

- **Alphabet knowledge**—Alphabet knowledge requires young learners to identify and name the upper- and lowercase letters of the alphabet. Alphabet books, magnetic letters, and the use of environmental print all enhance alphabet knowledge.

- **Concepts of print**—Knowledge of how print works is vital. Young learners should understand that print conveys meaning, directionality (left to right and top to bottom progression), concept of a word (word boundaries), letter knowledge, phonemic awareness, and literacy language (author, illustrations, title, and so on).

- **Voice-to-print matching**—Voice-to-print matching is essentially reading aloud and matching the voice to the print. This technique is often used with beginning readers in the primary grades.

Repetition and routine are key components of high-quality instruction for young students. Through daily read alouds, guided reading, and shared reading instruction, students can be exposed to basic concepts of print, word recognition skills, vocabulary, sight words, high-frequency words, literary elements, content knowledge, narrative and expository structure, and comprehension strategies, just to name a few. This type of routine and repetitive instruction provides students the opportunity to truly internalize the necessary skills to become successful readers. Specifically, the incorporation of these basic concepts in small group guided reading settings can prevent difficulties with emergent literacy skills or intervene when these skills pose difficulty to students. This being said, consistently monitoring their growth by using various assessments is not only mandated by the state, but it is also vital to the teacher's instructional goals. Whether formal or informal, assessments help the teacher identify students' strengths and weaknesses. In order to instruct and create lesson plans that meet the varying needs of the diverse population in the classroom, teachers must employ various assessment instruments. The following are examples of various assessment instruments and how they can be used with young students:

- **Concepts of print**—Checklist that identifies basic knowledge of print conventions and overall book structure (that is, letter identification, word boundaries, book cover, and so on).

- **Checklists**—High-frequency word checklists can be used as screening and progress monitoring tools to instantly assess what words students know.

- **Rubrics**—Retelling rubrics can be used to identify what important literary elements students are incorporating into their retelling.
- **Games**—Sight word bingo can be used to informally assess sight word recognition.
- **Surveys**—Interest and attitude surveys can be used to gauge attitudes about reading and identify topics of interest to the students.
- **Portfolios**—Working and/or growth portfolios can be used to collect work samples over time to gain true insight into how the students' skills have progressed.

Checkpoint

1. Fill in the blanks: Phonological awareness refers to the ability to _____ and _____ large parts of spoken language.

2. True or false: Oral language skills can be enhanced through songs, echo reading, and story retellings.

3. Fill in the blanks: _____ and _____ are two informal assessment instruments.

4. True or false: Emergent literacy refers to the *latter* part of the reading process.

5. True or false: Basic concepts of print include but are not limited to directionality, title page, and illustrations.

6. True or false: Oral language development can be enhanced through class and small group discussions.

7. Fill in the blank: _____ is a literary genre that is pleasant to the ear and contains short text that aids phonological awareness skills in young learners.

8. Fill in the blank: _____ is the concept of print that refers to the left to right and top to bottom progression of text on the printed page.

Checkpoint Answers

1. identify; manipulate

2. True

3. Any two of the following: checklists, rubrics, games, concepts of print, surveys, portfolios

4. False

5. True

6. True

7. Poetry

8. Directionality

The Five Major Components of Reading

The following are five critical skills necessary for success in reading:

1. **Phonemic awareness** is the ability to hear and manipulate the sounds of spoken language. This includes noticing rhyme and recognizing the separate, small sounds in words (phonemes).

2. **Phonics** is the understanding of the relationships between the written letters of the alphabet and the sounds of spoken language. This knowledge allows a reader to "decode" words by translating the letters into speech sounds.

3. **Fluency** is the ability to read at an appropriate rate, accurately, and with prosody (proper expression). Fluent readers can concentrate on understanding what they read because they don't have to focus on decoding.

4. **Vocabulary** includes all the words the reader can understand and use. The more words a child knows, the better he or she will understand what is read. Knowing how words relate to each other is a building block that leads to comprehension.

5. **Comprehension** is the ability to understand what one has read. This includes understanding the plot of a story or the information in an article. It also includes things like recognizing the main idea of an article or being able to compare and contrast different characters in a story. (www.justreadflorida.com/docs/Read_to_Learn.pdf)

Word Recognition Skills

Word recognition means that the student has the ability to visually identify words in isolation or context. The goal of enhancing word recognition is to enable students to understand how words work. The phases of word recognition are pre-alphabetic, partial-alphabetic, full-alphabetic, graphophonemic, and morphemic.

Critical Thinking Strategies

Critical thinking strategies include the following:

- **Making connections**—Teachers facilitate and encourage three types of connections to text to aid reading comprehension: text to self, text to text, and text to world. A text to self connection implies that the reader has made a connection from the reading to his or her own personal life. A text to text connection implies that the reader has made a connection from the reading to another book with a similar writing style, theme, or topic. A text to world connection implies that the reader has made a connection from the reading to a topic or an event that has taken or is taking place in the world. Whatever the connection, the act of making any connection helps the reader to better remember and comprehend the text.

- **Making predictions**—Making predictions about what a particular text is going to be about aids student comprehension. Prior to the reading of a particular text, the front cover, including the title and illustration or photograph, can be used by the teacher and students to predict what they think the text is going to be about. Then throughout the reading, these predictions can be affirmed or revised according to the content of the selection, both written and visual.

- **Questioning**—Questioning is the strategy that helps students make meaning of the text being read. Teachers must model a variety of questions for students to then internalize and implement in their own reading. Students should read with a purpose and question in mind. Questions about the content of the text, the author's intent, and questions that lead to further research about a particular topic are all appropriate. There are four key types of questions:
  - "Right there" questions (text explicit)—These are literal questions in which the answer is in the text itself.
  - "Think and search" questions (text implicit)—The answer is implicit in the text, but the student must synthesize, infer, or summarize to find the answer. Think and search questions tend to be more open-ended without set answers.
  - "Reader and author" questions (text implicit or experience-based)—The reader needs to generate the answer by combining his or her own experiences with what the text states, that is, the knowledge presented by the author.
  - "On my own" questions (text implicit or experience-based)—The reader needs to generate the answer from his or her prior knowledge. The reader may not need to read the text to answer, but the answer would certainly be shaped differently after reading the text.

- **Summarizing**—To summarize is to simply and concisely paraphrase what has been read. This takes place during and after the reading. Summarizing what has been read can be done orally (whole group, small group, pairs) or in writing.

- **Chunking**—To break down words for the purpose of decoding words in a text.

Reading Fluency

Components of reading fluency include the following:

- **Accuracy**—Ability to correctly read the words in a text
- **Automaticity**—Ability to instantly recognize a large bank of words and to quickly decode unfamiliar words
- **Rate**—Speed of reading
- **Prosody**—Ability to read with appropriate rhythm, intonation, and expression

To become fluent, students must have a strong foundation in word recognition and must spend time reading. The more students read, the more fluent they become. Fluent readers focus on comprehension and make connections, read with expression and phrasing, decode quickly, and self-correct when their reading does not make sense.

A sampling of instructional methods that aid fluency include repetitive or repeated reading, oral reading, echo reading, choral reading, timed reading, readers theater, audio books, poetry readings, independent reading, and paired reading.

Reading Comprehension

The following are skills essential to reading comprehension:

- **Recognizing the main idea**—Identifying the main idea means determining the essential message of a reading selection. The main idea can be constructed from the various supporting details in the text.
- **Finding supporting details and facts**—The supporting details and facts in a selection provide the reader with the vital information needed to synthesize and summarize what is being read.
- **Determining the author's purpose**—Identifying the author's purpose or point of view is vital to comprehension. For example, the author's purpose for writing the text could be to explain, inform, persuade, or entertain.
- **Distinguishing between fact and opinion**—A fact is a piece of information that is true and accurate. An opinion is a personal judgment. Students should be able to read a selection and identify what is fact and what is someone's opinion.
- **Determining point of view**—A point of view is a way of looking at something. Authors write from varying points of view. Student should be able to identify from which point of view an author is writing.
- **Making inferences**—Making an inference is often referred to as "reading between the lines" or deriving meaning from the implied or underlying theme/point of the text. An inference often includes merging what is already known about a topic to the new information being presented.
- **Visualizing**—To visualize a text means to create mental pictures in one's mind about the content of the reading.
- **Drawing conclusions or summarizing**—The conclusion is the end or summation of a reading selection. To summarize is to simply and concisely paraphrase what has been read. This takes place after the reading and can be done orally or in writing. This summation of the reading is often included in a retelling of the selection. Students can use the Think-Pair-Share technique to discuss their summaries with partners.

The following instructional methods and skills facilitate student reading comprehension:

- **Activating prior knowledge**—Students must connect what they hear, read, and view with what they already know. Making these connections to the text enables readers to process the information and add the new knowledge to what they already know. Students can use the Think-Pair-Share technique to discuss what they already know about a topic with partners. Teachers can use graphic organizers, like K-W-L charts, to elicit what students already know about a topic.
- **Self-monitoring**—Being aware of their thinking as they are reading is what self-monitoring is all about. Students must pause periodically to reflect and think about the information being presented in the text. This reflection may lead to students making adjustments to their thinking and inevitably gaining greater meaning from the text.

- **Questioning**—Questioning is the strategy that helps students make meaning of the text being read. Teachers must model a variety of questions for students to then internalize and implement in their own reading. Students should read with a purpose and question in mind. Questions that clarify the content of the text and the author's intent and questions that lead to further research about a particular topic are all appropriate.

- **Using graphic and semantic organizers**—Graphic and semantic organizers are used by teachers and students to highlight the big ideas in a text and to facilitate connections. These organizers synthesize and summarize the reading to aid comprehension.

- **Vocabulary**—Student understanding of literary and domain-specific vocabulary is vital to text comprehension. Pre-teaching vocabulary not specifically defined in context can aid student understanding while reading. Special attention to domain-specific vocabulary (i.e., math, science, and social studies) is particularly important in the content areas. These terms are not part of a student's daily oral or written vocabulary; therefore, they must be taught explicitly during units of study utilizing content area reading materials.

- **Think alouds**—Also known as "talking to the text," this instructional method involves the teacher modeling her thoughts *aloud* while reading text (fiction and informational) aloud to her students. Teachers often incorporate vocabulary into their think alouds to pre-teach new words and their meaning. Once modeled by the teacher, think alouds can be practiced by students with partners.

- **Recognizing story structure**—Narratives or stories have a beginning, middle, and end and incorporate such literary elements as setting, characters, and plot. Teachers highlight and facilitate the analyzing of story structure through questioning techniques before, during, and after a read aloud or shared reading.

Informational and Literary Text Structures

Unlike literary or narrative text, informational or nonfiction text is structured using organizational aids called text features. The following is a list of common text features used in informational text: title, table of contents, headings, subheadings, bold and italicized words, illustrations, photographs, labeled diagrams, charts, graphs, tables, glossary, and index.

These text features usually support the body of the text and help to synthesize and summarize the information being presented. Previewing the text, paying specific attention to these features, aids students in not only reading the body of the informational text but also in identifying the various features in place to aid their comprehension of the content. Text feature "scavenger hunts" can be performed to locate the text features present in a particular text. After reading, a variety of graphic organizers (cause and effect, Venn diagrams, double-entry journals, time-lines, and so on) can be used to further explore the content.

Most literary text or narratives have a logical sequence. Students can be taught to recognize the beginning, middle, and end of a story through story retellings after a read aloud.

Checkpoint

1. Fill in the blank: _____ is a vital part of understanding content area reading text because knowing the meaning of specific words is paramount to comprehension.

2. True or false: "Talking to the text" is also known as a strategy called a *think aloud*.

3. True or false: Graphophonemic is a phase of word recognition in elementary-age students that refers to the letter-sound relationship.

4. Fill in the blanks: _____ and _____ are two of the many essential skills related to reading comprehension.

5. Fill in the blank: Breaking down words for the purpose of decoding is known as _____.

6. Fill in the blank: A _____ is an example of a nonfiction/informational text feature.

Checkpoint Answers

1. Vocabulary

2. True

3. True

4. Any two of the following: recognizing the main idea, finding supporting details and facts, determining the author's purpose, distinguishing between fact and opinion, determining point of view, making inferences, visualizing, drawing conclusions or summarizing.

5. chunking

6. Any of the following: chart, table, graph, timeline, sidebar, inset, photograph, labeled diagram, bold print, etc.

Competency 2: Knowledge of Literary Analysis and Genres

Competency Description

According to the *Competencies and Skills Required for Teacher Certification in Florida,* 20th Edition (available at www.fldoe.org/asp/ftce/pdf/ftce20edition.pdf), **Competency 2** for the Elementary Education (K–6) Subject Area Examination (SAE) Language Arts and Reading subtest addresses the following key indicators:

1. Differentiate among characteristics and elements of a variety of literary genres (e.g., realistic fiction, fantasy, poetry, informational texts).
2. Identify and analyze terminology and intentional use of literary devices (e.g., simile, metaphor, personification, onomatopoeia, hyperbole).
3. Evaluate and select appropriate multicultural texts based on purpose, relevance, cultural sensitivity, and developmental appropriateness.
4. Identify and evaluate appropriate techniques for varying student responses to texts (e.g., Think-Pair-Share, reading response journals, evidence-based discussion).

Overview

Knowledge of literature and the ability to analyze literature's many genres and forms is of primary importance to elementary educators. There are approximately **10 questions** that address Competency 2. This section addresses the following areas related to **Competency 2** key indicators:

- Literary Genres
- Literary Elements and Devices
- Multicultural Children's Literature
- Literature Response

Literary Genres

Children's literature can be defined as books written primarily for children. The books can be categorized into several genres or types. There are eight main genres of children's literature: poetry, folklore, fantasy, science fiction, realistic fiction, historical fiction, biography, and nonfiction (Galda, et al, 2013). These genres of children's literature may be presented in picture book or chapter book form and include a wide variety of settings, cultures, and ethnicities in hopes of broadening the readers' or listeners' horizons. The genres are defined here:

- **Poetry**—Contains short lines, imagery, and elements of sound, such as rhythm and rhyme; some examples of poetic forms include **haiku** (three lines with 5-7-5 syllables), **limerick** (five-line humorous poem with aabba rhyme scheme), **ode** (a lyrical and expressive poem), **diamante** (seven lines; form diamond shape), and **clerihew** (humorous verse consisting of two rhyming couplets, one of which includes a person's name)
- **Traditional Literature/Folklore**—Stories that were told by word of mouth: nursery rhymes, fairy tales, fables, myths, legends, tall tales
- **Fantasy**—Stories that could not happen in the real world
- **Science fiction**—Stories that might happen in the future; common themes include space travel, cloning, and utopian societies
- **Realistic fiction**—Stories focusing on events that *could* happen in the real world
- **Historical fiction**—Realistic stories set in the past
- **Biography**—Stories that tell the tale of a person's life
- **Autobiography**—Stories that tell the tale of a person's life written by the person himself or herself

- **Nonfiction**—Books that present information
- **Hybrid**—Books that possess two or more genres, with each genre being easily identified separately in the text

Checkpoint

1. True or false: Nursery rhymes, fairy tales, legends, and myths are all considered folklore.

2. Fill in the blank: Realistic stories set in the past that usually incorporate significant time periods and/or events in history are considered _____ fiction.

3. Fill in the blank: _____ are stories written by the individual that tell the tale of his or her life.

4. True or false: A hybrid text includes two or more genres; however, they are interwoven throughout the text to provide the illusion of a seamless writing piece.

Checkpoint Answers

1. True

2. historical

3. Autobiographies

4. False

Literary Elements and Devices

Each genre of children's literature contains **literary elements** that are specific to that type of writing. Literary elements such as setting, characters, plot, theme, and style are present in most **narratives,** while nonfiction text features like labeled diagrams and photographs present informative text in a comprehensible manner. Nonfiction text features include but are not limited to the following: titles, headings, subheadings, bold print, captions, charts, graphs, timelines, table of contents, index, glossary, and drawings.

Literary elements:

- **Setting**—Where the story takes place
- **Characters**—People or animals in a story, novel, or play
- **Plot**—The events that take place in a story; often includes a climax and resolution
- **Theme**—The subject or central idea of the story
- **Style**—The vocabulary and syntax the author uses to create the story

A sampling of literary devices:

- **Alliteration**—Two or more words or syllables, near each other, with the same beginning consonant
- **Hyperbole**—An exaggeration used to emphasize a point
- **Onomatopoeia**—The use of words to imitate sounds to reinforce their meaning (for example, *smash, bang, boom*)
- **Analogy**—A detailed and sometimes lengthy comparison of two ideas or events
- **Irony**—Using words or situations that mean the opposite of what the author intends
- **Personification**—Giving human qualities to a thing or abstraction
- **Climax**—The point of highest dramatic interest or a turning point in the story
- **Metaphor**—A comparison of two distinctly different things suggesting a similarity between them
- **Simile**—A comparison using *like* or *as*
- **Metonym**—A word used in metonymy like *the wagon* being used instead of *sobriety*

- **Synonym**—A word that means the same as or similar to a given word
- **Antonym**—A word that means the opposite of the given word
- **Idiom**—an expression that is peculiar and cannot be understood by the literal meaning of its elements; *my heart's beating out of my chest*
- **Figurative language**—Language that utilizes figures of speech, especially metaphors
- **Pun**—A humorous play on words
- **Literal language**—Obvious or non-figurative language
- **Literary language**—A dialect of language used in literary writing

Checkpoint

1. Fill in the blank: The _____ is the events that take place in the story.
2. True or false: The literary element of style refers to the appearance of the words on the page.
3. True or false: *Her eyes twinkle like the stars* is an example of personification.
4. Fill in the blank: _____ is a literary device that usually contains the word *like* or *as*.

Checkpoint Answers

1. plot
2. False
3. False
4. Simile

Multicultural Children's Literature

Multicultural children's literature can be loosely defined as books written for children that illuminate the variety of cultures, ethnicities, and traditions present in a country of multicultural heritage (Norton, 2009). Many children's authors write multicultural children's books based on their own heritage. For example, Tomie dePaola writes books related to his Italian ancestry; Patricia Polacco writes books based on her Ukrainian background, and Carmen Agra Deedy uses her knowledge of growing up in Cuba to influence the content of her books. Other authors take popular traditional literature also known as folklore and recreate the stories utilizing the traditions and lore of other cultures. Such common tales as *Cinderella* and *Little Red Riding Hood* have been written reflecting numerous cultures around the world. The provision of books in classroom libraries containing characters and traditions from multiple ethnicities and locations around the world is important to the overall goal of supporting well-rounded readers. Criteria that must be considered in the selection of quality multicultural children's literature is as follows (Galda, et al, 2013):

- Depicts diversity but avoids stereotyping of a particular culture
- Explores cultural differences and similarities in a sensitive manner
- Provides an accurate and positive portrayal of the culture represented
- Provides language and setting that is consistent with the culture and avoids stereotyping.

Checkpoint

1. Fill in the blank: A book portraying all Asian children as being smart and disciplined would be considered _____ of this culture.
2. True or false: Classroom libraries should contain a wide variety of multicultural children's literature to aid in the exploration and understanding of various cultures.
3. True or false: Patricia Polacco and Tomie dePaola are two authors who write multicultural text for children.
4. True or false: *Lon Po Po* is the Chinese version of the classic folktale *Little Red Riding Hood*.

Checkpoint Answers

1. stereotypical

2. True

3. True

4. True

Literature Response

Responding to literature in a variety of ways assists students with deeply comprehending a text. These activities help children to understand the essence of the stories they are reading. These responses can take on many forms, such as artistic literature response, discussion, drama, inquiry, written response, and **multimedia.**

- Artistic literature response incorporates a variety of artistic mediums such as drawing, painting, collage, and scratchboard.
- A response that involves discussion might include **literature circles** or book clubs (face to face or online) that encourage small, temporary, and **heterogeneous** groups of students to talk about the story they are reading.
- Dramatic responses might include poetry readings, **readers theater,** or storytelling.
- Inquiry could include research about a particular author (an author study) or topic (inquiry circles).
- Written response involves readers responding to what has been read in writing. The use of independent **graphic organizers,** reading logs, learning logs, and reading response journals are all examples of written response.
- Multimedia tools such as computer software programs or online resources can enhance student reading comprehension. Students could create PowerPoint presentations, podcasts, **Wiki** pages, digital storytellings, or **WebQuests** in response to literature.

Checkpoint

1. Fill in the blank: Responding to a piece of literature by drawing is an example of _____ literature response.

2. True or false: Small groups of students talking about a book they are reading are called book chats.

3. Fill in the blank: Reading response journals assist students with text _____.

Checkpoint Answers

1. artistic

2. False

3. comprehension

Competency 3: Knowledge of Language and the Writing Process

Competency Description

According to the *Competencies and Skills Required for Teacher Certification in Florida,* 20th Edition (available at www.fldoe.org/asp/ftce/pdf/ftce20edition.pdf), **Competency 3** for the Elementary Education (K–6) Subject Area Examination (SAE) Language Arts and Reading subtest addresses the following key indicators:

1. Identify and evaluate the developmental stages of writing (e.g., drawing, dictating, writing).
2. Differentiate stages of the writing process (e.g., prewriting, drafting, revising, editing, publishing).
3. Distinguish among the modes of writing (e.g., narrative, informative/explanatory, argument).
4. Select the appropriate mode of writing for a variety of occasions, purposes, and audiences.
5. Identify and apply instructional methods for teaching writing conventions (e.g., spelling, punctuation, capitalization, syntax, word usage).
6. Apply instructional methods for teaching writer's craft across genres (e.g., precise language, figurative language, linking words, temporal words, dialogue, sentence variety).

Overview

Knowledge of the writing process and its applications is of primary importance to elementary educators. There are approximately **10 questions** that address Competency 3. This section addresses the following areas related to **Competency 3** key indicators:

- Writing: Stages, Process, Modes, and Conventions
  - Developmental Writing Stages
  - The Writing Process
  - Modes of Writing
  - Teaching Writing Conventions

Writing: Stages, Process, Modes, and Conventions

Developmental Writing Stages

The developmental stages of writing begin with scribbling and end with conventional spelling. These stages include but are not limited to scribbling, mock handwriting, mock letters, conventional letters, invented—temporary—or phonetic spelling, and conventional spelling.

The Writing Process

The writing process includes the following stages and components:

- **Prewriting**—Activating prior knowledge; gathering and organizing ideas; may include brainstorming a list of ideas and researching/reading about a topic; may include deciding upon the intended audience
- **Drafting**—Transfer of ideas to paper; focus is on getting all thoughts down (the content) rather than on spelling, grammar, and mechanics
- **Revising**—Refining and clarifying the draft; focus is on meaning and further developing the writing piece
- **Editing**—Proofreading the draft for misspelled words and grammatical and mechanical errors; focus is on the mechanics (punctuation, sentence fragments, capitalization, etc.)
- **Publishing**—Sharing a final product

Modes of Writing

The mode of writing reveals the purpose of the writing as well as the intended audience:

- **Narrative writing** recounts a personal or fictional experience or tells a story based on a real or imagined event.
- **Opinion/Argument writing** attempts to argue a particular topic using claims, including the validity of the reasoning as well as the relevance and sufficiency of the evidence (www.corestandards.org/).
- **Descriptive writing** attempts to "paint a picture" or describe a person, place, thing, or idea.
- **Expository/explanatory writing** gives information, explains why or how, clarifies a process, or defines a concept.
- **Informative writing** informs the reader in an attempt to create newfound knowledge.
- **Creative writing** uses the writer's imagination.

Teaching Writing Conventions

Writing conventions include such mechanics as spelling, punctuation, capitalization, and grammar. These conventions can be taught to a whole group through modeled, shared, and interactive writing opportunities or to small groups and individuals during writing conferences. Students apply their knowledge of writing conventions during the editing and publishing phases of the writing process. Teachers can provide insight into their expectations of writing by providing detailed rubrics. Rubrics assessing writing should include sections related to the writing process, mode of writing, and the importance of spelling, punctuation, capitalization, and grammar.

Checkpoint

1. True or false: The editing phase of writing requires the writer to modify his or her writing for content.

2. True or false: Expository/explanatory writing attempts to convince the reader of a particular point of view.

3. Fill in the blank: The _____ stage of writing includes brainstorming and gathering and organizing ideas.

4. Fill in the blank: _____ is the first developmental phase of writing.

Checkpoint Answers

1. False

2. False

3. prewriting

4. Scribbling

Competency 4: Knowledge of Literacy Instruction and Assessment

Competency Description

According to the *Competencies and Skills Required for Teacher Certification in Florida,* 20th Edition (available at www.fldoe.org/asp/ftce/pdf/ftce20edition.pdf), **Competency 4** for the Elementary Education (K–6) Subject Area Examination (SAE) Language Arts and Reading subtest addresses the following key indicators:

1. Distinguish among different types of assessments (e.g., norm-referenced, criterion-referenced, diagnostic, curriculum-based) and their purposes and characteristics.

2. Select and apply oral and written methods for assessing student progress (e.g., informal reading inventories, fluency checks, rubrics, story retelling, portfolios).

3. Analyze assessment data (e.g., screening, progress monitoring, diagnostic) to guide instructional decisions and differentiate instruction.

4. Analyze and interpret students' formal and informal assessment results to inform students and stakeholders.

5. Evaluate the appropriateness of assessment instruments and practices.

6. Select appropriate classroom organizational formats (e.g., literature circles, small groups, individuals, workshops, reading centers, multiage groups) for specific instructional objectives.

7. Evaluate methods for the diagnosis, prevention, and intervention of common emergent literacy difficulties.

Overview

Knowledge of reading methods, assessment in the area of reading, and the instructional methods related specifically to emergent literacy is of primary importance to elementary educators. There are approximately **13 questions** that address Competency 4. This section addresses the following areas related to **Competency 4** key indicators:

- Reading Assessment
- Classroom Organizational Formats

Reading Assessment

Assessment is defined as the process for gathering data about students to identify areas of strength and weakness in order to guide future instruction. There are two basic types of assessment: formal and informal. Formal assessments include intelligence tests, achievement tests (norm- and criterion-referenced), and diagnostic tests. Informal assessments include but are not limited to informal reading inventories, running records, cloze tests, anecdotal notes, checklists, rubrics, portfolios, and surveys. The following are key terms and definitions related to reading assessment:

- **Norm-referenced tests**—Assessment instruments that have been administered to students of various socio-economic backgrounds and in a variety of geographic locations in order to develop *norms*. These norms are the average scores of the populations and serve as a comparison point for teachers to compare their student results with those of a similar population.

- **Criterion-referenced tests**—Assessment instruments that determine the point at which the student has achieved mastery. These tests enable educators to assess whether or not a student has met a predetermined goal. The former high stakes test in Florida known as the Florida Comprehensive Assessment Test (FCAT) was a criterion-referenced test.

- **Percentile ranking**—This standardized test score ranking compares a student to other students his or her age. For example if Brett earned a 75%, this means that 25% of his peers scored better than he did on a particular assessment, while 74% scored below him. (Devries, 2004)

- **Stanine score**—A stanine score is a score quite similar to a percentile score. The stanine scores range from one through nine. Scores of four through six are considered to be average. (Devries, 2004)

- **Diagnostic assessment**—Standardized tests (carefully constructed and field-tested) that aim to determine a student's strengths and weaknesses.

- **Performance-based assessment**—Also known as authentic assessment, this form of assessment incorporates real-life applications of what has been taught and enables the teacher to assess meaningful and complex educational products and performances.

- **Fluency checks**—Quick (usually 1-minute timed readings) assessments that focus on accuracy, rate, and prosody; students' WPM (words per minute) or WCPM (words correct per minute) are calculated.

  - Words Per Minute (WPM) formula: $\dfrac{\text{Number of words} \times 60}{\text{Number of seconds}}$

  Example: A student read a 188-word piece in 4 minutes 30 seconds. His reading rate would be as follows:

  $\dfrac{188 \times 60}{270 \text{ (seconds)}} = 41.8$ WPM. Thus, this student reads at 41.8 words per minute.

  - Words Correct Per Minute (WCPM) formula: $\dfrac{\text{Number of words} - \text{errors } (x - E) \cdot 60}{\text{Number of seconds}}$

  Example: A student read a 188-word piece in 4 minutes 30 seconds with four recorded errors. Her accuracy

  rate would be as follows: $\dfrac{188 - 4(x - E) \cdot 60}{270 \text{ (seconds)}} = 40.9$ WCPM. Thus, the student reads 40.9 words correct per minute.

- **Informal reading inventories (IRIs)**—Individual tests that generally include lists of words or sentences and leveled reading passages with accompanying questions. These inventories can be performed quickly and provide valuable information on the students' independent, instructional, and frustration reading levels. Teachers calculate the student's accuracy rate, expressed as a percentage (see the following formula and table) to identify the appropriate reading level. You can use accuracy rate to determine whether the text (leveled selection) read is easy enough for independent reading, difficult enough to warrant instruction yet avoid frustration, or too difficult for the reader. Teachers then use this valuable information to guide reading instruction and provide for differentiated instruction.

  Teachers can calculate the accuracy rate by using the following formula:

  $$\dfrac{(\text{Total words read} - \text{total errors})}{\text{Total words read}} \times 100 = \text{Accuracy rate}$$

  OR

  $$\dfrac{(TW - E)}{TW} \times 100 = AR$$

  For example:

  $$\dfrac{(120 - 6)}{120} \times 100 = \text{accuracy rate}$$

  $$\dfrac{114}{120} \times 100 = \text{accuracy rate}$$

  $$.95 \times 100 = 95\%$$

Reading Level	Accuracy Rate Range*
Independent reading level	95–100%
Instructional reading level (appropriate for use in guided reading session)	90–94%
Frustration reading level	89% and below

*Depending on the IRI being used, the percentages could vary.

- **Rubric**—A rubric is a set of scoring guidelines or criteria for evaluating student work. Rubrics often provide specific guidelines regarding teacher expectations.
- **Running records**—Informal assessments that enable the teacher to observe, score, and interpret a student's reading behaviors. Observations include:
  - **Errors (E)**—Errors are tallied during the reading whenever a student does any of the following: Substitutes another word for a word in the text, omits a word, inserts a word, or has to be told a word by the person administering the running record.
  - **Self-corrections (SC)**—Self-correction occurs when a student realizes his error and corrects it. When a student makes a self-correction, the previous substitution is not scored as an error.
  - **Meaning (M)**—Meaning is part of the semantic cueing system in which the student takes her cue to make sense of text by thinking about the story background, information from pictures, or the meaning of a sentence. These cues assist in the reading of a word or phrase.
  - **Structure (S)**—Structure refers to the structure of language and is often referred to as syntax (syntactic cueing system). Implicit knowledge of structure helps the reader know whether what he reads sounds correct.
  - **Visual (V)**—Visual information (graphophonemic cueing system) is related to the look of the letter in a word and the word itself. A reader uses visual information when he studies the beginning sound, word length, familiar word chunks, and so on.
- **Analyzing a running record**—Qualitative analysis is based on observations the teacher makes during the running record. It involves observing how the student uses the meaning (M), structural (S), and visual (V) cues to help her read. It also involves paying attention to fluency, intonation, and phrasing. When a student makes an error in a line of text, record the source(s) of information used by the student in the second column from the right on the running record form. Write M, S, and V to the right of the sentence in that column. Then circle M, S, and/or V, depending on the source(s) of information the student used.
- **Scoring a running record**—Information gathered while doing a running record is used to determine error, accuracy, and self-correction rates. Directions for calculating these rates follow. The calculated rates, along with qualitative information and the student's comprehension of the text, are used to determine a student's reading level.

  Error rate is expressed as a ratio and is calculated by dividing the total number of words read by the total number of errors made.

  $$\frac{\text{Total words}}{\text{Total errors}} = \text{Error rate}$$

OR

  $$\frac{TW}{E} = ER$$

For example:

  $$\frac{120}{6} = 20$$

The ratio is expressed as 1:20. This means that for each error made, the student read 20 words correctly. For information on determining the accuracy rate, see the IRI bullet point on the previous page.

Self-correction is expressed as a ratio and is calculated by using the following formula:

  $$\frac{\text{Errors} + \text{self-correction}}{\text{self-correction}} = \text{Self-correction rate}$$

OR

  $$\frac{(E + SC)}{SC} = SC \text{ rate}$$

For example:

$$\frac{(10+5)}{5} = SC \text{ rate}$$

$$\frac{15}{5} = SC \text{ rate}$$

$$3 = SC \text{ rate}$$

The SC is expressed as 1:3. This means that the student corrects 1 out of every 3 errors. If a student is self-correcting at a rate of 1:3 or less, this indicates that she is self-monitoring her reading.

- **Screening**—A screening instrument is used to assess students at the beginning of the year to identify the students' reading level and capabilities. This screening tool can then be compared to the progress monitoring assessments to show growth over time.

- **Progress monitoring**—A progress monitoring instrument is used throughout the year to show gains in reading achievement and to provide information to the teacher that will help guide instruction.

- **Anecdotal notes (records)**—Anecdotal notes or records are short, concise, written observations made by the teacher while students work. Their purpose is to observe and record information that may be useful in guiding reading instruction and sharing student capabilities with parents. Dating these notes and filing them in a student portfolio or lesson plan book ensures easy access to ongoing informal information about the student.

- **Cueing systems**—There are three main cueing systems: semantic, syntactic, and graphophonemic. The semantic cueing system focuses on any meaning a student derives from a sentence that is primarily based on prior knowledge. Students using the semantic cueing system can identify sentences that make sense and those that do not. Teachers can ask, "Did that make sense?" when a semantic error is made. The syntactic cueing system focuses on the structure of the sentence and how language works. Students using the syntactic cueing system can identify sentences that sound correct. The teacher can ask, "Does that sound right?" when a syntactical error is made. The graphophonemic cueing system focuses on various visual cues and knowledge about the relationship between sounds and symbols. The student's phonological awareness is very important for this cueing system. If you were using the graphophonemic cueing system, you would want to investigate how students apply their knowledge of phonology as they read. Teachers can ask, "Does that look right?" when a graphophonemic error is made.

- **Miscue analysis**—A technique for recording and analyzing students' oral reading errors in order to gain insight into the reading process they employ. It is useful to ask comprehension questions or ask students to retell what they have read after the reading to determine how well students have understood the text.

- **Cloze test**—The cloze procedure involves getting students to fill in words deliberately omitted from a passage of text. This procedure assists students in the prediction and the use of context clues.

- **Response logs**—A response log is an informal assessment that documents students' reading, viewing, and listening. Students record thoughts and feelings as they read, listen to, or watch literary, factual, or media texts. It is important to encourage students to value their own responses to texts.

- **Retelling**—Retelling is a technique that involves reading, either silently or aloud, and then retelling what has been read. In the retelling, a student reveals the parts of the text that were more significant to him.

Checkpoint

1. True or false: A criterion-referenced test is an example of a formal assessment.

2. True or false: The three main cueing systems are semantic, syntactic, and graphophonemic.

3. Fill in the blank: _____ are short, concise written observations made while students work.

4. Fill in the blank: A _____ instrument is used to assess students at the beginning of the year to identify the students' reading level and capabilities.

Checkpoint Answers

1. True

2. True

3. Anecdotal notes

4. screening

Classroom Organizational Formats

- Literature circles are small, temporary, and heterogeneous groups of students that gather together to discuss a book of their choice with the goal of enhancing comprehension.

- A workshop approach to literacy provides a framework for teachers and students to learn together in a meaningful way. A workshop organizational format usually begins with teacher demonstration and modeling (mini-lessons), an opportunity for guided practice of the skills and content, independent practice (individual or small group), and ends with opportunities for sharing. While the independent practice takes place, teachers provide small group or individual differentiated instruction to meet the needs of their students. During this time in reading, the teacher usually provides guided reading lessons to primary students or facilitates literature circles in the intermediate grades. During a writing workshop, teachers usually conduct small group lessons or meet one on one with students to confer about their writing.

- Literacy centers/stations are essential to a balanced literacy program and offer a wide variety of learning opportunities to students. These centers allow the students time to practice and apply what they are learning in a small group setting. Examples of some literacy centers are poetry, listening, word work, writing, spelling, comprehension, literature response, vocabulary, art, and independent reading.

- Small groups are groups of students working together in order to expand their knowledge. Examples of small groups are jigsaw groups (small groups that are provided a task to become experts on the topics and later share their knowledge with the whole class), literature circles, and students working at centers.

- Partner/buddy reading takes place between two students of the same or differing ages/grade levels. The pair of students usually has a copy of the same text and read chorally or take turns reading to each other.

Checkpoint

1. True or false: The workshop approach to organizing your classroom provides time to meet with small groups of students and provide differentiated instruction to meet individual and small group needs.

2. True or false: Literature circles contain many students and many different books so that students can teach each other about what they are reading independently.

3. Fill in the blank: _____ groups are small groups that are provided a task to become experts on the topics and later share their knowledge with the whole class.

Checkpoint Answers

1. True

2. False

3. Jigsaw

Competency 5: Knowledge of Communication and Media Literacy

Competency Description

According to the *Competencies and Skills Required for Teacher Certification in Florida,* 20th Edition (available at www.fldoe.org/asp/ftce/pdf/ftce20edition.pdf), **Competency 5** for the Elementary Education (K–6) Subject Area Examination (SAE) Language Arts and Reading subtest addresses the following key indicators:

1. Identify characteristics of penmanship (e.g., legibility, letter formation, spacing).

2. Distinguish among listening and speaking strategies (e.g., questioning, paraphrasing, eye contact, voice, gestures).

3. Identify and apply instructional methods (e.g., collaborative conversation, collaborative discussion, presentation) for developing listening and speaking skills.

4. Select and evaluate a wide array of resources (e.g., Internet, printed material, artifacts, visual media, primary sources) for research and presentation.

5. Determine and apply the ethical process (e.g., citation, paraphrasing) for collecting and presenting authentic information while avoiding plagiarism.

6. Identify and evaluate current technology for use in educational settings.

Overview

Knowledge of oral and written communications skills is of primary importance to elementary educators. There are approximately **10 questions** that address Competency 5. This section addresses the following areas related to **Competency 5** key indicators:

- Penmanship
- Instructional Methods and Strategies
  - Listening
  - Speaking Strategies
- Media Literacy
- Educational Technology
  - Interactive Whiteboards
  - Computer Software
  - Web 2.0 Tools

Penmanship

Penmanship refers to the quality or style of one's handwriting. Legible or easily read handwriting is a developmental process, somewhat like reading. In the primary grades, students are taught manuscript handwriting techniques, and in the intermediate grades, they are taught cursive. Depending on your school or district, students may be taught traditional manuscript or D'Nealian, which is a more modern form of handwriting that incorporates more strokes. Being able to transfer thoughts to paper in a legible manner is of utmost importance in written communication. The following are several elements related to traditional and legible manuscript handwriting:

- **Letter formation**—Four basic strokes: circles, horizontal lines, vertical lines, and slant lines.
- **Spacing**—Should be consistent (to the eye) between letters, words, and sentences.
- **Letter size and alignment**—Should be roughly the same size on the writing lines, using the headline, midline, and baseline as instructed (that is, tall letters should touch the headline; "tail" letters should descend below the baseline; all letters should "sit" on the baseline and should not float above this designated line).
- **Line quality**—Strokes of the pencil should be of a consistent smoothness, color, and weight; line quality should not be too dark or wavy, too light or varied; smooth circles and straight lines are the goal.

Checkpoint

1. Fill in the blank: Students are taught to write in cursive in the _____ grades.

2. True or false: The element of legible handwriting that refers to consistency of the pencil strokes is letter alignment.

Checkpoint Answers

1. intermediate

2. False

Instructional Methods and Strategies

Listening and speaking opportunities should abound in elementary classrooms. Both listening and speaking are oral processes that are essential elements of high-quality language arts instruction. Students must be taught to listen and speak effectively for maximum success in the school environment and later life.

Listening

Listening is the language art used most often, yet it is also the one most often neglected. Listening requires the student to take in or receive what has been heard and seen, attend to what is most important, and then comprehend the message. Students must be provided multiple opportunities daily to listen effectively in order to gain meaning from the world around them. They must also know that there are several purposes of listening. *Efferent listening* refers to listening to learn new information, and *aesthetic listening* is listening that is more for pleasure and enjoyment. Listening to their teachers, other authority figures at the school, and their peers is vital to student success in school. Following are a variety of methods and strategies that should be used to enhance listening skills in the school environment:

- **Set a purpose**—Prior to a read aloud, storytelling, or class demonstration, ensure that students understand the objective of the lesson. Making predictions prior to the lesson helps to set a purpose for listening attentively to confirm or revise what has been stated. Activating prior knowledge related to the topic enhances the listeners' ability to make connections to the new information being presented and what was already known about a particular topic. The use of visuals help to engage the listeners as well.

- **Questioning and visualizing**—Before, during, and after a reading or class discussion, students should question the content of the lesson to ascertain the important concepts and begin to organize the newly learned information. Along with questioning, students need to visualize while listening. The questioning and visualizing strategies enhance critical thinking skills and aid in deeper comprehension.

- **Summarizing**—Concurrently and after questioning, students should begin to synthesize the information and see relationships among key concepts. Having students pair up to discuss what has been heard, as in a Think-Pair-Share, enables them to process the information and allows for another opportunity to listen.

- **Graphic organizers**—In order to solidify that last phase of listening, comprehension, many teachers encourage students to complete graphic organizers to synthesize and then evaluate the learning that has taken place.

Speaking Strategies

Listening and speaking often go hand in hand in elementary classrooms. Allowing students to process their learning through speaking is vital to deeply understanding the concepts being presented day in and day out. Speaking to an individual or group, using eye contact, taking turns, and projecting your voice are not only useful in the classroom, but necessary for effective communication in daily life. Following are a variety of methods and strategies that should be used to enhance speaking skills in the school environment:

- **Organizational format**—A combination of whole group lessons and small group discussions provides multiple and varying speaking opportunities for students. Students in classrooms with literacy centers or stations have many opportunities to speak and process their learning. The use of small groups in guided reading and literature circles again provides students the opportunity to not just recall what is being read and learned, but to critically think about the information and hear their classmates' points of view as well.

- **Questioning**—Listening and speaking go hand in hand; therefore, the questioning strategy is one that can be thought but also expressed orally. Teachers model varying levels of questioning (literal, inferential, and critical), and students then begin to add these types of questions to their own repertoire.
- **Retelling**—Retelling what has been heard helps students organize their thoughts into a logical sequence of beginning, middle, and end. Students are encouraged to focus on the big ideas and summarize or paraphrase the less important parts.
- **Drama**—Allowing students to role play, storytell, and share readers theater scripts with an audience provides an authentic way for students to elaborate on their learning, specifically enhancing fluency and comprehension. Students can manipulate visuals to add to the performance.

Checkpoint

1. Fill in the blank: The _____ strategy is useful in both effective listening and speaking.
2. True or false: Efferent listening is listening for pleasure or enjoyment.
3. Fill in the blank: In order to foster multiple opportunities for listening and speaking in the classroom, the day should be structured to incorporate both whole group and _____ lessons.
4. Fill in the blank: When using drama as a teaching method in the classroom, _____ aid(s) in fluency and comprehension.

Checkpoint Answers

1. questioning
2. False
3. small group
4. Any one of the following: role play, storytell, or readers theater scripts

Media Literacy

Media literacy refers to the ability of a student to interpret media messages. These media messages are provided in a variety of formats and for many purposes. These messages in the school environment are primarily meant to inform the reader. Following is a list of definitions related to information and media literacy:

- **Artifacts**—Real objects; usually representative of a particular culture or event
- **Internet**—A communication system that connects computers and their networks all over the world
- **Printed material**—Anything with printed text: books, magazines, journals, and so on
- **Primary sources**—A document or piece of work that was written, recorded, or created during a particular time period: photographs, speeches, interviews, diaries, video and audio recordings, and so on
- **Visual media**—Also known as nonprint media, this refers to anything that is not literally printed: television, video, some radio broadcasts, etc.

Safely and effectively navigating the Internet and all of its many tools is an important skill for elementary-age students. In this digital age, students are accessing and using mass amounts of information on the Web at younger and younger ages. Following are some basic guidelines for how elementary-age students can safely interact with the Internet:

- Primary students should be provided preselected sites to choose from in order to avoid exposure to inappropriate web content.

- Intermediate students can also be provided preselected sites, but should be taught advanced search skills to collect information helpful to their learning.
- Once a site is accessed, students should be taught to critically question and evaluate the site based on its content and their needs. Questions like "Does this site contain accurate information?" and "Does this site contain information I need for the subject I am studying?" should be considered when accessing information and media online.
- Older students must be taught proper citation skills and should understand copyright laws.

Checkpoint

1. True or false: An authentic arrowhead found on a Native American reservation is an example of an artifact.

2. True or false: Visual media refers to any print material including books, journals, and magazines.

3. True or false: The Internet is a safe environment for students of all ages.

Checkpoint Answers

1. True

2. False

3. False

Educational Technology

The use of educational technology is a rapidly growing trend in our schools. Preparing our students for working in the 21st century utilizing 21st century skills has become another vital aspect of daily classroom activity. Lack of educational funding still inhibits some teachers to provide such experiences to their students with current technologies. Outside entities like the Bill and Melinda Gates Foundation offer teachers in these situations grant opportunities to better fund their use of technology in the classroom. Students must be exposed to the many technological advancements and how these tools can positively impact their acquisition of knowledge. Following are some educational technology resources and tools.

Interactive Whiteboards

Interactive whiteboards are becoming more and more popular in educational settings. Lessons that would have taken place on a traditional whiteboard using erasable markers are now being accessed or created using new software that allows students to interact with the material in a digital fashion. Using this interactive whiteboard technology, students and teachers can read, write, click, drag, hide, and save all of their work on the computer. Educators can quiz and analyze student work instantaneously.

Computer Software

- Basic programs like the Microsoft Office package include computer software that can be used to simply word process information like stories students have written (Word) or create presentations (PowerPoint).
- Programs like Kidspiration offer students the opportunity to create their own graphic organizers including but not limited to charts, timelines, and webs.
- Programs like PhotoStory, Windows MovieMaker, and iMovie enable students to create digital stories to share their learning through visual media.

Web 2.0 Tools

- **E-mail**—Students can interact with other students around the country and the world using basic electronic mail. Programs like Epals aid teachers in setting up electronic correspondence with other classrooms.

- **Online book clubs**—Many publishing companies offer online book clubs to motivate students to discuss the books they have been reading online with other students outside of their classrooms and sometimes even with the authors.
- **WebQuests**—WebQuests are web-based learning experiences in which students navigate predetermined websites to glean further insight into a topic of study. Sample WebQuests can be found online, or teachers/students can create their own based on a topic of study.
- **Wiki sites**—Many web 2.0 tools allow students to create their own "mini-web pages." Wikispaces and Pbworks are two examples of such tools. Students can combine text, graphics, animation, and even hyperlinks to share and extend their knowledge.
- **Video conferencing**—Programs like Skype and FaceTime allow students to communicate, via video online, with other students regarding topics of study. These online video discussions allow for greater understanding and the expansion of knowledge.
- **Blogs**—A blog, short for weblog, is a user-friendly web page that allows students to post and comment on their work. Ongoing dialogue surrounding the work is encouraged. Classroom news blogs and literature response blogs have become common in elementary classrooms.
- **Glogs**—Glogs are virtual posters that offer an interactive experience for the viewer. Glogs can incorporate not only text but audio and video elements as well.
- **Podcasts**—Students and teachers have the ability to publish their audio recordings online for all to hear. These podcasts, like blogs, allow students a new way to share their learning.
- **Video projects**—Students share and expand on newfound knowledge by creating digital stories or videos related to student learning. Uploading these videos to safe video-hosting sites like TeacherTube allows students to share their knowledge with the masses.
- **SRS**—Student response systems (sometimes referred to as clickers) are used with or without interactive whiteboards to poll students or allow all students to respond/interact with content.
- **Tablets**—These include mobile computers that are often controlled via touchscreen technology. Teachers often use these devices for centers, partner, or whole group instruction.
- **Apps**—Short for applications, apps are inexpensive software that can be downloaded from the Internet and are typically used on mobile devices like tablets or smartphones.

Checkpoint

1. True or false: To aid comprehension, students can create their own graphic organizers using computer software.

2. Fill in the blank: The Internet provides such tools as _____ to promote discussion about books outside of the regular classroom.

3. True or false: Blogs tend to isolate students and do not allow for collaboration opportunities.

4. True or false: Podcasts are audio recordings of students learning that can be posted for stakeholders to hear.

5. True or false: A WebQuest allows students to safely navigate the Internet using websites provided by the teacher to meet standards in a content area.

Checkpoint Answers

1. True

2. online book clubs

3. False

4. True

5. True

Summary

The Language Arts and Reading subtest (Competencies 1–5) encompasses a variety of subcompetencies related to the basic knowledge required of educators teaching elementary-age students. Competency 1, knowledge of the reading process, entails emergent literacy and the five major components of reading: word recognition skills, critical thinking strategies, reading fluency, reading comprehension, and informational and literary text structures. Competency 2, knowledge of literary analysis and genres, includes genres of literature, literary elements and devices, multicultural children's literature, and literature response. Competency 3, knowledge of language and the writing process, means that the teacher understands the developmental stages of writing, the writing process, modes of writing, and writing conventions. Competency 4, knowledge of literary instruction and assessment, encompasses reading assessment and classroom organizational formats. Competency 5, knowledge of communication and media literacy, includes instructional methods and strategies for both listening and speaking, as well as identifying types of media and available educational technology tools and resources.

You should use the information in this section to complement your previous knowledge in the areas of language arts and reading. The general review of Language Arts and Reading competencies provided in this chapter should allow you to explore areas of strength and weakness that you might still need to review. To provide an opportunity for further practice and analysis, sample questions for the Language Arts and Reading competency area appear in the next section of this chapter. Answer explanations follow the sample questions.

Sample Questions

1. A primary source document is

    A. one that was created during that time period.
    B. nonprint media.
    C. a website.
    D. None of the above

2. The teacher has organized her classroom to allow for small groups. Students are listening to audio books, reading poetry, and responding to quality literature in writing. This is an example of what organizational format?

    A. literature circles
    B. shared reading
    C. interactive writing
    D. reading centers/stations

3. A third-grade class is reading *The Miraculous Journey of Edward Tulane* by Kate DiCamillo. Rather than reading this book as a whole group, the teacher has created small groups of students who have specific discussion roles. What organizational format is being used to encourage discussion and overall comprehension of this book?

    A. book talks
    B. guided reading
    C. literature circles
    D. independent reading

4. A teacher asks her students, "Which two words rhyme: fat, rag, cat?" Which area of emergent literacy does this illustrate?

    A. phonological awareness
    B. vocabulary
    C. concepts of print
    D. fluency

5. Identify the literary device used in the following example.

    Her stare was as cold as ice!
    A. onomatopoeia
    B. simile
    C. alliteration
    D. analogy

6. Graphic organizers are

    A. busy work.
    B. worksheets that require basic recall of facts.
    C. synthesizing and summarizing tools that aid comprehension.
    D. a waste of time.

7. In order to communicate in writing, penmanship must be legible. Which of the following contributes to legible handwriting?

   A. spacing
   B. letter formation
   C. letter alignment
   D. All of the above

8. An example of visual media is

   A. a book.
   B. a journal.
   C. the newspaper.
   D. a television program.

9. Classroom news and literature response _____ have become common web-based activities in elementary classrooms.

   A. blogs
   B. digital stories
   C. Word documents
   D. All of the above

10. Key features of descriptive writing include

   A. sensory language that refers to how something smells, looks, tastes, etc.
   B. vivid language that aids visualization.
   C. vague vocabulary.
   D. A and B only

11. Metamorphosis, pupa, and life cycle are all examples of

   A. domain-specific/academic vocabulary.
   B. butterfly words.
   C. scientific method.
   D. None of the above.

12. Some vocabulary terms have multiple meanings that can be understood in context. Read the passage below including the multiple meaning word in context (*in italics*) and identify the correct meaning below.

   The big sister walked into the baby's nursery when she heard her cries on the baby monitor. Knowing it was not time for the baby's nap to be over, she quickly turned on the *mobile* and exited the now quiet room.

   A. artistic object with moving parts
   B. cell phone
   C. capable of motion
   D. None of the above

13. There are many traits that create an effective writing piece. Which of the following is NOT one of these traits?

   A. word usage/choice
   B. voice
   C. prosody
   D. organization

14. The plot is known as the pattern or sequence of events that take place in a story. Which of the following elements are critical to a narrative plot?

    A. a problem or conflict involving the characters
    B. rising action that describes how the problem or conflict is building toward the climax
    C. resolution
    D. All of the above

15. A _____ is an online, collaborative web 2.0 tool that allows students to collaborate on a project by posting their work to pages for members to see and edit.

    A. Wikispace
    B. podcast
    C. digital story
    D. blog

Answer Explanations

1. **A.** Competencies 1 and 5. A primary source is a document or piece of work that was actually written, recorded, or created during the specific time under study.

2. **D.** Competency 4. Reading centers/stations allow students to construct meaning in a small group setting. For the teacher, this organizational format allows time to meet with guided reading groups and to differentiate instruction to meet the varying needs of students in the classroom.

3. **C.** Competency 2. Literature circles are small, temporary groups of students that gather together to discuss a book that each student is reading, with the goal of enhancing comprehension.

4. **A.** Competencies 1 and 4. Emergent literacy includes oral language development, print awareness, phonological awareness, and alphabet knowledge. Phonological awareness is the ability of a student to identify and manipulate large parts of spoken language (words, syllables, onset-rime units) and awareness of other aspects of sound in our language like alliteration, intonation, and rhyming.

5. **B.** Competency 2. Each of the options are literary devices. Although an analogy is a detailed and sometimes lengthy comparison of two ideas or events, simile is the correct answer. A simile is a comparison using *like* or *as*.

6. **C.** Competency 1. Graphic organizers are synthesizing and summarizing tools that aid student comprehension. They allow students to process what they have read, heard, or viewed. Graphic organizers can be completed individually or in small groups and can be an alternative form of assessment when completed.

7. **D.** Competency 5. Letter formation, spacing, letter size and alignment, and line quality all contribute to legible handwriting or penmanship.

8. **D.** Competency 5. Visual media is also known as nonprint media and refers to anything that is not literally printed: television, video, some radio broadcasts, and so on.

9. **A.** Competency 5. Blogs are user-friendly web pages that allow students to post and comment on their work.

10. **D.** Competency 3. Descriptive writing includes both sensory and vivid language.

11. **A.** Competency 1. Domain-specific/academic vocabulary refers to words or phrases that relate to a specific topic of study.

12. **A.** Competency 1. In this example, the meaning of *mobile* described in the passage is an artistic object with moving parts.

13. **C.** Competency 3. Prosody refers to the intonation used when reading fluently. All other answer choices are key traits in effective writing pieces.

14. **D.** Competency 2. Problems or conflicts, rising action and climax, and resolution are all key elements of a plot.

15. **A.** Competency 5. A Wikispace is a collaborative web 2.0 tool.

Chapter 3

Social Science

This chapter provides a general review of the Social Science subtest with sample questions and explanations at the end of the chapter. Checkpoint exercises are found throughout, giving you an opportunity to practice the skills addressed in this section. The answers to the Checkpoint exercises immediately follow the set of questions. We encourage you to cover the answers as you complete the Checkpoint exercises.

Competency 1: Knowledge of Effective Instructional Practice and Assessment of the Social Sciences

Competency Description

According to the *Competencies and Skills Required for Teacher Certification in Florida,* 20th Edition (available at www.fldoe.org/asp/ftce/pdf/ftce20edition.pdf), **Competency 1** for the Elementary Education (K–6) Subject Area Examination (SAE) Social Science subtest addresses the following key indicators:

1. Select appropriate resources for instructional delivery of social science concepts, including complex informational text.
2. Identify appropriate resources for planning for instruction of social science concepts.
3. Choose appropriate methods for assessing social science concepts.
4. Determine appropriate learning environments for social science lessons.

Overview

Knowledge of effective instructional practice and assessment of social sciences is of primary importance to elementary educators responsible for educating our youth in the social sciences. There are approximately **10 questions** that address Competency 1. This section addresses the following areas related to **Competency 1** key indicators:

- Instructional Resources
- Instructional Methods and Strategies
- Multiple Forms of Assessment

Instructional Resources

Elementary-age students not only need to know about the world before they were in it, but must also understand the basics of how the world works today and its many facets. A positive classroom learning environment that encourages collaboration and an appreciation for diverse points of view is vital to successful social studies instruction. The foundation you provide in the elementary school will positively impact further instruction in the social sciences.

Educators must first access their state standards and then know how and where to find the resources necessary to instruct students. Resources abound for this particular content area. In this digital age, using reputable websites can be one of the most efficient means of enhancing your knowledge of subject matter for topics needing to be taught to your grade level students. For example:

- Government agencies have websites, and most provide valuable information for educators.
  - www.usa.gov—The United States government's official web portal
  - www.loc.gov—The Library of Congress

- memory.loc.gov/ammem/index.html—The American Memory Project of the Library on Congress and National Endowment for the Humanities
- historyexplorer.si.edu—Smithsonian History Explorer and Verizon Thinkfinity
- bensguide.gpo.gov—Ben's Guide to U.S. Government for Kids, a service of the U.S. Government Printing Office
- Specialized organizations have websites and multiple links to additional reputable websites to assist educators in teaching in this content area. *Note:* Members of local, state, and national organizations often receive newsletters and journals that are valuable and current sources of information.
  - www.socialstudies.org—National Council for the Social Studies (NCSS)
  - www.readwritethink.org—International Reading (Literacy) Association, National Council of Teachers of English, and Verizon Thinkfinity
- Societies like National Geographic have educational divisions and publish valuable resources for students. They also have websites with multiple links that provide quality resources for educators. (www.national geographic.com)

More resources in print will be provided in school settings along with the adopted social studies textbook. Many schools have purchased supplemental resources like guided reading books and age-appropriate magazines or newspapers that include teacher's guides to help educators teach this vital subject. Using the local, school, and school-based professional libraries can be advantageous to the educator as well. An abundance of high-quality children's literature (of various genres like historical fiction and nonfiction) is available to not only young children, but also to educators. Sharing these books with students helps enlighten them about various ways of life, geographical locations, historical events, and more.

Instructional Methods and Strategies

Teachers often utilize a variety of teaching methods to differentiate instruction and meet the individual needs of students. The following methods can be used in isolation or in collaboration, depending on the specific subject matter, and are often employed while teaching social studies concepts (Chapin, 2012):

- Direct or expository teaching
- Problem-based learning
- Inductive thinking (related to the list-group-label technique)
- Cooperative learning
- Role play
- Simulation

Teachers also employ a host of strategies appropriate for learners in a specific content area. Please remember that many teaching strategies appropriate for teaching in the areas of reading and language arts are also appropriate for content area instruction. The following is a sampling of appropriate tools and strategies often used while teaching social studies:

- Story mapping—history frames or sequence of event charts
- Anticipation guides
- Double-entry journals
- K-W-L charts
- 5-W + H charts (Who, What, When, Where, Why, How)
- Semantic feature analysis charts
- Graphic organizers—Venn diagrams, sequence diagrams (timelines), and concept maps
- Content-specific learning logs
- Guest speakers

- Field trips and virtual field trips
- Learning centers/stations
- Community-based, service-learning experiences
- Digital media and educational software

Multiple Forms of Assessment

Assessment in the social studies classroom can be more traditional, using paper-and-pencil tests (teacher-created or published with the textbook); more technologically advanced, using interactive whiteboard quizzes, for example; or more performance-based, using a variety of authentic tasks and portfolios of student work to show the learning that has taken place over time. Often, performance-based assessments include the use of learning goals accompanied by scales and/or rubrics that delineate the expectations set forth by the teacher. Many educators choose to have the students assist in the creation of the rubrics to help the students take an active role in their learning. Please note that many of the instructional strategies aforementioned could also be used to alternatively assess learning gains.

Whatever method of assessment is used, it is vital to incorporate multiple forms of assessments including pre-assessment tools to gauge what the students already know and to help guide instruction (for example, K-W-L charts and anticipation guides) and post-assessments that, when compared to the pre-assessment, show growth over time. Effective educators base lesson plan development on pre-assessment results to maximize the learning opportunities for their students. Effective teachers also align learning goals and scales, essential questions, learning objectives, learning activities, and their assessment tools to ensure that students are being fairly assessed on content specifically taught based on the standards the students need to know.

Checkpoint

1. True or false: Many government agencies and specialized organizations provide valuable resources to members.

2. Fill in the blank: The use of _____ helps to synthesize and summarize informational text.

3. True or false: Many language arts and reading strategies are also appropriate for content area instruction.

4. Fill in the blanks: _____ and _____ are two teaching methods that can effectively teach social studies content.

Checkpoint Answers

1. True

2. graphic organizers

3. True

4. Any of the following two: direct/expository teaching, problem-based learning, inductive thinking, cooperative learning, role play, and simulation

Competency 2: Knowledge of Time, Continuity, and Change (i.e., History)

Competency Description

According to the *Competencies and Skills Required for Teacher Certification in Florida,* 20th Edition (available at www.fldoe.org/asp/ftce/pdf/ftce20edition.pdf), **Competency 2** for the Elementary Education (K–6) Subject Area Examination (SAE) Social Science subtest addresses the following key indicators:

1. Identify and analyze historical events that are related by cause and effect.
2. Analyze the sequential nature of historical events using timelines.
3. Analyze examples of primary and secondary source documents for historical perspective.
4. Analyze the impacts of the cultural contributions and technological developments of Africa; the Americas; Asia, including the Middle East; and Europe.
5. Identify the significant historical leaders and events that have influenced Eastern and Western civilizations.
6. Determine the causes and consequences of exploration, settlement, and growth on various cultures.
7. Interpret the ways that individuals and events have influenced economic, social, and political institutions in the world, nation, or state.
8. Analyze immigration and settlement patterns that have shaped the history of the United States.
9. Identify how various cultures contributed to the unique social, cultural, economic, and political features of Florida.
10. Identify the significant contributions of the early and classical civilizations.

Overview

Knowledge of history—specifically time, continuity, and change—is of primary importance to elementary educators responsible for educating our youth in the social sciences. There are approximately **14 questions** that address Competency 2. This section addresses the following areas related to **Competency 2** key indicators:

- Historical Events and Historic Figures
- Early Explorers
- Florida History
- Ancient Civilizations

Historical Events and Historic Figures

Today's world has been shaped by many notable occurrences and historic figures. The idea that some of these historical events are related by cause and effect is known as historic causation. The following is a list of some notable historical events and figures:

- **Columbus landing in the New World**—Christopher Columbus (1451–1506), perhaps one of the most famous early explorers, believed he could sail across the Atlantic to Asia. After much pleading, the King and Queen of Spain agreed to fund his expeditions. Columbus made four voyages in an effort to find a route to the East. During his expeditions he discovered the Bahamas, Hispaniola, Cuba, Dominica, Guadeloupe, Jamaica, Central America, and South America. Columbus's discoveries opened up the Western hemisphere to economic and political development by the Europeans, namely the Spanish, English, and French.
- **French and Indian War (1754–1763)**—This war, which was an extension of the European Seven Years War, was a battle over colonial territory and resources by the French and the English. This war effectively ended France's cultural and political influence in North America. In their victory, England gained massive amounts of land but also weakened its rapport with the Native Americans and with the English colonists.

In sum, although the war strengthened England's hold on the colonies, it also increased tensions in North America, which inevitably led to the Revolutionary War.

- **The Royal Proclamation of 1763**—Knowing that the colonists sought to expand to the west, King George forbid them to settle past the Appalachian Mountains. This proclamation offended the colonists, who wanted to be able to settle and live wherever they wanted, specifically on potential farmland.

- **The Quartering Act of 1765**—This act required the colonists to provide living quarters for British soldiers.

- **The Stamp Act (1765)**—This act placed a tax on paper products sold in the colonies. Items that were taxed, such as playing cards, legal documents, and newspapers, had to be made of paper embossed in England with a government stamp. Samuel Adams, who had already been arguing along with Patrick Henry for independence from British rule, began to protest this act and spread the word that "taxation without representation" should not be tolerated by the colonists.

- **The Townshend Acts of 1767**—These acts proposed by British government official Charles Townshend taxed the colonists on such products as tea, glass, lead, and paper. The taxes of the people in England at the time were decreased and the colonists once again were outraged by British rule.

- **The Boston Massacre (1770)**—In March 1770, some colonists approached a group of British soldiers, taunting them and throwing snowballs. The British soldiers opened fire on the colonists and killed five including Crispus Attucks, who is considered to be the first American to die in the Revolutionary War.

- **The Tea Act of 1773**—This restriction imposed on the colonists stated that they could only purchase tea (at an elevated price) that was sold by the British East India Company and taxed by the British government.

- **Sons of Liberty**—A group of Patriots formed with the support of Paul Revere to retaliate against the many injustices put upon them by King George and Britain.

- **The Boston Tea Party (December 16, 1773)**—The British tea tax and the Tea Act of 1773 angered the colonists, who wanted to be free to buy untaxed tea from other sources. Three British ships filled with tea cargo docked in Boston Harbor. To show their great disgust for this tax, Samuel Adams, John Hancock, and approximately 80 other men disguised themselves as Native Americans and threw all of the tea overboard into the Boston Harbor.

- **The Intolerable Acts (1774)**—After the tea incident in Boston Harbor, the King closed the harbor for any business. Massachusetts Colony lost its charter, and the King once again reinforced the Quartering Act, requiring colonists to house British soldiers.

- **American Revolutionary War (1775–1783)**—The Revolutionary War was also known as the American War of Independence. Due to rising tensions caused by the French and Indian War, colonists of the 13 original colonies (Massachusetts, Rhode Island, Connecticut, New Hampshire, New York, New Jersey, Pennsylvania, Delaware, Georgia, Maryland, North Carolina, South Carolina, and Virginia) desired to form self-governing independent states. These states, in order to defend their right to self-governance, fought the British. Some important historical figures involved include Samuel Adams, Ethan Allen, Benjamin Franklin, John Hancock, Patrick Henry, Thomas Jefferson, Thomas Paine, Paul Revere, Deborah Sampson (who joined the Continental Army dressed as a man), Dr. Joseph Warren, and George Washington. The war ended with the signing of the Treaty of Paris, which recognized the sovereignty of the United States.

- **Patriots, Loyalists, and Redcoats (1775–1783)**—Patriots were revolutionary rebels who fought against British control during the American Revolution. Loyalists were colonists who remained steadfast in their allegiance to British rule during the American Revolution. The Redcoats were the British soldiers who fought to retain control over the colonies.

- **Paul Revere's Midnight Ride (April 18, 1775)**—Sent by Dr. Joseph Warren, Paul Revere is famous for the "Midnight Ride" he took on horseback to warn the Patriots that the British were coming "by sea," rowing across the Charles River in Massachusetts. In case this express rider was captured, William Dawes also made this important trip via horseback, taking a different route to Lexington and Concord.

- **Important battles of the Revolutionary War (1775–1776)**—The following is a list of important battles that took place during the American Revolutionary War: Ticonderoga (May 1775), Bunker Hill (June 1775), Trenton (December 1776), Saratoga (October 1777), Charleston (April–May 1780), and Yorktown (October 1781).

- **The Battle at Bunker Hill (June 17, 1775)**—This battle is historically recognized as the first major battle of the American Revolutionary War. The British are heralded as winning this battle; however, they sustained great losses in soldiers and weaponry. On the Patriot side, a great loss occurred in the battle with the death of Dr. Joseph Warren.

- *Common Sense* **(1776)**—This historic booklet or pamphlet, originally published anonymously but written in clear language by Thomas Paine, inspired the colonists to seek freedom from British rule.

- **Declaration of Independence (1776)**—This historic document, written by Thomas Jefferson and adopted by the Second Continental Congress, begins with a preamble or reason for the necessity of the document and then establishes the reasons why the original colonies sought freedom from British rule. This declaration laid the foundation for their new government and severed ties to Great Britain. The Continental Congress would later name the new nation the United States of America.

- **American Revolution Allies (1778)**—The newly formed states in America had assistance in their fight against the British from foreign allies. Specifically, the French, Dutch, and Spanish lent financial support and manpower in the form of soldiers.

- **Benjamin Banneker (1731–1806)**—As the son of a slave in Maryland Colony, self-taught Benjamin Banneker grew up to become an astronomer who could predict lunar eclipses, an inventor of irrigation systems for crops, and a mathematician who wrote almanacs filled with useful information.

- **The Industrial Revolution (1760s–1830s)**—This period was characterized by the transition from manual labor to the use of machines, specifically water-powered and then steam-powered machines used in the creation of textiles and iron goods. It initially began in Great Britain and within a few decades spread through Western Europe and inevitably to the United States.

- **The Civil War (1861–1865)**—The American Civil War was a conflict between the North (the Union) and the South (the Confederacy). Eleven southern slave states wanted to secede from the Union. Although noted as the deadliest war in American history, this war ended slavery (Lincoln's Emancipation Proclamation, 1862), restored the union, and strengthened the role of the federal government.

- **Westward Expansion (1807–1912)**—After the War of 1812, Americans wanted to explore and settle the land to the west. This territory had been expanded due to the Louisiana Purchase. Famous explorers like Lewis and Clark, followed by pioneer families, swept westward and founded new communities. Another component of settling the west involved the removal of Native Americans from the most desirable lands in the south and west (under the authority of President Andrew Jackson and subsequent administrations). They were cruelly and violently driven from their homes and pushed to concentrated areas called reservations. By the early 20th century, the west was settled, and the United States consisted of 48 contiguous states.

- **World War I (1914–1918)**—This First World War was initiated by a conflict between Austria-Hungary and Serbia. As a result of a system of alliances, it became a global conflict that involved major world powers. The two opposing military alliances were the Entente (Allied) Powers (Russian Empire, United Kingdom, France, Canada, Australia, Italy, the Empire of Japan, Portugal, and the United States) and the Central Powers (German Empire, the Austrian-Hungarian Empire, the Ottoman Empire (Turkey), and the Kingdom of Bulgaria). The Allied Powers were victorious, but lasting effects and repercussions from the war led to WWII.

- **World War II (1939–1945)**—The Second World War was again a global military conflict between two opposing forces: The Allies (Leaders)—Great Britain (Churchill), United States (Roosevelt/Truman), Russia (Stalin), Free France (de Gaulle), and China (Chiang Kai-shek)—and the Axis Powers (Leaders)—Germany (Hitler), Italy (Mussolini), and Japan (Hirohito). Japan's attack on Pearl Harbor resulted in the United States' involvement in the war. In 1945, the Allies defeated the Axis, with the USSR and the United States emerging as the world's superpowers. This led to the Cold War, which lasted for the next 45 years. After WWII, the United Nations was formed in an effort to prevent further global conflicts.

- **Korean War (1950–1953)**—Due to a division in Korea (communist North and American-occupied South) caused by WWII, war began in 1950. The United States came to South Korea's aid, but to no avail. In 1953, the war ended with a signing of a peace treaty at Panmunjom and with Korea remaining divided, just as it was at the beginning of the conflict.

- **Civil Rights Act of 1964**—This statutory law was the result of a 100-year quest by African Americans for racial equality. This landmark piece of legislation outlawed racial segregation in the United States. Specifically, it voided Jim Crow laws in the southern states and prohibited racial discrimination in schools, public places, and places of employment.
- **Vietnam War (U.S. involved 1959–1975)**—This war was fought between communist North Vietnam and the government of South Vietnam. The United States, again in an effort to oppose communism, supported the South Vietnamese forces until 1973, when Congress passed the Case-Church Amendment in response to the anti-war movement. North Vietnam captured the capital of South Vietnam, Saigon (Fall of Saigon), which marked the end of the war and the beginning of a reunified Vietnam under communist rule.
- **Persian Gulf War (August 1990–February 1991)**—Also known simply as the Gulf War, this military conflict authorized by the United Nations was between Iraq and a coalition force made up of 34 nations. The purpose of this war was to liberate Kuwait and expel Iraqi forces. Operation Desert Storm was the name for the United States' land and air operations involved in the Gulf War effort.

There have been a significant number of historical events and leaders that have helped to influence and shape Eastern and Western civilization as we know it. The following is a sampling of just a few of those leaders and events:

Historical Leaders	Influential Events
Alexander the Great	King of Macedonia in 336 B.C.; conquered the Persian Empire; founded the city of Alexandria in Egypt, a center of learning and culture; created a massive empire and restored order in Ancient Greece
Nicolaus Copernicus (1473–1543)	First astronomer to place the Sun at the center of the universe
Galileo Galilei (1564–1642)	Italian physicist, mathematician, astronomer, and philosopher responsible for the birth of modern science
John Locke (1632–1704)	British Enlightenment writer whose ideas influenced the Declaration of Independence, state constitutions, and the United States Constitution; believed that people are born free with certain natural rights including the right to life, liberty, and property
Isaac Newton (1642–1727)	English physicist, mathematician, astronomer, natural philosopher, alchemist, and theologian known for defining gravity and the laws of motion
Samuel Adams (1722–1803)	Outspoken Patriot during the American Revolution; sometimes referred to as the Father of the American Revolution; protested against British rule and taxation; designed and carried out the famous Boston Tea Party incident
Patrick Henry (1736–1799)	Patriotic founding father; Governor of Virginia; famous for saying "Give me liberty or give me death!"
Benjamin Franklin (1706–1790)	Patriot, writer (wrote under pen names like Poor Richard and Silence Dogood), publisher, scientist, inventor, and diplomat; noted as one of the United States founding fathers; signed the Declaration of Independence, the Treaty of Paris, and the United States Constitution
George Washington (1732–1799)	Commander-in-Chief of the Continental Army during the American Revolution (1775–1783); first President of the United States
Thomas Jefferson (1743–1826)	Third President of the United States; considered one of the Founding Fathers of the United States; principal author of the Declaration of Independence; played a role in the Louisiana Purchase and the Lewis and Clark expedition

Checkpoint

1. True or false: The defeat of the Axis Powers in WWII led to the emerging of two world superpowers and inevitably the Cold War.

2. Fill in the blank: The _____ War led to the start of the American Revolutionary War.

3. True or false: The Boston Tea Party was the last of many events that caused King George to impose the Intolerable Acts, which soon after led to the Revolutionary War.

4. Fill in the blank: _____ was the first astronomer to place the Sun at the center of the universe.

5. Fill in the blank: _____ was one of the many women who dressed like a man to fight for independence in the American Revolutionary War.

6. True or False: The Industrial Revolution initially began in Great Britain.

Checkpoint Answers

1. True

2. French and Indian

3. True

4. Nicolaus Copernicus

5. Deborah Sampson

6. True

Early Explorers

The following table provides dates, explorers, their nationality, and their most notable achievements:

Date	Explorer	Nationality	Achievement
1492–1504	Christopher Columbus	Italian	Made four voyages to West Indies and Caribbean Islands
1497–1503	Amerigo Vespucci	Italian	Sailed to West Indies and South America
1497–1498	John Cabot	Italian	Explored the shores of Newfoundland, Nova Scotia, and Labrador; his voyages gave England claim to North America and paved the way for the settlement of the English colonies in the early 1600s
1498	Vasco da Gama	Portuguese	First to travel to India around Africa's Cape of Good Hope
1513	Vasco Núñez de Balboa	Spanish	Led expedition across Panama and found the Pacific Ocean
1513	Juan Ponce de Leon	Spanish	Explored Florida looking for the Fountain of Youth
1515	Prince Henry the Navigator	Portuguese	Pioneered sponsored exploration and cartography
1520–1521	Ferdinand Magellan	Portuguese	Circumnavigated the globe with five ships and 270 men
1519–1521	Hernando Cortez	Spanish	Conquered Aztecs in Mexico

Date	Explorer	Nationality	Achievement
1523–1535	Francisco Pizarro	Spanish	Conquered Incas of Peru, which added lands to the Spanish Empire
1534–1542	Jacques Cartier	French	Traveled St. Lawrence River
1539–1542	Hernando de Soto	Spanish	Explored American Southeast; discovered the Mississippi River
1540–1542	Francisco Vazquez de Coronado	Spanish	Explored American Southwest; opened up the Southwest to Spanish colonization
1577–1580	Sir Frances Drake	English	First Englishman to sail around the world; defeated the Spanish Armada; claimed California for England
1603–1616	Samuel de Champlain	French	Explored eastern coast of North America and the coast of the St. Lawrence River to Lake Huron; reached Lake Champlain
1609–1611	Henry Hudson	English	Explored Hudson Bay, Hudson River, and Hudson Strait

Checkpoint

1. True or false: John Cabot traveled around the Cape of Good Hope to reach the West Indies.

2. Fill in the blank: _____ explored Florida in search of the Fountain of Youth.

3. Fill in the blank: Hernando de Soto explored the present-day American Southeast and discovered the _____ River.

4. True or false: Explorers came from various parts of the world including France, Portugal, Spain, and Italy.

Checkpoint Answers

1. False

2. Juan Ponce de Leon

3. Mississippi

4. True

Florida History

Florida history is the main topic of social studies education in fourth grade in the state of Florida, according to the Next Generation Sunshine State Standards. The following list highlights important information regarding Florida's history:

- Initially inhabited by various tribes like the Timicuan.
- Named Florida by Juan Ponce de Leon in 1513.
- The English, Spanish, and French established settlements in Florida during the 1500s and 1600s.
- St. Augustine, founded by the Spanish, came to serve as the capitals of the British (East) and Spanish (West) colonies of Florida.
- The Spanish brought many goods like spices and citrus to the New World but also brought disease, which wiped out much of the Native American population.
- Britain tried to develop Florida through the importation of immigrants for labor.

- Spain regained control of Florida after the American Revolutionary War.
- In 1845, Florida became the 27th state in the United States of America.
- The Florida East Coast Railway, founded by Henry Flagler, was integral in the development of Florida's Atlantic Coast.
- Florida's land was intensely developed prior to the Great Depression of the 1930s.
- Florida's economy was positively affected by WWII.
- Present-day Florida is one of the most populous states in the south.

Checkpoint

1. True or false: Juan Ponce de Leon discovered Florida.

2. True or false: Florida became the 17th state in the union in 1845.

3. Fill in the blank: Florida was inhabited by _____ prior to its later discovery by Europeans.

4. Fill in the blank: Florida's east coast was developed in the late 1800s due to the Florida East Coast Railway, whose founder was _____.

Checkpoint Answers

1. False

2. False

3. Native American tribes

4. Henry Flagler

Ancient Civilizations

The following table highlights important information regarding early civilizations and their significant contributions:

Civilization	Historical Contributions
Mesopotamia	Often referred to as the "cradle of civilization"; origin of organized societies; first civilization to gather and live together in large communities/cities (in the area around the Tigris and Euphrates rivers in the Middle East); created a system of government and learned to write
Greece	Influenced present-day language, the arts and sciences, education, philosophy, and politics; origin of the Olympic games; influenced the ancient Romans, who modeled many aspects of ancient Greek society
Rome	Influenced politics and forms of government (monarchy and republics), literature and the arts, architecture, warfare, society (highly developed civilization for its time—8th century B.C.), engineering and technology
Egypt	Influenced government (pharaoh/king as ruler with an administration to assist), religion, writing (hieroglyphics), irrigation of crops, warfare tactics, art, architecture and construction techniques (pyramids), mathematics (decimal system), medicine, and technology
China	Known as one of the oldest civilizations; formed dynasties (powerful ruling families) beginning with the Shang Dynasty; influenced government and politics, culture, warfare, art (painting, poetry, and calligraphy), forms of writing, religion, and architecture

Checkpoint

1. True or false: Ancient Rome was the site of the very first Olympic Games.

2. True or false: Ancient Mesopotamia located in the Middle East (present-day Iraq), was the first known civilization to live in relatively large groups in cities.

3. Fill in the blank: Ancient _____ developed a highly effective irrigation system to water crops.

4. True or false: Ancient Chinese people practiced calligraphy as a form of artistic expression.

Checkpoint Answers

1. False

2. True

3. Egyptians

4. True

Competency 3: Knowledge of People, Places, and Environment (i.e., Geography)

Competency Description

According to the *Competencies and Skills Required for Teacher Certification in Florida,* 20th Edition (available at www.fldoe.org/asp/ftce/pdf/ftce20edition.pdf), **Competency 3** for the Elementary Education (K–6) Subject Area Examination (SAE) Social Science subtest addresses the following key indicators:

1. Identify and apply the six essential elements of geography (i.e., the world in spatial terms, places and regions, physical systems, human systems, environment and society, uses of geography), including the specific terms for each element.

2. Analyze and interpret maps and other graphic representations of physical and human systems.

3. Identify and evaluate tools and technologies (e.g., maps, globe, GPS, satellite imagery) used to acquire, process, and report information from a spatial perspective.

4. Interpret statistics that show how places differ in their human and physical characteristics.

5. Analyze ways in which people adapt to an environment through the production and use of clothing, food, and shelter.

6. Determine the ways tools and technological advances affect the environment.

7. Identify and analyze physical, cultural, economic, and political reasons for the movement of people in the world, nation, or state.

8. Evaluate the impact of transportation and communication networks on the economic development in different regions.

9. Compare and contrast major regions of the world, nation, or state.

Overview

Knowledge of geography, specifically people, places, and the environment, is of primary importance to elementary educators responsible for educating our youth in the social sciences. There are approximately **10 questions** that address Competency 3. This section addresses the following areas related to **Competency 3** key indicators:

- Essential Elements of Geography
- Map and Globe Terminology

Essential Elements of Geography

Geography can be defined as the study of the Earth's surface, atmosphere, and people. The following web identifies the six essential elements of geography (Chapin, 2012):

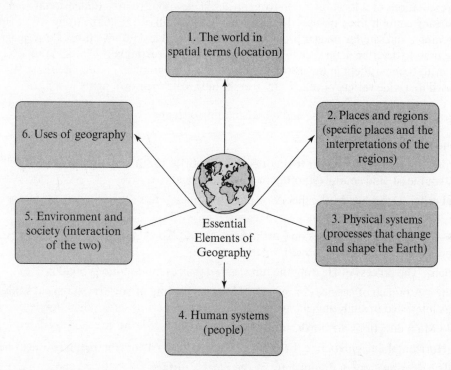

1. **The world in spatial terms (location)**
2. **Places and regions (specific places and the interpretations of the regions)**
3. **Physical systems (processes that change and shape the Earth)**
4. **Human systems (people)**
5. **Environment and society (interaction of the two)**
6. **Uses of geography**

Essential Elements of Geography

1. The world in spatial terms refers to location. Location refers to the position on the Earth's surface. These locations can be either **relative** or **absolute**. A relative location is defined as the location of something in relation to another place, while an absolute location is the specific location of a place. Spatial terms reference organization of people and places on Earth.

2. Places and regions refers to the physical characteristics of specific places and how they form and change.

3. Physical systems are processes that change and shape the Earth.

4. Human systems are the people or inhabitants.

5. Environment and society refers to the relationships and interactions that take place between people and their surroundings.

6. Uses of geography include interpreting the past and present along with planning for the future.

Checkpoint

1. Fill in the blank: There are _____ essential elements of geography.

2. True or false: One of the six essential elements of geography is environment and society.

3. Fill in the blank: A(n) _____ location is described by general terms and area landmarks.

Checkpoint Answers

1. six

2. True

3. relative

Map and Globe Terminology

Maps and globes are valuable educational tools in the elementary classroom. Teachers use maps to not only teach map skills, but also to provide information to their students about places all over the world. Many maps are two-dimensional representations of a location, often from an aerial viewpoint. Three-dimensional maps can be created by **cartographers** using contour lines, or lines that show the rise and fall of the land. Along with maps, graphs, diagrams, photographs, and satellite images provide valuable geographical information. These geographical representations can be used to describe natural changes (that is, volcanoes, earthquakes, floods) that occur and affect the world. In order to become adept in the use of maps and other geographical representations, students should not only be exposed to a wide variety of maps, but also should create their own maps.

The following terms are essential to the use and understanding of maps:

- **Cartographers**—Mapmakers
- **Compass rose**—Indicator of the four main directions —north, south, east, and west—as well as northeast, northwest, southeast, and southwest; often part of the legend
- **Continental drift**—Described by the theory of plate tectonics; refers to the movement of the Earth's crust over time
- **Continents**—Seven mainland masses on Earth: Asia, Africa, North America, South America, Antarctica, Europe, and Australia; Asia is the largest in terms of area
- **Deforestation**—The process of clearing the forests; destabilizes mountainous regions
- **Demography**—A branch of science concerned with the well-being of society; statistical study of human populations interested in analyzing changes in size, movement, crime rates, education levels, and so on
- **Directions**—Main directions are north, south, east, and west
- **Equator**—Horizontal, imaginary line that divides the Earth into its northern and southern halves
- **Erosion**—The wearing away or diminishing of the Earth's surface
- **Globe**—Small model of the Earth; considered the most accurate representation of Earth
- **GPS**—Global Positioning System; satellite navigation systems that involve multiple satellites and computers working together to compute locations on Earth
- **Grid**—Vertical and horizontal lines on a map
- **Hemispheres**—Northern and southern halves of the Earth divided by the equator
- **International Date Line**—Largely vertical, imaginary line that marks where the date officially changes each day
- **Latitude and longitude**—The grid lines on a map; longitude lines run from the poles, north and south; latitude lines run parallel to the equator, east and west
- **Legend**—Also known as the key; explains what the symbols, colors, lines, and so on mean on a map
- **Map**—Flattened-out representation of a globe or portion of a globe
- **Oceans**—Largest expanses of sea water on Earth: Atlantic, Pacific, Indian, Southern (identified in 2000), and Arctic; in terms of area, the Pacific is the largest
- **Physical maps**—Show country borders, major cities, significant bodies of water, and major landforms like deserts, mountains, and plains
- **Political maps**—Show governmental boundaries of counties, states, and countries; identify major cities and significant bodies of water
- **Population**—People living in a particular geographic area
- **Prime meridian**—Vertical, imaginary line that divides the Earth into its eastern and western halves; runs through Greenwich, England (1884 site of the Royal Observatory; at that time housed the most advanced geographic equipment)
- **Regions**—A wide-ranging geographic area; usually contains similar physical features (for example, caverns, deltas, deserts, hills, mesas, mountains, plains, plateaus) or unifying characteristics (for example, common language, government)

- **Relief maps**—Show the shape of the land's surface; provide detail through use of color and contour lines
- **Satellite imagery**—Images obtained via space-based satellites that provide an accurate view of Earth and other objects and planets in space
- **Scale**—Items on a map are drawn to size; when compared to each other, they are the right size and distance apart; the larger the scale, the more detail shown (for example, a theme park map), the smaller the scale, the more area shown but the less detail (for example, a world map); shown on a map in fractions or words and figures (that is, 1 inch: 16 miles; 1: 1,000)
- **Symbol**—Representations of real things on a map (for example, dots for cities, stars for capitals); usually small simple shapes and pictures
- **Thematic maps**—Show specific topics or subjects (for example, human or animal populations, climate)

Checkpoint

1. Fill in the blank: The _____ is the imaginary line that divides the Earth into its eastern and western halves.

2. True or false: Demography is the statistical study of human populations.

3. Fill in the blank: _____ maps are those that specify a particular topic or subject.

4. Fill in the blank: A _____ represents real items on a map.

5. True or false: Beach erosion occurs on the Florida coastlines due to severe weather occurrences.

Checkpoint Answers

1. prime meridian

2. True

3. Thematic

4. symbol

5. True

Competency 4: Knowledge of Government and the Citizen (i.e., Government and Civics)

Competency Description

According to the *Competencies and Skills Required for Teacher Certification in Florida,* 20th Edition (available at www.fldoe.org/asp/ftce/pdf/ftce20edition.pdf), **Competency 4** for the Elementary Education (K–6) Subject Area Examination (SAE) Social Science subtest addresses the following key indicators:

1. Distinguish between the structure, functions, and purposes of federal, state, and local government.
2. Compare and contrast the rights and responsibilities of a citizen in the world, nation, state, and community.
3. Identify and interpret major concepts of the U.S. Constitution and other historical documents.
4. Compare and contrast the ways the legislative, executive, and judicial branches share powers and responsibility.
5. Analyze the U.S. electoral system and the election process.
6. Identify and analyze the relationships among social, economic, and political rights and the historical documents that secure these rights in the United States.
7. Identify and analyze the processes of the U.S. legal system.

Overview

Knowledge of our government and what it means to be a responsible citizen is of primary importance to elementary educators responsible for educating our youth in the social sciences. There are approximately **11 questions** that address Competency 4. This section addresses the following areas related to **Competency 4** key indicators:

- Government
  - Local and State Government
  - Federal (National) Government
  - Local, State, and Federal Powers
  - Federal Court System
  - State Courts
  - Election Process/Electoral College
- Civics

Government

Government can be defined as the agency in which a governing body functions and exercises authority. The government in the United States of America is a **democracy** or government by the people. A democratic form of government provides for equality and inalienable rights of its citizens. These citizens elect officials to make important decisions on their behalf. The government is primarily responsible for administering justice, the education system, maintaining roads, maintaining statistics about society, and overseeing the national defense. The various levels of government in the United States are local, state, and federal (national).

Local and State Government

- In the mayor-council form of local government, the leader or chief executive is the **mayor.** The mayor is an elected official and works in collaboration with the **city council.** Two other forms of local government are the council-manager form and commission form.
- The leader of the state government is the **governor.** The governor is also an elected official who works cooperatively with state senators of the **Senate** and state representatives of the **House of Representatives.** Nebraska is the only exception to this, with a single law-making body called the Nebraska Legislature.

Federal (National) Government

The three branches of the federal government are legislative, judicial, and executive. All branches are concerned with upholding the laws set forth by the Constitution of the United States of America and representing the citizens of this country. These branches provide for a system of checks and balances (each branch has the ability to check or limit the other; see "Election Process/Electoral College") and the separation of powers (each branch has specific powers and cannot interfere with the powers of another).

- **Legislative (Congress)**—Comprised of the Senate and the House of Representatives; established by Article I of the Constitution; the Senate has the sole power to conduct impeachment trials, which have occurred 17 times since 1789
- **Judicial (Supreme Court)**—Can determine established laws to be unconstitutional; led by supreme court justices appointed by the President of the United States; established by Article III of the Constitution
- **Executive**—Led by the President and Vice President; leads the country and the military; appoints justices; can veto bills passed by Congress; established by Article II of the Constitution; contains 15 departments (i.e., Department of Defense, Department of Justice, Department of Education); if the President dies, resigns, or is impeached, the Vice President is the next to assume command

Note: The Constitution of the United States of America lists three rules related to who can become president. The individual must be a natural born citizen of the United States, reside in the U.S. for at least 14 years, and must be a minimum of 35 years of age.

Concerning international relations and the executive branch of government:

- Both the Secretary of State (appointed by the president) and the National Security Council advise the president on matters of foreign policy.
- Ambassadors are also executive branch members who reside in other countries in order to lobby for the United States in international meetings.

Note: The Magna Carta of 1215 (England) is considered the very first modern document that sought to limit the powers of the governing body.

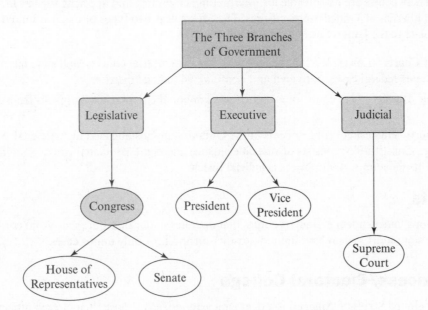

Local, State, and Federal Powers

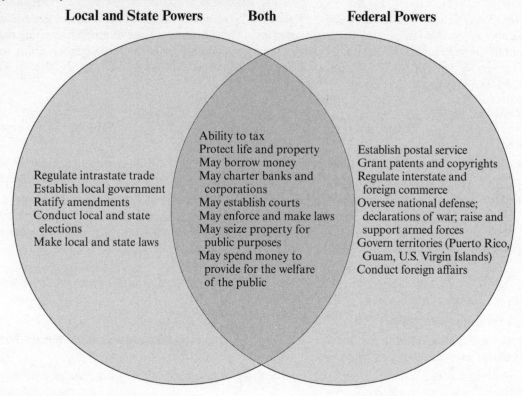

Local and State Powers   Both   Federal Powers

Local and State Powers
Regulate intrastate trade
Establish local government
Ratify amendments
Conduct local and state
 elections
Make local and state laws

Both
Ability to tax
Protect life and property
May borrow money
May charter banks and
 corporations
May establish courts
May enforce and make laws
May seize property for
 public purposes
May spend money to
 provide for the welfare
 of the public

Federal Powers
Establish postal service
Grant patents and copyrights
Regulate interstate and
 foreign commerce
Oversee national defense;
 declarations of war; raise and
 support armed forces
Govern territories (Puerto Rico,
 Guam, U.S. Virgin Islands)
Conduct foreign affairs

Federal Court System

There are three levels of federal courts in the Unites States: U.S. District Courts, U.S. Court of Appeals, and the Supreme Court. These courts are responsible for interpreting, enforcing, and applying the law in an effort to protect the rights and liberties of United States citizens. The courts hear two types of cases: criminal and civil. The following terms relate to the Unites States legal system:

- **U.S. District Courts**—Lowest level in the federal court system; trial courts; each state has at least one district court; hears federal cases, both civil and criminal; 94 judicial districts

- **U.S. Court of Appeals**—One court for each of the 12 regional circuits; hears appeals from courts within its circuit

- **Supreme Court**—Highest court of appeals in the United States; established in Article III, Section 1 of the United States Constitution; consists of one chief justice and eight associate justices appointed by the president; one of its most important powers is **judicial review**

State Courts

Each state has its own independent system of courts that operates under that state's laws and constitution. The local courts in the state court system have limited jurisdiction and hear only minor cases.

Election Process/Electoral College

Knowing that the United States of America is a democracy, its citizens choose their elected officials and make decisions about laws, statutes, and referenda by voting. Citizens must register to vote and may declare membership to a political party when registering. There are many political parties in the United States, but the two main parties are the Republican and Democratic political parties. In order to become an elected official, candidates for office campaign to inform the public about the candidate's views and intentions if elected. Elections take place on a regular basis.

The Electoral College, also known as the College of Electors, was established by Article II in the United States Constitution in 1787. It is the country's system for electing the president and vice president. The Electoral College was included in Article II as one of the checks and balances in the system of government for two reasons: to give more equal weight to states with small populations and to assist voters in making an informed decision regarding our highest elected officials. The following is basic knowledge related to the Electoral College:

- Body of elected representatives (electors) is chosen by the voters in each state.
- Electors pledge in advance to vote for the candidate of their party based on the popular vote.
- Meet after the citizen vote; cast ballots based on the public vote for president and vice president.
- Currently (2009) there are 538 electors in the United States; 270 electoral votes are required to win.
- Each state is assigned a number of electoral votes based on the number of senators and representatives it has (for example, Florida currently has 2 senators and 25 representatives for a total of 27 electoral votes).
- Electors actually elect the president and vice president.

Checkpoint

1. True or false: Supreme Court Justices are elected officials in the judicial branch of government.

1. Fill in the blank: The _____ government has the ability to regulate intrastate trade.

1. Fill in the blank: Article _____ of the United States Constitution established the legislative branch of government.

1. True or false: The Electoral College, also known as the College of Electors, gives the states with small populations more of an equal weight in presidential elections.

2. Fill in the blank: There are _____ U.S. District Courts.

Checkpoint Answers

1. False
2. local/state
3. I
4. True
5. 94

Civics

Civic education, also known as citizenship education, has been said to be one of the most important components of social studies education. The development of good citizens is imperative to the future of the country. Students should be exposed to social studies concepts that foster a need for becoming responsible, functioning members of their community. They should understand that they have certain rights as citizens and particular responsibilities as well. www.icivics.org is an excellent resource for engaging students in civic education.

Civic education is imperative to the democratic way of life. Because democratic society is founded on the principles set forth in the Constitution of the United States, following is a summary of that important historical document:

- Comprised of a **preamble,** 7 articles, and 27 amendments
  - Article I—Legislative Branch; includes nine sections
  - Article II—Executive Branch; includes four sections
  - Article III—Judicial Branch; includes three sections
  - Article IV—The relationship between the states; includes four sections
  - Article V—Amendments

- Article VI—Supreme Law, Oaths of Office and Debts
- Article VII—Approving the Constitution

The **Bill of Rights,** amendments (legally adopted changes) 1 through 10 of the Constitution of the United States of America, lays the foundation for the civic rights of citizens in this country and limits the power of the federal government. Briefly, the following describes the basic rights noted in the first ten amendments to the United States Constitution known as the Bill of Rights:

- First Amendment—Provides for five basic freedoms: religion, speech, the press, assembly, and petition the government
- Second Amendment—States the right of citizens to keep and bear arms
- Third Amendment—States that citizens do not have to provide housing to soldiers during peacetime
- Fourth Amendment—States the right to privacy
- Fifth Amendment—States the right to due process of the law
- Sixth Amendment—States the right to a public and speedy trial in front of an impartial jury
- Seventh Amendment—States, in civil lawsuits (that is, lawsuits dealing with significant property or money), the right to a jury trial
- Eighth Amendment—States that punishment cannot be excessive (cruel and unusual) and should fit the crime
- Ninth Amendment—States that citizens have other rights not necessarily stated in the Bill of Rights
- Tenth Amendment—Limits the national government to only the powers provided in the United States Constitution

Checkpoint

1. True or false: Civic education is not important in the overall social studies curriculum.

2. Fill in the blank: The _____ Amendment to the Constitution states that persons convicted of a crime must be mandated fair punishment that fits the crime.

3. True or false: The Bill of Rights only provides for the rights and freedoms of the citizens of the United States and does not limit governmental control.

4. True or false: Articles I, II, and III of the United States Constitution required a balance of powers; namely, the Executive, Legislative, and Judicial branches of government.

Checkpoint Answers

1. False

2. Eighth

3. False

4. True

Competency 5: Knowledge of Production, Distribution, and Consumption (i.e., Economics)

Competency Description

According to the *Competencies and Skills Required for Teacher Certification in Florida,* 20th Edition (available at www.fldoe.org/asp/ftce/pdf/ftce20edition.pdf), **Competency 5** for the Elementary Education (K–6) Subject Area Examination (SAE) Social Science subtest addresses the following key indicators:

1. Determine ways that scarcity affects the choices made by governments and individuals.
2. Compare and contrast the characteristics and importance of currency.
3. Identify and analyze the role of markets from production through distribution to consumption.
4. Identify and analyze factors to consider when making consumer decisions.
5. Analyze the economic interdependence between nations (e.g., trade, finance, movement of labor).
6. Identify human, natural, and capital resources and evaluate how these resources are used in the production of goods and services.

Overview

Knowledge of economics, specifically production, distribution, and consumption, is of primary importance to elementary educators responsible for educating our youth in the social sciences. There are approximately **10 questions** that address Competency 5. This section addresses the following areas related to **Competency 5** key indicators:

- Economics
  - Types of Economies
  - Economic Institutions
  - Currency

Economics

Economics is defined as the science that deals with the production, consumption, and distribution of goods and services. All categories in the social sciences are somehow related to economics. For example, significant historical events like the Great Depression (1930s) were spawned by the fall of the economy (history). Human beings have chosen locations to settle based on whether or not they were appropriate for production of goods they needed for survival and for ease of distribution (geography).

In the United States, we operate in a mixed (market/command) economy or one in which the government and private businesses both play vital roles. The majority of goods and services are produced by the private sector. The prices of these goods and services are determined by supply and demand for those items. When a population demands more of something, the supply is increased, as is the price. Often, an increase in competition can be seen among producers of the sought-after items or services. When demand for an item decreases, the supply is reduced and again, so is the price. Producers of less popular goods and services often go out of business or choose to produce other items.

Along with voting for officials who help to shape economic policy, the choices consumers make regarding goods and services have a significant impact on our overall economy. Consumer decision making entails several steps, including comparing needs versus wants, searching for high-quality products, studying the attributes of those items to ascertain whether or not they meet the need, comparing prices, and eventually making an informed purchase. Historically, bitter confrontations over economic systems have unfolded. For example, in the late 1980s the Soviet Union fell due to the collapse of their command economy. Teaching youth (future consumers) problem solving and strategic thinking skills in relation to economics will help them to make better decisions in the modern global economy.

Types of Economies

There are four basic economies operating around the world: traditional, command, market, and mixed. Knowledge of these economic systems is crucial in an interdependent global economy.

- **Traditional economy**—This original form of economic systems is characterized by bartering and trading and is usually employed in rural or farm-based areas. Cultural traditions, beliefs, and customs largely affect the production, distribution, and consumption of goods. The Inuit tribes of the Artic regions including Greenland, Canada, and the northern United States along with the people of Southern India practice a traditional economy.

- **Command economy**—This economic system is controlled by the government. Decisions about what to produce and how to disseminate and use the goods are decided by government officials. The former Soviet Union (socialism) and Cuba both practice a command or planned economy.

- **Market economy**—This economic system is controlled by individuals. In a pure market economy, the government has no say in economic affairs whatsoever. Individuals interact with companies to decide how to allocate resources and distribute goods. During the late 1800s, the United States practiced a market economy, nearly a pure market economy, for a short period of time.

- **Mixed economy**—This economic system is a mixture of both the market and command economies. Individuals and the government make decisions regarding production, distribution, and consumption of goods and services. The United States practices a mixed economy, as does the People's Republic of China.

In an effort to simplify some of the abstract ideas related to economics, the Council on Economic Education, CEE, created this simplified list of economic principles (www.councilforeconed.org):

1. People choose.
2. People's choices involve costs.
3. People respond to incentives in predictable ways.
4. People create economic systems that influence individual choices and incentives.
5. People gain when they trade voluntarily.
6. People's choices have consequences that lie in the future.

In addition to the preceding information, the following are key terms related to economics:

- **Capital resource**—Any asset used in the production of goods and services
- **Consumption**—The use and intake of goods and services
- **Depression**—Long-lasting and painful recession or slowing of economic activity
- **Distribution**—The dissemination or dispersing of goods and services
- **Finance**—The managing of monetary resources
- **Fiscal policy**—Government spending policies that affect interest rates, tax rates, and government spending; policies aid in governmental control of economy
- **Free enterprise**—Emphasizes private ownership; supply and demand
- **Gross Domestic Product (GDP)**—Formerly known as the "gross national product"; total monetary value of all goods and services produced in a nation during a specific time frame (for example, 1 year)
- **Human resource**—A person used to accomplish a goal
- **Inflation**—A persistent, general increase in prices over a period of time
- **Limited resource**—An item that is in short supply
- **Monopoly**—One company or institution that has exclusive control of a particular good or service in a market
- **Natural resource**—An available supply of something (land, water, oil) occurring in nature; often used to create wealth
- **Production**—The creation of goods and services

- **Recession**—A slowing of economic activity
- **Scarcity**—Insufficient supply or shortage of goods and services; often affected by consumer decision making
- **Stagflation**—High rate of inflation accompanied by rising unemployment
- **Trade**—The exchange of goods and services

Economic Institutions

Economic institutions (organizations created to pursue particular endeavors, like banking by financial institutions) are vital components of our overall economy. Following are a list of various economic institutions with a description of their overall purpose in our economy:

- **Bank**—Depository; financial institution; an establishment authorized by the government that mediates financial transactions and provides other financial services (loans, checking/savings accounts, pay interest, and so on)
- **Credit union**—Depository; financial institution; an establishment owned, controlled, and operated by its members; provides financial services much like commercial banks but often provides lower interest rates for some of those services
- **Stock market**—A place (virtual or physical) where stocks and bonds are exchanged, also known as the stock exchange; the two largest stock exchanges are the New York Stock Exchange and the National Association of Securities Dealers Automated Quotations (NASDAQ); activity in these exchanges are an indicator of the state of the economy
- **Federal Reserve banks**—The central bank of the United States federal banking system located in each of the 12 districts; regulates and supervises member banks in the 12 regions; maintains funds for future use, issues bank notes, controls credit, lends money, and so on; involved in the setting of national monetary policy

Currency

Currency is defined as a unit of exchange. Money is a form of currency. The following is a short list of currencies currently used around the world:

United States	dollar
United Kingdom	pound
Spain, Portugal, Netherlands, Germany, etc.	euro
Mexico	peso
Japan	yen

Checkpoint

1. True or false: The Great Depression of the 1930s was considered a long-lasting and painful slowing of the overall economy.

2. True or false: Consumer decision making has no effect on the supply and demand of products in this country and all over the world; therefore, teaching our youth economic reasoning skills is futile.

3. Fill in the blanks: Both _____ and _____ are depository financial institutions that mediate financial transactions and provide a variety of financial services.

4. True or false: A market economy operates on the concepts of supply and demand.

5. Fill in the blank: The former Soviet Union's _____ economy self-destructed in the late 1980s.

6. True or false: Comparing the prices of an item is an important part of consumer decision making.

7. True or false: Many European countries use a form of currency called the euro.

Checkpoint Answers

1. True
2. False
3. banks; credit unions
4. True
5. command
6. True
7. True

Summary

The Social Science subtest encompasses a variety of subcompetencies related to the basic knowledge required of educators teaching elementary-age students. This section of competencies begins with the knowledge of effective instructional practices and assessment that are effective in the teaching and learning of the social sciences. Knowledge of time, continuity, and change (the study of history) involves the influences that prominent historical figures and events have had on the United States and the world. The knowledge of people, places, and their environment, also known as the study of geography, encompasses map and globe skills, the essential elements of geography, and how the environment has impacted human life and continues to do so today. Knowledge of government and the citizen (civics) relates to major historical documents that have shaped the country, structure and purposes for government, and basic knowledge of how the U.S. government functions. The study of economics (production, distribution, and consumption) covers basic information related to financial institutions and the role of markets in the United States and the world.

You should use the information in this section to complement your previous knowledge in the area of social science. The general review of social science provided in this chapter should allow you to explore areas of strength. In addition, you are encouraged to note areas of weakness that you might still need to review. To provide an opportunity for further practice and analysis, sample questions for the Social Science competency area appear in the next section of this chapter. Answer explanations follow the sample questions.

Sample Questions

1. Although not the first to set foot on the land we now know as America, what early explorer opened up the Western hemisphere to economic and political development by the Europeans?

   A. Hernando Cortez
   B. Vasco da Gama
   C. Christopher Columbus
   D. John Cabot

2. Many government agencies and specialized organizations provide valuable resources related to the social sciences. Choose one such agency/organization that could be used to enhance your knowledge of subject matter in this content area.

   A. NCTM
   B. NCSS
   C. IRA
   D. NCTE

3. A market economy functions around the concepts of supply and

   A. consumer.
   B. fiscal responsibility.
   C. product.
   D. demand.

4. A primary source document is

   A. one that was created during that time period.
   B. nonprint media.
   C. a website.
   D. a blog.

5. "Power to the people" is a phrase that describes the function of a republic. The Bill of Rights was not only enacted to protect the citizens of the United States but also to

   A. enhance government control.
   B. place sanctions on exporting goods.
   C. limit government power.
   D. control the choices citizens make.

6. What early explorer named Florida in the year 1513?

   A. Juan Ponce de Leon
   B. Ferdinand Magellan
   C. Sir Francis Drake
   D. Vasco Núñez de Balboa

7. In the 1930s, the United States experienced a long-lasting and painful slowing of the overall economy. This is called a

    A. regression.
    B. repression.
    C. depression.
    D. recession.

8. GDP stands for

    A. Gross Daily Product.
    B. Gross Domestic Product.
    C. Good Dogs Play.
    D. Good Domestic Producers.

9. In what year did the United States became involved in the Vietnam War?

    A. 1973
    B. 1959
    C. 1965
    D. 1937

10. What distinct portion of the population produces the majority of goods and services?

    A. the public sector
    B. the private sector
    C. the northwest sector
    D. the unknown sector

11. After what war did Americans want to explore and settle land to the west?

    A. Vietnam War
    B. French and Indian War
    C. War of 1812
    D. Korean War

12. What is considered to be the first modern document written to limit governmental power?

    A. the Treaty of Paris
    B. the United States Constitution
    C. the Bill of Rights
    D. the Magna Carta of 1215

13. What vocabulary term is used to describe the statistical study of human populations?

    A. topography
    B. biography
    C. ethnography
    D. demography

14. Which of the following resources can educators use to enhance the comprehension of content area material?

    A. guest speakers
    B. direct instruction
    C. literature circles
    D. storytelling

15. In the U.S. government, some government officials are elected by the population while others are appointed by executive officials. Of the following, which government position is appointed?

    A. President of the United States
    B. mayor
    C. Supreme Court Justice
    D. senator

16. The two largest stock exchanges are the New York Stock Exchange and

    A. the National Consortium of Stocks.
    B. the National Association of Securities Dealers Automated Quotations.
    C. Wall Street.
    D. Main Street.

17. What was the name of the United States air and land operations involved in the Persian Gulf War?

    A. Operation Enduring Freedom
    B. Operation Liberation
    C. Operation United Nations
    D. Operation Desert Storm

18. Who was the King of Macedonia in 336 B.C. who was credited with conquering the Persian Empire and restoring order to Ancient Greece?

    A. Ivan the Terrible
    B. Catherine the Great
    C. Alexander the Great
    D. Louis XII

19. Democracy, monarchy, oligarchy, and dictatorship are four types of government structures employed around the world. Which of the following best defines an oligarchy?

    A. government by the few
    B. government by the people
    C. government by one exercising absolute power
    D. government by royalty

20. During the Revolutionary War, _____ commanded the Continental Army.

    A. George Washington
    B. Patrick Henry
    C. Deborah Sampson
    D. Ethan Allen

Answer Explanations

1. **C.** Competency 2. Christopher Columbus's discoveries opened up the Western hemisphere to economic and political development by the Europeans, namely the Spanish, English, and French.

2. **B.** Competency 1. NCTM stands for the National Council of Teachers of Mathematics. NCSS stands for the National Council of the Social Studies. IRA stands for the International Reading Association, and finally, NCTE stands for the National Council of Teachers of English. Although most of these national organizations offer suggestions that cross the curriculum, NCSS specifically references the social science content area.

3. **D.** Competency 5. Supply and demand are the concepts that provide the foundation of a market economy.

4. **A.** Competency 2. A primary source document is one that was written during that time period or shortly thereafter. It could be a photograph, article, book, diary entry, and so on.

5. **C.** Competencies 2 and 4. The Bill of Rights was not only enacted to protect the rights of U.S. citizens but also to limit the power of the government. A true republic's power lies in its people.

6. **A.** Competency 2. Juan Ponce de Leon, a Spanish explorer who was searching for the Fountain of Youth, inevitably named Florida. All other choices were also early explorers of the world.

7. **C.** Competency 5. A long-lasting and painful slowing of economic activity that inevitably has negative effects on the population is known as a depression.

8. **B.** Competency 5. Gross Domestic Product (GDP), formerly known as the "gross national product," is the total monetary value of all goods and services produced in a nation during a specific time frame (for example, 1 year).

9. **B.** Competency 2. The United States became involved in order to prevent the communist takeover of South Vietnam in the year 1959.

10. **B.** Competency 5. The majority of goods and services are produced by the private sector.

11. **C.** Competency 2. After the War of 1812, Americans wanted to explore and settle the land to the west. This movement was known as westward expansion.

12. **D.** Competency 2. The Magna Carta of 1215 (England) is considered the very first modern document that sought to limit the powers of the governing body.

13. **D.** Competency 3. Demography is the study of demographics or population data regarding, for example, the income, age, and education of a population.

14. **A.** Competency 1. The use of guest speakers, field trips, virtual field trips, learning centers, community-based service-learning experiences, and digital media/educational software are all examples of resources that educators can use to enhance comprehension of content area material. The other choices are examples of teaching strategies or methods.

15. **C.** Competency 4. Of the choices provided, the only appointed position is that of a Supreme Court Justice. All other officials listed are elected.

16. **B.** Competency 5. The two largest stock exchanges are the New York Stock Exchange and the National Association of Securities Dealers Automated Quotations (NASDAQ).

17. **D.** Competency 2. Operation Desert Storm was the name for the U.S. land and air operations involved in the Gulf War effort.

18. **C.** Competency 2. Alexander the Great was King of Macedonia in 336 B.C., conquered the Persian Empire, founded the city of Alexandria in Egypt as a center of learning and culture, and created a massive empire that restored order in Ancient Greece.

19. **A.** Competency 4. An oligarchy is best defined as a government by the few.

20. **A.** Competency 2. George Washington was the commander of the Continental Army during the Revolutionary War.

Chapter 4

Science

This chapter provides a general review of the Science subtest with sample questions and explanations at the end of the chapter. Checkpoint exercises are found throughout, giving you an opportunity to practice the skills addressed in each section. The answers to the Checkpoint exercises immediately follow the set of questions. We encourage you to cover the answers as you complete the Checkpoint exercises.

Competency 1: Knowledge of Effective Science Instruction

Competency Description

According to the *Competencies and Skills Required for Teacher Certification in Florida,* 20th Edition (available at www.fldoe.org/asp/ftce/pdf/ftce20edition.pdf), **Competency 1** for the Elementary Education (K–6) Subject Area Examination (SAE) Science subtest addresses the following key indicators:

1. Analyze and apply developmentally appropriate researched-based strategies for teaching science practices.
2. Select and apply safe and effective instructional strategies to utilize manipulatives, models, scientific equipment, real-world examples, and print and digital representations to support and enhance science instruction.
3. Identify and analyze strategies for formal and informal learning experiences to provide a science curriculum that promotes students' innate curiosity and active inquiry (e.g., hands-on experiences, active engagement in the natural world, student interaction).
4. Select and analyze collaborative strategies to help students explain concepts, to introduce and clarify formal science terms, and to identify misconceptions.
5. Identify and apply appropriate reading strategies, mathematical practices, and science-content materials to enhance science instruction for learners at all levels.
6. Apply differentiated strategies in science instruction and assessments based on student needs.
7. Identify and apply ways to organize and manage a classroom for safe, effective science teaching that reflect state safety procedures and restrictions (e.g., procedures, equipment, disposal of chemicals, classroom layout, use of living organisms).
8. Select and apply appropriate technology, science tools and measurement units for students' use in data collection and the pursuit of science.
9. Select and analyze developmentally appropriate diagnostic, formative and summative assessments to evaluate prior knowledge, guide instruction, and evaluate student achievement.
10. Choose scientifically and professionally responsible content and activities that are socially and culturally sensitive.

Overview

This section provides a look at important instructional strategies and methods for teaching science. There are approximately **11 questions** that address Competency 1. This section addresses the following areas related to **Competency 1** key indicators:

- Instructional Strategies and Classroom Teaching Tools
- Methods of Assessment
- Interrelationship of Science and Technology
- Technology Use by Students in Science

Students should be evaluated in their demonstration of acceptable scientific ethics and procedures; ability to identify inventions; ability to analyze and evaluate data collected or found in databases; and ability to critique scientific findings and reports. Some ways to evaluate students' growth are the following: documenting experiments by keeping notes or writing reflections related to personal experiences in science and presenting findings from experiments using valid and reliable data. Students should also be evaluated in their ability to describe findings using inquiry-based methods. They should be able to explain what science means personally and tell how science connects to society and other subjects.

Instructional Strategies and Classroom Teaching Tools

Students should be evaluated in their demonstration of acceptable presentation of scientific work, ability to communicate with others, and ability to analyze and evaluate scientific work. Some ways to evaluate students' growth are the following: documenting personal growth by keeping scientific notes, collecting data, or writing reflections related to personal experiences in science. Students should also be evaluated in their ability to describe scientific principles as they occur in experiments to describe data findings.

Student scientific findings should be displayed and evaluated in a detailed and analytical way. All students should participate in offering critiques that are guided by the teacher. This type of assessment should increase the viewpoints from which students' scientific work is evaluated and promote the inquiry-based skills of all the students. Student responses to scientific work will vary. This critique process is a way for students to learn from each other, learn from analyzing successful and less successful problem solving strategies, and find creative and aesthetic solutions to scientific issues or problems.

The *National Science Education Standards* reported, "Scientific inquiry refers to the diverse ways in which scientists study the natural world and propose explanations based on the evidence derived from their work. Inquiry also refers to the activities of students in which they develop knowledge and understanding of scientific ideas, as well as an understanding of how scientists study the natural world" (NSES, 1996, National Academy Press, Washington, D.C., p. 23). The inquiry process involves the following:

- Observation (close analysis of information, procedures, and evidence)
- Measurement (involving quantitative description of evidence and value placed on precision and accuracy)
- Experimentation (testing questions and ideas)
- Communication (relaying results, writing, speaking, and explaining)
- Mental processes (inductive reasoning, formulating hypotheses, analogy, extrapolation, classification, prediction, inference, synthesis, and deductive reasoning)

The inquiry-based learning approach is more focused on using and learning content as a means to develop information-processing and problem solving skills. The process should be more of a student-centered approach, as opposed to a teacher-centered approach. In this type of process, the teacher becomes a facilitator of learning. It also places more emphasis on "how we come to know" and less emphasis on "what we know." Students need to be more involved, motivated, engaged, and responsible as they construct knowledge through active involvement. The more involved in, motivated by, engaged in, and responsible students are in a subject, experiment, or project, the more likely they will be able to construct in-depth knowledge of a subject, experiment, or project. An inquiry-based learning environment must model appropriate scientific processes, allow for creative thinking, provide flexibility, use effective questioning strategies, and empower thinking skills and content. Teachers should encourage students to explain and justify their answers using data, manipulate data to distinguish patterns and trends (graphs, tables, and charts), and explain what they see, including, if needed, the possibility of data points that are outside the normal patterns (called outliers).

When trying to use an inquiry-based approach as part of the learning process, you should provide opportunities for students to use relevant data to answer research questions by analyzing the data. It is not enough that students collect data or use equipment. For example, constructing a molecular Solar System scale model is not an inquiry-based activity in itself, unless it also involves research questions and discussion of findings. Drill and practice activities for a particular concept or skill are not considered inquiry-based activities.

The *5-Step Experiential Learning Cycle* has been suggested as a method to support science learning. It may be repeated as needed for different scientific concepts. The five steps are presented and discussed here:

1. *Exploration* ("Do it"): Perform an activity with limited or no help from the teacher; for example, making products or models, role playing, presenting findings, problem solving, or playing a game.

2. *Sharing* ("What Happened?"): Publicly share the results, reactions, and observations; talk freely about experiences; and discuss feelings generated by the experience (as a group or individually).

3. *Processing* ("What's Important?"): Discuss, analyze, and reflect on how the experience was carried out, how issues were brought out by the experience, how specific problems or issues were addressed, what personal experiences were involved, and what recurring themes were encountered.

4. *Generalizing* ("So What?"): Connect the experience with real-world examples, find general trends or common truths in the experience, identify "real-life" principles that surfaced, and list key terms that capture the learning.

5. *Application* ("Now What?"): Apply what was learned to a similar or different situation, learn from past experiences, discuss how new learning can be applied to other situations, discuss how issues raised can be useful in the future, discuss how more effective behaviors can develop from the new learning, and develop a sense of ownership for what was learned.

Another suggested method to support science learning is the 5-E's Learning Cycle. This is a method of structuring science lessons that is based on cognitive psychology and constructivist learning theory. Bybee (1997, *Achieving Science Literacy: From Purposes to Practices*. Portsmouth, NH: Heinemann) described what this five-step learning cycle involves: *Engagement, Exploration, Explanation, Elaboration,* and *Evaluation*. Note that *Evaluation* is not the last step of this cyclical process. It is more like a recurring step within the other four stages of this learning cycle. Examples of the evaluation aspects for each stage are given for each description here:

- *Engagement*—The cyclical process starts with engagement. At this stage, the teacher presents the problem, pre-assesses the students, helps students make connections, and informs students of the research questions, relevant information, procedures, goals, and objectives of the activity. The evaluation of students' engagement revolves around the pre-assessment and students' proper understanding of the activity, and motivation to engage in the activity. The context of the activity and students' mastery of prior knowledge and prerequisites are very important at this point. This evaluation could involve teacher's field notes and observations (formal or informal), and students' oral and written responses. Note that the effectiveness of the activity is directly related to the level of students' engagement.

- *Exploration*—In this phase, students should be actively engaged in collecting or finding data to solve the problem, and the teacher should make sure students are doing so effectively and appropriately. Evaluation during this stage should focus on the process itself, including students' proper and logical use of data collection and recording procedures instead of focusing on the product resulting from their data collection.

- *Explanation*—At this point, students should use the data they have collected to solve the problem and answer research questions; they should report their procedures and thinking process as they solve the problem. The teacher could also introduce new vocabulary, ideas, concepts, skills, phrases, or sentences to label what the students have already figured out. Evaluation during this stage should focus on the processes the students are using, including how well they use the collected information and develop new ideas. The teacher could ask comprehension questions dealing with new vocabulary and concepts.

- *Elaboration*—Elaboration is the last step of the cycle, before it goes back to the engagement stage. Students are given new information questions and problems in order to extend what they have learned in the earlier parts of the learning cycle and posed problems to be solved by applying what they have learned, including examples and non-examples. Evaluation during this stage should focus on the overall performance and final application problems, answers to and discussion of research questions, products, reports, or presentations (individually or as small groups).

Methods of Assessment

Assessment can be used for a variety of purposes. Each purpose presents its own opportunities and challenges. The five most common types of assessment are as follows:

- **Diagnostic assessment** (pretests) are used to help determine what students know when they begin any educational task.
- **Formative assessments** help guide day-to-day classroom activities.
- **Student outcome** or **summative assessment** is used to find out what students have learned and mastered in their individual programs.
- **Comparative assessments** determine how an individual's or a group's outcome compares to another group's outcome.
- **Student assessment** is used to help determine the effectiveness of a program, curriculum innovation, pedagogic strategy, professional development, or policy initiative.

Other terms used to describe assessment are the following:

- **Traditional assessment** involves students selecting responses from a multiple-choice list, true/false list, or matching list, or working out the full solution of an equation.
- **Standardized testing** involves the administration of tests under controlled conditions and using consistent scoring procedures.
- **Performance assessment** involves the direct, systematic observation of an actual student's performance and rating of that performance according to pre-established performance criteria or a rubric, and assessment of both the results and process.
- **Alternative assessment** involves students' derived responses to a task or question; for example, demonstrations, exhibits, portfolios, oral presentations, or essays; not traditional assessment.
- **Authentic assessment** involves presenting tasks that reflect the kind of mastery demonstrated by experts or in real-world situations.

As part of an inquiry-based learning environment, assessment is focused on determining students' progress and development in reasoning skills, in addition to content understanding. Inquiry-based learning is concerned with in-school success, and students' preparation as life-long learners. Inquiry-based classrooms are open learning environments in which students search and make use of resources beyond the classroom and the school, and use technology to connect appropriately with local and world communities. Students learn to use an inquiry approach to help them connect science with the scientific method.

Abstract concepts like potential and kinetic energy are difficult for students to understand. Studies have shown that one of the most effective ways to introduce and reinforce abstract scientific concepts is by using manipulatives (blocks, rods, beans, and sticks, among others). They include objects that can be touched and moved around by students in ways that enable descriptions to come alive; for example, using race vehicles powered by springs or rubber bands down a ramp to illustrate potential and kinetic energy. Students should have opportunities to investigate ways to solve problems and share and discuss their solutions and procedures. They should also have opportunities to make sound connections between new information and previously acquired information. An effective way to provide the possibility of making this type of connection is the use of small groups of students working cooperatively or collaboratively with manipulatives. Activities like this one allow students to design and experiment with their own vehicles in an environment that encourages social interaction and active learning. They allow for cooperation and collaboration, creativity, self-esteem, and self-efficacy. Also, physical models can be used to develop an intuition related to fundamental scientific ideas and processes. Physical models can serve as the basis for short, in-class demonstrations or for course projects.

Many "virtual" versions of manipulatives (called virtual manipulatives or applets) and simulations of activities are now available on a number of websites, and used in science and mathematics education. Virtual manipulatives are interactive, Web-based visual representations of objects that provide opportunities for constructing mathematical or scientific knowledge. Some virtual manipulatives are available online from the following sources: *National Library of Virtual Manipulatives* and *National Council of Teachers of Mathematics (NCTM) Illuminations*.

Virtual manipulatives can be used to help students learn some of the underlying ideas of mathematics modeling and computer simulation. They should not be used as a substitute for real, concrete manipulatives, models, or simulations. Static and dynamic virtual models can be found online. Static virtual models are not considered true virtual manipulatives. They are pictorial representations of the physical concrete manipulatives that cannot be manipulated. Virtual manipulatives should be more than pointing and clicking to get results on the computer and providing answers at an abstract level. For example, a virtual manipulative should provide some control by allowing slides, flips, turns, and/or rotations.

Computer simulations are the technique of representing the real world via a computer program. They can represent real or imaginary situations and may allow users to study or try things that would be difficult or impossible to do in real life. They should imitate the internal processes and not merely the results of what they are simulating. Some simulations are available online from the following sources:

- *Lions and Antelopes* (by Jo Edkins, 2004: explores the relationship between predators, herbivores, and vegetation)
- *Plants-in-motion* (by Roger P. Hangarter, 2000: uses time-lapsed photography to show the movement of Arabidopsis plants in response to stimuli, and that plants are living organisms)
- *Science Simulations on the Internet from Kent County Council* (biology, physics, health, astronomy, and virtual experiments)

Checkpoint

1. Fill in the blank: _____ learning should be of a more student-centered approach than a teacher-centered approach.

2. Fill in the blank: _____ assessment is used to help determine what students know when they begin any educational task.

3. Fill in the blank: A type of assessment used to help guide day-to-day classroom activities is called _____ assessment.

4. Fill in the blank: _____ refers to the precision of an assessment instrument.

5. Fill in the blank: _____ refers to the accuracy of an assessment instrument.

Checkpoint Answers

1. Inquiry or Inquiry-based
2. Diagnostic
3. formative
4. Reliability
5. Validity

Interrelationship of Science and Technology

Science is the systematic and logical investigation of observable events. Its goals include to identify and establish principles and theories that may be used in the solution of problems by using formal techniques, such as systematic studies, observations, experimentations, and inquiry methods. In order to establish knowledge, scientific findings must be repeatable, susceptible to disagreement and change, disprovable, and submitted to a rigorous peer-reviewed process. Science also involves the development of theories, laws, and hypotheses. Their development is driven by the quality of data that is available and how it is interpreted at a given time. The following is a description of theory, hypothesis, and law as defined in science:

- A **scientific theory** is a well-validated and well-supported explanation of some aspect of the natural world; for example, Theory of Relativity, Quantum Mechanics, Germ Theory of Disease, or Theory of Evolution.

- A **hypothesis** is a tentative and testable insight into the natural world that is not yet verified; but if it were found to be true, it would explain certain aspects of the natural world and might become a scientific theory. A hypothesis is typically situation-dependent; however, theories began as hypotheses prior to being validated.

- A **scientific law** is a truthful explanation of different events that happen with uniformity under certain conditions; for example, laws of nature, laws of gravitation, Kepler's three laws of planetary motion, or laws of thermodynamics. A law is a description of how things behave, but it does not necessarily explain why they behave the way they do.

The use of scientific and inquiry-based methods is very important. These methods refer to techniques used to investigate phenomena, acquire new knowledge, or correct and integrate previous knowledge. Methods of inquiry must be based on gathering observable, empirical, and measurable evidence subject to specific principles of ethics and reasoning. A scientific method consists of the collection of data through observation and experimentation, and the formulation and testing of hypotheses; new researchable questions or hypotheses usually come out of the testing of hypotheses, and the process is carried out all over again. The issues of validity and reliability of data, findings, and interpretations need to be considered:

- **Validity** refers to the degree to which a measure accurately assesses the specific concept it is designed to measure.

- **Reliability** refers to the consistency of a set of measurements or a measuring instrument. This can refer to whether the measurements of the same instrument provide the same measurement (test-retest), or whether two independent investigators give consistently similar scores (this is called inter-rater reliability).

Note that an instrument may be reliable but not valid. A reliable instrument might be measuring something consistently, but not necessarily what it is supposed to be measuring validly. Reliability refers to the precision of the instrument, and validity refers to the accuracy of the instrument.

Technology Use by Students in Science

Technologies are not usually exclusive products of or tools for science. The development of technology limits or expands the development of scientific discoveries. Technologies have to satisfy their own utility, usability, and safety requirements, among other things, which takes time, money, and effort. Engineers are an important factor when it comes to the interrelationship between science and technology. Engineering is a more goal-oriented or result-oriented process for the design, improvement, and development of tools and systems. One of its goals is to investigate natural observable events for practical human means. In many cases, engineering uses and integrates results and techniques from science, but it draws knowledge from many areas, such as scientific, mathematical, linguistic, social, and historical. Technology is often a combination of science and engineering, but as a human activity, technology precedes science and engineering. For instance, when studying the flow of electrons in electrical conductors, scientists might use already existing tools and knowledge, and then engineers might use the newfound knowledge to develop and improve tools.

Students' use of technology gets them ready to participate in tomorrow's rapidly evolving world. They should learn to analyze and intervene creatively to improve the quality of life. Science requires that students become independent and creative problem solvers, individually and as team members. Students must have opportunities to respond and develop a range of ideas, science products, and systems. These opportunities should combine practical skills, understanding of aesthetics, social and environmental issues, and industrial practices. Students should also analyze and evaluate uses and effects of present and past technologies. They should become discriminating and informed consumers of scientific products as well as innovators, using science as a tool.

An example of the interrelationship of science and technology is the late 1600s development of the technology to make precision magnifying lenses. These magnifying glasses, in turn, helped scientists discover the existence of tiny organisms, such as bacteria. Lately, a great deal of attention has been given to nanotechnology. Advances in nanoscale science and technology have revolutionized manufacturing procedures, medicine, and energy discoveries. "Nano" comes from the Latin word "nanus," meaning dwarf, and is used to describe very small quantities of mass, time, and length. It indicates a scaling factor in exponential notation of 10^{-9} or one billionth; for example, a nanogram (one billionth of a gram), nanosecond (one billionth of a second), and nanometer (one billionth of a meter). In general, nanoscience studies the chemical and physical consequences of manipulating materials on the nanometer (nm) length scale, is concerned with the development of tools for manipulating materials on this scale, and exploits these tools for the development of new products and processes.

Computer software and hardware are very important in the collection, manipulation, and analysis of data; for example:

- Word processors facilitate the preparation, manipulation, modification, and arrangement of electronically developed text, tables, and images for reports and documents.
- Spreadsheets allow tabulation and performance of simple and complicated calculations, mathematical manipulations, and plots and graphs on various types of data, such as numbers, names, alphabetical information, scientific measurements, statistical information, and budget information.
- Database software allows easy collection, access, organization, and retrieval of data, such as inventories, experiments, and records.
- Online databases allow access to essential tools for research in science and other areas, including scientific associations and scientists from around the world, massive bibliographic databases, print material, and interlibrary loans.
- The Internet allows access to online resources and faster communication and sharing of information, including social networking and online communities (e.g., e-mail, instant messaging, YouTube, TeacherTube, Facebook, MySpace, Twitter, LinkedIn, and Wiki).

Graphing calculators also provide an incredible tool for this purpose when placed in the hands of students. Also, tools like spectometers and sensors facilitate the collection of data, which might also be used with computer software to manage data. Spectometers are instruments that can be used to measure the absorbance spectrum of a liquid, conduct kinetic studies of absorbance versus time, conduct equilibrium studies of absorbance versus time and/or absorbance versus concentration, measure emissions of gas discharge tubes or other light sources, and other experiments.

Sensors are also instruments used to collect data; for example:

- Accelerometers are small devices that can be mounted on moving objects to study one-dimensional motions, such as the motion of a car, elevator, mass on a string undergoing simple harmonic motion, or amusement park rides.
- Barometers are used for either weather studies or lab experiments involving pressures close to normal atmospheric pressure.
- Blood pressure sensors are designed to measure human blood pressure.
- Temperature probes are used for data collection during temperature-related experiments.

Checkpoint

1. Fill in the blank: A _____ is a well-validated and well-supported explanation of some aspect of the natural world.

2. Fill in the blank: A _____ is a truthful explanation of different events that happen with uniformity under certain conditions.

3. Fill in the blank: The _____ allows access to online resources and faster communication and sharing of information, including social networking and online communities.

4. Fill in the blank: A _____ is a tentative and testable insight into the natural world.

5. True or false: Gloria constructed a reliable instrument for her experiment. She concluded that since her instrument is reliable it would also be a valid instrument.

Checkpoint Answers

1. theory

2. law

3. Internet

4. hypothesis

5. False: A reliable instrument might be measuring something consistently, but not necessarily what it is supposed to be measuring validly. Reliability refers to the precision of the instrument, and validity refers to the accuracy of the instrument. They do not depend on each other.

Competency 2: Knowledge of the Nature of Science

Competency Description

According to the *Competencies and Skills Required for Teacher Certification in Florida,* 20th Edition (available at www.fldoe.org/asp/ftce/pdf/ftce20edition.pdf), **Competency 2** for the Elementary Education (K–6) Subject Area Examination (SAE) Science subtest addresses the following key indicators:

1. Analyze the dynamic nature of science models, laws, mechanisms, and theories that explain natural phenomena (e.g., durability, tentativeness, replication, reliance on evidence).

2. Identify and apply science and engineering practices through integrated process skills (e.g., observing, classifying, predicting, hypothesizing, designing and carrying out investigations, developing and using models, constructing and communicating explanations).

3. Differentiate between the characteristics of experiments (e.g., multiple trials, control groups, variables) and other types of scientific investigations (e.g., observations, surveys).

4. Identify and analyze attitudes and dispositions underlying scientific thinking (e.g., curiosity, openness to new ideas, appropriate skepticism, cooperation).

5. Identify and select appropriate tools, including digital technologies, and units of measurement for various science tasks.

6. Evaluate and interpret pictorial representations, charts, tables, and graphs of authentic data from scientific investigations to make predictions, construct explanations, and support conclusions.

7. Identify and analyze ways in which science is an interdisciplinary process and interconnected to STEM disciplines (i.e., science, technology, engineering, mathematics).

8. Analyze the interactions of science and technology with society including cultural, ethical, economic, political, and global factors.

Overview

Knowledge of the nature of science includes scientific processes, inquiry, and procedures for teaching science. There are approximately **10 questions** that address Competency 2. This section addresses the following areas related to **Competency 2** key indicators:

- Scientific Processes and Inquiry
- Laboratory Safety and Procedures

Scientific Processes and Inquiry

Scientific methods are ways in which scientists answer questions and solve problems systematically. The steps for any scientific method are the same, but the order may differ based on what is needed to answer the question posted. The scientific method includes the following steps: 1) ask a question, 2) make observations, 3) hypothesize, 4) predict, 5) test, and 6) conclude.

The first step is to *ask a question.* In order to answer the question, observations are needed (step 2). *Observations* may include collecting observed data such as the number of a specific species of frogs in an area. Once the question is formulated and observations are conducted, a *hypothesis* is created (step 3). A hypothesis is a possible answer to the question. Hypotheses are not based on blind guessing; they are based on what was observed and are testable. Answers are *predicted* (step 4) and an **experiment** is formulated to *test the hypothesis* (step 5). **Controlled experiments** are designed so that there is an **experimental group** and a **control group.** The two groups are identical except for one factor, the **variable,** which is used with the experimental group. This allows for conclusions to be made that are directly related to the factor being tested. Once the experiment is conducted, analysis of the data is done, and *conclusions* are made (step 6) based on the results of the experiment.

Checkpoint

1. What are the six steps in any scientific method?

2. What two groups are in a controlled experiment?

Checkpoint Answers

1. ask a question, make observations, hypothesize, predict, test, and conclude

2. experimental and control

Laboratory Safety and Procedures

When conducting experiments in laboratory settings, safety procedures must be followed. Procedures should be clearly explained to students prior to engaging in laboratory experiments. The teacher should have experience with the laboratory situation. It is recommended that teachers perform any experiment prior to asking students to conduct it.

Students must be taught how to properly use tools in experiments including microscopes, graduated cylinders, two-balance scales, thermometers, scalpels, and Bunsen burners.

Eye protection should be worn during all laboratory experiments. Safety goggles that are shared among students should be sterilized between uses. When using heat sources, long hair should be tied back and loose clothing should be secured.

Laboratory space should contain safety equipment including eyewash stations, shower stations, emergency blankets, first-aid kits, and fire extinguishers. Students should not be allowed to eat or drink in the laboratory. Laboratory space should be well ventilated. Chemicals should be stored and disposed of properly. Hazardous chemicals should be stored in locked cabinets that are low to the ground. Students must wash their hands after handling any type of plant or animal. Gloves should be worn to protect the skin from chemicals used in preserved specimens, and gowns should be worn to protect the student's clothing and body.

Most science supply companies have resources that can assist teachers with educating children for laboratory safety and procedures.

Checkpoint

1. True or false: Hair should be tied back when conducting science experiments.

2. True or false: Safety goggles can be shared among students without sanitizing.

3. True or false: It is okay to have the laboratory fire extinguisher located in an adjacent classroom.

Checkpoint Answers

1. True

2. False

3. False

Competency 3: Knowledge of Physical Sciences

Competency Description

According to the *Competencies and Skills Required for Teacher Certification in Florida,* 20th Edition (available at www.fldoe.org/asp/ftce/pdf/ftce20edition.pdf), **Competency 3** for the Elementary Education (K–6) Subject Area Examination (SAE) Science subtest addresses the following key indicators:

1. Identify and differentiate among the physical properties of matter (e.g., mass, volume, texture, hardness, freezing point).
2. Identify and differentiate between physical and chemical changes (e.g., tearing, burning, rusting).
3. Compare the properties of matter during phase changes through the addition and/or removal of energy (e.g., boiling, condensation, evaporation).
4. Differentiate between the properties of homogeneous mixtures (i.e., solutions) and heterogeneous mixtures.
5. Identify examples of and relationships among atoms, elements, molecules, and compounds.
6. Identify and compare potential and kinetic energy.
7. Differentiate among forms of energy, transformations of energy, and their real-world applications (e.g., chemical, electrical, mechanical, light, heat, sound).
8. Distinguish among temperature, heat, and forms of heat transfer (e.g., conduction, convection, radiation).
9. Analyze the functionality of an electrical circuit based on its conductors, insulators, and components.
10. Identify and apply the characteristics of contact forces (e.g., push, pull, friction) at-a-distance forces (e.g., magnetic, gravitational, electrostatic), and their effects on matter (e.g., motion, speed).

Overview

Knowledge of the nature of matter is a very important area of science education. The word *science* comes from the Latin word "scientia," which means knowledge. Science uses study, observation, experimentation, and practice to acquire knowledge in an organized manner. There are approximately **11 questions** that address Competency 3. This section addresses the following areas related to **Competency 3** key indicators:

- Physical and Chemical Properties of Matter
- Classification of Matter
- Phase Change
- Temperature, Heat, and Heat Transfer
- Contact Forces and At-a-Distance Forces
- Light and Optics
- Electrical Currents, Circuits, Conductors, Insulators, and Static Electricity
- Types of Energy and Motion
- Balanced and Unbalanced Forces

Physical and Chemical Properties of Matter

There are several fundamental physical properties of matter: mass, volume, density, physical change, and chemical change. **Matter** is what makes up everything in the world: rocks, people, chairs, buildings, water, oxygen, animals, and chemical substances, among others. It takes up space (**volume**) and has mass. It not only involves molecules and atoms, but also subatomic particles such as protons, neutrons, and electrons. The **mass** of objects is always the same and is independent of gravity; for example, two rocks with the same amount of mass placed on a pan balance scale here on Earth will also be balanced on the Moon even though the gravitational pull on the rocks is different. **Gravity** (an attractive force that draws objects toward the center of the Earth) does not change the mass of the rocks. Weight is often confused with mass. The measure of the Earth's pull of gravity on an object is called **weight.** It is the force of gravity on objects and is measured in pounds (English or traditional system), or newtons (International System of Units, SI). The weight of a rock on Earth would be different on the Moon. The gravitational pull would be different on Earth than it is on the Moon.

Volume is another property of matter together with mass. The amount of cubic space that an object occupies is called **volume. Density** (symbol: ρ, which is the Greek "rho") is defined as mass per unit of volume, or the ratio of total mass (m) to total volume (V): $\rho = \dfrac{m}{v}$ (for example, kilogram per cubic meter or kg/m^3, and grams per cubic centimeter or g/cm^3). In other words, it defines how closely the molecules are packed together. It depends on the *type* of matter you are using but not the *amount* of matter you are using. For example, an object made of iron, which is very dense, will have less volume than an object of equal mass made of some less dense substance like water. The higher an object or a substance density is, the higher the ratio of total mass to total volume would be. To calculate an object's density, you need to use a balance to measure its mass and then measure its volume (multiply together the object's length, width, and height if it is rectangular). The volume of an object may also be measured by seeing how much water it displaces when it is submerged in water. You will need to measure the water in the container before and after the object is submerged in the water, and then calculate the difference between these two numbers, which results in the volume of the object. An object's buoyancy is directly related to its density. An object will sink in a liquid or gas if it is denser than the liquid or gas that surrounds it. An object will float in a liquid or gas if its density is less than the density of the liquid or gas that surrounds it.

Matter is in constant change. A **physical change** does not produce a new substance (for example, freezing and melting water), and a **chemical change or reaction** does produce one or more substances. The following are examples of physical changes:

- Water boils out of a metal pot.
- Water condenses on a cold glass.
- A metal pot is put on a burner and gets hot.
- Dry ice is altered from a solid to a gaseous form of carbon dioxide.
- Gold melts or solidifies.
- Sand is mixed in with salt.
- A piece of chalk is ground to dust.
- A glass breaks.
- An iron rod gets magnetized.
- A lump of sugar dissolves into water.

The physical and chemical properties of matter describe the appearance and behavior of substances. The physical properties may be observed without altering the identity of a substance or its molecular structure (for example, changes in size, form, or appearance of the substance or object). These physical changes may include melting, bending, or cracking. The chemical properties of a substance indicate the ability of a substance to be altered into new substances and involve changes in the molecular structure of the substance or object. These chemical changes may include **burning, rusting,** and digestion. Under some conditions, a chemical reaction may involve breaking apart, combining, recombining, or decomposing substances. For example, baking powder is chemically altered as it changes into carbon dioxide gas during the baking process. Chemical equations may be used to represent chemical reactions.

The following are examples of chemical changes (the elements and compounds to the left of the arrow are the reactants, and those to the right side of the arrow are called products):

- The silver in a silver spoon combines with sulfur in the air to produce silver sulfide, which is the black material we call tarnish: $2\,Ag + S \rightarrow Ag_2S$
- The iron in an iron bar combines with oxygen in the air to produce rust: $4\,FE + 3\,O_2 \rightarrow 2\,Fe_2O_3$
- As it burns, methane combines with oxygen in the air to produce carbon dioxide and water vapor: $CH_4 + 2\,O_2 \rightarrow CO_2 + 2\,H_2O$

Checkpoint

1. Fill in the blank: If an object is more dense than the liquid that surrounds it, it will _____ (sink or float) in the liquid.

2. True or false: A physical change reaction produces one or more substances.

3. True or false: A glass broken into pieces is an example of a physical change.

Checkpoint Answers

1. sink

2. False

3. True

Classification of Matter

The classification of matter also involves elements, compounds, mixtures, and solutions. An **element** is a substance that consists of only one type of atom and is represented by a symbol consisting of one or more letters. An element cannot be broken down into other substances of that element. For example, oxygen (O), iron (Fe), and carbon (C) are elements. An **atom** is the smallest particle of the element, which retains the properties of that element. It is the basic building block of matter. The atoms of each element are the same, but different from the atoms of other elements. Under most conditions, they are indivisible, but they may be split or combined during atomic reactions to form new atoms. These reactions change the number of protons and neutrons of an atom. Atomic reactions may take place in the Sun, nuclear power reactors, nuclear bombs, and radioactive decay. Atoms are made of three components of subatomic particles: protons, neutrons, and electrons. The **protons** and **neutrons** are in the nucleus (or solid center) of the atom. **Electrons** are in the outer part of the atom. A **molecule** is the smallest particle of substance that may exist independently and maintains all the properties of the substance.

The three main states or phases of matter are gas, liquid, and solid.

- **Gas** is distinguished from liquid and solid by its relatively low density and viscosity, relatively great expansion and contraction with changes in pressure and temperature, ability to diffuse easily, and spontaneous tendency to distribute uniformly throughout space. It has no definite volume and takes the shape of the container; for example, water vapor or steam.

- **Liquid** is distinguished from gas and solid by its readiness to flow, little or no tendency to disperse in the air, and relatively high difficulty to compress. It has a definite volume, and takes the shape of the container; for example, water.

- **Solid** is not gaseous or liquid. It is firm or compact in substance. It has definite volume and shape; for example, ice.

Other phases are crystal, glass, and plasma.

At the elementary-school level, children should have many opportunities to observe and describe a variety of objects, focusing on the object's physical properties as well as what the object is made of, and demonstrate knowledge that all matter is composed of parts too small to be seen; for example, electrons, protons, and neutrons. An activity that might help with this is to have children view salt under varied magnifications. They should observe salt with the naked eye, under a hand lens, a microscope, and the electron microscope (the electron image is available via the Internet). This way they can begin to construct the understanding that materials may be composed of parts that are too small to be seen with or without magnification, make detailed observations, and discover the unexpected details at smaller scales. This type of discovery prepares them for learning that all matter is made up of atoms, tiny moving parts too small to be seen.

A **compound** is matter that combines atoms chemically in definite weight proportions. Water (represented by the shorthand formula H_2O) is an example of a compound that has the ratio of two hydrogen atoms (represented by the subscript after the H, which tells the number of hydrogen atoms) and one oxygen atom (represented by the O; notice that no subscript is written in this case, which implies that the number of oxygen atoms is 1). A **mixture** is any combination of two or more substances, not chemically combined and without any definite weight proportions. In this case, the substances keep their own chemical properties. For example, milk is a mixture of water and butterfat particles. There are homogeneous and heterogeneous mixtures. **Homogeneous mixtures** are called **solutions.** They are uniform and consistent throughout. For example, seawater is a solution containing water and salt, which could be separated through the evaporation process. **Heterogeneous mixtures** contain dissimilar elements or parts. The following table provides a comparison between compounds and mixtures:

Category	Compounds	Mixtures
Number of elements	Two or more	Two or more
Type of particles	One kind	Two or more kinds
Chemical changes	Chemically combined	Not formed by chemical changes
Elements' chemical properties	Elements lose their individual entities	Elements keep their own chemical properties
Weight proportions	Combine in definite weight proportions	Combine without any definite weight proportions
Amount	Specific amount for each element	Does not have a definite amount for each element
Examples	Acids (vinegar, lemons), bases, salts, oxides, water	Seawater, milk

Checkpoint

1. Fill in the blank: A(n) _____ is a substance that consists of only one type of atom.

2. Fill in the blanks: The three main states of matter are _____, _____, and _____.

3. Fill in the blank: A(n) _____ is matter that combines atoms chemically in definite weight proportions.

Checkpoint Answers

1. element

2. gas, liquid, solid

3. compound

Phase Change

There are several transitions that take place within all the three main phases of matter. They might not be apparent by just looking at a substance. The transitions are processes that take place over time and might develop slowly. The different phases of matter are related to each other in terms of changes in temperature and/or pressure. Therefore, matter can undergo a **phase change** through heating and cooling, shifting from one form to another: for example, melting (changing from a solid to a liquid), **freezing** (changing from a liquid to a solid), evaporating (changing from a liquid to a gas), **boiling** (past the boiling point, which is the temperature at which a liquid boils at a fixed pressure; for example, boiling of water to form steam), and **condensing** (changing from a gas to a liquid). When the temperature of a solid is raised enough or the pressure is reduced enough, the result is a liquid.

The following table presents the transitions between the solid, liquid, and gaseous phases of matter due to the effect of temperature and/or pressure:

Transformation From	To		
	Solid	Liquid	Gaseous
Solid	Solid–solid transformation	Melting/fusion	Sublimation
Liquid	Freezing	N/A	Boiling/evaporation/ vaporization
Gaseous	Deposition	Condensation	N/A

Checkpoint

1. Fill in the blank: _____ is a phase change that involves changing from a liquid to a solid.

2. Fill in the blank: _____ happens when the temperature of a solid is raised enough and the result is a liquid.

3. Fill in the blank: The transition from water to steam due to the effect of temperature is _____.

Checkpoint Answers

1. Freezing

2. Melting

3. boiling

Temperature, Heat, and Heat Transfer

The concepts of heat and temperature are not the same. **Temperature** is a measure related to the average kinetic energy of the molecules of a substance. It has to do with the degree of hotness or coldness of the substance. This is how hot or cold an object is with respect to a standard unit of measurement. A common type of thermometer is the one that uses a glass tube containing mercury or a liquid, such as colored alcohol. Temperature is not energy, but it is a number that relates to the kinetic energy possessed by the molecules of a substance (measured in Kelvin, Fahrenheit, or Celsius degrees). This measure is directly proportional to the average kinetic energy of the molecules. On the Celsius scale, the freezing point of water is set at 0 degrees and the boiling point is 100 degrees. The Celsius symbol is C. On the Kelvin scale, absolute zero is set at 0 degrees (the theoretical absence of all thermal energy), the freezing point of water at 273.15 degrees, and the boiling point of water at 373.15 degrees. The Kelvin symbol is K. On the Fahrenheit scale, the freezing point of water is set at 32 degrees, and the boiling point of water is 212 degrees. The Fahrenheit symbol is F.

Heat is a measurement of the total energy in a substance. That total energy is made up of the kinetic and the potential energies of the molecules of the substance. Temperature does not tell you anything about the potential energy. When heat (or energy) goes into a substance, one of two things may happen: The substance can experience a raise in temperature (the heat can be used to speed up the molecules of the substance), or the substance can change its state (for example, if the substance is ice, it can melt into water). The faster the molecules of the substance are moving, the hotter the temperature becomes.

Checkpoint

1. Fill in the blank: _____ is a measurement of the total energy in a substance.

2. Fill in the blank: _____ is a measure related to the average kinetic energy of the molecules of a substance.

3. True or false: The concepts of heat and temperature define the same thing.

Checkpoint Answers

1. Heat

2. Temperature

3. False

Contact Forces and At-a-Distance Forces

Dynamics is the branch of mechanics that studies the relationship between motion and the forces affecting motion of bodies. **Force** is a **pull** or a **push** upon an object that results from the object's interaction with another object. If there is interaction between objects, then there is a force upon each of the objects. When the interaction is over, so is the force. Force is necessary to make a machine work. When a force is unbalanced (or kinetic friction), the object accelerates (there is relative motion between the surfaces); for example, the thrust of an airplane's engine moves the airplane forward. When a force is a balanced net force on the object (or static force), the object does not accelerate; it remains still or continues to move at the same speed. Two main types of forces are contact force (for example, frictional, tension, air resistant, applied, and mechanical), and at-a-distance force (for example, magnetic, gravitational, and electrostatic forces).

Contact forces require physical contact and interaction between objects. Some examples of contact forces include the following:

- **Friction** is the force involved when surfaces that touch each other have a certain resistance to motion. In a machine, friction reduces the mechanical advantage, or the ratio of output to input. For instance, an automobile uses one-quarter of its energy on reducing friction; but also friction in the tires and clutch allows the car to stay on the road and makes it possible to drive.

- An **applied force** is a force that is applied to an object by a person or another object. For example, when a person is pushing a desk across the room, there is an applied force exerted upon the object.

Mechanical force is the application of force to bend, dent, scratch, compress, or break something; for example, machines in general multiply force or change the direction of force.

At-a-distance forces result even when the interacting objects are not in physical contact, but they exert a push or pull despite their physical separation. Some examples of at-a-distance forces include the following:

- **Gravitational forces** are involved when the Sun and planets exert a gravitational pull on each other despite their large spatial separation. The gravitational pull is still present even when you have no physical contact with the Earth.

- **Centripetal force** is also involved when an object moves in a circular path, and force is directed toward the center of the circle in order to keep the motion going; for example, centripetal force keeps a satellite circling Earth.

- **Electrical forces** are involved when the protons in the nucleus of an atom and the electrons outside the nucleus exert an electrical pull toward each other despite the spatial separation.

- **Magnetic forces** are involved when two magnets can exert a magnetic pull on each other even when a short distance separates them.

- **Nuclear force** is present in the nucleus of atoms. It is released by fission (the breaking of a heavy nucleus into two lighter nuclei), fusion (two atomic nuclei fuse together to form a heavier nucleus), or radioactive decay (a neutron in the radioactive nucleus decays spontaneously by emitting either particles, electromagnetic radiation, or gamma rays, or all of these).

Checkpoint

1. Fill in the blank: _____ forces result even when the interacting objects are not in physical contact, but they exert a push or pull despite their physical separation.

2. Fill in the blank: _____ forces are the result of the physical interaction between objects.

3. Fill in the blank: _____ forces are involved in the application of force needed to bend, dent, scratch, compress, or break something.

Checkpoint Answers

1. At-a-distance

2. Contact

3. Mechanical

Light and Optics

Light is a type of energy that has a comparatively low level of physical weight or density. It is considered an electromagnetic radiation that has a wavelength (electromagnetic waves); for example, radiant waves, X-rays, radio waves, and ultraviolet rays. The Sun provides radiant energy. The constancy and universality of the speed of light in a vacuum is recognized to be 299,792,458 meters per second or 186,000 miles per second, which is faster than the speed of sound. It can go through some materials like transparent materials (such as air, water, and clear glass), but not through others like opaque materials (a brick wall that allows the passage of no light) or only partially through translucent materials (like frosted glass that allows the passage of some light). Light travels in a straight line. It can change direction, but it still keeps traveling in a straight line; for example, when a light ray strikes a mirror, it changes direction, but continues traveling in a straight line. In this case, the mirror reflects light. Each surface reflects light differently. Rough surfaces tend to scatter light in many directions, and smooth surfaces tend to reflect light in one direction. **Refraction** occurs when light passes through a transparent material such as water at a slant angle; the ray of light bends or changes speed. **Diffraction** occurs when a ray of light bends around the edges of an object; the ray of light has been diffracted.

Optics is a branch of physics that studies the physical properties of light. It provides information about the behavior and properties of light and its interaction with matter. A **lens** is a piece of transparent and curved material; for example, glass. Light bends when it passes through this material. Convex lenses are thicker in the middle and are used as magnifying glasses and to help correct the vision of nearsighted persons. This vision correction is accomplished by using the concave lens to spread the light rays before they enter the eye and allow the light rays to merge farther back in the eye to form a clear image on the retina. Lenses are used for monoculars, binoculars, telescopes, microscopes, cameras, and projectors. A **prism** is a transparent object with flat polished surfaces that refract or diffuse (break apart) light. The exact angles between the surfaces depend on the application or possible use of the prism. They are usually triangular prisms with a triangular base and rectangular sides and are made out of glass (other transparent materials can be used). They can also be used to break light up into its constituent spectral colors (the colors of the rainbow).

Checkpoint

1. Fill in the blank: _____ is a branch of physics that studies the physical properties of light.

2. Fill in the blank: A type of energy that has a comparatively low level of physical weight or density is called _____.

3. Fill in the blank: A _____ is a piece of transparent and curved material.

Checkpoint Answers

1. Optics

2. light

3. lens

Electrical Currents, Circuits, Conductors, Insulators, and Static Electricity

Electricity is a physical occurrence related to stationary and moving electrons and protons. The electric energy is made available by the flow of an electric charge through a conductor. A **conductor** allows electricity to flow freely through it (for example, copper is a good conductor of electricity). On the other hand, an **insulator** does not allow the electrons to flow freely (for example, glass, rubber, and air). It can be used to transform the chemical makeup of a substance; for example, passing electricity through water to break the water down into hydrogen and oxygen gases. Atoms may transmit electrical energy. Neutral atoms contain an equal number of protons and electrons because they cancel each other out and provide no net charge. Atoms with a negative charge contain more electrons than protons, and atoms with a positive charge contain fewer electrons than protons. When two objects are rubbed against each other, electrons transfer from one object to the other, and leave both of them charged. **Electric current** is the flow of electricity through a conductor. Electrical cables are usually made of conductors (for example, copper) and insulation (for example, rubber on the outside part). An **electrical circuit** is a path or combination of paths that allow the flow of the electrical current from one place to another. **Series circuits** use only one electrical path. **Parallel circuits** use several electrical paths. For example, this type of circuit allows the distribution of the electric current throughout a house. Circuit breakers may be used in a house to monitor its electric flow, and if there is an overload of electricity the flow of electricity will stop.

An electrical circuit must have a continuous flow of electricity going through a complete loop (circuit), returning to its original position, and cycling through again. An example that illustrates the necessity of a complete loop utilizes a battery, a small light bulb, and a connecting wire. Students should observe the effect of connecting and disconnecting a wire in a simple arrangement of the battery, light bulb, and wire. If appropriate connections are made, then the light bulb will light up. The lighting of the bulb should occur immediately after the final connection is made appropriately. There should be no perceivable time delay between when the last connection is made and when the light bulb is perceived to light up. If the light bulb lights up and remains lit, this is evidence that the charge is flowing through the light bulb filament and that an electric circuit has been established. A circuit is a closed loop through which electrical charges can continuously move. Students should explore different ways to set up the electric circuit by rearranging the placement of the wire, battery, and light bulb.

Using friction can produce static electricity. **Static electricity** refers to the accumulation of excess electric charge in a region that has poor electrical conductivity (like an insulator). It refers to the build-up of electric charge on the surface of objects (stationary electric charges). For example, a plastic stick that is rubbed with silk will become electrically charged and attract small pieces of paper. Electrically charged objects share the following characteristics: like charges repel one another, opposite charges attract each other, and charge is conserved.

Checkpoint

1. Fill in the blank: A _____ is a closed loop through which electrical charges can continuously move.

2. Fill in the blank: The accumulation of excess electric charge in a region that has poor electrical conductivity is called _____ electricity.

3. Fill in the blank: A _____ allows electricity to flow freely through it.

Checkpoint Answers

1. circuit

2. static

3. conductor

Types of Energy and Motion

Several types of energy are presented in this section. Notice that many energy sources might produce more than one form of energy. For example, the Sun produces light and heat, a light bulb also produces some heat energy, and an oven also produces some light energy. Also, notice that energy cannot be created or destroyed, but it can be transformed from one form to another. This process is called **energy transformation,** which occurs every day and everywhere. The following are some examples of energy transformations:

- A person uses mechanical energy to clap, producing sound energy.
- The Sun provides light energy to help plants produce chemical energy.
- The mechanical energy used to rub our hands together is transformed into heat or thermal energy.
- The wind provides mechanical energy, which can be transformed into electrical energy.
- A battery is chemical energy that becomes electrical energy in a CD player; the CD player emits sound energy.
- Electrical energy is transformed into heat energy in an oven.
- Wood provides chemical energy, which changes to light energy and heat energy in a fire.
- A plane uses chemical energy from gasoline to fly (mechanical energy).
- A person uses chemical energy from food to ride a bike (mechanical energy).
- A car transforms chemical energy (gasoline) and/or electrical energy (battery in hybrid cars) to mechanical energy.
- A man uses mechanical energy to ring the doorbell, producing sound energy.
- A windmill turns mechanical energy from the wind into electrical energy.
- Traffic signals turn electrical energy into light energy.
- A lightning bolt's electrical energy transforms into light energy and sound energy.
- Solar panels transform light energy into electrical energy.

The following are some examples of different types of energy:

- **Chemical energy** is the energy stored in the chemical bonds of molecules; for example, the combustion (burning) of gasoline provokes a chemical reaction that releases chemical energy. The molecules are broken to produce heat and light. Combustion is used to power automobiles and other machines. Examples of chemical energy can be found in food, gasoline, oil, wood, and coal.
- **Electrical energy** is energy stored in electric fields that results from the presence of electric charges; it is produced by moving electrons and made available by the flow of electrical charge through a conductor. The stream of electrons moving through a conductor is an electric current. This current is the source of what we call electricity, which is an application of electrical energy that we use to operate telephones, televisions, and computers, among other things. Lightning is a natural result of an increase of electrical energy in the atmosphere. Power plants transform chemical, mechanical, or other forms of energy into electrical energy. By connecting electricity to a machine, you are converting it to another type of energy:
  - Motor-electrical energy to mechanical energy (with heat energy byproduct)
  - Lamp-electrical energy to light energy (with heat energy byproduct)
  - Heater coil-electrical energy to heat energy (with light energy byproduct)
  - Oven-electrical energy to heat energy (with light energy byproduct)
  - Speaker-electrical energy to sound energy (with heat energy byproduct)

  In most cases, energy changes produce heat, even when they are not the intended target energy. This is because the machines do not work with complete efficiency—some energy is lost as heat in the transformation process.
- **Magnetic energy** is the force (pull or push) of a magnet. This energy is stored in magnetic fields that are produced by moving electric charges. If the poles of two magnets near each other are alike, then they repel each other. If the poles of two magnets near each other are different, then they attract each other. For

example, a compass is a navigational tool for determining direction relative to the Earth's magnetic poles, which consists of a magnetized pointer free to align itself with Earth's magnetic field. Compasses greatly improved the safety and efficiency of travel.

- **Mechanical energy** is the energy of the moving parts of machines or humans; for example, a moving bike or a handshake. It is the energy that machines create. Mechanical energy is the sum of **potential** (stored energy of position) and **kinetic energy** (energy of motion) of a mechanical system. It also describes the energy of an object if it is moving, or if it has the potential to move. For example, a moving car and a car stopped on a hill both have mechanical energy. The moving car has kinetic energy (energy of motion), and the stopped car has potential energy because gravity can pull the car down the hill. Or, a moving baseball has mechanical energy because of both its high speed (kinetic energy) and its vertical position above the ground (gravitational potential energy). Other examples of mechanical energy include a moving windmill and a book resting on a shelf.

- **Nuclear energy** is present in the nucleus of atoms. Dividing, combining, or colliding of nuclei can result in the release of nuclear energy. It is released by fission (the breaking of a heavy nucleus into two lighter nuclei), fusion (two atomic nuclei fuse together to form a heavier nucleus), or radioactive decay (a neutron or proton in the radioactive nucleus decays spontaneously by emitting either particles, electromagnetic radiation, or gamma rays, or all of these).

- **Radiant or light energy** is the energy transmitted in the form of electromagnetic waves or radiation; for example, visible light that the brain interprets as color, radio waves, infrared rays, ultraviolet rays, or X-rays.

- **Solar energy** is the energy from the Sun that can be converted into thermal or electrical energy. It can have the form of electromagnetic waves (or "light"). Daylight is a result of solar energy. The Sun warms the Earth. Energy from the Sun enables plants to synthesize food and allows for evaporation. Solar power is the conversion of sunlight into electricity.

- **Sound or acoustic energy** is the energy in the form of mechanical waves transmitted through materials (such as plastic or air). These waves can be audible or inaudible. The brain interprets audible wave sounds as they enter through the ears. The sound is less intense as it moves farther and farther from the source. For example, a ringing telephone changes sound energy into electrical energy and then back into sound energy.

- **Thermal energy** is considered the most internal energy of objects, which is created by vibration and movement. It is a form of kinetic energy and transferred as heat. It manifests itself as an increase in temperature. Heat is thermal energy that is transferred due to a difference in temperature between two objects.

Students should also demonstrate knowledge that forces can change motion of all matter, observed, described, and measured. They should have opportunities to observe airplanes, baseballs, planets, or people, and analyze how the motion of all bodies is governed by the same basic rules. They also need multiple opportunities to experience, observe, and describe (in words and pictures) motion, including the factors (pushing and pulling) that affect motion. They should have opportunities to do the following:

- Measure and record changes (for example, vary the height of a ramp and roll spheres down it, measure the speed or the distance the sphere rolls, and collect data).

- Investigate the effects of adding or removing mass to an object on its motion (for example, use different sizes and masses of objects dropped from the same height at the same time to explore the force of gravity, or roll a metal sphere and a wooden sphere down a ramp, and collect data to explore the impact of mass on speed and distance traveled).

- Explain how force causes movement (for example, describe and predict the path of moving objects, identify the variables that change the direction and rate of moving objects, and use common sport activities to demonstrate how the rate of motion is affected by the strength of a push or pull).

- Use tools to collect data (for example, design an experiment where the amount of force applied to an object is the independent variable and time or distance traveled is the dependent variable: Drag a tub full of metal washers and a tub full of cotton balls a certain distance and use a spring scale to measure the force needed to move the two masses).

Checkpoint

1. Fill in the blank: The combustion (burning) of gasoline provokes a reaction that releases _____ energy.

2. Fill in the blank: _____ energy is considered the most internal energy of objects, which is created by vibration and movement.

3. Fill in the blank: Daylight is a result of _____ energy.

4. True or false: Pushing and pulling are the two main factors effecting motion.

Checkpoint Answers

1. chemical

2. Thermal

3. solar

4. True

Balanced and Unbalanced Forces

The development of **force** involves a push or a pull. This process can give energy to an object, causing it to start moving, stop moving, or change its motion. Forces occur in pairs and can be either balanced or unbalanced. **Balanced forces** do not cause a change in motion. They are in opposite directions and equal in size.

For example, if Person A arm-wrestles with Person B, and Person A is just about as strong as Person B, then there will probably be a time when both of them are pushing as hard as they can, but their arms stay in the same place. In other words, the force exerted by each person is equal, but they are pushing together in opposite directions. Because the force that each person is exerting is equal, the two forces cancel each other out and the resulting force is zero, which produces no change in motion, as illustrated by the following two arrows:

Person A's force	Person B with equal force, in an opposite direction	
→	←	Stay in the same place, and the force exerted by each person is equal.

Similarly, balanced forces could be in action during a tug of war, but in this case the forces are pulling away from each other. As with arm wrestling, if Team A and Team B have equal strength or force, then the rope stays at about the same place, the resulting force is zero, and there is no change in motion, as illustrated by the following two arrows:

Team A's force	Team B with equal force, in an opposite direction	
←	→	Stay in the same place, and the force exerted by each team is equal.

In contrast, **unbalanced forces** always cause a change in motion. They are often in opposite directions and not equal in size. When two unbalanced forces are exerted in opposite directions, their combined force is equal to the difference between the two forces, and exerted in the direction of the larger force. For example, if Person A arm-wrestles with Person C, but this time Person C is the stronger person, the arm of Person A with less arm strength moves in the direction of Person C, who is pushing with a stronger force. The resulting force is equal to the force of Person C minus the force of Person A, as illustrated by the following arrows:

Person A with weaker force	Person C with stronger force		Difference between forces with the direction of stronger person
→	←	=	←

Similarly, two teams are having a tug of war against each other, with Team C being stronger than Team A. The weaker team moves in the direction that the stronger team is pulling with a force that is equal to the stronger team's force minus the force of the weaker team, as illustrated by the following arrows:

Team A with weaker force	Team C with stronger force		Difference between forces with direction of stronger team
⟵	⟶	=	⟶

Unbalanced forces can also happen with forces in the same direction and still cause movement. For example, a car breaks down on the road and two people have to push it out of the way. If the two people push the car, the resulting force on the car is the sum of the two people's forces and in the direction that they are applying the force, as illustrated by the following arrows:

Person 1	Person 2		Sum of the two forces with the same direction
⟶	⟶	=	⟶

Notice that when working with balanced and unbalanced forces, the strength of forces moving in the same direction are combined by adding them, and the strength of forces moving in opposite directions are combined by subtracting the smaller one from the larger one. If two forces are of equal magnitude and in opposite directions, then they balance each other. In this case, the object is said to be at equilibrium, with no unbalanced force acting upon it; and thus, an object in equilibrium maintains its state of motion.

Checkpoint

1. True or false: Unbalanced forces can only happen with two forces in opposite directions.

2. True or false: Balanced forces do not cause a change in motion.

3. Fill in the blank: When working with balanced and unbalanced forces, the strength of forces moving in the same direction are combined by _____ them.

Checkpoint Answers

1. False

2. True

3. adding

Competency 4: Knowledge of Earth and Space

Competency Description

According to the *Competencies and Skills Required for Teacher Certification in Florida,* 20th Edition (available at www.fldoe.org/asp/ftce/pdf/ftce20edition.pdf), **Competency 4** for the Elementary Education (K–6) Subject Area Examination (SAE) Science subtest addresses the following key indicators:

1. Identify characteristics of geologic formations (e.g., volcanoes, canyons, mountains) and the mechanisms by which they are changed (e.g., physical and chemical weathering, erosion, deposition).
2. Identify and distinguish among the major groups and properties of rocks and minerals and the processes of their formations.
3. Identify and analyze the characteristics of soil, its composition and profile, and the process of soil formation.
4. Identify and analyze processes by which energy from the Sun is transferred (e.g., radiation, conduction, convection) through Earth's systems (e.g., biosphere, hydrosphere, geosphere, atmosphere, cryosphere).
5. Identify and analyze the causes and effects of atmospheric processes and conditions (e.g., water cycle, weather, climate).
6. Identify and analyze various conservation methods and their effectiveness in relation to renewable and nonrenewable natural resources.
7. Analyze the Sun-Earth-Moon system in order to explain repeated patterns such as day and night, phases of the Moon, tides, and seasons.
8. Compare and differentiate the composition and various relationships among the objects of our Solar System (e.g., Sun, planets, moons, asteroids, comets).
9. Identify major events in the history of space exploration and their effects on society.

Overview

Knowledge of Earth and space includes an understanding of the systems of the Earth (geology) as well as those interacting in space. The interactions of the Earth within the Solar System are important. There are approximately **10 questions** that address Competency 4. This section addresses the following areas related to **Competency 4** key indicators:

- Earth Science
  - Geologic Formations
  - Rocks and Minerals
  - Water, Air, and Land
  - Heat Transfer
- Space Science
  - Planets
  - Celestial Bodies
  - History

Earth Science

Earth science encompasses all aspects of knowledge of **geology** and the Earth. This includes geologic formations; rocks and minerals; the interactions of land, air, and water; and heat transfer.

Geologic Formations

The Earth is divided into three main layers—the **core,** the **mantle,** and the **crust.** The core is the innermost part of the Earth. It is approximately 1,800 miles (2900 km) below the surface of the Earth. The core is made up of iron and nickel and is divided into two sections—the **inner core** and the **outer core.** The inner core is solid and approximately 780 miles (1260 km) thick. It is made up of iron, nickel, and other light elements. The pressure in the inner core is so great that, despite the high temperatures, it will not melt. The outer core is always **molten,** or melted. The outer core is made up of mostly iron with some nickel and other elements and makes up the remainder of the core, approximately 1,300 miles (2090 km). Since the Earth rotates, the outer core rotates while the inner core remains stationary due to its solid nature, creating the Earth's magnetism.

The layer above the core is called the mantle. The mantle begins about 6 miles (10 km) under the ocean's crust and 19 miles (30 km) below the continent's crust. The mantle makes up a majority of the Earth's volume.

The top layer of the Earth is called the crust. The crust is the hard outer shell of the Earth and is the thinnest layer of the Earth. The crust floats on the mantle and is solid material. There are two types of crusts—**oceanic crust** and **continental crust.** The oceanic crust is that part of the crust under the oceans. The oceanic crust is 4–7 miles (6–11 km) thick. The rock in the oceanic crust is generally younger and consists mainly of basalt. Seventy-one percent of the Earth's surface is oceanic crust. The continental crust (20–40 miles thick, or 35–70 km), the remaining 29 percent, is that part of the crust that contains the continents. There are six regions, called continents, namely Eurasia (Europe and Asia), Africa, North America, South America, Antarctica, and Australia.

Because the core is so hot, heat develops a current that radiates to the Earth's crust through **convection currents.** These currents cause the plates of the Earth's crust to move, called **plate tectonics.** Plate tectonics move the continents around the surface of the Earth and cause **geological formations** to occur. Due to plate tectonics, the continents have changed over time. Alfred Wegener proposed a theory that the continental plates have been joined into one plate at different periods in time, forming a supercontinent, one of which was called **Pangea.**

Geologic formations include volcanoes, canyons, and mountains.

Volcanoes form when hot material called **magma** rises from below the Earth's surface to break through the Earth's crust. Magma gathers in a reservoir called the **magma chamber.** In many cases, this reservoir eventually erupts onto the surface of the Earth, creating the volcano. When the magma reaches the surface of the Earth, it is called **lava.** As the lava cools, it creates a cone of rock, the volcano.

Canyons form when **erosion** changes the face of the Earth's surface. In canyons, the erosion occurs due to water, often rivers, running through a dry region. The rocks in the dry region provide resistance, which causes the canyon to be created. In some cases, the water removes rock material and transports it to a different location. As this happens, the river digs deeper into the Earth's crust, forming a canyon. As the plates of the Earth shift, there is a phenomenon called uplift, which causes the plateau to rise, causing the river to be lower relative to the surface of the plateau.

When plates of the Earth's surface intersect, different phenomena may occur depending on the type of intersection and the type of plate. **Mountains** are formed when two continental plates collide with each other and force both plates upward. **Earthquakes** occur when plates slide against each other in opposite directions. As the plates slide, pressure is created. When this pressure is released, an earthquake occurs. This point is called the **focus.** The point on the Earth's surface directly above the focus where the earthquake begins is called the **epicenter.** The amount of energy released during the earthquake is measured by a **seismometer** and uses the **Richter Scale.** When an earthquake occurs under water, it often causes a **tsunami,** or tidal wave.

Rocks and Minerals

Various types of rocks are formed in different ways. These include igneous rocks, sedimentary rocks, and metamorphic rocks.

Igneous rocks are formed from the cooling of magma. As the magma cools, it changes from a liquid to a solid state. Igneous rocks are named by composition and texture and are usually coarse. They make up the majority of the Earth's crust. Examples of igneous rocks include granite and basalt.

Sedimentary rocks cover igneous rocks with loose sediment. Sedimentary rocks are created when layers of debris, or sediment, are compacted and fuse together. Sedimentary rocks are called secondary because they are made when small pre-existing rocks accumulate. There are three types of sedimentary rocks: clastic, chemical, and organic. **Clastic rocks** are basic sedimentary rocks and are accumulations of broken pieces of rocks. **Chemical rocks** form when standing water evaporates and leaves dissolved **minerals** behind. **Organic rocks** are formed by organic material such as calcium from shells, bones, and teeth.

Metamorphic rocks form when a pre-existing rock is moved into an environment of intense heat and/or pressure, in which the minerals that make up the rock become unstable, often burial. The rock changes form as it seeks to regain equilibrium, forming a new rock. Common metamorphic rocks are slate, gneiss, and marble.

Soil is formed by the **physical weathering** of rocks and minerals. As rocks at the surface of the Earth are broken down by weathering, the smaller pieces mix with organic material like mosses and eventually create soil. Decaying organic matter adds to the thin layer of soil, creating a rich environment for plants to grow.

Water, Air, and Land

The interaction of water, air, and land determines many aspects of **weather.**

Water

Water is not a **renewable resource**—there is a limited amount of water on the Earth. The water that is present on the Earth follows a cycle called the **water cycle.** It is made up of four steps—evaporation, condensation, precipitation, and collection.

1. **Evaporation** occurs when the Sun heats up the water on the surface of the Earth. This water turns into vapor and goes into the air.
2. **Condensation** occurs when the water vapor in the air cools and changes back into liquid, forming clouds.
3. **Precipitation** occurs when the amount of water that has condensed in the air is too much for the air to hold. The clouds that hold the water become heavy and the water falls back to the surface of the Earth in the form of rain, hail, sleet, or snow.
4. **Collection** occurs when the water returns to the surface of the Earth and falls back into water sources like oceans, lakes, or rivers. When the water falls back to land, it either soaks into the Earth and becomes ground water or runs over the soil and returns back to the water sources.

Air

Air masses determine weather patterns. In the United States, five types of air masses determine the weather: Continental Arctic, Continental Polar, Maritime Polar, Maritime Tropical, and Continental Tropical.

- Continental Arctic air masses bring extremely cold temperatures and little moisture. They generally originate in the Arctic Circle and move south across Canada and the United States during winter.
- Continental Polar air masses bring cold and dry weather, but not as cold as Continental Arctic masses. They generally form south of the Arctic Circle and affect the weather in the United States in the winter. In the summer, Continental Polar air masses affect only the northern portion of the United States.
- Maritime Polar air masses are cool and moist and bring cloudy, damp weather to the United States. They form over the northern Atlantic and Pacific oceans and can form at any time of the year. They are usually warmer than Continental Polar air masses.
- Maritime Tropical air masses bring warm temperatures and moisture. They are most common over the eastern United States and are created over the southern Atlantic Ocean and the Gulf of Mexico. They can form year-round but are most common in the summer.

- Continental Tropical air masses form over the Southwest desert and northern Mexico in the summer. They begin over the equator, where moist air is heated and rises. As this air moves away from the equator, it begins to cool, causing precipitation in the tropics and leaving the air dry. This dry air then forms a Continental Tropical air mass, creating the deserts of the Southwest and Mexico. These air masses rarely form in the winter but keep temperatures in the Southwest above 100 degrees in the summer.

An additional aspect of weather patterns is wind. **Wind** is the horizontal movement of air. The equator receives direct rays from the sun. The moist air is heated and rises, leaving low-pressure regions called **doldrums**—regions of little steady air movement. As this air moves north and south of the equator, it begins to cool and sink. Some of that air moves back toward the equator forming **trade winds**—warm, steady breezes that blow continuously. Trade winds act as the steering force for tropical storms. The remaining winds move toward the poles, appearing to curve to the east. Since they come out of the west, they are called **prevailing westerlies.** These winds are responsible for many of the weather movements in the United States and Canada. As the winds continue to travel north and south, prevailing westerlies join with polar easterlies that originate from the poles.

As winds and air interact, they form clouds. There are four main types of clouds—stratus, cumulus, cirrus, and nimbus. Most clouds are a combination of the three types.

- **Stratus clouds** are horizontal, layered clouds that appear to blanket the sky. Stratus clouds form where warm, moist air passes over cool air.
- **Cumulus clouds** are puffy and look like cotton balls. They generally form when warm, moist air is forced upward. As the air rises, it cools. The size of a cumulus cloud depends on the force of upward movement. These clouds produce heavy thunderstorms in the summer.
- **Cirrus clouds** are wispy and feathery. They only form at high altitudes and are composed of ice crystals.
- **Nimbus clouds** produce precipitation.

Land

As water interacts with the land, various phenomena can occur:

- **Runoff** is rain water that falls to land and moves across the land to rivers, streams, or other water sites. Runoff occurs when the quantity of rainfall exceeds the rate at which the soil can absorb the water.
- **Percolation** is the downward movement of water through the soil and rock in the ground.
- **Leaching** is the process by which materials in the soil are transferred into the water.
- **Sinkholes** are formed when cavities form under the surface of the Earth. These cavities are formed when water filling the space is removed through evaporation or absorption. The weight of the soil or other material above the cavity collapses it, forming a sinkhole. Sinkholes are very common in Florida.
- The **aquifer** is a formation that transmits water under the surface of the Earth. When digging a well, the aquifer is the water source.
- A **reservoir** is a lake-like area where water is kept until needed. These may be canals or retention ponds and may be naturally formed or man-made.

Heat Transfer

There are three ways heat is transferred through the Earth's system—radiation, conduction, and convection.

- **Radiation** is when heat is transferred through electromagnetic waves. Examples of radiation are the heating of the skin by the Sun and the heat of a bonfire. The heat is transferred through the movement of electromagnetic waves, as is the case with the Sun's energy reaching the Earth.
- **Conduction** occurs when heat transfers through molecular movement. For example, when you pick up a metal bar, it is cold. As you hold it, the warmth of your body conducts heat to the metal bar through solid-to-solid contact.

- **Convection** occurs through the movement of masses, either air or water. Convection occurs when hot air rises, cools, and then falls. This cycle is what makes ceiling fans warm the air in the winter. The ceiling fan forces the cooler air in the lower parts of the room to move toward the ceiling, pushing the warm air from the ceiling downward, warming the room. This helps to distribute the heat evenly throughout the room.

Checkpoint

1. What are the four stages of the water cycle?

2. True or false: Trade winds form at the poles.

3. What are three methods for heat transfer?

Checkpoint Answers

1. evaporation, condensation, precipitation, and collection

2. False

3. radiation, conduction, and convection

Space Science

Space science includes the study of the Solar System, which consists of various elements. Our Solar System is called the **Milky Way,** which is made up of about 400 billion stars. The shape of the Milky Way is spiral, with arms extending out from the center. Within the Milky Way are planets and other celestial bodies.

Planets

There are eight **planets**—Mercury, Venus, Earth, Mars, Jupiter, Saturn, Uranus, and Neptune.

- **Mercury** is the smallest planet and is closest to the Sun. It has no moons. The planet has hardly any atmosphere and is most like the Moon's surface.
- **Venus** is the second planet from the Sun. Venus is very hot due to thick gases in the atmosphere causing a greenhouse effect.
- **Earth** is the third planet from the Sun. Oceans cover nearly three-quarters of the Earth's surface. The Earth has one moon.
- **Mars** is the fourth planet from the Sun. It has the nickname of the Red Planet because it is covered with rusty colored soil. Mars has two moons, Phobos and Diemos.
- **Jupiter** is the fifth planet from the Sun and is by far the largest. Jupiter has small rings, at least 50 moons, and is known for its large red spot.
- **Saturn** is the sixth planet from the Sun and is the second largest planet. Saturn has about 53 moons and is known for its rings.
- **Uranus** is the seventh planet from the Sun and is the third largest. It is a bluish-green planet made up of hydrogen, helium, and methane gases. It has nine faint rings that are made up of rocks and dust. Its poles point sideways, and it has an angle of 98 degrees. Uranus has 27 moons.
- **Neptune** is the eighth planet from the Sun and is the fourth largest. It has 13 moons.

The planets move around the Sun in elliptical orbits. In addition, many planets, including Earth, are tilted on their own axis. The tilt of the Earth accounts for the **seasons.** The intensity of the rays from the Sun change as the Earth orbits the Sun, making spring, summer, fall, and winter. The seasons are opposite in the **Northern hemisphere** than in the **Southern hemisphere.** In June, July, and August, the Northern hemisphere is exposed to more direct sunlight, making the temperatures warmer so it is summer in the Northern hemisphere. At the same time, the Southern hemisphere is exposed to less direct sunlight, making it cooler so it is winter in the Southern hemisphere.

Celestial Bodies

Pluto was once considered a planet but is now considered a dwarf planet. It is smaller than Earth's Moon and yellowish in color. Pluto's orbit around the Sun is tilted, unlike the other planets whose orbits are flat, and its path is extremely elliptical. As a result, there are times that Pluto is closer to the Sun than Neptune.

Comets are bodies in space that orbit the Sun and are made of rocks, frozen water, frozen gases, and dust. Each comet has a tail. The most famous comet is Halley's Comet.

Asteroids are made up of rock, metal, or ice and are like planets in that they orbit the Sun. A belt of asteroids exists between Mars and Jupiter and separates the planets.

Meteoroids are objects that rotate around the Sun but are too small to be called asteroids or comets. They are made from bits and pieces of the Solar System and are called meteors when they fall through the Earth's atmosphere. Pieces that reach the surface of the Earth are called meteorites.

Stars are made up entirely of gases, mostly hydrogen. Stars are born in hot gas and dust. A star's color, temperature, and size depend on its mass. Star colors can vary from slightly reddish, orange, and yellow to white and blue. These colors are easy to see, especially on dark nights. The Sun is a mid-sized star and is the closest star to the Earth. The Sun is the center of our Solar System and provides heat and light to Earth.

Moons are satellites of planets. They generally orbit around a planet. Some planets have a large number of moons, but the Earth has one moon. The Moon is subjected to the gravitational pull of the Earth, keeping it in orbit around the Earth. Additionally, the Moon's pull on the Earth affects the **tides** of the oceans.

The **phases of the Moon** are a result of sunlight hitting the Moon's surface and then reflecting toward Earth. The Moon does not create its own light. The amount of the Moon that is visible through reflection is measured by the lunar phase. A Full Moon occurs when the Moon and Sun are on opposite sides of the Earth, giving a full reflection of the Moon's surface. A New Moon occurs when the Moon and Sun are on the same side of the Earth, giving no reflection of the Moon's surface toward the Earth. The time between Full Moons is approximately 29 days. Between a New Moon and a Full Moon is a First Quarter Moon, in which the right 50 percent of the moon's lit-up surface is visible. Between a Full Moon and a New Moon is a Last Quarter Moon, in which the left 50 percent of the Moon's illuminated surface is visible. The side of the Moon that is visible is reversed for the Southern hemisphere.

History

The beginnings of space exploration began in 1914 when Robert Goddard received two patents for rockets. Prior to that, publications by Isaac Newton and others indicated space travel was theoretically possible. In 1926, Robert Goddard successfully applied his rocketry theories and launched the first liquid-fueled rocket in Massachusetts. The 4-foot rocket, called "Nell," reached an altitude of 41 feet and a speed of about 60 miles per hour. The flight lasted 2.5 seconds. This began the long road that continues today into exploration of space:

Date	Country	Accomplishment
1942	Germany	Launched first rocket to reach suborbital spaceflight
1946	United States	Launched American-made rocket in White Sands, New Mexico
1957	Soviet Union	Launched Sputnik, the first satellite to be placed into orbit; Sputnik transmitted radio signals back to Earth for a short time
1957	Soviet Union	Launched Sputnik 2, which housed a dog contained in a pressurized container with food supplies and an atmosphere; showed it was possible to survive in space
1958	United States	Launched first satellite, Explorer 1
1958	United States	National Aeronautics and Space Administration (NASA) was created
1961	Soviet Union	Cosmonaut Yuri Alekseyevich Gagarin became the first human in space; made one complete orbit around the Earth and his flight lasted 1 hour 48 minutes
1961	United States	Astronaut Alan Shepard was launched into space and completed a suborbital flight of 15 minutes; experienced weightlessness for about 5 minutes

Date	Country	Accomplishment
1962	United States	Astronaut John Glenn became first American to orbit the Earth; made three orbits
1966	Soviet Union followed by United States	Landed unmanned spacecraft on the Moon
1967	United States	Gus Grissom, Ed White, and Roger Chaffee were killed during a routine test on the launch pad when a spark caused a fire to start in the crew compartment of the command module
1968	United States	*Apollo 7* becomes first manned mission; orbited Earth once
1968	United States	*Apollo 8* is first manned spacecraft to orbit the Moon; makes 10 orbits on 6-day mission
1969	United States	*Apollo 11* lands on the Moon; Neil Armstrong and Edwin "Buzz" Aldrin, Jr., become first human beings to walk on the Moon
1970	United States	*Apollo 13* aborts mission to the Moon after explosion of oxygen tanks; astronauts James A. Lovell, Jr., John L. Swigert, Jr., and Fred W. Haise, Jr., return safely
1971	Soviet Union	First space station, Salyut 1, placed in orbit
1971	United States	*Apollo 15* astronauts become first to drive a rover on the surface of the Moon
1973	United States	First U.S. space station, Skylab, placed in orbit
1981	United States	First space shuttle, *Columbia,* launched in Space Transportation System-1 (STS-1)
1983	United States	Space shuttle *Challenger* makes first mission; first American spacewalk in 9 years
1983	United States	Sally Ride becomes first woman astronaut on *Challenger* mission STS-7
1984	United States	Space shuttle *Discovery* launches first mission
1985	United States	Space shuttle *Atlantis* launches first mission
1986	United States	Space shuttle *Challenger* explodes during liftoff, killing all crew
1986	Soviet Union (Russia)	Space station Mir is successfully placed into Earth's orbit
1990	United States	Hubble Space Telescope is deployed in order to image space
1992	United States	Space shuttle *Endeavor* launches first mission
1995	United States/ Russia	Space shuttle *Atlantis* rendezvous with space station Mir
2001	United States	100th U.S. spacewalk
2003	United States	Space shuttle *Columbia* breaks up in the atmosphere over Texas on re-entry, killing the entire crew
2005	United States	Space shuttle *Discovery* returns to flight after 2-year hiatus as a result of the *Columbia* disaster; changes to space protocol are enacted to increase safety

Checkpoint

1. What are the four phases of the Moon?

2. What two space shuttles were destroyed during missions?

3. In which Apollo mission did Armstrong and Aldrin walk on the Moon?

Checkpoint Answers

1. New Moon, First Quarter Moon, Full Moon, Last Quarter Moon

2. *Challenger* and *Columbia*

3. *Apollo 11*

Competency 5: Knowledge of Life Science

Competency Description

According to the *Competencies and Skills Required for Teacher Certification in Florida,* 20th Edition (available at www.fldoe.org/asp/ftce/pdf/ftce20edition.pdf), **Competency 5** for the Elementary Education (K–6) Subject Area Examination (SAE) Science subtest addresses the following key indicators:

1. Identify and compare the characteristics of living and nonliving things.
2. Analyze the cell theory as it relates to the functional and structural hierarchy of all living things.
3. Identify and compare the structures and functions of plant and animal cells.
4. Classify living things into major groups (i.e., Linnaean system) and compare according to characteristics (e.g., physical features, behaviors, development).
5. Compare and contrast the structures, functions, and interactions of human and other animal organ systems (e.g., respiration, reproduction, digestion).
6. Distinguish among infectious agents (e.g., viruses, bacteria, fungi, parasites), their transmission, and their effects on the human body.
7. Identify and analyze the processes of heredity and natural selection and the scientific theory of evolution.
8. Analyze the interdependence of living things with each other and with their environment (e.g., food webs, ecosystems, pollution).
9. Identify and analyze plant structures and the processes of photosynthesis, transpiration, and reproduction (i.e., sexual, asexual).
10. Predict the responses of plants to various stimuli (e.g., heat, light, gravity).
11. Identify and compare the life cycles and predictable ways plants and animals change as they grow, develop, and age.

Overview

Knowledge of life science includes an understanding of the systems of the body as well as how plants and animals interact in the world. There are approximately **13 questions** that address Competency 5. This section addresses the following areas related to **Competency 5** key indicators:

- Living and Nonliving Things
- Cells
  - Eukaryotic Cells
- Prokaryotes
  - Bacteria and Viruses
- Eukaryotes
  - Protists
  - Fungi
  - Plants
  - Animals
- Heredity, Evolution, and Natural Selection

Living and Nonliving Things

In order to be considered a **living thing,** six criteria must be met:

1. Made up of cells
2. Obtain and use energy

3. Grow and develop
4. Reproduce
5. Respond to stimuli in environment
6. Adapt to environment

Nonliving things may have some of the criteria of living things, but if they do not meet all six criteria, they are not living things. For example, a crystal can grow and develop, but it is not made up of cells, so it is not living.

Living things can be further categorized. **Taxonomy** is the classification of living things into categories based on physical characteristics. The taxonomical classification was originally developed by Carolus Linnaeus and is known as the **Linnaean system.** This system includes eight levels, listed from the broadest to the most specific: domain, kingdom, phylum, class, order, family, genus, and species.

Domains	Archaea	Bacteria	Eukarya			
Kingdoms	Archaebacteria	Eubacteria	Protists[1]	Fungi	Plants	Animals

[1]*Some references no longer list "Protists" as a kingdom.*

Checkpoint

1. What are the eight levels of taxonomy?
2. What are the three domains?
3. What are the six characteristics of living things?

Checkpoint Answers

1. Domain, kingdom, phylum, class, order, family, genus, and species
2. Archaea, Bacteria, and Eukarya
3. Made up of cells; obtain and use energy; grow and develop; reproduce; respond to stimuli in environment; adapt to environment

Cells

All living things are made up of cells. **Cells** are the smallest unit of living things and were not discovered until microscopes were invented in the mid-1600s. Cells come in many different shapes and sizes and can perform different functions, but they all have many parts in common. All cells contain cell membranes, cytoplasm, organelles, and DNA.

Cell membranes surround the cell and provide a protective layer that covers the surface of the cell and acts as a barrier to its environment. The cell membrane controls what materials go into and out of the cell. Inside the cell is a fluid called the **cytoplasm.**

Within cells are **organelles,** which carry out the life processes within the cell. Organelles perform specific functions within the cell, and different cell types have different organelles. Some organelles float in the cytoplasm; others have membranes; still others are attached to membranes or other organelles.

All cells contain **DNA,** the genetic material that contains information needed to make new cells. DNA is passed from parent cells to new cells and determines the type and function of a cell. In some cells, the DNA is enclosed inside an organelle called the **nucleus.** These cells are called **eukaryotic cells.** In other cells, a nucleus does not exist. These cells are called **prokaryotic cells.**

Eukaryotic Cells

Eukaryotic cells can have **cell walls,** a rigid structure that gives support to the cell. The cell wall is the outermost part of the cell. Cell walls in plants and algae are made up of **cellulose,** a complex sugar that animals cannot digest without help. Cell walls in plants allow the plants to stand upright. When a plant droops over, it is often due to the cells lacking water, which causes the cell walls to collapse and the plant to droop. In cells without a cell wall, the cell membrane is the outermost part of the cell. In cells with a cell wall, the cell membrane is just inside the cell wall.

The cell membrane of eukaryotic cells contains **proteins, lipids,** and **phospholipids.** Proteins and lipids control the movement of larger materials into and out of the cell. Small nutrients and water move into the cell, while wastes move out of the cell by diffusion. The web of proteins inside the cytoplasm is called the **cytoskeleton.** The cytoskeleton acts both as muscles and a skeleton for the cell. It keeps the cell membrane from collapsing and helps cells move.

Eukaryotic cells also contain a nucleus, a large organelle containing the cell's DNA. The cell's DNA contains the information on how to make the cell's proteins. The proteins are not made in the nucleus; instead the instructions for making the protein are copied from the DNA and sent out through pores in the nucleus. The nucleus of many cells contains the **nucleolus,** a dark area in which the cell begins to make **ribosomes.** Ribosomes are the smallest of all organelles. Some ribosomes float in the cytoplasm, while others are attached to membranes or the cytoskeleton. Ribosomes are not covered by a membrane. In all cases, ribosomes build proteins, which are made of **amino acids.** All cells need proteins to live, so all cells have ribosomes.

Chemical reactions take place in a cell, many of which take place on the **endoplasmic reticulum,** or ER, a system of folded membranes in which proteins, lipids, and other materials are made. The folded membranes contain many tubes and passageways for delivering substances to different parts of the cell. There are two types of ER, rough and smooth. **Rough ER** is covered in ribosomes and is usually found near the nucleus. **Smooth ER** does not contain ribosomes; it makes lipids and breaks down toxic material that could damage the cell.

The power source of the cell is the **mitochondrion,** the organelle in which sugar is broken down to produce energy. Mitochondria are covered by two membranes, the outer membrane and the inner membrane. Mitochondria make a substance called **ATP,** the form of energy that cells can use. Most of a cell's ATP is made in the inner membrane of the mitochondria.

The organelle that packages and distributes proteins is called the **Golgi complex.** The Golgi complex looks like smooth ER, but its job is to take the lipids and proteins made from the ER and deliver them to the other parts of the cell. The Golgi complex might modify lipids and proteins to do different jobs. The final product is enclosed in a piece of the Golgi complex's membrane that then pinches off in a small bubble called a **vesicle,** which transports the lipids and proteins to other parts of the cell or outside the cell. The vesicles responsible for digestion inside a cell are called **lysosomes.** Lysosomes are organelles that contain digestive enzymes that destroy worn-out or damaged organelles, get rid of waste, and protect the cell from invaders. **Vacuoles** are large vesicles. In plant and fungal cells, some vacuoles act like large lysosomes by storing digestive enzymes and aiding in digestion within the cell. Other vacuoles in plant cells store water and other liquids.

Plant cells contain **chloroplasts,** which animal cells do not. Chloroplasts are organelles present in plant and algae cells and allow the plant to harness energy from the Sun. **Photosynthesis** takes place in the chloroplasts. The process of photosynthesis allows plants and algae to use sunlight, carbon dioxide, and water to make sugar and oxygen. Chloroplasts are green because they contain **chlorophyll,** a green pigment found inside the inner membrane of a chloroplast. Chlorophyll traps the energy from sunlight, which is then used in photosynthesis to make the sugar glucose. Glucose is then used by the mitochondria to make ATP.

Checkpoint

1. True or false: Cells are present in all living things.

2. What parts do all cells contain?

3. Fill in the blank: Cells which have a nucleus are called _____.

Checkpoint Answers

1. True

2. cell membranes, cytoplasm, organelles, and DNA

3. eukaryotes

Prokaryotes

Prokaryotes are single-celled organisms. Prokaryotic cells are small and simple cells that do not have a nucleus or membrane-bound organelles. Prokaryotes are divided between two domains—**Archaea** and **Bacteria.**

Bacteria and Viruses

Archaeabacteria are single-celled microorganisms. They have no cell nucleus or complex organelles, but their cells contain DNA and ribosomes to carry on the functions of life. They are similar in shape to bacteria, but have some notable differences. They live in a variety of harsh, oxygen-deprived habitats including hot springs, salt lakes, soils, oceans, and marshlands.

Eubacteria are large groups of single-celled organisms that grow in nearly every environment on Earth. They are typically micrometers in length and can be classified based on their shape, type of cell wall, methods of movement, or way of obtaining energy. In terms of shape, bacteria can be spheres (**cocci**), rods (**bacilli**), or spirals (**spirilla**).

Bacteria have three basic roles in nature. They act as decomposers in order to return raw materials and nutrients to the soil for other life. Bacteria are also nitrogen fixers, meaning that they can turn nitrogen in the atmosphere into nitrogen that is in a form useful for life. These bacteria form a symbiotic relationship with a plant in which the bacteria consume nutrients and produce nitrogen that the plant needs, but cannot create on its own. Lastly, there are bacteria that cause disease; these are called pathogens. Examples of human diseases include tetanus, syphilis, leprosy, and tuberculosis. Each pathogen produces specific diseases when interacting with the host human body. Staphylococcus and streptococcus are two common bacteria that cause skin infections, pneumonia, meningitis, and other minor or serious diseases. These same bacteria, however, are commonly found on the skin and are not pathogenic at all. Infections caused by bacteria can usually be treated with antibiotics.

Another major infectious agent is the **virus.** Viruses and bacteria are similar in some ways, but also different. Bacteria can live outside a host; viruses cannot. Bacteria are made of cells; viruses use the cells they infect and do not have cells of their own. Instead, viruses are made of a protein coat that surrounds either DNA or RNA. Viruses spread in many ways, including human contact, airborne contact, and surface contact. Viruses are the cause of diseases such as the common cold, influenza, chickenpox, Ebola, AIDS, and SARS. Viruses cannot be treated with antibiotics. Because viruses live in the host cell and take it over, the virus cannot be killed without killing the host cell. This is not always practical, so some viruses are never eliminated from the body. The most effective method of controlling viruses is vaccination. The body's immune system must eliminate the virus. Vaccination gives the body's immune system a boost in fighting viruses.

Checkpoint

1. True or false: Bacteria can live outside a host.

2. True or false: Viruses can be treated with antibiotics.

Checkpoint Answers

1. True

2. False

Eukaryotes

Eukaryotes are organisms whose cells contain complex structures, including membrane-bound organelles and a nucleus containing DNA. These cells are typically much larger than prokaryotes. Eukaryotic cells are still microscopic, but they are about 10 times larger than bacteria. All living things that are not eubacteria or archaebacteria are made up of eukaryotic cells. Most eukaryotes are multicellular, although some are single-cellular. Eukaryotes include protists, fungi, plants, and animals.

Protists

Protists are organisms that are similar to plants, fungi, and animals, but do not fit neatly into those kingdoms. They come in many shapes and sizes, but they have a few traits in common. All protists are eukaryotic. Most protists are single-celled organisms, but some are multicellular and others live in colonies. Some protists produce their own food, while others eat other organisms or decaying matter. Some protists control their own movement, while others cannot. Protists are less complex than other eukaryotic organisms. They do not have specialized tissues.

Protists obtain food in many ways. Protists that produce their own food have special structures called chloroplasts. Similar to plants, these chloroplasts provide the structure to capture energy from the Sun through photosynthesis. Some protists consume food in their environment. These protists are **heterotrophs.** Protist heterotrophs eat small living organisms like bacteria, yeast, or other protists. Some are decomposers that get energy from breaking down dead organic matter. Other protist heterotrophs are **parasites,** namely organisms that invade other organisms called hosts to obtain the nutrients they need.

Protists reproduce in several ways. Some protists reproduce asexually, while others reproduce sexually. In **asexual reproduction,** offspring come from one parent and are an identical copy of the parent. Asexual reproduction in protists occurs through fission. **Sexual reproduction** requires two parents and often involves a process called conjugation, in which two individuals join together and exchange genetic material using a second nucleus. They then divide to produce four protists that have new combinations of genetic material.

Protists can be divided into three types—plant-like protists, which act as producers; animal-like protists; and fungus-like protists.

There are two categories of plant-like protists: unicellular algae and multicellular **algae.** All algae have chlorophyll and most have other pigments that give them color. Most algae live in water. Red algae have a pigment that makes them red, allowing them to absorb the light deep in clear water. Green algae (now part of the plant kingdom) can be unicellular or multicelluluar and live in water or moist soil. Brown algae are found in cool climates. Free-floating single-celled protists are called **phytoplankton.** Phytoplankton are microscopic and usually float near the water's surface and produce much of the world's oxygen.

Animal-like protists are heterotrophs and are called **protozoans.** Amoebas are an example of a protozoan. They are found in fresh and salt water and as parasites in animals. They appear shapeless but are actually highly structured. Many amoebas eat bacteria and small protists, but some are parasites. Amoebas move with **pseudopodia,** or false feet. To move, an amoeba stretches out a pseudopod from the cell. The cell then flows into the pseudopod, providing movement. They also use pseudopodia to catch food. Another protozoan is the **zooflagellate.** Zooflagellates move with **flagella,** whiplike strands extending out from the cell that move back and forth. Some zooflagellates are parasites that cause disease, while others are mutualists. **Ciliates** are complex protists that have hundreds of tiny, hairlike structures called **cilia,** which beat back and forth, causing the ciliate to move. They also use cilia for obtaining food. The most common ciliate is the paramecium.

Fungus-like protists are heterotrophs that are similar to fungi but do not fit in the fungi kingdom. They can be parasites that do not move about or move only at certain phases of life. Spore-forming protists are parasites that absorb nutrients from their host. They have no cilia or flagella and cannot move on their own. Water molds are also heterotrophs that do not move. Water molds live in water, moist soil, and other organisms. Slime molds move only at certain phases of their life cycle. They live in cool, moist places in the woods. When environmental conditions are favorable, slime molds use pseudopodia to move. When environmental conditions are unfavorable, slime molds form spores that do not move.

Fungi

Fungi are eukaryotic heterotrophs that have rigid cell walls and no chlorophyll. Fungi come in a variety of shapes, sizes, and colors. As heterotrophs, fungi find food in their environment, but they cannot catch or surround food. They must live on or near their food supply. Most fungi are consumers and obtain nutrients by dissolving food with digestive juices. Many fungi are decomposers and feed on dead plant or animal matter. Others are parasites. Still others are mutualists.

Fungi are made up of eukaryotic cells. Multicellular fungi are made up of chains of cells called **hyphae.** Most of the hyphae that make up a fungus grow together to form a **mycelium,** a twisted mass of hyphae. The mycelium makes up most of the fungus, but is hidden from view underground.

Reproduction in fungi is either asexual or sexual. Asexual reproduction occurs in two ways—breaking apart or producing **spores,** which form new fungi. Sexual reproduction in fungi happens when sex cells are formed and then joined together to make sexual spores that grow into new fungi.

There are four main groups of fungi, classified based on their shape and how they reproduce:

- Threadlike fungi live in soil and are decomposers. Some are parasites. They reproduce both asexually using spore cases called **sporangia** and sexually when hypha from one individual joins with hypha from another individual. A common example of threadlike fungi is black bread mold.
- Sac fungi include yeasts, mildews, truffles, and morels. Sac fungi reproduce both asexually though a sac called an ascus and sexually through spores developed within the ascus. Many sac fungi are helpful to humans. Yeasts are used in making bread and alcohol through fermentation. Some antibiotics and vitamins come from sac fungi. Some sac fungi are not helpful to humans, however. Many sac fungi are parasites that can cause plant diseases.
- Club fungi are most commonly recognized as mushrooms. They produce sexually. Some club fungi are edible, but others are not. There are other forms of club fungi as well. Bracket fungi grows outward from wood to form shelves. Smuts and rusts are common fungal plant pathogens and often attack crops.
- Imperfect fungi include all other species of fungi. These fungi reproduce asexually. Most are parasites that cause disease in plants and animals. Athlete's foot is caused by imperfect fungi. Penicillin derives from penicillium, an imperfect fungi.

Plants

A **plant** is a eukaryotic, multicellular autotroph. Almost all food originates from plants, whether the food is the plant itself or animals that eat the plants; therefore, plants form the basis of many **food webs.** Plants come in various shapes and sizes, but they all have several characteristics in common. Plants are **autotrophs** (meaning they create their own food), have a two-stage life cycle, and have cell walls.

The two stages of a plant's life cycle are the **sporophyte stage** and the **gametophyte stage.** During the sporophyte stage, plants make spores, which then can grow in a suitable environment. During the gametophyte stage, male and female parts make gametes. The female gametophytes produce eggs, and male gametophytes produce sperm. Sperm must fertilize the egg, which then grows into a sporophyte, creating spores.

Plants are classified into two major groups—**nonvascular plants** and **vascular plants.** Nonvascular plants do not have specialized tissues to move water and nutrients through the plant. Mosses, liverworts, and hornworts are nonvascular plants. Nonvascular plants must rely on **diffusion** to move materials from one part of the plant to another. As a consequence, nonvascular plants are very small. Vascular plants have tissues, called **vascular tissues,** which move water and nutrients from one part of the plant to another. Vascular tissues can move water and nutrients to any part of the plant, so vascular plants can be very large. There are two types of vascular tissues: **xylem** and **phloem.** Vascular plants are divided into **seedless plants, nonflowering seed plants,** and **flowering seed**

plants. Seedless plants include ferns, horsetails, and club mosses. Nonflowering seed plants are called **gymnosperms.** Flowering seed plants are called **angiosperms.** Angiosperms are then divided into monocots and dicots.

Nonvascular	Vascular			
Mosses Liverworts Hornworts	Seedless plants	Seed plants		
	Ferns	Gymnosperm	Angiosperms	
		Cone-bearing plants	Flowering plants	
			Monocots	Dicots

Plant cells contain **chlorophyll,** a green pigment that captures energy from sunlight. Plants use the energy from sunlight to make food from carbon dioxide and water in a process called **photosynthesis.** Plants are protected by a **cuticle,** a waxy layer that coats the plant surfaces that are exposed to air. The cuticle prevents the plant from drying out. Plant cells contain rigid cell walls that keep the plant upright.

Photosynthesis

Photosynthesis is the process by which plants make food. Plants use chlorophyll to capture energy from the Sun. The light energy captured by chlorophyll helps form glucose molecules. In the process, oxygen is given off. Photosynthesis is represented by the following chemical equation:

$$6\ CO_2 + 6\ H_2O \longrightarrow C_6H_{12}O_6 + 6\ O_2$$

Carbon dioxide and water are used to form sugar and oxygen. The sugar is used for food by the plant, and the oxygen is released from the leaves.

Transpiration

In order for photosynthesis to occur, carbon dioxide must be absorbed by the plant. Plant surfaces above ground are covered by a waxy cuticle that protects the plant from water loss. Carbon dioxide enters the plant's leaves through **stomata,** openings in the leaf's surface that can open and close. When stomata are open, carbon dioxide enters the leaf, oxygen produced during photosynthesis exits the leaf, and water vapor exits the leaf. The loss of water through leaves is called **transpiration.** Water absorbed through the roots replaces the water lost through transpiration.

Reproduction

Plants can reproduce with either sexual or asexual reproduction.

In flowering plants, sexual reproduction occurs within the flowers. The male part of the flower is the **stamen,** which is made of the **anther** that makes pollen and the **filament** that holds up the anther. The female part of the flower is the **pistil,** which is made of the **stigma, style,** and **ovary.** Pollination occurs when pollen is moved from anthers to stigmas. This movement often happens through wind or animals. Pollen contains sperm. Once pollen lands on the stigma, a tube grows from the pollen through the style to an **ovule** inside the ovary. Each ovule contains an egg. When the sperm fuses with the egg, **fertilization** occurs. Once fertilization occurs, the ovule develops into a seed containing a tiny, undeveloped plant. The ovary surrounding the ovule becomes a fruit that swells and ripens to protect the developing seed. Once the seed is developed, the young plant inside the seed stops growing. When the seed is dropped or planted in a suitable environment, the seed sprouts and forms a new plant. This process is called **germination.**

Flowering plants may also reproduce asexually without flowers. This may occur through plantlets, tubers, or runners. **Plantlets** occur when tiny plants grow along the edges of a plant's leaves. The plantlets then fall off and grow new plants. **Tubers** are underground stems that can produce new plants. **Runners** are above-ground stems that form new plants.

Respiration

Cellular respiration is the process by which plants convert the energy that is stored in glucose molecules into energy that cells can use. This happens in the mitochondria. Plant cells use oxygen in this process and create carbon dioxide and water as waste. Any excess glucose that is not used in cellular respiration is converted into sucrose, another sugar, or stored as starch. Cellular respiration is not unique to plant cells. All eukaryotic organisms need to convert energy storage molecules like sugars into usable energy (ATP).

Responses to Environment

Plants have various responses to their environment. When a plant is placed so that light only comes from one direction, the plant tips will most likely bend toward the light. Plant growth also changes with the direction of gravity. Roots will grow toward the center of the Earth, and shoots will grow upward away from the center of the Earth. If a plant is placed on its side, the shoots will begin to move upward and the roots will begin to move downward relative to the new position.

Plants also respond to environmental changes through the seasons. Plants living in regions with cold winters can detect the change in seasons. As the seasons change, so do the length of days and nights. As fall and winter approach, days get shorter and nights get longer. Plants respond to the changes in length of day/night and will begin reproducing at the appropriate time of the year. All trees lose their leaves; however, some will lose some of their leaves year-round but keep most of them (**evergreen trees**), while others will lose all of their leaves at specific times of the year, typically fall (**deciduous trees**). The loss of leaves allows the plants to survive cold temperatures or long dry spells.

As deciduous trees prepare to lose their leaves, their leaves often change color. The green chlorophyll breaks down, so the color of the leaves changes to orange or yellow.

Animals

Animals are eukaryotic, multicellular heterotrophs that come in various shapes and sizes. Some animals are microscopic. Others are bigger than a car. Unlike plant cells, animal cells do not have cell walls. Animal cells are surrounded only by cell membranes.

There are two types of animals—vertebrates and invertebrates. **Vertebrates** are animals that have a backbone and include fish, amphibians, reptiles, birds, and mammals. Invertebrates do not have a backbone and include insects, snails, jellyfish, worms, and sponges. Less than 5 percent of animals are vertebrates.

An animal's body is formed by distinct parts that have different functions. Some cells are skin cells. Others are muscle cells, nerve cells, or bone cells. When different kinds of cells combine, they become tissues. Most animals also have **organs,** a group of tissues that carry out a specific function within the body. Each organ has a unique role in the function of the body.

Most animals can move from place to place. They may move differently—fly, run, or swim, for example. Animals cannot make their own food; movement often assists in the search for food. They survive by eating other organisms.

Invertebrates

Animals without a backbone are called **invertebrates.** Invertebrates have three basic body symmetries—bilateral, radial, or asymmetrical. Most animals have bilateral symmetry, meaning the two sides of the body mirror each other. Radial symmetry occurs when the body is organized around a center. Asymmetry occurs when there is no symmetry in the structure of the body. Invertebrates are classified into six distinct categories, with three categories of worms.

Sponges	Cnidarians	Worms			Mollusks	Echinoderms	Arthropods
		Flatworms	Roundworms	Segmented worms			

- **Sponges** are the simplest invertebrates. They are asymmetrical and have no tissues. They are marine animals.
- **Cnidarians** have stinging cells. They are more complex than sponges. They have complex tissues and a simple network of nerve cells. Jellyfish, sea anemone, and coral are cnidarians.
- Worms:
    - **Flatworms** are the simplest kind of worms. Flatworms have bilateral symmetry. There are three types of flatworms: planarians and marine flatworms, flukes, and tapeworms. Planarians live in freshwater lakes and streams or in damp places on land. Most planarians eat other animals. Flukes are parasites that have suckers and hooks, allowing them to attach to animals. Tapeworms are similar to flukes and are also parasites. They live and reproduce in other animals and feed on these animals. Tapeworms, however, do not have a gut. They attach to the intestines of another animal and absorb nutrients.
    - **Roundworms** have bodies that are long, slim, and round. They have bilateral symmetry and a simple nervous system. Most species of roundworms are small, and they typically break down dead tissues of plants and animals. Many roundworms are also parasites.
    - **Segmented worms** have bilateral symmetry but are more complex than flatworms and roundworms. They have a closed circulatory system and a complex nervous system. Segmented worms can live in salt water, fresh water, or on land. They eat plant material or animals and are grouped into earthworms, marine worms, and leeches.
- Most **mollusks** live in the ocean, but some live in fresh water and some live on land. Mollusks fit into three categories: gastropods, bivalves, and cephalopods. Gastropods include slugs and snails. Bivalves include clams and shellfish that have two shells. Cephalopods include squids and octopuses.
- **Echinoderms** are spiny-skinned invertebrates that include sea stars, sea urchins, and sand dollars. They are marine animals and live on the sea floor. Adult echinoderms have radial symmetry.
- **Arthropods** are the largest group of animals. At least 75 percent of all animal species are arthropods. All arthropods have a segmented body with specialized parts, jointed limbs, an **exoskeleton,** and a well-developed nervous system. The segmented body includes structures such as wings, claws, and antennae. There are three main body parts: the head, thorax, and abdomen. Arthropods include centipedes, millipedes, crustaceans (lobsters), arachnids (spiders), and insects.

Vertebrates

Vertebrates are animals with a backbone. Vertebrates include fish, amphibians, reptiles, birds, and mammals.

There are two main types of vertebrates—**endotherms** and **ectotherms.** Endotherms are warm-blooded animals. They are able to regulate their own body temperature. Birds and mammals are endotherms. Ectotherms are cold-blooded animals. They are unable to regulate their own body temperature and rely on the environment to regulate their temperature. Amphibians, reptiles, and fish are ectotherms.

There are more than 25,000 species of **fish,** but all share several characteristics. All fish live in water. Fish have strong muscles attached to their backbone that allow them to swim quickly. They have fan-shaped **fins** that help them to steer, stop, and balance in the water. Many fish have scales covering their bodies to protect them and lower friction as they swim through the water. Fish have a brain that keeps track of information obtained through **senses,** of which all fish have at least three—vision, hearing, and smell. Fish breathe using **gills,** an organ that removes oxygen from the water. Water passes through the gills, and the oxygen in the water passes through a membrane into the blood, which then carries the oxygen to the rest of the body. Most fish reproduce by external fertilization. The female lays unfertilized eggs in the water, and the male drops sperm onto the eggs to fertilize them. Some species of fish reproduce by internal fertilization, in which the male deposits sperm inside the female. The female then usually lays fertilized eggs called **embryos,** although some embryos develop inside the female fish. There are three types of fish—jawless fish, cartilaginous fish, and bony fish. Jawless fish include hagfish and lampreys; they are typically eel-like. Cartilaginous fish include sharks and rays. Bony fish are the largest group and include goldfish, tuna, trout, catfish, and cod.

Amphibians are animals that live in water or on land during different stages of their life cycle. Unlike fish, they have **lungs** and legs as adults. The lungs allow the amphibian to get oxygen from the air and deliver that oxygen to the blood. Most amphibians live part of their life in water and part on land. Amphibian eggs do not have a shell or protective membrane so they must be laid in a moist environment to prevent dehydration. Embryos must also develop in wet environments, and most amphibians continue to live in water after hatching. Later, they develop into adults that live on land. The skin of amphibians is thin, smooth, and moist. Water helps amphibians to regulate their body temperature and moisture content of their skin. Amphibians do not drink water; instead, they absorb it through the skin. Due to their double life, amphibians change dramatically as they grow. For example, a frog or toad embryo becomes a **tadpole** that must live in water. Tadpoles obtain oxygen through gills like fish and have a long tail for swimming. As the tadpole develops, it loses its gills and tail and develops lungs and limbs so that it can live on land as a frog or toad. This transformation is referred to as **metamorphosis.**

There are more than 5,400 species of amphibians, and they are categorized into three groups: caecilians, salamanders, and frogs and toads. Caecilians live in tropical areas of Asia, Africa, and South America and look like earthworms or snakes; however, they have the thin, moist skin of amphibians. Salamanders generally live in the woods of North America. They have four strong legs and a long tail. Frogs and toads encompass about 90 percent of all amphibians. Toads are actually a type of frog. Frogs and toads live all over the world. They are found in regions from deserts to rain forests. They have strong leg muscles for jumping and well-developed ears and vocal cords for hearing and calling.

Reptiles live entirely on land. All reptiles have lungs to breathe air and have thick, dry skin. Their skin has a watertight layer that keeps cells from losing water by evaporation. The eggs of reptiles are called **amniotic eggs;** they hold a fluid that protects the embryo. They also have a shell, allowing the eggs to be laid under rocks or in the ground. Reptiles reproduce by internal fertilization. The egg is fertilized inside the female and a shell is formed prior to the female laying her eggs. In a few cases, reptiles do not lay eggs; instead, the embryo develops inside the mother, and the young are born alive. There are four groups of reptiles: turtles and tortoises, crocodiles and alligators, lizards and snakes, and tuataras. Turtles and tortoises have a shell, making it hard to outrun predators. Many turtles can pull their head and legs into the shell to protect themselves. Tortoises live on land, while turtles spend all or much of their life in water. Some turtles, like the sea turtle, come on land to lay eggs. Crocodiles and alligators spend most of their time in the water. They have a flat head, and their eyes and nostrils are positioned on the top of their head. They are meat eaters, with their diet consisting of invertebrates, fish, turtles, birds, and mammals. Snakes and lizards are the most common reptiles today. Snakes are **carnivores** (meat eaters), and their tongue allows them to smell. Some snakes kill their prey by squeezing it until it suffocates, while others have fangs that inject venom into their prey. Snakes can open their mouths extremely wide to swallow whole animals that are larger than the snake is. Lizards are generally carnivores, eating primarily insects and worms, but some eat plants. Lizards do not swallow their prey whole. Tuataras live only on a few islands off the cost of New Zealand. They look similar to lizards, but are classified into a different group. They do not have visible ear openings like lizards do.

Birds share many characteristics with reptiles—their legs and feet are covered by scales and their eggs have an amniotic sac like reptiles. However, bird eggs have harder shells, and birds have feathers and wings. They can usually fly and can regulate their own body temperature. Birds require a lot of energy to fly, so their body breaks down food quickly to generate energy. Most birds eat insects, nuts, seeds, or meat. To enable flight, birds have wings and lightweight bodies. Birds can be grouped into four categories—flightless birds, water birds, perching birds, and birds of prey. **Flightless birds** do not have the muscles for flight. They often run very fast or are skilled swimmers. Flightless birds include penguins, ostriches, and kiwi. **Water birds** have webbed feet for swimming or long legs for wading. Water birds fly, are comfortable in the water, and find food on land and in water. They include cranes, ducks, geese, swans, pelicans, and loons. **Perching birds** have adaptations for resting on branches. They include songbirds like robins and sparrows. Their feet are able to wrap around a branch when they land in a tree. **Birds of prey** hunt and eat mammals, fish, reptiles, and other birds. They have sharp claws and a sharp beak. Birds of prey include owls, ospreys, eagles, and hawks.

Mammals live in almost every climate on Earth. All mammals have hair and **mammary glands,** which are structures that make milk. Although all mammals have mammary glands, only mature females actually produce milk. Mammals have lungs to get oxygen from the air. The hair on mammals helps them to regulate their body temperature. Mammals that live in cold climates have thick coats of hair, called fur. Mammals that live in warmer climates do not need as much hair, but all mammals have hair. Mammals also have teeth with different shapes and sizes for different jobs. All mammals reproduce sexually, and in most cases, mammals give birth to live young. A mammal's brain is larger than most other animals, allowing the mammal to learn and think quickly. Mammals have five senses—sight, hearing, smell, touch, and taste—which allow them to examine the world around them. There are three categories of mammals—placental mammals, monotremes, and marsupials. The embryos of **placental mammals** develop inside the mother's body and are attached to the mother through a placenta. Most mammals are placental, including rodents, rabbits, bats, walruses, elephants, giraffes, whales, apes, and humans. **Monotremes** are mammals that lay eggs. These include echidnas and the platypus. **Marsupials** carry their young in a pouch. They give birth to live young that are underdeveloped and finish their development in a pouch for several more months. Marsupials include koalas, opossums, and kangaroos.

Physiological Processes

Two or more tissues working together to carry out a specific function of the body form an **organ.** Different organs work together to create an **organ system.** There are 11 organ systems in the human body: integumentary, muscular, skeletal, cardiovascular and circulatory, respiratory, urinary, reproductive, nervous, digestive, lymphatic, and endocrine. These are detailed in the following table:

System	Function
Integumentary	Skin, hair, and nails, which protect the tissue beneath them; skin has two main layers—**epidermis** (the top layer) and **dermis** (the bottom layer).
Muscular	Three types of muscles cause movement in the body: **Skeletal muscles** (voluntary, striated) attach to bones with tendons for body movement; **smooth muscles** (involuntary, not striated) move food through the digestive system; and **cardiac muscle** (involuntary, striated) is in the heart.
Skeletal	Provides the frame for the body and protects body parts; made up of **bones, cartilage,** and **ligaments.**
Cardiovascular and circulatory	Transports materials in the blood around the body. The heart pumps blood throughout vessels in the body, namely arteries, capillaries, and veins. Blood is pumped to the lungs in order to pick up oxygen and remove carbon dioxide.
Respiratory	Air moves down the **trachea** to the **lungs** to the alveoli for the absorption of oxygen into the blood and removal of carbon dioxide waste from the blood; oxygen goes into the blood for transport to the cells of the body for cellular **respiration.**
Urinary	The **kidneys** filter waste from the blood and send the urine into the **bladder** to await removal. The kidneys also regulate the body's water balance.
Reproductive	Provides the components for creating new life.
Nervous	Senses the environment and controls the body. It receives and sends electrical signals throughout the body along **neurons;** two parts—**central nervous system** (brain and spinal cord) and **peripheral nervous system** (nerves of the body that connect all parts of the body to the central nervous system and sense organs).
Digestive	Digests food into small particles in the mouth, stomach, and small intestine so that nutrients can be absorbed in the small intestine; the large intestine absorbs water and vitamins while preparing waste for removal.
Lymphatic	Lymphatic vessels remove excess fluid from around cells and return it to the circulatory system, while eliminating bacteria and viruses; contains **lymph nodes,** small bean-shaped masses of tissue that remove pathogens from the **lymph.**
Endocrine	Comprised of glands that send out hormones, chemical messengers control body functions (e.g., pituitary, thyroid, ovaries, testes, and adrenal glands).

Checkpoint

1. What are the four categories of eukaryotes?

2. What two things do plant cells have that animal cells do not have?

3. True or false: Eukaryotes have a nucleus.

4. Fill in the blank: _____ is the process by which plants make food.

5. What are the two types of animals?

6. What are the five categories of vertebrates?

7. Which organ system removes waste from the body?

Checkpoint Answers

1. protists, fungi, plants, and animals

2. chloroplasts and cell walls

3. True

4. Photosynthesis

5. vertebrates and invertebrates

6. fish, amphibians, reptiles, birds, and mammals

7. urinary system

Heredity, Evolution, and Natural Selection

Heredity is the passing of traits from parents to their offspring. The principles of heredity used today were discovered by **Gregor Mendel.** Mendel began his work by selectively mating pea plants. He examined traits of the parents and of their offspring by studying one characteristic (for example, flower color) at a time and examining how the parents' traits were passed on to the offspring. He determined that there were factors that were passed from one generation to the next that, when combined, created either **dominant traits** or **recessive traits.** For example, when Mendel bred a purple-flowered plant with a white-flowered plant, he discovered that all of the offspring had purple flowers. Purple flowers are a dominant trait. However, when he crossed the first generation of purple-flowered plants with themselves, then the white flowers reappeared, meaning that white flowers are a recessive trait or one that is hidden by factors that cause a dominant trait. The factors that Mendel investigated are now called **genes.** One set of genes is given from each parent to their offspring. The characteristics of the offspring are then determined by the dominant and recessive **alleles** received from the parents. An allele is a form that a gene can take; e.g., there is a gene for flower color, where the dominant allele is for purple flowers and the recessive allele is for white flowers.

In asexual reproduction, one parent cell is needed. The structures of the cell are copied identically in a process called **mitosis.** Most cells in the body make copies of themselves through this process when they need to divide (e.g., skin cell growth). In sexual reproduction, two **gametes** (e.g., egg and sperm) join together to form an offspring that is different from both parents. Each parent cell contributes half of its genetic material to the gamete. In sexual reproduction, gametes are made through a process called **meiosis.** In meiosis, cells are produced that contain half the genetic material of the parent sex cells.

As species reproduce, various traits are passed from parents to children. Some traits are advantageous to the species in that they help the organism survive and reproduce in its environment. A trait that is advantageous to the species is known as an **adaptation.** As species adapt over time, they can turn into a new species in a process called **evolution.** Scientists use **fossils,** imprints of once-living organisms found in rock layers, to examine changes in species over time. The **fossil record** is the timeline of life gathered from examining fossils. As scientists examine the fossil record, they make conclusions about the ancestry of species and how they have adapted over time. The most famous scientist who created the theory of evolution was **Charles Darwin.** Darwin examined plants and animals in varying places around the world on his voyage on the H.M.S. *Beagle* and noticed that animals and plants in different places had similar adaptations, but also had differences. As a result of his observations, he developed a theory of **natural selection** to explain how evolution occurs over time to create new species from existing species. The theory of natural selection proposes that nature selects species to survive and reproduce because they are the most fit to do so, i.e., they have the best adaptations or **survival of the fittest.** Over geologic time, new species will arise from pre-existing ones, as organisms continue to adapt to a changing environment.

Checkpoint

1. What are the two ways cells can divide?

2. Who was the father of modern genetics?

3. Who was the father of evolution?

Checkpoint Answers

1. mitosis and meiosis

2. Gregor Mendel

3. Charles Darwin

Summary

The Science subtest encompasses a variety of subcompetencies related to the basic knowledge required of educators teaching elementary-age students. Knowledge of effective science instruction entails understanding methods for assessing scientific understanding in the classroom, the use of technology and other tools in scientific experimentation and instruction, strategies for connecting science to other content areas including reading and mathematics, and classroom management related specifically to the science classroom. Knowledge of the nature of science entails understanding **scientific inquiry** and use of laboratory equipment and analysis of data from scientific experimentation. Knowledge of physical sciences includes understanding the physical and chemical properties of matter; physical and chemical change; properties of solids, liquids, and gases; forces; temperature change; light; electricity; energy; and balanced and unbalanced forces. Knowledge of Earth and space means that the teacher understands the structure of the Earth, geological processes, the Earth's place in the Solar System, and interactions of the Sun, planets, and other celestial bodies. Knowledge of life science entails understanding living and nonliving things, the structure of plants and animals, the interaction of living things with their environment, and heredity.

You should use the information in this chapter to complement your previous knowledge in the area of science. The general review of science provided in this chapter should allow you to explore areas of strength and weakness that you might still need to review. To provide an opportunity for further practice and analysis, sample questions for the Science competency area appear in the next section of the chapter. Answer explanations follow the sample questions.

Sample Questions

1. The topmost layer of the Earth is called the

   A. crust.
   B. inner core.
   C. outer core.
   D. mantle.

2. Which of the following is a component of evolution?

   A. global warming
   B. greenhouse gases
   C. hurricanes
   D. natural selection

3. The geological phenomena of plate tectonics is most likely caused by

   A. solar energy heating the crust of the Earth.
   B. the mantle of the Earth shrinking and cooling.
   C. convection currents in the core.
   D. ocean currents moving the plates.

4. Pam says that CO_2 is matter. Is she correct?

   A. She is not correct because CO_2 is a gas.
   B. She is not correct because CO_2 does not have a specific shape like a rock.
   C. She is correct because CO_2 is composed of molecules, and molecules are matter.
   D. She is not correct because you can't see CO_2.

5. Rocks formed when existing rocks undergo change are called

   A. sedimentary rocks.
   B. metamorphic rocks.
   C. igneous rocks.
   D. river rocks.

6. Which organ system breaks down food into nutrients for the body?

   A. muscular system
   B. skeletal system
   C. digestive system
   D. respiratory system

7. It is summer in the Northern hemisphere from June through August. What is the cause of this?

   A. the Earth moving closer to the Sun, causing the Sun's rays to be more intense
   B. the tilt of the Earth, causing the Sun's rays to hit the Northern hemisphere directly
   C. the rotation of the Earth, causing the Northern hemisphere to be closer to the Sun
   D. the Sun becoming hotter between June and August

8. Ralph is on a diet. Which of the following is he trying to lose with this diet?

   A. density
   B. mass
   C. weight
   D. buoyancy

9. Jonathan is conducting an experiment to test whether or not the Sun has an effect on the growth of a particular plant. He sets up an experiment in which he has two plants that are identical. One plant is exposed to the Sun, while the other is not exposed to the Sun. What type of experiment is Jonathan conducting?

   A. controlled experiment
   B. single-subject experiment
   C. descriptive experiment
   D. dissection

10. A tugboat exerts a force of 4500 newtons on a large boat, and another tugboat exerts a force of 6300 newtons in the opposite direction on the same large boat. What is the combined force of these two tugboats on the large boat?

   A. 4500 newtons
   B. 6300 newtons
   C. 10,800 newtons
   D. 1800 newtons

11. Which of the following is NOT a component of every cell?

   A. cell membrane
   B. cell wall
   C. DNA
   D. cytoplasm

12. Hector is concerned with the precision of a thermometer he is using for an experiment. His concern is related to the

   A. validity of the instrument.
   B. clarity of the instrument.
   C. reliability of the instrument.
   D. acceptability of the instrument.

13. Mrs. Spalding is conducting a scientific experiment with her fourth-grade class. She is heating water to boiling to begin her experiment. Which of the following should Mrs. Spalding be sure to do with her students?

   A. allow her students to run in the laboratory room
   B. have the fire extinguisher available in the room next door
   C. require her students to wear safety goggles
   D. allow the students in the back of the room to not wear safety goggles

14. Which of the following is NOT an appropriate formative assessment for evaluating student performance in a laboratory experiment?

   A. unit exam
   B. journal entry
   C. student presentation
   D. student video

15. Which conclusion can be drawn from the following chart?

Plant Growth: Week 2

Controlled variable: light
Independent variable: water
Dependent variable: growth

Amount of light	Amount of water	Amount of growth
8 hours	0 ml	0 inches
8 hours	2 ml	2 inches
8 hours	5 ml	3 inches
8 hours	7 ml	6 inches
8 hours	10 ml	3.5 inches

A. Adding 7 ml of water provided the most growth.
B. The more water a plant received, the taller the plant grew.
C. The more sunlight a plant received, the taller the plant grew.
D. For each ml of water added, the plant grew 1 inch.

16. A toy car is stationary at the top of an inclined ramp. Which type of energy is demonstrated?

A. electrical
B. potential
C. solar
D. kinetic

17. Which of the following is a heterogeneous mixture?

A. salt water
B. balsamic vinaigrette salad dressing
C. coffee
D. laundry detergent

18. Which of the following is a NOT a kingdom in the Linnaean classification system?

A. animal
B. plant
C. bacteria
D. fungi

19. What makes plants green?

    A. photosynthesis
    B. chloroplasts
    C. carbon dioxide
    D. chlorophyll

20. What is the difference between viruses and bacteria?

    A. Bacteria can live outside a host and viruses cannot.
    B. Viruses can live outside a host and bacteria cannot.
    C. Viruses are made up of cells and bacteria are not.
    D. Vaccination prevents bacteria but not viruses.

21. Which of the following is a chemical change?

    A. melting
    B. boiling
    C. rusting
    D. tearing

22. What would be an appropriate unit of measure for the amount of water in a swimming pool?

    A. square yards
    B. ounces
    C. pounds
    D. gallons

Answer Explanations

1. **A.** Competency 4. The layers of the Earth are, from center to surface, the inner core, the outer core, the mantle, and the crust.

2. **D.** Competency 5. Natural selection is a component of evolution where an adaptation by a species allows it to survive as its surroundings change.

3. **C.** Competency 4. Plate tectonics is caused by convection currents, which radiate from the core of the Earth. These currents cause the plates to move.

4. **C.** Competency 3. Yes, she is correct because CO_2 is composed of molecules, and molecules are matter, even when they are not easily seen.

5. **B.** Competency 4. Metamorphic rocks are formed when existing rocks undergo change, often due to burial. Sedimentary rocks are formed when layers of debris fuse together. Igneous rocks form when magma cools.

6. **C.** Competency 5. The digestive system breaks down food for nutrients. The muscular and skeletal systems allow for movement. The respiratory system exchanges gases.

7. **B.** Competency 4. The seasons are caused by the tilt and revolution of the Earth. In the summer months in the Northern hemisphere, the Sun's rays are more direct, causing it to be warmer.

8. **B.** Competency 3. Ralph is most likely on a diet because he wants to reduce the amount of matter on his body. He most likely wishes to lose mass. If he wishes to lose weight, he would need to go to another planet.

9. **A.** Competency 2. Jonathan has set up an experimental group and a control group. This is a controlled experiment.

10. **D.** Competency 3. Since the tugboats provide unbalanced forces in opposite directions, you need to subtract 4500 from 6300, which provides a difference of 1800 newtons.

11. **B.** Competency 5. All cells contain a cell membrane, cytoplasm, organelles, and DNA.

12. **C.** Competency 2. Hector's concern is related to the reliability of the instrument, which involves the precision of the instrument. Validity refers to the accuracy of the instrument.

13. **C.** Competency 1. Safety goggles should be worn by all students at all times.

14. **A.** Competency 1. A unit exam is a summative assessment. Journal entries, student presentations, and videos show pieces of student learning.

15. **A.** Competency 2. The graphic indicates that the largest plant growth occurred with 7 ml of water over the 2-week period. If more water was given, the growth was less after this point. The sunlight was held constant and growth was not linear.

16. **B.** Competency 3. The car exhibits potential energy. It is not moving yet, so it has potential energy. Once the car begins moving, the potential energy would be transformed to kinetic energy.

17. **B.** Competency 3. Salt water, coffee, and laundry detergent are homogeneous mixtures—they are uniform in composition and cannot be separated by physical means. Balsamic vinaigrette salad dressing separates naturally into its component ingredients; therefore, it is a heterogeneous mixture.

18. **C.** Competency 5. Bacteria is a domain in the Linnaean classification system, not a kingdom. The six kingdoms are archaebacteria, eubacteria, fungi, plants, and animals (and possibly protists).

19. **D.** Competency 5. Chlorophyll is the pigment found inside the chloroplast that makes plants green. The chlorophyll traps the energy from sunlight, which, along with carbon dioxide and water, is used to make sugar and oxygen through photosynthesis.

20. **A.** Competency 5. Bacteria can live outside a host and are made up of cells. They can be treated with antibiotics. Viruses must have a host cell, and they do not have cells of their own. They use the cells they infect and cannot be treated with antibiotics. Vaccination helps to treat viruses by building immunity prior to exposure to the virus.

21. **C.** Competency 3. Rusting changes the chemical composition from metal to iron oxide. Melting, boiling, and tearing are physical changes. They do not change the chemical composition of the material.

22. **D.** Competency 2. The amount of water in a swimming pool is the volume of the pool. Gallons is an appropriate unit of measure for volume. Square yards measures area; ounces and pounds measure weight.

Mathematics

This chapter provides a general review of the Mathematics subtest with sample questions and explanations at the end of the chapter. Checkpoint exercises are found throughout, giving you an opportunity to practice the skills addressed in each section. The answers to the Checkpoint exercises immediately follow the set of questions. We encourage you to cover the answers as you complete the Checkpoint exercises.

Competency 1: Knowledge of Student Thinking and Instructional Practices

Competency Description

According to the *Competencies and Skills Required for Teacher Certification in Florida,* 20th Edition (available at www.fldoe.org/asp/ftce/pdf/ftce20edition.pdf), **Competency 1** for the Elementary Education (K–6) Subject Area Examination (SAE) Mathematics subtest addresses the following key indicators:

1. Analyze and apply appropriate mathematical concepts, procedures, and professional vocabulary (e.g., subitize, transitivity, iteration, tiling) to evaluate student solutions.

2. Analyze and discriminate among various problem structures with unknowns in all positions in order to develop student understanding of operations (e.g., put-together/take apart, arrays/area).

3. Analyze and evaluate the validity of a student's mathematical model or argument (e.g., inventive strategies, standard algorithms) used for problem solving.

4. Interpret individual student mathematics assessment data (e.g., diagnostic, formative, progress monitoring) to guide instructional decisions and differentiate instruction.

5. Select and analyze structured experiences for small and large groups of students according to the cognitive complexity of the task.

6. Analyze learning progressions to show how students' mathematical knowledge, skills, and understanding develop over time.

7. Distinguish among the components of math fluency (i.e., accuracy, automaticity, rate, flexibility).

Overview

This section provides a look at important instructional strategies and methods. There are approximately **13 questions** that address Competency 1. This section addresses the following areas related to **Competency 1** key indicators:

- Instructional Strategies for Teaching
- Methods for Assessing Mathematical Knowledge
- Concept versus Procedure
- Components of Math Fluency
- Levels of Content Complexity/Depth of Knowledge for Mathematics

Instructional Strategies for Teaching

An important aspect of teaching mathematics is the ability to identify appropriate instructional strategies. These strategies provide ways to accommodate and meet students' needs, differences, and interests. **Cooperative** or **collaborative** learning are ways of organizing the classroom, supporting and facilitating students' development. In these approaches, the classroom is organized in small groups of two to five students each. The students are also assigned roles or duties to perform during activities. A more **learner-centered instruction** is being advocated and supported by the constructivist learning theory as a framework. This is based on the premise that the student actively constructs knowledge, not in a passive manner. The process of solving problems and applying mathematical ideas becomes very relevant. The cognitive levels involved in the learning process are concrete (involving manipulative materials and/or real-life objects, which implies a more hands-on descriptive and exploratory process); pictorial (involving static drawing, images or pictures of the manipulative materials or objects); and abstract (involving written or spoken words or symbols). In geometry, the Van Hiele levels of geometric reasoning (described in the bulleted list that follows) is an example of a learning progression from descriptive, to analytic, to abstract:

- Visualization (descriptive): Can name and recognize shapes by their appearance and characteristics, but cannot specifically identify properties of shapes, and does not use them to recognize and sort shapes:
  - Sort, identify, and describe shapes; manipulate physical models; see different sizes and orientations of the same shape to distinguish characteristics of a shape and the features that are not relevant; build, draw, make, put together, and take apart shapes

- Analysis (analytic): Able to identify properties of shapes and is learning to use appropriate vocabulary related to properties, but does not make connections between different shapes and their properties; is able to focus on all shapes within a class (for example, able to think about what properties make a rectangle); and begins to talk about the relationship between shapes and their properties:
  - Use models to define, measure, observe, and change properties; use models to focus on defining properties, making property lists, and discussing sufficient conditions to define a shape; solve problems, including tasks in which properties of shapes are important components

- Informal deduction (abstract): Can recognize relationships between and among properties of shapes or classes of shapes and follow logical arguments using such properties:
  - Solve problems, including tasks in which properties of shapes are important components; use models, and properly list and discuss which group of properties constitute a necessary and sufficient condition for a specific shape; use informal, deductive language ("all," "some," "none," "if-then," "what if," etc.); investigate certain relationships among polygons to establish if the converse is also valid (for example, "If a quadrilateral is a rectangle, it must have four right angles; if a quadrilateral has four right angles, must it also be a rectangle?"); use models and drawings (including dynamic geometry software) as tools to look for generalizations and counter-examples; make and test hypotheses using properties to define a shape or determine if a particular shape is included in a given set

- Deduction: Able to go beyond identifying characteristics of shapes and constructs proofs using postulates or axioms and definitions (high school geometry course).

- Rigor: Can work in different geometric or axiomatic systems (college-level geometry course).

In this type of learning environment, the teacher's role is to facilitate the active learning of students. Students should have opportunities to answer questions involving classifying, hypothesizing, specializing (giving examples of how something works), generalizing, convincing, and analyzing. **Educational coaching** or **scaffolding** is used to provide guidance and support to a student as he or she learns, without limiting the student's investigation abilities. Other strategies are the following:

- Think alouds: A student or teacher says out loud what he/she is thinking about when reading, solving math problems, or simply responding to questions, and makes visible the mental processes.

- Peer tutoring: Students work in pairs or small groups to master academic skills or content as well as social development. It could involve pairing "high achieving" students with lower achieving students or those with comparable achievement for structured learning. Also, it can involve partners who are the same age or different ages (cross-age).

- Problem-based instruction: Students actively solve complex problems in realistic situations and emphasize the use of a problem solving process. The problem-solving process involves four steps initially developed by Polya (1957): understanding the problem, devising a plan, carrying out the plan, and looking back.

- Simulations: Simulations are a form of experiential learning or scenario where students interact in a reality defined by the teacher. They encourage students to use critical and evaluative thinking and to contemplate the implications of a scenario. They may contain elements of a game, role-play, or an activity that acts as a metaphor. Board games such as Monopoly or Careers are a type of simulation.

- Games: Games involve competition, social interaction, and some form of prize or award at the end of the game.
- Role playing: Students act out characters in a given "situation." It allows them to take risk-free positions by acting out characters in hypothetical situations.

Manipulatives are tools used to help students internalize mathematics concepts and skills. They help students work with abstract ideas at a concrete level. They are designed as a means to help understand mathematical abstractions and learn more conceptually. For example, students could count meaningfully the number of objects in a set and eventually instantly recognize without counting (**subitize**), or measure the size of an object using an **iteration** process with non-standard units and eventually use written symbols to represent the estimated size. The following table lists some manipulatives available for different mathematical ideas. Many of these manipulatives are now available as virtual manipulatives (also known as apps or applets) through the National Council of Teachers of Mathematics (NCTM) Illuminations (illuminations.nctm.org) and the National Library of Virtual Manipulatives (NLVM) (nlvm.usu.edu/en/nav/vLibrary.html). Calculators and computers are other important teaching tools. Geometer's Sketchpad (www.dynamicgeometry.com) and GeoGebra (www.geogebra.org) are dynamic geometry software that allow students to construct or draw dynamic geometric shapes (allowing for animation and movement) with points, vectors, segments, lines, polygons, conic sections, and functions.

Examples of Manipulatives and Mathematical Concepts

Manipulative	Mathematical Concepts
Algebra tiles	equations, estimation, expressions, factoring, integers, inequalities, operations, polynomials, similar terms, …
Attribute blocks	classifying, congruence, geometry, investigation of attributes (size, shape, color, thickness), logical reasoning, organization of data, patterns, problem solving, sequencing, similarity, sorting, symmetry, thinking skills, …
Balance scale	equality, equations, estimation, inequality, measurement, operations, mass, variables, weight, …
Base-ten blocks	area, classification, comparing, computation (whole numbers and decimals), decimal-fractional-percent equivalencies, metric measurement, number concepts, ordering, percent, perimeter, place value, polynomials, sorting, square and cubic numbers, …
Capacity containers	capacity, estimation, geometry, measurement, volume, …
Centimeter cubes	area, decimals, equations, expressions, fractions, mass, measurement, operations, patterns, volume, …
Chronometers	decimals, fractions, measurement, speed, time, …
Clocks	fractions, measurement, modular arithmetic, multiplication, time, …
Color tiles	area, color, counting, equality, estimation, even and odd numbers, inequality, integers, measurement, number concepts, operations, patterns, percent, perimeter, probability, proportion, ratio, shapes, spatial visualization, square numbers, tiling, …
Compasses	angle measurement, constructions, geometry, measurement, proof, …
Cubes	area, averages, classification, colors, counting, cubic numbers, equalities, even and odd numbers, frequencies, graphs, inequalities, mean, median, mode, number concepts, operations, patterns, percent, perimeter, prime and composite numbers, probability, proportion, ratios, sorting, spatial visualization, square numbers, surface area, symmetry, transformational geometry, volume, …
Cuisenaire rods	classification, common factors and multiples, comparisons, counting, decimals, estimation, even and odd numbers, factors, fractions, greatest common factors, least common multiple, logical reasoning, multiples, number concepts, operation concepts, ordering, patterns, place value, prime and composite numbers, proportions, ratios, sorting, …

(continued)

Examples of Manipulatives and Mathematical Concepts (*continued*)

Manipulative	Mathematical Concepts
Decimal squares	decimals—classification, comparing, number concepts, place value, operations, ordering, sorting, ...
Fraction tiles and circles	computation, decimals, fractions, operations, ...
Geoboards	geometric concepts, measurement, ...
Hands-on equations	algebra, equations, functions, operations, ...
Multilinks	area, averages, classification, colors, counting, cubic numbers, equalities, even/odd numbers, frequencies, graphs, inequalities, mean, median, mode, number concepts, operations, patterns, percent, perimeter, prime/composite numbers, probability, proportion, ratios, sorting, spatial visualization, square numbers, symmetry, transformational geometry (flips, turns, slides), volume, ...
Pattern blocks	area, classifying, equations, expressions, geometry, measurement, numeration, patterns, perimeter, sorting, tiling, variables, ...
Tangrams	area, decimals, fractions, geometry, measurement, percent, ...
Two-color chips	integers, number combinations, operations, ...
Unifix cubes	area, averages, classification, colors, counting, cubic numbers, equalities, even and odd numbers, frequencies, graphs, inequalities, mean, median, mode, number concepts, operations, patterns, percent, perimeter, prime and composite numbers, probability, proportion, ratios, sorting, spatial visualization, square numbers, surface area, symmetry, transformational geometry, volume, ...

Checkpoint

1. Fill in the blank: _____ learning is a way of organizing a classroom to support and facilitate students' development.

2. Fill in the blank: _____ help in making visible the mental processes that might be invisible to students in the reading or problem solving process.

3. Fill in the blank: _____ are concrete-level tools used to help students internalize mathematics concepts.

4. Fill in the blank: _____ is a student's ability to look at a number pattern and instantly recognize that number without counting.

5. Which is the most appropriate sequence for the following learning progression through the levels of geometric thinking? a-b-c; a-c-b; b-a-c; b-c-a; c-a-b; or c-b-a.

    a. The student makes and tests hypotheses using geometric shape properties.
    b. The student classifies geometric shapes using the properties of the shapes.
    c. The student sorts, identifies, and describes shapes by manipulating concrete models.

Checkpoint Answers

1. Cooperative or Collaborative

2. Think alouds

3. Manipulatives

4. Subitizing

5. The most appropriate sequence for the learning progression is c-b-a.

Methods for Assessing Mathematical Knowledge

The *Assessment Standards for School Mathematics Assessment* (NCTM, 1995) indicates that assessment is "the process of gathering evidence about a student's knowledge of, ability to use, and disposition toward mathematics and of making inferences from that evidence for a variety of purposes" (p. 3). In this manner, it should support and enhance the learning of important mathematics, and provide valuable information to both teachers and students. This implies that assessment should be more than just a score on a test. Instead, assessment should involve a more holistic view of each student's understanding, skills, and readiness. Assessment should:

- Reflect the mathematics that all students need to know.
- Enhance mathematics learning.
- Be a means of fostering growth toward high expectations.
- Promote equity.
- Be an open process.
- Promote valid inferences about mathematics learning (NCTM).

This assessment process involves the use of valid and reliable assessment measures and making valid inferences from the data collected. Different types of assessment and evaluative techniques should be considered and selected according to the situation at hand. One type of assessment might be appropriate for one situation but not for another. The students should be considered as a whole. Teachers should always be aware of the students' backgrounds. For example, a student may know the concept but not the terminology. The teachers should make sure the student understands the question or task. A variety of types of assessment, evaluative techniques, and sources of information should be considered and used with students as necessary:

- Observation (including observational checklists)
- Considerations of family life variables
- Consideration of student's readiness
- Review of school records and student files
- Oral responses
- Dramatizations
- Drawings
- Interviews
- Student's demonstrations
- Projects or project-based activities
- Checklists
- Rubrics
- Games
- Application items
- Problem solving items
- Peer evaluation
- Student writing and journals
- Self-assessment
- Portfolios
- Multiple-choice items
- Regular classroom tests
- Fill-in-the-blank with word bank

There are different useful types and models of assessment; several of them are listed below:

- *Objective assessment* refers to testing that requires the selection of one item from a list of choices provided with the question. This type of assessment includes true-false responses, yes-no answers, and questions with multiple-choice answers.
- *Alternative assessment* refers to other (non-traditional) options used to assess students' learning. When using this type of assessment, the teacher is not basing student progress only on the results of a single test or set of evidence. Some of the forms of this type of assessment include portfolios, journals, notebooks, projects, and presentations.
- *Authentic assessment* is a form of alternative assessment that incorporates real-life functions and applications.
- *Performance assessment* (often used interchangeably with authentic assessment) requires the completion of a task, project, or investigation; communicates information; or constructs a response that demonstrates knowledge or understanding of a skill or concept.

- *Naturalistic assessment* involves evaluation that is based on the natural setting of the classroom. It involves the observation of students' performance and behavior in an informal context.

- *Achievement test battery* is composed of subtests of mathematics concepts and skills and usually includes technical aspects of mathematics.

- *Standardized tests* include content areas and provide useful information about students' mathematics skills. Their validity and reliability depend on three basic assumptions: students have been equally exposed to the test content in an instructional program, students know the language of the test directions and the test responses, and students just like those taking the test have been included in the standardization samples to establish norms and make inferences.

- *Diagnostic tests* are used within the diagnostic-prescriptive teaching of mathematics. This process is an instructional model that consists of diagnosis, prescription, instruction, and ongoing assessment. Diagnostic test results could help identify specific problem areas. The tests can be teacher-made or commercially developed.

- *Progress monitoring* is a systematic and scientifically based assessment practice that involves students' academic performance and evaluates the effectiveness of instruction. It can be implemented with individual students, small groups, or an entire class. Students' current levels of performance are determined on a regular basis (weekly or monthly), goals are identified for learning that will take place over time, and progress toward meeting those goals is measured by comparing expected and actual rates of learning. Based on findings from the collected data and students' needs, instruction is adjusted if necessary.

- *Response to Intervention (RtI) and Multi-tier System of Support (MTSS)* are educational models used in the United States to provide early, effective assistance to children who are having difficulty learning. They were also designed to function as a databased process of diagnosing for learning disabilities. They may be used at group and individual levels and seek to prevent academic failure through early intervention, frequent progress measurement, and increasingly intensive research-based instructional interventions for children who continue to have difficulty. They also help with providing high-quality intervention matched to student needs, using learning rate over time and level of performance and making important educational decisions based on data.

We should also consider what any type of assessment and learning of mathematics model is *not*:

- Learning mathematics is not mastering a fixed set of basic skills, and, as a result, mathematics assessment should not focus on whether or not students have mastered these basic skills.

- Problem solving and application of mathematics does not come only after mastery of skills. The application of mathematics and the implementation of interesting contexts should be used to motivate and engage students. A natural learning environment should provide the basis for teaching, learning, and assessment.

- We should not teach then assess. Assessment should be ongoing and summative. The best assessment also instructs, and the best instructional tasks are rich diagnostic opportunities.

Checkpoint

1. Fill in the blank: _____ assessment is a form of alternative assessment that incorporates real-life functions and applications.

2. True or false: Problem solving and application of mathematics should come only after mastery of skills.

3. True or false: Assessment should be more than just a score on a test.

Checkpoint Answers

1. Authentic

2. False

3. True

Concept versus Procedure

A *concept* represents a big idea, understanding, or strategy in which relationships of key elements are developed. For example, addition operation is a key mathematical concept that involves joining together two sets. When the understanding of the addition operation concept is developed, it evolves into efficient and effective procedures. Understanding a concept underlies the development and usage of skills and procedures to be learned later and leads to proper connections and transfer. On the other hand, skills and *procedures* are rules, series of steps, routines, or processes. Skills and procedures should evolve from the understanding and usage of concepts. A **learning progression** (1) proposes a sequence for a topic across a number of grade levels, (2) is informed by research on children's cognitive development and logical structure of mathematics, (3) is used to explain why standards are sequenced in a given manner, (4) points out cognitive difficulties and pedagogical solutions, and (5) gives more detail on particularly challenging areas of the topic. A learning progression for the concept of addition could be the following:

- Counts a set with five cubes and another set with three cubes to represent $5 + 3 = ?$
- Joins the two sets together and counts each one of the cubes to find the sum
- Uses a count on strategy to find the sum by counting five objects in the first set and then counting on the other three cubes: 6, 7, 8
- Recalls $1 + 1$, $2 + 1$, etc.
- Recalls small totals like $5 + 3 = 8$
- Uses thinking strategies for larger numbers by recalling various totals: makes a ten ($9 + 6 = 10 + 5 = 15$) or uses doubles plus 1 ($6 + 7 = 6 + 6 + 1 = 12 + 1 = 13$)

Mastery of the addition operation concept is necessary to properly understand the addition computation algorithm (for example, $27 + 69 = ?$, or $123 + 67 = ?$). Another aspect involved in computation is memorization of basic facts (two one-digit addends or factors and a one- or two-digit sum or product: $4 + 3 = 7$, $9 + 8 = 17$, $3 \times 2 = 6$, or $6 \times 5 = 30$). Computational **fluency** involves rate, flexibility, automaticity, and accuracy. The memorization of basic facts provides for proper speed and accuracy when calculating sums, differences, products, or quotients involving large numbers. The recall rate of the basic fact answers is an important aspect in the calculation process. When solving mental or paper-and-pencil calculations, children carry out two main tasks: *choose* the most appropriate strategy to solve it (or strategy selection), and *execute* the chosen strategy with reasonable speed and accuracy (strategy efficiency or fluency). The students can use automatic recall, but they can also use a compensation strategy for calculating; for example, $35 + 9$ could be calculated by adding 10 to 35 and then subtracting 1: $35 + 10 - 1 = 44$ (which is the same as adding 9, but easier for mental calculation). In this context, automaticity means instant recall of a math fact without having to think about it.

Checkpoint

1. Does the following objective involve a concept or a skill?

   The students will use ratio language to describe a ratio relationship between two quantities.

2. Does the following standard involve a concept or a skill?

   Find a percent of a quantity as a rate per 100 (e.g., 30% of a quantity means $\frac{30}{100}$ times the quantity); solve problems involving finding the whole, given a part and the percent.

3. _____ is involved when students can recite basic fact answers with speed and accuracy.

Checkpoint Answers

1. Concept
2. Skill
3. Automaticity

Components of Math Fluency

Efficiency is involved when students do not get caught up in too many steps or get confused with the logic of the strategy or conceptual meaning. An efficient algorithm is carried out easily and without confusion.

Accuracy involves careful recording of the computational algorithm, memorizing basic facts, knowing number relationships and place value, and checking reasonableness or correctness of the results.

Flexibility is involved when the students are able to use and understand more than one computational algorithm for a particular exercise. The students are able to choose the most appropriate approach for a given exercise. They are also able to use one approach to solve an exercise and another to check correctness, accuracy, or reasonableness of the result. In this case, the students are able to use computational algorithms and tools that are appropriate for a given context and purpose. This process could include mental calculations, estimations, calculators, and paper-and-pencil recording.

Rate is involved in tracking how many exercises were correctly done in a fixed amount of time. It tells you how many problems per minute were solved. This rate could change from one student to another. The teacher might want to consider how laborious solving a set of exercises is for a student instead of just how fast they were solved.

Levels of Content Complexity/Depth of Knowledge for Mathematics

(Adapted from Webb, N. L., n.d., Depth-of-Knowledge Levels for Four Content Areas, University of Wisconsin Center for Educational Research)

It is important to assign depth of knowledge levels to objectives and assessment activities. The following table provides a general definition for each of the four levels of content complexity/depth of knowledge for mathematics, and examples of activities, possible products, and the student's roles.

Level	Activities	Possible Products	Student's Roles
1. Recalls information such as facts, definitions, terms, properties, rules, procedures, algorithms, rote response, …	Counts to 100 by ones. Counts to 100 by tens. Adds, subtracts, multiplies, or divides with basic facts fluently. Identifies place value of numbers.	Quiz, definition, fact, test, label, list, workbook, reproduction, vocabulary, recitation, example, collection, explanation, outline, categorizing, commenting, searching, Googling	Responds, remembers, absorbs, recognizes, memorizes, describes, explains, translates, restates, interprets
2. Basic application of concepts and skills requires engagement of some mental processing beyond a habitual response, and making some decisions as to how to approach the problem or activity, following a defined series of steps.	Compares data by first identifying characteristics of the objects and then grouping or ordering the objects. Reads and interprets information from a simple graph. Expresses the length of an object as a whole number of length units by iterating unit. Measures and estimates liquid volumes. Applies properties of operations as strategies to add. Measures and records data and produces graphs of relevant variables.	Photograph, illustration, simulation, sculpture, demonstration, presentation, interview, performance, diary, journal, reverse-engineering, cracking codes, linking, mashing, commenting, moderating, testing, validating	Solves problems, demonstrates use of knowledge, calculates, compiles, completes, illustrates, constructs

Level	Activities	Possible Products	Student's Roles
3. Strategic thinking and complex reasoning requires reasoning, planning, using evidence, and a higher level of thinking than the previous two levels; making conjectures is also at this level.	Interprets information from a complex graph that requires some decisions. Explains why addition strategies work. Interprets the rate of change and initial value of a linear function. Given a real-world situation, formulates a problem. Organizes, represents, and interprets data obtained through experiments. Formulates a mathematical model to describe a complex phenomenon.	Graph, spreadsheet, checklist, chart, outline, survey, database, mobile, abstract, report, debate, panel, evaluating, investigation, conclusion, program, film, animation, video cast, podcast, publishing, Wiki	Discusses, uncovers, argues, debates, thinks deeply, tests, examines, questions, calculates, judges, disputes, compares, assesses, decides, selects, justifies
4. Extended thinking and complex reasoning to incorporate demands from other content areas (e.g., English, science), in the development and support of real-world mathematical arguments.	Derives a mathematical model to explain a complex phenomenon or make a prediction. Completes a project requiring the formulation of questions, devising a plan, collecting data, analyzing the data, and preparing a written report describing the justification of the conclusions.	Film, story, project, plan, new game, song, newspaper, media product	Designs, formulates, plans, takes risks, modifies, creates, proposes, evaluates

Checkpoint

For each of the following tasks, identify the level of content complexity:

1. Given an ill-defined problematic situation, a student finds a mathematical solution by applying information in a novel manner.

2. A group of students makes models of geometric shapes they know and shares them with the whole class.

3. A group of students writes a list of keywords they know about geometric shapes.

4. A student makes a Venn diagram that shows how two topics are the same and different.

Checkpoint Answers

1. Level 4: Extended thinking and complex reasoning

2. Level 2: Basic application of concepts and skills

3. Level 1: Recalls information

4. Level 3: Strategic thinking and complex reasoning

Competency 2: Knowledge of Operations, Algebraic Thinking, Counting, and Numbers in Base Ten

Competency Description

According to the *Competencies and Skills Required for Teacher Certification in Florida,* 20th Edition (available at www.fldoe.org/asp/ftce/pdf/ftce20edition.pdf), **Competency 2** for the Elementary Education (K–6) Subject Area Examination (SAE) Mathematics subtest addresses the following key indicators:

1. Interpret and extend multiple representations of patterns and functional relationships by using tables, graphs, equations, expressions, and verbal descriptions.
2. Select the representation of an algebraic expression, equation, or inequality that models a real-world situation.
3. Analyze and apply the properties of equality and operations in the context of interpreting solutions.
4. Determine whether two algebraic expressions are equivalent by applying properties of operations or equality.
5. Evaluate expressions with parentheses, brackets, and braces.
6. Analyze and apply strategies (e.g., models, estimation, reasonableness) to solve multistep word problems.
7. Apply number theory concepts (e.g., primes, composites, multiples, factors, parity, rules of divisibility).
8. Identify strategies (e.g., compensation, combining tens and ones) based on place value to perform multidigit arithmetic.

Overview

Knowledge of **numbers** and **operations** is one of the most important areas of mathematics education. It involves different types of **cognitive levels** (concrete, pictorial, and abstract), number sets and their equivalent forms, estimation, problem solving, and number theory. Rational or meaningful counting skills, as well as numbers in base ten, are important components of this learning progression. This knowledge sets the stage for students' understanding of many algebraic thinking concepts and skills, including variables, expressions, equations, and functions. There are approximately **14 questions** that address Competency 2. This section addresses the following areas related to **Competency 2** key indicators:

- Select and Perform Operations to Solve Problems
- Apply Number Theory Concepts
- Apply the Order of Operations
- Algebraic Thinking
  - Linear Relationships
  - Properties

Select and Perform Operations to Solve Problems

The major operations on rational numbers are addition, subtraction, multiplication, and division. When solving word problems, it is important to take the time to select the appropriate operation involved in the problem. This requires the ability to translate the word problem into a mathematical sentence and solving the mathematical sentence accordingly. Some word problems might require multiple steps and operations. The examples provided in this section involve only whole numbers, but decimals or fractions could be used in a similar manner. Make sure you practice operations with integers, fractions, decimals, ratios, and percents.

For addition and subtraction, we have four types of problems: *join, separate, part-part-whole,* and *compare. Join problems* involve adding or joining elements to a set. Three quantities are involved: *the starting amount, the change amount,* and *the resulting amount.* Variations of the join problems include situations when the result is unknown, the change amount is unknown, or the starting amount is unknown. *Separate problems* involve removing elements from a set. Similar to join problems, we have three quantities involved and three variations of the separate problems. *Part-part-whole problems* involve no action or change over time as happens with join and separate problems; these problems focus on the relationship between a set and its two subsets (or a whole and two parts). Variations of these problems involve situations when *the whole is unknown* or *part of the whole is unknown*. *Compare problems* also involve no action, but involve comparisons between two different sets. These comparisons can be made in terms of how much more or how much less is one set than another set. Variations of the compare problems are *difference unknown, larger amount unknown,* and *smaller amount unknown.* For any of these types of problems, always remember to relate your answer to the initial question of the problem. The following table provides examples for each type of problem (Carpenter, et al., 1999; Carpenter & Moser, 1992; Cathcart, et al., 2010; Greer, 1992).

Addition and Subtraction Problems

Type of Problem	Example of Problem	Mathematical Sentence	Solution
Addition and Subtraction Problems That Involve Actions			
Join	Result unknown: Carla had 29 apples, and Frank gave her 56 apples. How many apples does Carla have now?	$29 + 56 = $ ___	Carla has 85 apples now.
	Change unknown: Carla had 29 apples, and Frank gave her some more apples. If Carla has 85 apples now, how many apples did Frank give her?	$29 + $ ___ $= 85$	Frank gave her 56 apples.
	Start unknown: Carla had some apples, and Frank gave her 56 more apples. If Carla has 85 apples now, how many apples did she have to start with?	___ $+ 56 = 85$	Carla started with 29 apples.
Separate	Result unknown: Mary had 85 apples. If she gave 29 apples to Albert, how many apples does she have left?	$85 - 29 = $ ___	Mary has 56 apples left.
	Change unknown: Mary had 85 apples. If she gave some apples to Albert and now she has 29 apples left, how many apples did Mary give to Albert?	$85 - $ ___ $= 29$	Mary gave 56 apples to Albert.
	Start unknown: Mary had some apples. If she gave 56 apples to Albert and now she has 29 apples, how many apples did Mary have to start with?	___ $- 56 = 29$	Mary had 85 apples to start with.
Addition and Subtraction Problems That Involve No Actions			
Part-part-whole	Whole unknown: Samuel has a combination of 29 red apples and 56 green apples in a box. How many apples does he have in the box?	$29 + 56 = $ ___	Samuel has 85 apples in the box.
	Part unknown: Samuel has a total of 85 apples in a box, with 29 of them being red apples and the rest green apples. How many green apples does he have?	$29 + $ ___ $= 85$	Samuel has 56 green apples.
Compare	Difference unknown: Samuel has 85 apples, and Frank has 56 apples. How many more apples does Samuel have than Frank? Or how many fewer apples does Frank have than Samuel?	$56 + $ ___ $= 85$, or $85 - 56 = $ ___	Samuel has 29 more apples than Frank.
	Larger unknown: Frank has 56 apples, and Samuel has 29 more apples than Frank. How many apples does Samuel have?	$56 + 29 = $ ___	Samuel has 85 apples.
	Smaller unknown: Samuel has 85 apples. Samuel has 29 more apples than Frank. How many apples does Frank have?	$29 + $ ___ $= 85$, or $85 - 29 = $ ___	Frank has 56 apples.

The types of problems for multiplication and division are fundamentally different than those for addition and subtraction. The types of problems are *equal groups* or *repeated addition, area and array, multiplicative comparison,* and *combination. Equal groups problems* involve making a certain number of equal-sized groups. The three numbers involved are the number of groups (factor), size of the groups (factor), and total number of the objects (product). For example, 3×6 is 3 groups of 6 objects each. Equal groups can also be interpreted in

Chapter 5: Mathematics

relation to repeated additions: $3 \times 6 = 6 + 6 + 6$. *Partitive or sharing division* and *measurement or subtractive division* are two models for division modeling related to equal groups problems. *Area and array problems* involve finding the area of a rectangular area or arrangement. For example, such a problem could involve finding the area of a rectangle that is 3 feet wide by 6 feet long, or the number of chairs in a 3 rows by 6 columns arrangement. *Multiplicative comparison problems* involve the comparison of two quantities multiplicatively. They involve finding "how many times as much" of one quantity is compared in another quantity, or "stretching" the original quantity by a certain quantity. *Combination problems* involve different combinations that can be made from two sets, like shirts and pants. The following table provides examples for each type of problem.

Multiplication and Division Problems

Type of Problem	Example of Problem	Mathematical Sentence	Solution
Equal groups or repeated addition	Multiplication: Oscar has 5 bags of apples with 17 apples in each bag. How many apples does Oscar have altogether?	$5 \times 17 =$ ___	Oscar has 85 apples altogether.
	Partition or sharing division: Oscar has 85 apples. He arranges the apples into 5 bags with the same amount of apples in each bag. How many apples are in each bag?	$85 \div 5 =$ ___	Oscar has 17 apples in each bag.
	Measurement or subtractive division: Oscar has 85 apples. He arranges the apples into bags of 17 apples each. How many bags of apples did he make?	$85 \div 17 =$ ___	Oscar has 5 bags containing 17 apples each.
Area and array	Multiplication: Oscar has a farm of apple trees planted in 5 rows of 17 apple trees in each row. How many apple trees does he have on his farm?	$5 \times 17 =$ ___	Oscar has 85 apple trees on his farm.
	Division: Oscar planted 85 palm trees on his farm. He wants to plant the trees in 5 equal rows of palm trees. How many palm trees will he need to plant in each row?	$85 \div 5 =$ ___	Oscar will need to plant 17 palm trees in each row.
Multiplicative comparison	Multiplication: Oscar has 17 apples and Tom has 5 times as many apples as Oscar does. How many apples does Tom have?	$5 \times 17 =$ ___	Tom has 85 apples.
	Division: Tom has 85 apples. This is 5 times as many as what Oscar has. How many apples does Oscar have?	$85 \div 5 =$ ___	Oscar has 17 apples.
Combination	Multiplication: How many combinations of shirts and pants can be made out of 5 shirts and 17 pants?	$5 \times 17 =$ ___	You can have 85 combinations.
	Division: If you have 5 shirts, how many pants are needed to make 85 combinations of pants and shirts?	$85 \div 5 =$ ___	You need 17 pants.

Checkpoint

For each of the following scenarios, write a mathematical sentence, and solve the problem.

1. Gloria has 120 basketballs. She wants to put 30 basketballs into each box. How many boxes does she need?

2. Bob has 12 times as many baseball cards as his friend Carlos. Carlos has 34 baseball cards. How many baseball cards does Bob have?

3. Nancy has 123 papers and Mary has 67 papers. How many fewer papers does Mary have than Nancy?

4. Martha has 108 M&M's to be shared equally among her and her 8 friends. How many M&M's would each one get?

Checkpoint Answers

1. $120 \div 30 = 4$. Gloria needs 4 boxes.

2. $12 \times 34 = 408$. Bob has 408 baseball cards.

3. $123 - 67 = 56$. Mary has 56 fewer papers than Nancy.

4. $108 \div 9 = 12$. Martha and her friends would get 12 M&M's each.

Apply Number Theory Concepts

Factors and **multiples** are important ideas related to number theory. Factors are any of the numbers or symbols that you multiply together to get another number or product. For example, 5 and 6 are factors of 30 because $5 \times 6 = 30$; similarly, 1 and 30 are factors of 30 because $1 \times 30 = 30$. Other possible factors of 30 are 2, 3, 10, and 15. This is because $2 \times 15 = 30$ and $3 \times 10 = 30$. So all the possible whole number factors of 30 are 1, 2, 3, 5, 6, 10, 15, and 30. The number itself and 1 are always factors of a given number, as you can see in the factors of 30. In a similar manner, you can say that 30 is a multiple of 5 because $5 \times 6 = 30$. So 30 is a multiple of 1, 2, 3, 5, 6, 10, 15, and 30. The number itself is always a multiple of a number. For example, the multiples of 5 are 5, 10, 15, 20, 25, 30, … There is an infinite number of multiples for a given number.

A number with exactly two whole-number factors (1 and the number itself) is considered a **prime number. Whole numbers** are natural numbers and zero. **Natural numbers** are the counting numbers (1, 2, 3, 4, 5, ...). The first few prime numbers are 2, 3, 5, 7, 11, 13, and 17. On the other hand, **composite numbers** are numbers composed of several whole-number factors. For example, 30 is a composite number because it is composed of several whole-number factors other than 1 and itself, like 2, 3, 5, 6, 10, and 15. The number 1 is not considered a prime or a composite number because it only has one whole-number factor, itself.

The **greatest common factor (GCF)** of a set of numbers is the largest number that is a factor of all the given numbers. For example, find the GCF of 30 and 20, or GCF (30, 20). First, find the factors of 30: 1, 2, 3, 5, 6, 10, 15, and 30. Second, find the factors of 20: 1, 2, 4, 5, 10, and 20. The GCF of 30 and 20 is 10, which is the largest common factor that divides both numbers evenly. The **least common multiple (LCM)** of a set of numbers is the smallest non-zero multiple that is divisible by all of the given numbers. For example, find the LCM of 30 and 20, or LCM (30, 20). First, find the non-zero multiples of 30: 30, 60, 90, 120, … Second, find the non-zero multiples of 20: 20, 40, 60, 80, 100, 120, … As you can see, the least common multiple of 30 and 20 is 60. There are other common multiples of 30 and 20, like 120, but only 60 is the least common multiple of these two numbers.

The *rules of divisibility* are also important in the area of number theory. The following is a list of the most common divisibility rules:

- Division by zero is undefined or not possible.
- Only whole numbers ending in 0, 2, 4, 6, or 8 are divisible by 2. For example, 256 is divisible by 2 because it ends in 6, and 257 is not divisible by 2 because it does not end in 0, 2, 4, 6, or 8.
- Only whole numbers ending in 0 or 5 are divisible by 5. For example, 255 is divisible by 5 because it ends in 5, and 257 is not divisible by 5 because it does not end in 0 or 5.
- Only whole numbers whose digits add up to a number divisible by 3 are also divisible by 3. For example, to check if 234 is divisible by 3, add $2 + 3 + 4$, which is equal to 9. Since 9 is divisible by 3, then 234 is also divisible by 3.
- Only whole numbers whose digits add up to a number divisible by 9 are also divisible by 9. For example, to check if 234 is divisible by 9, add $2 + 3 + 4$, which is equal to 9. Since 9 is divisible by 9, then 234 is also divisible by 9.
- A number is divisible by 6 if it is divisible by both 2 and 3. For example, 252 has digits that add up to 9, which is divisible by 3, which makes 252 divisible by 3; it ends in 2, which makes it divisible by 2. So it is divisible by both 2 and 3, which makes it also divisible by 6.
- A number is divisible by 4 if the number formed by the last two digits is evenly divisible by 4. For example, 3,480 has 80 as its last two digits, and 80 is divisible by 4. Therefore, 3,480 is also divisible by 4.

- A number is divisible by 8 if the number formed by the last three digits is evenly divisible by 8. For example, 3,480 has 480 as its last digits, and 480 is divisible by 8. Therefore, 3,480 is also divisible by 8.

- Only whole numbers ending in 0 are divisible by 10. For example, 250 is divisible by 10 because it ends in 0, and 257 is not divisible by 10 because it does not end in 0.

Number properties are another important aspect of number theory. The following is a list of some of the number properties for addition, subtraction, multiplication, and division:

Commutative property:	Addition: $a + b = b + a$	Multiplication: $ab = ba$
Associative property:	Addition: $a + (b + c) = (a + b) + c$	Multiplication: $a(bc) = (ab)c$
Identity property:	Additive identity: $a + 0 = a$	Multiplicative identity: $a \cdot 1 = a$
Inverse property:	Additive inverse: $a + (-a) = 0$	Multiplicative inverse: $a \cdot \left(\dfrac{1}{a}\right) = 1$
Distributive property:	Multiplication over addition:	$a(b + c) = ab + ac$

Checkpoint

1. Find the whole-number factors of 240.

2. Find the first five multiples of 35.

3. What is the GCF and LCM of 45 and 15?

4. If the GCF $(a, b) = 1$, then the LCM $(a, b) = $ _____

Checkpoint Answers

1. The whole-number factors of 240 are 1, 2, 3, 4, 5, 6, 8, 10, 12, 15, 16, 20, 24, 30, 40, 48, 60, 80, 120, and 240.

2. The first five multiples of 35 are 35, 70, 105, 140, and 175.

3. The factors of 45 are 1, 3, 5, 9, 15, and 45; the factors of 15 are 1, 3, 5, and 15. The common factors of 45 and 15 are 1, 3, 5, and 15. The GCF of 45 and 15 is 15, and the LCM of 45 and 15 is 45 ($5 \times 3 \times 3 = 45$).

4. If the GCF $(a, b) = 1$, then the LCM $(a, b) = a \cdot b$ or ab.

Apply the Order of Operations

The order of operations must be followed when several operations are involved in mathematical sentences or algebraic expressions. The mnemonic PEMDAS can help you remember the order of operations:

- **P** (parentheses): Simplify inside the grouping characters such as parentheses, brackets, square roots, fraction bars, and others.

- **E** (exponents): Apply exponents. You should treat exponential expressions ("powers") as multiplication.

- **M** (multiplication) and **D** (division): Do multiplication and division, working from left to right.

- **A** (addition) and **S** (subtraction): Do addition and subtraction, working from left to right.

Be careful with operations on integers, fractions, and decimals. Pay special attention to the sign (positive or negative value) of the answers.

- For addition and subtraction, the rules are the following:
  - Adding or subtracting when at least one negative number is involved, you may think of adding as gaining, subtracting as losing, positive numbers as credits, and negative numbers as debits. Adding or gaining -9 is actually losing 9: $-4 + -9 = -13$, $4 + -9 = -5$.

- For multiplication and division, the rules are the following:
  - Multiplying or dividing two positive or two negative numbers gives a positive value.
  - Multiplying or dividing a positive by a negative (or a negative by a positive) gives a negative number: $-4 \times 8 = -32$, or $-45 \div 5 = -9$.

Following the order of operations, solving the expression $25 + 9 \times 5 - 7$ requires that you multiply 9×5 before performing addition and subtraction from left to right: $25 + 45 - 7 = 63$. This is different when parentheses are involved. For example, $(25 + 9) \times 5 - 7$ requires that you add $25 + 9$, then multiply this sum by 5, and finally subtract 7: $34 \times 5 = 170$, $170 - 7 = 163$.

Checkpoint

Simplify the following expressions.

1. $5^3 - 4x - 9$
2. $34 - 12 \times 3^2 - 4(3 - 7 \times 5)$

Checkpoint Answers

1. $5^3 - 4x - 9 = 125 - 4x - 9 = 116 - 4x$

2. $$\begin{aligned}
34 - 12 \times 3^2 - 4(3 - 7 \times 5) &= 34 - 12 \times 9 - 4(3 - 35) \\
&= 34 - 108 - 4(-32) \\
&= 34 - 108 - (-128) \\
&= -74 - (-128) \\
&= -74 + 128 \\
&= 54
\end{aligned}$$

Algebraic Thinking

Algebraic reasoning begins in elementary grades with continuing and generalizing repeating and growing patterns, identifying and using properties to show that expressions are equivalent, and representing linear equations and inequalities in real-world settings. This section addresses the following areas related to algebraic thinking:

- Linear Relationships
- Properties

Linear Relationships

A relationship is linear if the relationship between two **variables** is a constant rate of change of one variable in relation to another. For example, a rate of 55 miles per hour is a constant rate of change. For each hour, the distance changes by 55 miles. Relationships can be represented in multiple ways, the most common of which are tables, **graphs,** and equations/expressions. Many of these relationships are first displayed as patterns.

Example: For the following pattern, find the perimeter (P) of the train in terms of the number of octagons (n).

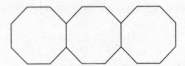

Solution: This pattern can be thought of in numerous ways. We can represent the pattern visually. If you separated each of the octagons, there would be 8 sides for each figure. This gives a perimeter of $8n$ for n octagons. When the octagons are connected, two sides are lost at each connection. There is one fewer connection than the number of octagons. This gives a formula of $P = 8n - 2(n - 1)$.

This can also be thought of visually by looking at the end shapes and the middle shapes. Each of the end shapes has 7 sides. That gives 14 sides. The shapes in the middle give 6 more sides each. There are two fewer sides in the middle than the total. This gives the formula of $P = 14 + 6(n - 2)$.

A table could also be used, which might look like this:

# Octagons (n)	Perimeter (P)
1	8
2	14
3	20
4	26

For each additional octagon, the perimeter increases by 6. This means the **slope** (or rate of change) is 6. The value for 1 octagon is 8, which is 2 more than the slope, so the formula would become $P = 6n + 2$.

Checkpoint

1. A square garden measures $n \times n$. The gardener wants to place a tile border around the garden, which is 1 tile wide. How many 1×1 tiles are needed?

2. Find the number of squares (S) in the nth figure:

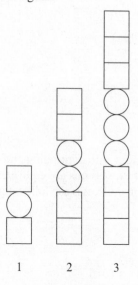

1   2   3

Checkpoint Answers

1. $4n + 4$

   There are n tiles for each side of the garden, so 4 sides of length n. There are also 4 corners of the border that are not sides of the garden.

2. The number of squares is twice the figure number. Therefore, $S = 2n$.

Properties

There are three main properties that are necessary for symbolic manipulation of algebraic expressions.

The **commutative property** says that the order in which you add two terms together or multiply two terms together does not affect the sum or product. If the numbers are a and b, then $a + b = b + a$ and $a \times b = b \times a$. This property only applies to addition and multiplication.

The **associative property** says that when more than two terms are added together or multiplied together, the order in which the terms are paired does not affect the sum or product. If the numbers are a, b, and c, then $(a + b) + c = a + (b + c)$ and $a(bc) = (ab)c$. This property only applies to addition and multiplication.

The **distributive property** says that when a sum or difference is multiplied by a common term, each part of the sum or difference can be multiplied by the common term and then added or subtracted. If the numbers are a, b, and c, then $a(b + c) = ab + ac$ and $a(b - c) = ab - ac$.

These properties can be used to demonstrate that two expressions are equivalent.

Example: Show that the expressions given to the octagon train problem are equivalent.

Solution: The equations were: $P = 8n - 2(n - 1)$, $P = 14 + 6(n - 2)$, and $P = 6n + 2$.

In the first expression, the distributive property can be used first, followed by the associative property in combining like terms: $P = 8n - 2(n - 1) = 8n - 2n + 2 = 6n + 2$. The same can be done on the second expression: $P = 14 + 6(n - 2) = 14 + 6n - 12 = 6n + (14 - 12) = 6n + 2$. These three expressions are all equivalent to each other.

These properties can also be used to solve one- and two-step linear equations and inequalities. The first approach to solving linear equations and inequalities is the idea of balance. When two expressions are equivalent, we must change them in the same ways or they do not remain equivalent. Therefore, if you subtract something from one expression, for it to continue to be equal to the other expression, you must also subtract it from the second expression. The commutative, associative, and distributive properties can continue to be used in these situations as well.

Example: Solve $3x + 8 = 14$ for x.

Solution: First, the term with x must be isolated. In order to eliminate $+8$, 8 needs to be subtracted from each side. If you only subtracted 8 from $3x + 8$, the expressions would no longer be equal. Once $3x$ is isolated, the multiplication needs to be undone through division.

$$3x + 8 = 14$$
$$3x + 8 - 8 = 14 - 8$$
$$3x = 6$$
$$\frac{3x}{3} = \frac{6}{3}$$
$$x = 2$$

Checkpoint

1. True or false: The commutative property can be used with subtraction.

2. Fill in the blank: The associative property says that $(5 + 2) + 8 = 5 + ($_____$)$.

3. Solve $7x = 2x + 35$ for x.

Checkpoint Answers

1. False

2. $2 + 8$

3. $x = 7$

   Starting with $7x = 2x + 35$, subtract $2x$ from each side: $7x - 2x = 2x + 35 - 2x$. Then simplify: $5x = 35$. Next, divide both sides by 5: $\frac{5x}{5} = \frac{35}{5}$. Then simplify: $x = 7$.

Competency 3: Knowledge of Fractions, Ratios, and Integers

Competency Description

According to the *Competencies and Skills Required for Teacher Certification in Florida,* 20th Edition (available at www.fldoe.org/asp/ftce/pdf/ftce20edition.pdf), **Competency 3** for the Elementary Education (K–6) Subject Area Examination (SAE) Mathematics subtest addresses the following key indicators:

1. Compare fractions, integers, and integers with integer exponents and place them on a number line.

2. Convert among standard measurement units within and between measurement systems (e.g., metric, U.S. customary) in the context of multistep, real-world problems.

3. Solve problems involving addition, subtraction, multiplication, and division of fractions, including mixing whole numbers and fractions, decimals and percents by using visual models and equations to represent the problems and their solutions.

4. Select the representation (e.g., linear, area, set model) that best represents the problem and solution, given a word problem or equation involving fractions.

5. Solve real-world problems involving ratios and proportions.

Overview

Knowledge of **fractions, ratios,** and **integers** is less natural than cardinal numbers. They are more algebraic in nature and require a deeper conceptual understanding in order to understand some possible generalizations and basic properties. There are approximately **9 questions** that address Competency 3. This section addresses the following areas related to **Competency 3** key indicators:

- Associate Multiple Representations of Real Numbers
- Compare the Relative Size of Numbers
- Apply Ratios, Proportions, and Percents
- Represent Numbers in a Variety of Equivalent Forms
- Use Estimation in Problem Solving Situations

Associate Multiple Representations of Real Numbers

Real numbers are the set of both **rational numbers,** which can be expressed as a ratio of two integers, $\frac{a}{b}$, where $b \neq 0$, and **irrational numbers,** which include nonrepeating, nonterminating decimals like π or $\sqrt{2}$. You can basically have three forms of representing or **modeling** a number (and other mathematical concepts and skills): **concrete, pictorial** (also known as **representational** and graphic representations), and **symbolic** (also known as **abstract**) levels. Children seem to learn best when early learning experiences start with the use of concrete materials (such as toys, cubes, and other objects) to represent numerical ideas. However, concrete activities should not be used exclusively. Children should also have experiences involving the representational and abstract levels. The representational level involves pictorial representations of the manipulative materials or objects used for learning. Number lines, pie graphs, bar graphs, and charts can also be used as representation of numerical values. The abstract level involves the use of symbols to represent ideas.

For example, numbers can be modeled in a way that children come to understand and know. At the concrete level, manipulative materials are used to facilitate this learning. The manipulative materials could be cubes, pencils, books, or people they count to find how many are in a set or group. In this manner, students find the numberness or cardinality of the set. Other counting number–related ideas are equality, more than, less than, combining groups, and separating groups, which could be modeled similarly. In a similar way, pictures (or pictorial representations) or drawings are used to model number ideas. The symbolic form of a number is called a **numeral.** The cardinality of a set with three objects is represented by using the numeral "3" at the symbolic level. The number name "three" is also considered to be at the symbolic level. The abstract level is involved when you say words and read or write symbols. Children's ability to transfer ideas from one mode or level of a number idea demonstrates their degree of understanding of the idea.

Examples of Multiple Representations of Numbers

Set of Numbers	Word Name	Standard Numeral	Pictorial Model
Whole numbers	Five	5	Let each square equal one unit:
Integers	Negative three	–3	Let gray represent negative numbers and white represent positive numbers: Note that +1 + –1 = 0:
Fractions	One-fifth	$\dfrac{1}{5}$	Let each square equal one out of five pieces:
Decimals	Five-tenths	0.5	Let each square equal one out of ten pieces:

Checkpoint

1. Fill in the blank: The _____ cognitive level is involved when children are trying to find out how many crayons are contained in a box of crayons.

2. Peter wrote the following symbol on the board: 3. Is he writing a number or a numeral?

3. True or false: A number is a symbolic representation of a numerical quantity.

Checkpoint Answers

1. concrete

2. numeral

3. False

Compare the Relative Size of Numbers

When you compare numbers, you need to keep in mind the equivalent ways a quantity could be represented. For example, $\dfrac{1}{2}$ is a fraction that could be expressed as $\dfrac{2}{4}$ using an equivalent fraction, 0.5 or 0.50 using decimals, and 50% using percents. The following are other examples of multiple representations of numbers:

$$\sqrt{144} = \sqrt{12^2} = 12$$

$$200 = 200.00 = \frac{400}{2} = 20,000\% = 2 \times 100 = 2 \times 10^2$$

A fraction can be converted into a decimal by dividing the **numerator** by the **denominator**. For example, $\dfrac{3}{4}$ is equivalent to 0.75 because 3 divided by 4 is equal to 0.75. Similarly, $9\dfrac{1}{4}$ is equivalent to 9.25. The **decimal** numbers are terminating or non-terminating repeating decimals. A non-terminating non-repeating number is called an irrational number, which is a subset of the real numbers (the square root of 2 is an example of an

171

irrational number). A simple fraction can be converted into a terminating (for example, 0.45, 0.5, and 0.010) or a non-terminating repeating decimal (for example, 0.66... or $0.\bar{6}$, where the line on top of the 6 indicates that 6 is repeating). A terminating decimal can be converted into a fraction by writing the decimal number as a fraction with the denominator as a power of 10, and then simplifying this fraction to lowest terms. For example, 0.245 is equivalent to $\dfrac{245}{1,000}$ (use as many zeroes as digits in the decimal part of the number; in this case, 3 zeroes for 3 digits in 0.245). This can be simplified to $\dfrac{49}{200}$ by dividing the numerator and denominator by 5 (the greatest common factor of 245 and 1,000).

A decimal (or fraction after being converted into a decimal) can be converted into a percent by shifting the decimal point two places to the right and adding the percent sign (%) to it. For example, 0.39 can be written as 39%, 0.436 as 43.6%, 5.49 as 549%, or .005 as 0.5%. The process of converting a percent to a decimal is the reverse of converting a decimal to a percent. You can convert a percent to a decimal by shifting the decimal point two places to the left without the percent sign. For example, 78% can be written as 0.78, 978% as 9.78, 65.7% as 0.657, and 0.6% as 0.006.

Exponential notation is another way to represent equivalent versions of a number. It is a way to represent repeated multiplication in a simple format. In this sense, **exponents** are used to indicate the number of times an expression is multiplied by itself. For example, $5 \times 5 \times 5$ can be written in exponential form as 5^3, indicating the number of times 5 is multiplied by itself three times. The number 4,329 can be expressed using expanded notation using number name form as 4 thousands, 3 hundreds, 2 tens, and 9 ones; using numeric form as $4 \times 1,000 + 3 \times 100 + 2 \times 10 + 9 \times 1$, and using exponential form as $4 \times 10^3 + 3 \times 10^2 + 2 \times 10^1 + 9 \times 10^0$, where $10^0 = 1$. Here are other examples of expressions with exponents: $y^2 = y \cdot y$ ("$\cdot$" is used to express multiplication), $\dfrac{1}{a \cdot a} = \dfrac{1}{a^2} = a^{-2}$, $a^3 \cdot a^2 = a^5$ (add exponents), $(a^2)^3 = a^6$, and $\sqrt{a} = a^{\frac{1}{2}}$.

Checkpoint

1. Order the following numbers from least to greatest: 60%, 1, –0.75, 0.64, –1.5, $\dfrac{7}{9}$, 2^{-2}, and 1×10^{-2}.

2. Express 83,476 in exponential notation.

3. Is $-\dfrac{1}{4}$ an integer? Explain.

4. Convert $\dfrac{5}{8}$ to a percent.

5. Convert 0.54 to a fraction.

Checkpoint Answers

1. –1.5, –0.75, 1×10^{-2}, 2^{-2}, 60%, 0.64, $\dfrac{7}{9}$, and 1

   $$1 \times 10^{-2} = 1 \times \frac{1}{10^2} = 1 \times \frac{1}{100} = 1 \times 0.01 = 0.01$$

   $$2^{-2} = \frac{1}{2^2} = \frac{1}{4} = 0.25$$

   $$60\% = 0.6 = 0.60$$

   $$\frac{7}{9} = 0.777... \text{ or } 0.\bar{7}$$

2. $8 \times 10^4 + 3 \times 10^3 + 4 \times 10^2 + 7 \times 10^1 + 6 \times 10^0$

3. No, because not all fractions are integers. Negative and positive fractions are not integers unless they are equivalent to whole numbers or their negative counterpart. In this case, $-\dfrac{1}{4}$ (or –0.25 in decimal form) cannot be expressed as a whole number or the negative of a whole number.

4. 62.5%

Since $5 \div 8 = 0.625$, then $\dfrac{5}{8}$ is equal to 62.5%.

5. $\dfrac{27}{50}$

$0.54 = \dfrac{54}{100} = \dfrac{27}{50}$

Apply Ratios, Proportions, and Percents

A **ratio** is another way to represent or use fractions. Ratios are involved when you compare two numbers or quantities. The following are four real-world examples of ratios: four bicycles cost $480.00, the map scale is 1 centimeter per kilometer, the speed limit is 70 miles per hour, the sale tax for the sofa is 7% (notice that a **percent** is a type of ratio). A **rate** is a specific case of ratios. A rate is involved when the measuring units in describing two quantities being compared are different. For example, speed situations: I ran 200 meters in 25 seconds, or I bought a six-pack of cola for $1.50. The **unit rate** is involved when the second term in the rate is equal to 1. For example, Lourdes can type 36 words per minute, or Paul earns $15.00 per hour.

A **proportion** involves a statement that indicates that two ratios are equal. For example, at the market today, four apples cost $1.20, then eight apples should cost $2.40. This could be stated in the following proportion:

$$\frac{4}{1.20} = \frac{8}{2.40}$$

Notice that the relationship between quantities on each side of the proportion (or for each ratio) is presented in the same manner: number of apples to number of dollars. This order could be changed as long as you do the same on both sides of the proportion. For example, an equivalent form of this proportion using the ratio of dollars to apples is the following:

$$\frac{1.20}{4} = \frac{2.40}{8}$$

Checkpoint

1. Does the following statement represent a proportion?

$$\frac{4}{20} = \frac{8}{50}$$

2. What value of x would make the following proportion true?

$$\frac{4}{8} = \frac{x}{24}$$

3. David said that 20% is a unit rate. Is he right?

4. Find the item with the best unit price:

$1.45 for 12 ounces

$1.90 for 15 ounces

$4.34 for 45 ounces

Checkpoint Answers

1. No, because the two ratios are not equivalent.

2. 12

3. No, it is a rate but is not a unit rate.

4. To solve, first find the unit price for each situation:

   $1.45 for 12 ounces: 1.45 ÷ 12 is about $0.12 per ounce

   $1.90 for 15 ounces: 1.90 ÷ 15 is about $0.13 per ounce

   $4.34 for 45 ounces: 4.34 ÷ 45 is about $0.10 per ounce

   The best unit price is $4.34 for 45 ounces.

Represent Numbers in a Variety of Equivalent Forms

Besides multiple representations of number quantities using word names and standard numerals, we can also represent numbers in different equivalent forms using whole numbers, fractions, decimals, percents, and exponents. The following table offers some examples.

Examples of Equivalent Forms of Numbers

Form	Two hundred thirty-four cubes in a set	Seven-eighths of a region
Whole number	234	
Integer	234 or +234	
Fraction	$\dfrac{234}{1}$	$\dfrac{7}{8}$
Decimal	234.0	0.875
Percent	23,400%	87.5%
Exponential	$2 \times 10^2 + 3 \times 10^1 + 4 \times 10^0$	$8 \times 10^{-1} + 7 \times 10^{-2} + 5 \times 10^{-3}$

Checkpoint

Complete the following table by expressing the numbers in their equivalent forms:

Form	One hundred sixty-eight pencils in a box	One-fourth of a region	Five-eighths of a region
Whole number			
Integer			
Fraction			
Decimal			
Percent			
Exponential			

Checkpoint Answers

Form	One hundred sixty-eight pencils in a box	One-fourth of a region	Five-eighths of a region
Whole number	168		
Integer	168 or +168		

Form	One hundred sixty-eight pencils in a box	One-fourth of a region	Five-eighths of a region
Fraction	$\dfrac{168}{1}$	$\dfrac{1}{4}$	$\dfrac{5}{8}$
Decimal	168.0	0.25	0.625
Percent	16,800%	25%	62.5%
Exponential	$1 \times 10^2 + 6 \times 10^1 + 8 \times 10^0$	$2 \times 10^{-1} + 5 \times 10^{-2}$	$6 \times 10^{-1} + 6 \times 10^{-2} + 5 \times 10^{-3}$

Use Estimation in Problem Solving Situations

Estimation is a very important part of problem solving. It can be used to test the reasonableness of possible solutions to problems, calculator results, and mental calculations. This is especially relevant for multiple-choice items like the ones included on the Mathematics subtest. Five types of estimation strategies are described in this section: *front-end, rounding, clustering, compatible numbers,* and *special numbers.* The *front-end strategy* involves the left-most or highest place value digits. For example, you can estimate the sum of 345 + 675 by adding the front-end digits of these numbers, in this case 3 + 6 = 9, and estimating 900 for the sum. Using the *rounding strategy,* this same exercise would round 345 as 300 (the number is closer to 300 than to 400) and 675 as 700 (the number is closer to 700 than to 600), and find the estimated sum to be 1,000 instead. The *clustering strategy* works well when the set of numbers involved are close together. For example, you can estimate the sum of 37 + 68 + 13 by noticing that 37 + 13 is equal to 50. As a result, the sum is close to 50 + 70 (by rounding 68), and the estimated sum is 120. In the *compatible* (or "friendly") *numbers strategy,* you adjust the numbers in order to make them easier to work with. For instance, when dividing numbers, you would need to adjust the divisor, the dividend, or both in order to make them easier to work with mentally. For example, to estimate the answer to 73 ÷ 5 using this strategy, you need to notice that 75 is close to 73 and divisible by 5, then solve 75 ÷ 5, which is equal to 15 and your estimate. With the *special numbers strategy,* you need to look for numbers that are close to "special" values that are easy to work with, like one-half, one-fourth, or powers of ten. For example, to estimate 54% of 243, you could notice that 54% is close to one-half (or 50%) and 243 is close to 240. One-half of 240 is 120, so 54% of 243 is about 120.

Checkpoint

Estimate the answers to the following problems:

1. 16 + 11 + 24 + 35

2. 25 + 44 + 35 + 80 + 57 + 60

3. 367 + 532

4. 37 + 41 + 39 + 39 + 44 + 42

Checkpoint Answers

1. 86

   Using the compatible numbers strategy, 16 + 24 = 40, 40 + 35 = 75, and 75 + 11 = 86. Or, 11 + 24 = 35, 35 + 35 = 70, and 70 + 16 = 86.

2. 300

   Using the compatible numbers strategy, 25 + 80 is about 100, 44 + 57 is about 100, and 35 + 60 is about 100. So your estimate would be about 300.

3. 900

   Using the rounding strategy, we would have 400 + 500 = 900.

4. 240

   Using the clustering strategy, notice that all the numbers are close to 40, so a good estimate would be 6 × 40, or 240.

Competency 4: Knowledge of Measurement, Data Analysis, and Statistics

Competency Description

According to the *Competencies and Skills Required for Teacher Certification in Florida,* 20th Edition (available at www.fldoe.org/asp/ftce/pdf/ftce20edition.pdf), **Competency 4** for the Elementary Education (K–6) Subject Area Examination (SAE) Mathematics subtest addresses the following key indicators:

1. Calculate and interpret statistics of variability (e.g., range, mean, absolute deviation) and central tendency (e.g., mean, median).
2. Analyze and interpret data through the use of frequency tables and graphs.
3. Select appropriate measurement units to solve problems involving estimates and measurements.
4. Evaluate the choice of measures of center and variability, with respect to the shape of the data distribution and the context in which the data were gathered.
5. Solve problems involving distance, time, liquid volume, mass, and money, which may include units expressed as fractions or decimals.

Overview

This section provides a look at important applications of mathematics. It involves the ideas of variability, central tendency, use of data and graphs, making predictions, and drawing conclusions. There are approximately **8 questions** that address Competency 4. This section addresses the following areas related to **Competency 4** key indicators:

- Concepts of Variability and Central Tendency
- Frequency Tables and Graphs

Concepts of Variability and Central Tendency

Range is a measure of variability. The range of a set of scores or quantities is a measure of the spread or variation of the numbers. It is the difference between the highest quantity and lowest quantity in the data set. The measures of central tendency of a set of quantities include the **mean, mode,** and **median.** The mean is the sum of a set of quantities divided by the total number of quantities. The median is the middle quantity of a set of quantities when arranged according to size (or numerical order); for an even number of quantities, the median is the **average** of the middle two quantities. The mode is the number that occurs with the greatest **frequency** in a set of quantities. There may be one or more modes or no mode for a set of data. A data set with two modes is *bimodal.*

Checkpoint

The following is a data set based on test scores:

78	78	67	85	92	78	95	72	72	74	85
60	95	78	92	85	65	92	66	78	78	92

Using this set of data, find each of the following:

1. Range
2. Mode
3. Mean
4. Median

Checkpoint Answers

Order data from least to greatest: 60, 65, 66, 67, 72, 72, 74, 78, 78, 78, 78, 78, 78, 85, 85, 85, 92, 92, 92, 92, 95, 95

1. Range: 95 – 60 = 35. The range is 35.

2. Mode: 78 has the highest frequency, with 6.

3. Mean: $(60 + 65 + 66 + 67 + 2(72) + 74 + 6(78) + 3(85) + 4(92) + 2(95)) \div 22 = 1{,}757 \div 22 = 79.8636...$

4. Median: The middle of the data is the 11th score ($22 \div 2 = 11$). Since the number of values for this data set is an even number, the median is the average of the middle two scores. Counting from left to right 78 is the 11th value, and counting from right to left 78 is also the 11th value. Since they are the same value, the middle number is 78. Thus, the median is 78.

Frequency Tables and Graphs

Frequency tables are used to organize a set of data. They show the number of pieces of data that fall within given intervals or categories. The information in the frequency table can be used to organize the data in graphs. **Bar graphs, line graphs,** and **pictographs** are types of statistical graphs. Bar graphs are used to compare quantities and may be made up of all vertical bars or all horizontal bars. This type of graph is used mainly for purposes of comparison. Line graphs involve lines to show how values change over time. Pictographs are diagrams or graphs that involve pictured objects, icons, or symbols to convey ideas or information.

Checkpoint

The following is a data set based on test scores:

78	78	67	85	92	78	95	72	72	74	85
60	95	78	92	85	65	92	66	78	78	92

Using this set of data, find each of the following:

1. Make a frequency table using this data set.

2. Construct a bar graph using this data set.

Checkpoint Answers

1. Frequency table:

Scores	Frequency
60	1
65	1
66	1
67	1
72	2
74	1
78	6
85	3
92	4
95	2

2. Construct a bar graph using this data set.

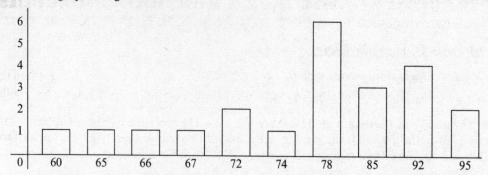

Competency 5: Knowledge of Geometric Concepts

Competency Description

According to the *Competencies and Skills Required for Teacher Certification in Florida,* 20th Edition (available at www.fldoe.org/asp/ftce/pdf/ftce20edition.pdf), **Competency 5** for the Elementary Education (K–6) Subject Area Examination (SAE) Mathematics subtest addresses the following key indicators:

1. Apply geometric properties and relationships to solve problems involving perimeter, area, surface area, and volume.

2. Identify and locate ordered pairs in all four quadrants of a rectangular coordinate system.

3. Identify and analyze properties of three-dimensional shapes using formal mathematical terms such as volume, faces, edges, and vertices.

4. Classify two-dimensional figures in a hierarchy based on mathematical properties.

Overview

Geometry is the study of shapes. Knowledge of geometry also includes spatial sense. In elementary grades, knowledge of geometry includes identification of attributes, classifications, and properties of shapes as well as connections between geometry and other areas of mathematics such as algebraic ideas of the **coordinate system.** Measurement is the assignment of a numerical value to an attribute of an object (that is, length, **area, perimeter,** distance, volume). Measurement is practical and pervasive in aspects of everyday life. Development of measurement ideas also provides opportunities to connect concepts in mathematics. There are approximately **6 questions** that address Competency 5. This section will address the following areas related to **Competency 5** key indicators:

- Geometry
  - Attributes, Properties, and Classifications
  - Congruence and Similarity
- Measurement
  - Geometric Measurement
  - Scientific Measurement
- Coordinate Plane or Grid

Geometry

Geometry is defined as "the branch of mathematics that deals with the deduction of the properties, measurement, and relationships of points, lines, angles, and figures in space from their defining conditions by means of certain assumed properties of space" (geometry in Dictionary.com, n.d.). Aspects of geometry in elementary grades include:

- Identification of attributes, properties, and classifications of two- and three-dimensional shapes
- Similarity and congruency

Attributes, Properties, and Classifications

Attributes are those aspects of a shape that are particular to a specific shape. For example, in the figure shown below, attributes may include that both shapes have four sides. The shape on the left is large and gray while the shape on the right is small and black.

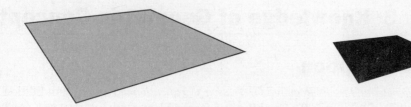

Properties are those aspects of a shape that define the shape. For example, a property of the shapes shown above is that they each have four sides, making them both quadrilaterals. Properties define a type of shape (for example, rectangle, square, circle). Properties are true for any shape falling into that shape type. All rectangles have right angles. All squares have four equal sides.

Classifications use the properties of shapes to lead to a hierarchical structure. Classifications are those names given that use properties to classify but also take into account the relationships between different classifications of shapes. An example of the hierarchical structure can be seen in quadrilaterals. All **quadrilaterals** have four sides, a defining property for the classification of a quadrilateral; however, there are also more specific names for quadrilaterals with different defining properties. A **trapezoid** is a specific type of quadrilateral in which exactly one set of sides is parallel. This is a defining property for the classification of trapezoid. Likewise, a **parallelogram** is a specific type of quadrilateral in which exactly two sets of sides are parallel. This is a defining property for the classification of parallelogram and makes parallelograms different from trapezoids.

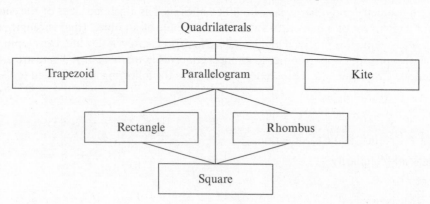

The most common classification for shapes is a polygon, which is then further classified by the number of sides. A **polygon** is a two-dimensional figure that is closed and contains at least three straight sides that meet only at corners. Under polygons, classifications are determined solely based on how many sides the shape has, not on any particular relationship between the sides (that is, they don't have to be all the same length).

Name	Number of Sides
Triangle	3
Quadrilateral	4
Pentagon	5
Hexagon	6
Heptagon	7

Name	Number of Sides
Octagon	8
Nonagon	9
Decagon	10
Dodecagon	12

All other polygons are named based on the number of sides. For example, an 11-sided polygon is an 11-gon. An 18-sided polygon is an 18-gon.

Under triangles and quadrilaterals, there are more specific classifications. **Triangles** include classifications based on angles (**acute, obtuse, right**) and on sides (**scalene, isosceles, equilateral**). Quadrilaterals include **trapezoids, kites, parallelograms, rectangles, rhombuses,** and **squares**.

Three-dimensional figures are classified as **polyhedron** (plural, polyhedra) or non-polyhedron. Polyhedra are three-dimensional figures whose **faces** are all polygons. **Edges** are where faces intersect. A **vertex** is where edges intersect.

Polyhedra are divided into prisms and pyramids. **Prisms** are polyhedra that have two congruent and parallel faces. The other faces are rectangles or parallelograms. A prism is named by the shape of its base (for example, triangular prism, rectangular prism). **Pyramids** are polyhedra that have one base with all other faces intersecting at one point. Pyramids are also named by the shape of their base (for example, triangular pyramid, rectangular pyramid).

Non-polyhedra include cylinders, cones, and spheres. **Cylinders** can be thought of as prism-like with circular bases. A **cone** can be thought of as pyramid-like with a circular base. In **spheres,** all points on the surface are the same distance from the center, such as a ball.

Checkpoint

1. What is the difference between attributes and properties?

2. What are the two special types of polyhedra?

3. How many sides does a nonagon have?

Checkpoint Answers

1. Attributes are aspects related to a specific shape. Properties define a set of shapes.

2. Prisms and pyramids

3. Nine

Congruence and Similarity

Two shapes are **congruent** ($\cong$) if all aspects of the shapes are identical. They have the same side lengths, same angle measurements, area, etc. If you were to cut one shape out, it would fit exactly over the other: same shape, same size.

Two shapes are **similar** ($\sim$) if the side lengths are proportional. Angle measurements are the same in both shapes, but the sides are proportional: same shape, different size.

Similarity can also be thought of as a dilation. **Dilation** is one of four geometric transformations: **translation** (slide), **reflection** (flip), **rotation** (turn), and dilation.

When shapes are congruent, side lengths and angles can be determined by examining the figures themselves. For example, if $\triangle ABC \cong \triangle DEF$, then $AB = DE$, $BC = EF$, and $AC = DF$. Likewise, $\angle A \cong \angle D$, $\angle B \cong \angle E$, and $\angle C \cong \angle F$.

Example: If $\triangle ABC \cong \triangle DEF$, find the values of x, y, and z as well as the measures of $\angle C$, $\angle D$, $\angle E$, and $\angle F$.

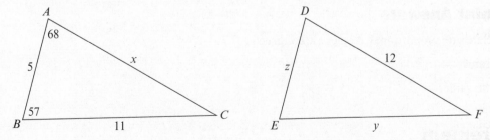

Solution: Since $\triangle ABC \cong \triangle DEF$, then $AB = DE$, $BC = EF$, and $AC = DF$. Then $x = 12$, $y = 11$, and $z = 5$. The measure of $\angle C$ can be found by using the fact that the angles of a triangle add up to 180 degrees. There are two angles given: 57 degrees and 68 degrees. These total 125 degrees. A triangle's angles total 180 degrees, so m∠C = 180 − 125 = 55 degrees. Since the triangles are congruent, m∠D = 68, m∠E = 57, and m∠F = 55.

When shapes are similar, side lengths can be determined by establishing and solving a proportion. Angle pairs are still congruent.

Example: If △ABC ~ △DEF, find the value of x and y as well as the measures of ∠A, ∠B, ∠D, and ∠F.

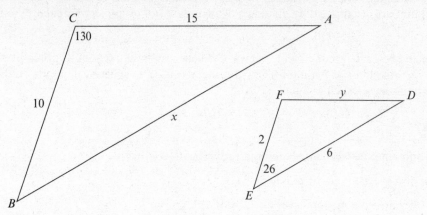

Solution: Since △ABC ~ △DEF, the sides are proportional. Set up ratios for each side and set them equal to each other. Be sure to remain consistent with the ratios. The three side ratios are $\frac{10}{2}$, $\frac{15}{y}$, and $\frac{x}{6}$. Set these ratios equal to each other in pairs: $\frac{10}{2} = \frac{15}{y}$. If you look at the first ratio, 10 is 5 times 2. Therefore, 5 times y would be 15.

This gives $y = 3$. Similarly, $\frac{10}{2} = \frac{x}{6}$. Since 10 is 5 times 2, then x is 5 times 6, so $x = 30$. The angles are congruent in pairs. Therefore, m∠B = 26 and m∠F = 130. To find the measures of ∠A and ∠D, use the fact that the angles of a triangle add to 180 degrees. So, 26 + 130 + m∠A = 180. This gives 156 + m∠A = 180, so measure of ∠A = 24. m∠D is also 24 degrees.

Checkpoint

1. True or false: The angles in similar figures are proportional.

2. Fill in the blank: Congruent shapes are (same; different) _____ size and (same; different) _____ shape.

3. Fill in the blank: Similar shapes are (same; different) _____ size and (same; different) _____ shape.

Checkpoint Answers

1. False. Sides are proportional. Angles are congruent.

2. same; same

3. different; same

Measurement

Measurement includes both geometric measurement and scientific measurement.

Geometric Measurement

Geometric measurement includes perimeter, circumference, area, and volume.

Perimeter is the distance around a polygon. It can be found by adding the lengths of all the sides of the polygon together.

Example: Find the perimeter of the shapes shown below (not drawn to scale).

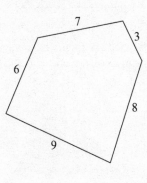
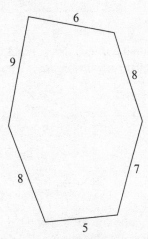

Solution: Perimeter is the distance around the shape. For the figure on the left, the perimeter is 6 + 7 + 3 + 8 + 9, which totals 33 units. For the figure on the right, the perimeter is 6 + 8 + 7 + 5 + 8 + 9, which totals 43 units.

Circumference is the distance around a circle. Circumference can be thought of as perimeter for circles. The ratio of the circumference to the diameter of a circle is defined as π, so $\dfrac{c}{d} = \pi$. This gives $C = \pi d = 2\pi r$. The value of π is approximately 3.14. For an exact value, leave the answer in terms of π (that is, 5π units).

Example: Find the circumference of the circle shown below.

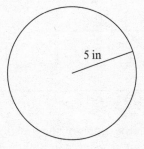

5 in

Solution: Circumference is the distance around the circle. The radius of the circle is 5 inches. $C = 2\pi r = 2\pi(5) = 10\pi$ inches.

Area is the amount of surface that a shape covers. It is measured in square units. There are many formulas for finding the area of various shapes.

Rectangles: The area of a rectangle can be found by multiplying the **base** times the **height.** For any figure, the height must form a right angle with the base.

Parallelograms: If a triangle is cut off the end of a rectangle, it can be shifted to the opposite side and a parallelogram is created. The area has not changed, so the formula for the area of a parallelogram is also base times height.

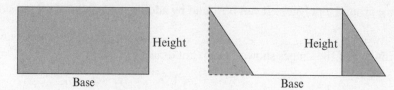

Triangles: If a diagonal is drawn in a parallelogram, two identical triangles are formed. The area of each triangle is half of the area of the parallelogram. Therefore, the formula for the area of a triangle is the base times the height divided by 2: $A = \frac{1}{2}bh$.

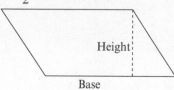 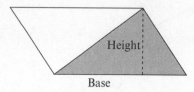

Trapezoids: The area of a trapezoid can be found by breaking the trapezoid into figures for which we know how to find the area. There are multiple ways to do this.

The figure can be divided into two triangles. The formula would then be $A = \frac{1}{2}(\text{base}_1)(\text{height}) + \frac{1}{2}(\text{base}_2)(\text{height})$.

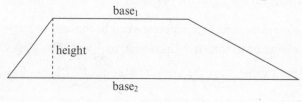

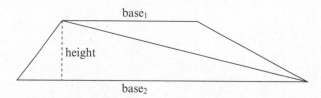

Alternatively, a rectangle can be cut out from the center of the trapezoid, leaving two triangles. If these two triangles are connected, we can find the area of each piece to find the area of the trapezoid.

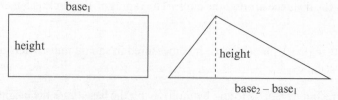

Then the area will be $A = (\text{base}_1)(\text{height}) + \frac{1}{2}(\text{base}_2 - \text{base}_1)(\text{height})$.

One can also make a copy of the original trapezoid and connect it with the original. This makes a parallelogram whose area is twice that of the trapezoid.

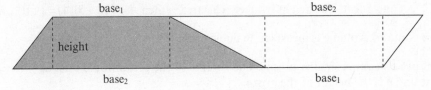

Then the area will be $A = \dfrac{(\text{base}_1 + \text{base}_2)(\text{height})}{2}$.

Circles: A circle can be cut into slices that can be placed together to approximate a parallelogram. The area is then $A = \pi r^2$.

The following table summarizes the area formulas:

Shape	Area Formula
Rectangle	$A = (\text{base})(\text{height}) = bh$
Parallelogram	$A = (\text{base})(\text{height}) = bh$
Triangle	$A = \dfrac{1}{2}(\text{base})(\text{height}) = \dfrac{1}{2}bh$
Trapezoid	$A = \dfrac{1}{2}(\text{base}_1 + \text{base}_2)(\text{height}) = \dfrac{1}{2}(b_1 + b_2)(h)$
Circle	$A = \pi r^2$

The areas of other shapes can often be found by breaking down the figure into shapes of which there are known formulas.

Example: Find the area of the shapes shown below (not drawn to scale).

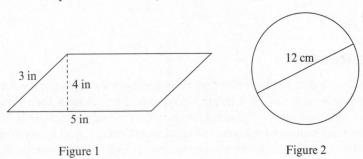

Figure 1   Figure 2

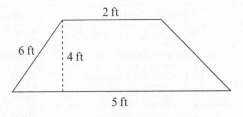

Figure 3

Solution: Figure 1 is a parallelogram. The base is 5 inches and the height is 4 inches. The area is the base times the height, so the area of figure 1 is $5 \times 4 = 20$ in^2.

Figure 2 is a circle. The diameter of the circle is 12 cm. The radius is half of the diameter, so the radius is 6 cm. The area of figure 2 is $A = \pi(6)^2 = 36\pi$ cm².

Figure 3 is a trapezoid. The bases are 2 feet and 5 feet. The height is 4 feet. The area is then $A = \frac{1}{2}(2+5)(4) = 14$ ft².

Volume is the amount of space a shape contains. Volume is measured in cubic units.

The volume of a prism can be thought of as stacking smaller prisms. The volume of the prism would then be $V = Bh$, where B is the area of the base and h is the height of the prism.

If a pyramid and a prism have the same base and same height, 3 pyramids will fit inside the prism. Therefore, the volume of a pyramid is $V = \frac{1}{3}Bh$.

A cylinder is similar to a prism. The base is a circle, so the volume of a cylinder is $V = (\pi r^2)h$.

A cone is similar to a pyramid. The base is a circle, so the volume of a cone is $V = \frac{1}{3}(\pi r^2)h$.

Checkpoint

1. Find the volume of a cone with a height of 4 cm and a diameter of 6 cm.

2. Find the perimeter and area of a rectangle with a base of 4 cm and a height of 8 cm.

3. Find the volume of a prism whose base is a triangle with a base of 3 cm and a height of 6 cm and the height of the prism is 7 cm.

Checkpoint Answers

1. $V = \frac{1}{3}(\pi r^2)h = \frac{1}{3}(\pi(3)^2)4 = \frac{1}{3}(9\pi)4 = 12\pi$ cm³

2. $P = 4 + 8 + 4 + 8 = 24$ cm; $A = (b)(h) = (4)(8) = 32$ cm²

3. $V = Bh = \left(\frac{1}{2}(3)(6)\right)(7) = (9)(7) = 63$ cm³

Scientific Measurement

Measurement can be direct or indirect. The concept of measurement with tools like a ruler involves creating a counting unit and then repeating that unit. If a length is said to be 3 inches long, then 1 inch is the unit and it is repeated 3 times to get a length of 3 inches. Standard measurement includes dimensions of inches, feet, yards, and miles. Metric measurement includes dimensions of centimeters, meters, and kilometers. Conversions can be made both within and between standard and metric measurement. The following conversions are helpful to know.

12 inches = 1 foot	3 feet = 1 yard	5,280 feet = 1 mile
60 minutes = 1 hour	60 seconds = 1 minute	24 hours = 1 day
1 cup = 8 fluid ounces	1 pint = 2 cups	1 quart = 2 pints
1 gallon = 4 quarts	1 pound = 16 ounces	1 ton = 2,000 pounds
1000 mg = 1 g	1000 g = 1 kg	1000 mL = 1 L
100 cm = 1 m	1000 mm = 1 m	1000 m = 1 km

To convert within a system of measurement, use the conversion and either multiply or divide by the conversion factor. Whether you multiply or divide depends on what unit you begin with compared to what unit you would like to end with. For example, if the measure was given in feet with a goal of inches, you would multiply the number of feet by 12 inches per foot. You can think of this as multiplying by 1 as well. The units must match in the numerator and denominator to cancel themselves out.

Example: How many inches are in 4 feet?

$$4 \text{ feet} \times \frac{12 \text{ inches}}{1 \text{ foot}} = 48 \text{ inches}$$

Since 12 inches = 1 foot, the fraction $\frac{12 \text{ inches}}{1 \text{ foot}}$ is equivalent to 1. Since the unit of feet is in both the numerator and the denominator, the unit cancels itself out.

Checkpoint

1. Convert 3 hours to minutes.

2. How many milligrams (mg) are in 3 grams (g)?

3. How many gallons are 32 cups?

Checkpoint Answers

1. $3 \text{ hours} \times \dfrac{60 \text{ minutes}}{1 \text{ hour}} = 180 \text{ minutes}$

2. $3 \text{ g} \times \dfrac{1000 \text{ mg}}{1 \text{ g}} = 3000 \text{ mg}$

3. $32 \text{ cups} \times \dfrac{1 \text{ pint}}{2 \text{ cups}} = 16 \text{ pints}$; $16 \text{ pints} \times \dfrac{1 \text{ quart}}{2 \text{ pints}} = 8 \text{ quarts}$; $8 \text{ quarts} \times \dfrac{1 \text{ gallon}}{4 \text{ quarts}} = 2 \text{ gallons}$

Coordinate Plane or Grid

The *coordinate plane or grid* is a plane that has a horizontal number line (*x*-axis) and a vertical number line (*y*-axis) intersecting at their zero points (also known as the *origin*). See the following illustration of a coordinate plane.

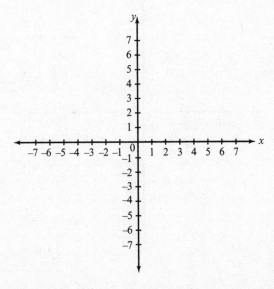

An *ordered pair* is a pair of numbers used to locate a point in a coordinate plane. It is written (*x*, *y*), in which the first term is for the *x-coordinate* (the horizontal number line of the coordinate plane) and the second term is for the *y-coordinate* (the vertical number line of the coordinate plane). The *x-coordinate* is the first number, and it corresponds to the number on the *x*-axis. For example, in the ordered pair (4, 5), 4 is the *x*-coordinate. The *y-coordinate* is the second number, 5. The *origin* is the point where the *x*-axis and *y*-axis intersect, and a *quadrant*

is one of the four sections that the coordinate plane forms by using the two perpendicular axes. The coordinate plane is separated into four quadrants (see next figure). Axes are not located in any of the quadrants.

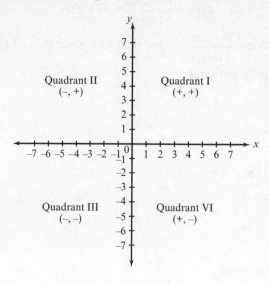

Checkpoint

1. How many quadrants are included in a coordinate plane?

2. What are the names of the coordinate plane quadrants?

3. What is the name of the horizontal number line in the coordinate plane?

4. What is the name of the vertical number line in the coordinate plane?

5. Name the ordered pair for each of the points on the following coordinate plane. Then identify the quadrant in which each point lies.

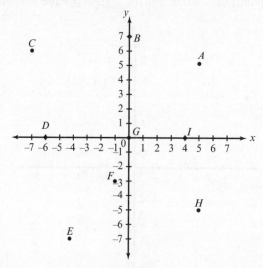

Checkpoint Answers

1. Four

2. Quadrants I, II, III, and IV

3. *x*-axis

4. *y*-axis

5. Point *A*: (5, 5) Quadrant I

Point *B*: (0, 7) No quadrant, it is on the *y*-axis

Point *C*: (–7, 6) Quadrant II

Point *D*: (–6, 0) No quadrant, it is on the *x*-axis

Point *E*: (–4, –7) Quadrant III

Point *F*: (–1, –3) Quadrant III

Point *G*: (0, 0) No quadrant, it is on the origin

Point *H*: (5, –5) Quadrant IV

Point *I*: (4, 0) No quadrant, it is on the *x*-axis

Summary

The Mathematics subtest encompasses a variety of subcompetencies related to the basic knowledge required of educators teaching elementary-age students.

Knowledge of student thinking and instructional practices entails analyzing and applying appropriate mathematical concepts and professional concepts to evaluate student solutions to problems; analyzing and discriminating among various problem structures with unknowns in all positions in order to develop student understanding of operations; analyzing and validating a student's mathematical model or argument used for problem solving; interpreting individual student mathematics assessment data to guide instructional decisions and differentiate instruction; selecting and analyzing structured experiences for small and large groups of students according to the cognitive complexity of the task; analyzing learning progressions to show how students' mathematical knowledge, skills, and understanding develop over time; and distinguishing among the components of math fluency.

Knowledge of operations, algebraic thinking, counting, and numbers in base ten includes aspects of interpreting and extending multiple representations of patterns and functional relationships by using tables, graphs, equations, expressions, and verbal descriptions; selecting the representation of an algebraic expression, equation, or inequality that models a real-world situation; analyzing and applying the properties of equality and operations in the context of interpreting solutions; determining whether two algebraic expressions are equivalent by applying properties of operations or equality; evaluating expressions with parentheses, brackets, and braces; analyzing and applying strategies to solve multistep word problems; applying number theory concepts; and identifying strategies based on place value to perform multidigit arithmetic.

Knowledge of fractions, ratios, and integers entails comparing fractions, integers, and integers with integer exponents and placing them on a number line; converting among standard measurement units within and between measurement systems in the context of multistep, real-world problems; solving problems involving addition, subtraction, multiplication, and division of fractions, including mixing whole numbers and fractions as well as decimals and percents by using visual models and equations to represent the problems and their solutions; selecting the representation (such as linear, area, set model) that best represents the problem and solution, given a word problem or equation involving fractions; and solving real-world problems involving ratios and proportions.

Knowledge of measurement, data analysis, and statistics entails calculating and interpreting statistics of variability (e.g., range, mean, absolute deviation) and central tendency; analyzing and interpreting data through the use of frequency tables and graphs; selecting appropriate measurement units to solve problems involving estimates and measurements; evaluating the choice of measures of center and variability, with respect to the shape of the data distribution and the context in which the data were gathered; and solving problems involving distance, time, liquid volume, mass, and money, which may include units expressed as fractions or decimals.

Finally, knowledge of geometric concepts includes applying geometric properties and relationships to solve problems involving perimeter, area, surface area, and volume; identifying and locating ordered pairs in all four quadrants of a rectangular coordinate plane system; identifying and analyzing properties of three-dimensional shapes using formal mathematical terms; and classifying two-dimensional figures in a hierarchy based on mathematical properties.

You should use the information in this chapter to complement your previous knowledge in the area of mathematics. The general review of mathematics provided in this chapter should allow you to explore areas of strength and weakness that you might still need to review. To provide an opportunity for further practice and analysis, sample questions for the Mathematics competency area appear in the next section of the chapter. Answer explanations follow the sample questions.

Sample Questions

1. $\sqrt{144} =$ _____

   A. 720
   B. 288
   C. 72
   D. 12

2. The dimensions of a rectangular garden are 14 feet by 12 feet. What will happen to the area of the garden if the length is doubled and the width is tripled?

   A. It becomes 2 times larger.
   B. It becomes 3 times larger.
   C. It becomes 5 times larger.
   D. It becomes 6 times larger.

3. $5^{4-2} =$ _____

   A. 5^2
   B. $\sqrt{5}$
   C. 5^8
   D. 5^{-8}

4. What is the eighth number in the following pattern: 2, 4, 8, 16, . . . ?

   A. 32
   B. 64
   C. 128
   D. 256

5. $\dfrac{3}{10} \times \dfrac{5}{9} =$ _____

   A. $\dfrac{15}{9}$
   B. $\dfrac{8}{19}$
   C. $\dfrac{8}{90}$
   D. $\dfrac{1}{6}$

6. $5.03 \times 4.9 =$ _____

   A. 9.93
   B. 246.47
   C. 24.647
   D. 2.4647

7. Alternative assessment may include

   A. multiple-choice items.
   B. portfolios.
   C. true/false items.
   D. All of the above

8. What is the least common multiple of 60 and 90?

    A. 30
    B. 180
    C. 360
    D. 90

9. Mike made the following table based on the number of hours he worked per day last month. Find the median number of hours he worked per day last month.

Number of Hours	Tally	Frequency
7	ЖІ ЖІ ІІ	12
8	ІІІ	3
9	ІІ	2
10	ЖІ ІІ	7

    A. 7 hours
    B. 8 hours
    C. 7.5 hours
    D. 2.5 hours

10. Select the most appropriate unit for measuring the height of an adult basketball player.

    A. centimeters
    B. feet
    C. inches
    D. kilometers

11. Change the fraction $\frac{3}{8}$ to a decimal.

    A. 0.375
    B. 0.0375
    C. 37.5
    D. 3.75

12. A rectangle can also be called which of the following?

    A. parallelogram
    B. pentagon
    C. trapezoid
    D. triangle

13. What is the greatest common factor of 60 and 90?

    A. 10
    B. 6
    C. 15
    D. 30

14. Find the mean for the data set given in the following table. Round your answer to the closest hundredth.

Number of Hours	Frequency
1	23
2	13
3	2
4	7

    A. 20.75 hours

    B. 2.5 hours

    C. 11.25 hours

    D. 1.84 hours

15. A mason was tiling a living room. To add to the appearance of the floor, the designer decided to use similar triangles within the tile.

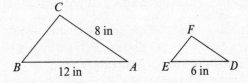

    Given $\triangle ABC \sim \triangle DEF$, find the length of DF.

    A. 2 inches

    B. 4 inches

    C. 6 inches

    D. 8 inches

16. $((-3)^2)^3 =$ _____

    A. 729

    B. −729

    C. 2,187

    D. 27

17. Which of the following expressions is NOT equivalent to $4 + 2(x + 5)$?

    A. $4 + 2x + 10$

    B. $2(x + 5) + 4$

    C. $4 + 2x + 5$

    D. $4 + 2(5 + x)$

18. Solve for x: $2x - 6 = 14$

    A. $x = 10$

    B. $x = 4$

    C. $x = 20$

    D. $x = 16$

19. Tom is a first-grade student playing with pattern blocks and making geometric patterns. Tom is working at the _____ cognitive level.

    A. concrete

    B. representational

    C. abstract

    D. symbolic

20. $2^3 \cdot 3^{-2} =$ _____

    A. 72

    B. $\dfrac{8}{9}$

    C. $-\dfrac{8}{9}$

    D. -72

21. Which of the following sequences is the most appropriate learning progression through the levels of geometric thinking?

    A. **First:** Understands the concept of multiplication using manipulative materials
    Second: Recalls multiplication facts without hesitation
    Third: Uses strategies to find the answer to basic facts (such as $8 \cdot 7 = 7 \cdot 7 + 7 = 56$)
    Fourth: Solves a problem like $23 \cdot 5$ using a computational algorithm with speed and accuracy

    B. **First:** Understands the concept of multiplication using manipulative materials
    Second: Uses strategies to find the answer to basic facts (such as $8 \cdot 7 = 7 \cdot 7 + 7 = 56$)
    Third: Recalls multiplication facts without hesitation
    Fourth: Solves a problem like $23 \cdot 5$ using a computational algorithm with speed and accuracy

    C. **First:** Uses strategies to find the answer to basic facts (such as $8 \cdot 7 = 7 \cdot 7 + 7 = 56$)
    Second: Recalls multiplication facts without hesitation
    Third: Understands the concept of multiplication using manipulative materials
    Fourth: Solves a problem like $23 \cdot 5$ using a computational algorithm with speed and accuracy

    D. **First:** Uses strategies to find the answer to basic facts (such as $8 \cdot 7 = 7 \cdot 7 + 7 = 56$)
    Second: Understands the concept of multiplication using manipulative materials
    Third: Recalls multiplication facts without hesitation
    Fourth: Solves a problem like $23 \cdot 5$ using a computational algorithm with speed and accuracy

Answer Explanations

1. **D.** Competency 2. This question is about finding the square root of 144, which means that you need to find a number that when multiplied by itself you get 144. The number is 12 because $12 \times 12 = 144$.

2. **D.** Competency 5. The area of the original garden is 14 feet $\times$ 12 feet $= 168$ feet^2. If the length is doubled and the width is tripled, the dimensions would then be 28 feet $\times$ 36 feet. This gives an area of 1,008 feet^2. To find how the area of the garden has changed, divide: $1,008 \div 168 = 6$. After doubling the length and tripling the width, the area of the new garden is 6 times larger. Alternately, the area of a rectangle is (length) $\times$ (width). This would become ($2 \times$ length) $\times$ ($3 \times$ width). Using the associative property, this can be written as $2 \times 3 \times$ length $\times$ width $= 6 \times$ length $\times$ width.

3. **A.** Competency 3. Since we have 5^{4-2}, you subtract the exponents $4 - 2 = 2$ to get 5^2.

4. **D.** Competency 2. Each term is doubled of the term before, so the next four terms are 32, 64, 128, and 256. The eighth term in the pattern is 256.

5. **D.** Competency 3. $\frac{3}{10} \times \frac{5}{9} = \frac{(3 \times 5)}{(10 \times 9)} = \frac{15}{90}, \frac{(15 \div 15)}{(90 \div 15)} = \frac{1}{6}$, or $\frac{3}{10} \times \frac{5}{9} = \frac{(3 \times 5)}{(10 \times 9)} = \frac{\overset{1}{\cancel{3}}}{\underset{2}{\cancel{10}}} \times \frac{\overset{1}{\cancel{5}}}{\underset{3}{\cancel{9}}} = \frac{1}{6}$.

6. **C.** Competency 2. One way to solve this problem is by estimating the answer: $5 \times 5 = 25$. The closest answer to 25 is 24.647.

7. **B.** Competency 1. The question asks about a type of alternative assessment; the only choice of this type is portfolios. The others are traditional types of assessment.

8. **B.** Competency 2. The multiples of 60 are 60, 120, 180, 240, 300, 360, ... The multiples of 90 are 90, 180, 270, 360, ... The least common multiple is 180. Or, using prime factorization: $60 = 2^2 \times 3 \times 5$, and $90 = 2 \times 3^2 \times 5$. The least common multiples are $2^2 \times 3^2 \times 5 = 4 \times 9 \times 5 = 180$.

9. **C.** Competency 4. The median is a measure of central tendency of data. The median of a set of data is the middle number of the ordered data, or the mean of the middle two numbers:

   $$7, 7, 7, 7, 7, 7, 7, 7, 7, 7, 7, \textbf{7, 8}, 8, 8, 9, 9, 10, 10, 10, 10, 10, 10, 10$$

   The median divides the data in half. In this case, the middle of the data is between the 11th and the 12th numbers because we have 24 numbers: $\frac{(7+8)}{2} = 7.5$. The median number of hours that Mike worked per day last month is 7.5 hours.

10. **B.** Competency 4. Feet is the best unit to measure the height of an adult basketball player. Centimeters and inches are smaller than necessary. Kilometers are longer than necessary.

11. **A.** Competency 3. Divide 3 by 8 to get the decimal, which is equal to 0.375.

12. **A.** Competency 5. A rectangle is a special type of parallelogram with four sides, opposite sides being parallel to one another and forming four right angles. A pentagon has five sides. A trapezoid only has one set of parallel sides. A triangle has three sides.

13. **D.** Competency 2. The factors of 60 are 1, 2, 3, 4, 5, 6, 10, 12, 15, 20, 30, and 60. The factors of 90 are 1, 2, 3, 5, 6, 9, 10, 15, 18, 30, 45, and 90. The greatest common factor of 60 and 90 is 30. Or, using prime factorization: $60 = 2^2 \times 3 \times 5$, and $90 = 2 \times 3^2 \times 5$. The common factors are 2, 3, and 5; and the greatest common factor is $2 \times 3 \times 5 = 30$.

14. **D.** Competency 4. To find the mean, multiply each number of hours by its frequency, add the products, and divide the sum by the total frequency (in this case 45): $(23 \cdot 1 + 13 \cdot 2 + 2 \cdot 3 + 7 \cdot 4) \div 45 = 83 \div 45 \approx 1.84$ (to the closest hundredth). The mean is 1.84 hours.

15. **B.** Competency 5. Since the triangles are similar, the sides are proportional in length. The length of a side in the smaller triangle (ΔDEF) is half the length of the corresponding side of the larger triangle (ΔABC). Since side AC corresponds with side DF, DF is half the length of AC. AC is 8 inches, so DF is 4 inches.

16. **A.** Competency 3. $((-3)^2)^3 = (-3 \times -3)^3 = 9^3 = 9 \times 9 \times 9 = 729$.

17. C. Competency 2. Choice A uses the distributive property $2(x + 5) = 2x + 2 \times 5 = 2x + 10$. Choice B uses the commutative property in switching the order of adding 4 and $2(x + 5)$. Choice D uses the commutative property to switch the order of $x + 5$. Choice C is incorrect; it does not use the distributive property correctly.

18. A. Competency 2. First add 6 to both sides, so $2x = 20$. Then divide both sides by 2, so $x = 10$.

19. A. Competency 1. Since the student is using pattern blocks, which are concrete objects, he is working at the concrete level.

20. B. Competency 3. $2^3 \cdot 3^{-2} = 2 \cdot 2 \cdot 2 \cdot \dfrac{1}{3^2} = 8 \cdot \dfrac{1}{9} = \dfrac{8}{9}$. A negative exponent indicates that the base (in this case, 3) is on the wrong side of the fraction line, so you need to flip the base to the other side (in this case, $3^{-2} = \dfrac{1}{3^2}$).

21. B. Competency 1. This question is about learning progressions. It is necessary that students develop proper understanding of the operation concept prior to trying to memorize facts, and eventually work with the computation algorithm. Memorization strategies will facilitate the students' memorization of facts.

Practice Test 1

Answer Sheet

Language Arts and Reading

1 Ⓐ Ⓑ Ⓒ Ⓓ	31 Ⓐ Ⓑ Ⓒ Ⓓ
2 Ⓐ Ⓑ Ⓒ Ⓓ	32 Ⓐ Ⓑ Ⓒ Ⓓ
3 Ⓐ Ⓑ Ⓒ Ⓓ	33 Ⓐ Ⓑ Ⓒ Ⓓ
4 Ⓐ Ⓑ Ⓒ Ⓓ	34 Ⓐ Ⓑ Ⓒ Ⓓ
5 Ⓐ Ⓑ Ⓒ Ⓓ	35 Ⓐ Ⓑ Ⓒ Ⓓ
6 Ⓐ Ⓑ Ⓒ Ⓓ	36 Ⓐ Ⓑ Ⓒ Ⓓ
7 Ⓐ Ⓑ Ⓒ Ⓓ	37 Ⓐ Ⓑ Ⓒ Ⓓ
8 Ⓐ Ⓑ Ⓒ Ⓓ	38 Ⓐ Ⓑ Ⓒ Ⓓ
9 Ⓐ Ⓑ Ⓒ Ⓓ	39 Ⓐ Ⓑ Ⓒ Ⓓ
10 Ⓐ Ⓑ Ⓒ Ⓓ	40 Ⓐ Ⓑ Ⓒ Ⓓ
11 Ⓐ Ⓑ Ⓒ Ⓓ	41 Ⓐ Ⓑ Ⓒ Ⓓ
12 Ⓐ Ⓑ Ⓒ Ⓓ	42 Ⓐ Ⓑ Ⓒ Ⓓ
13 Ⓐ Ⓑ Ⓒ Ⓓ	43 Ⓐ Ⓑ Ⓒ Ⓓ
14 Ⓐ Ⓑ Ⓒ Ⓓ	44 Ⓐ Ⓑ Ⓒ Ⓓ
15 Ⓐ Ⓑ Ⓒ Ⓓ	45 Ⓐ Ⓑ Ⓒ Ⓓ
16 Ⓐ Ⓑ Ⓒ Ⓓ	46 Ⓐ Ⓑ Ⓒ Ⓓ
17 Ⓐ Ⓑ Ⓒ Ⓓ	47 Ⓐ Ⓑ Ⓒ Ⓓ
18 Ⓐ Ⓑ Ⓒ Ⓓ	48 Ⓐ Ⓑ Ⓒ Ⓓ
19 Ⓐ Ⓑ Ⓒ Ⓓ	49 Ⓐ Ⓑ Ⓒ Ⓓ
20 Ⓐ Ⓑ Ⓒ Ⓓ	50 Ⓐ Ⓑ Ⓒ Ⓓ
21 Ⓐ Ⓑ Ⓒ Ⓓ	51 Ⓐ Ⓑ Ⓒ Ⓓ
22 Ⓐ Ⓑ Ⓒ Ⓓ	52 Ⓐ Ⓑ Ⓒ Ⓓ
23 Ⓐ Ⓑ Ⓒ Ⓓ	53 Ⓐ Ⓑ Ⓒ Ⓓ
24 Ⓐ Ⓑ Ⓒ Ⓓ	54 Ⓐ Ⓑ Ⓒ Ⓓ
25 Ⓐ Ⓑ Ⓒ Ⓓ	55 Ⓐ Ⓑ Ⓒ Ⓓ
26 Ⓐ Ⓑ Ⓒ Ⓓ	56 Ⓐ Ⓑ Ⓒ Ⓓ
27 Ⓐ Ⓑ Ⓒ Ⓓ	57 Ⓐ Ⓑ Ⓒ Ⓓ
28 Ⓐ Ⓑ Ⓒ Ⓓ	58 Ⓐ Ⓑ Ⓒ Ⓓ
29 Ⓐ Ⓑ Ⓒ Ⓓ	59 Ⓐ Ⓑ Ⓒ Ⓓ
30 Ⓐ Ⓑ Ⓒ Ⓓ	60 Ⓐ Ⓑ Ⓒ Ⓓ

Social Science

1 Ⓐ Ⓑ Ⓒ Ⓓ	31 Ⓐ Ⓑ Ⓒ Ⓓ
2 Ⓐ Ⓑ Ⓒ Ⓓ	32 Ⓐ Ⓑ Ⓒ Ⓓ
3 Ⓐ Ⓑ Ⓒ Ⓓ	33 Ⓐ Ⓑ Ⓒ Ⓓ
4 Ⓐ Ⓑ Ⓒ Ⓓ	34 Ⓐ Ⓑ Ⓒ Ⓓ
5 Ⓐ Ⓑ Ⓒ Ⓓ	35 Ⓐ Ⓑ Ⓒ Ⓓ
6 Ⓐ Ⓑ Ⓒ Ⓓ	36 Ⓐ Ⓑ Ⓒ Ⓓ
7 Ⓐ Ⓑ Ⓒ Ⓓ	37 Ⓐ Ⓑ Ⓒ Ⓓ
8 Ⓐ Ⓑ Ⓒ Ⓓ	38 Ⓐ Ⓑ Ⓒ Ⓓ
9 Ⓐ Ⓑ Ⓒ Ⓓ	39 Ⓐ Ⓑ Ⓒ Ⓓ
10 Ⓐ Ⓑ Ⓒ Ⓓ	40 Ⓐ Ⓑ Ⓒ Ⓓ
11 Ⓐ Ⓑ Ⓒ Ⓓ	41 Ⓐ Ⓑ Ⓒ Ⓓ
12 Ⓐ Ⓑ Ⓒ Ⓓ	42 Ⓐ Ⓑ Ⓒ Ⓓ
13 Ⓐ Ⓑ Ⓒ Ⓓ	43 Ⓐ Ⓑ Ⓒ Ⓓ
14 Ⓐ Ⓑ Ⓒ Ⓓ	44 Ⓐ Ⓑ Ⓒ Ⓓ
15 Ⓐ Ⓑ Ⓒ Ⓓ	45 Ⓐ Ⓑ Ⓒ Ⓓ
16 Ⓐ Ⓑ Ⓒ Ⓓ	46 Ⓐ Ⓑ Ⓒ Ⓓ
17 Ⓐ Ⓑ Ⓒ Ⓓ	47 Ⓐ Ⓑ Ⓒ Ⓓ
18 Ⓐ Ⓑ Ⓒ Ⓓ	48 Ⓐ Ⓑ Ⓒ Ⓓ
19 Ⓐ Ⓑ Ⓒ Ⓓ	49 Ⓐ Ⓑ Ⓒ Ⓓ
20 Ⓐ Ⓑ Ⓒ Ⓓ	50 Ⓐ Ⓑ Ⓒ Ⓓ
21 Ⓐ Ⓑ Ⓒ Ⓓ	51 Ⓐ Ⓑ Ⓒ Ⓓ
22 Ⓐ Ⓑ Ⓒ Ⓓ	52 Ⓐ Ⓑ Ⓒ Ⓓ
23 Ⓐ Ⓑ Ⓒ Ⓓ	53 Ⓐ Ⓑ Ⓒ Ⓓ
24 Ⓐ Ⓑ Ⓒ Ⓓ	54 Ⓐ Ⓑ Ⓒ Ⓓ
25 Ⓐ Ⓑ Ⓒ Ⓓ	55 Ⓐ Ⓑ Ⓒ Ⓓ
26 Ⓐ Ⓑ Ⓒ Ⓓ	
27 Ⓐ Ⓑ Ⓒ Ⓓ	
28 Ⓐ Ⓑ Ⓒ Ⓓ	
29 Ⓐ Ⓑ Ⓒ Ⓓ	
30 Ⓐ Ⓑ Ⓒ Ⓓ	

Tip: For the Mathematics section, you may consult the Mathematics Reference Sheet in Appendix C (pages 343–344) for common formulas.

CUT HERE

Science

1 Ⓐ Ⓑ Ⓒ Ⓓ	31 Ⓐ Ⓑ Ⓒ Ⓓ
2 Ⓐ Ⓑ Ⓒ Ⓓ	32 Ⓐ Ⓑ Ⓒ Ⓓ
3 Ⓐ Ⓑ Ⓒ Ⓓ	33 Ⓐ Ⓑ Ⓒ Ⓓ
4 Ⓐ Ⓑ Ⓒ Ⓓ	34 Ⓐ Ⓑ Ⓒ Ⓓ
5 Ⓐ Ⓑ Ⓒ Ⓓ	35 Ⓐ Ⓑ Ⓒ Ⓓ
6 Ⓐ Ⓑ Ⓒ Ⓓ	36 Ⓐ Ⓑ Ⓒ Ⓓ
7 Ⓐ Ⓑ Ⓒ Ⓓ	37 Ⓐ Ⓑ Ⓒ Ⓓ
8 Ⓐ Ⓑ Ⓒ Ⓓ	38 Ⓐ Ⓑ Ⓒ Ⓓ
9 Ⓐ Ⓑ Ⓒ Ⓓ	39 Ⓐ Ⓑ Ⓒ Ⓓ
10 Ⓐ Ⓑ Ⓒ Ⓓ	40 Ⓐ Ⓑ Ⓒ Ⓓ
11 Ⓐ Ⓑ Ⓒ Ⓓ	41 Ⓐ Ⓑ Ⓒ Ⓓ
12 Ⓐ Ⓑ Ⓒ Ⓓ	42 Ⓐ Ⓑ Ⓒ Ⓓ
13 Ⓐ Ⓑ Ⓒ Ⓓ	43 Ⓐ Ⓑ Ⓒ Ⓓ
14 Ⓐ Ⓑ Ⓒ Ⓓ	44 Ⓐ Ⓑ Ⓒ Ⓓ
15 Ⓐ Ⓑ Ⓒ Ⓓ	45 Ⓐ Ⓑ Ⓒ Ⓓ
16 Ⓐ Ⓑ Ⓒ Ⓓ	46 Ⓐ Ⓑ Ⓒ Ⓓ
17 Ⓐ Ⓑ Ⓒ Ⓓ	47 Ⓐ Ⓑ Ⓒ Ⓓ
18 Ⓐ Ⓑ Ⓒ Ⓓ	48 Ⓐ Ⓑ Ⓒ Ⓓ
19 Ⓐ Ⓑ Ⓒ Ⓓ	49 Ⓐ Ⓑ Ⓒ Ⓓ
20 Ⓐ Ⓑ Ⓒ Ⓓ	50 Ⓐ Ⓑ Ⓒ Ⓓ
21 Ⓐ Ⓑ Ⓒ Ⓓ	51 Ⓐ Ⓑ Ⓒ Ⓓ
22 Ⓐ Ⓑ Ⓒ Ⓓ	52 Ⓐ Ⓑ Ⓒ Ⓓ
23 Ⓐ Ⓑ Ⓒ Ⓓ	53 Ⓐ Ⓑ Ⓒ Ⓓ
24 Ⓐ Ⓑ Ⓒ Ⓓ	54 Ⓐ Ⓑ Ⓒ Ⓓ
25 Ⓐ Ⓑ Ⓒ Ⓓ	55 Ⓐ Ⓑ Ⓒ Ⓓ
26 Ⓐ Ⓑ Ⓒ Ⓓ	
27 Ⓐ Ⓑ Ⓒ Ⓓ	
28 Ⓐ Ⓑ Ⓒ Ⓓ	
29 Ⓐ Ⓑ Ⓒ Ⓓ	
30 Ⓐ Ⓑ Ⓒ Ⓓ	

Mathematics

1 Ⓐ Ⓑ Ⓒ Ⓓ	26 Ⓐ Ⓑ Ⓒ Ⓓ
2 Ⓐ Ⓑ Ⓒ Ⓓ	27 Ⓐ Ⓑ Ⓒ Ⓓ
3 Ⓐ Ⓑ Ⓒ Ⓓ	28 Ⓐ Ⓑ Ⓒ Ⓓ
4 Ⓐ Ⓑ Ⓒ Ⓓ	29 Ⓐ Ⓑ Ⓒ Ⓓ
5 Ⓐ Ⓑ Ⓒ Ⓓ	30 Ⓐ Ⓑ Ⓒ Ⓓ
6 Ⓐ Ⓑ Ⓒ Ⓓ	31 Ⓐ Ⓑ Ⓒ Ⓓ
7 Ⓐ Ⓑ Ⓒ Ⓓ	32 Ⓐ Ⓑ Ⓒ Ⓓ
8 Ⓐ Ⓑ Ⓒ Ⓓ	33 Ⓐ Ⓑ Ⓒ Ⓓ
9 Ⓐ Ⓑ Ⓒ Ⓓ	34 Ⓐ Ⓑ Ⓒ Ⓓ
10 Ⓐ Ⓑ Ⓒ Ⓓ	35 Ⓐ Ⓑ Ⓒ Ⓓ
11 Ⓐ Ⓑ Ⓒ Ⓓ	36 Ⓐ Ⓑ Ⓒ Ⓓ
12 Ⓐ Ⓑ Ⓒ Ⓓ	37 Ⓐ Ⓑ Ⓒ Ⓓ
13 Ⓐ Ⓑ Ⓒ Ⓓ	38 Ⓐ Ⓑ Ⓒ Ⓓ
14 Ⓐ Ⓑ Ⓒ Ⓓ	39 Ⓐ Ⓑ Ⓒ Ⓓ
15 Ⓐ Ⓑ Ⓒ Ⓓ	40 Ⓐ Ⓑ Ⓒ Ⓓ
16 Ⓐ Ⓑ Ⓒ Ⓓ	41 Ⓐ Ⓑ Ⓒ Ⓓ
17 Ⓐ Ⓑ Ⓒ Ⓓ	42 Ⓐ Ⓑ Ⓒ Ⓓ
18 Ⓐ Ⓑ Ⓒ Ⓓ	43 Ⓐ Ⓑ Ⓒ Ⓓ
19 Ⓐ Ⓑ Ⓒ Ⓓ	44 Ⓐ Ⓑ Ⓒ Ⓓ
20 Ⓐ Ⓑ Ⓒ Ⓓ	45 Ⓐ Ⓑ Ⓒ Ⓓ
21 Ⓐ Ⓑ Ⓒ Ⓓ	46 Ⓐ Ⓑ Ⓒ Ⓓ
22 Ⓐ Ⓑ Ⓒ Ⓓ	47 Ⓐ Ⓑ Ⓒ Ⓓ
23 Ⓐ Ⓑ Ⓒ Ⓓ	48 Ⓐ Ⓑ Ⓒ Ⓓ
24 Ⓐ Ⓑ Ⓒ Ⓓ	49 Ⓐ Ⓑ Ⓒ Ⓓ
25 Ⓐ Ⓑ Ⓒ Ⓓ	50 Ⓐ Ⓑ Ⓒ Ⓓ

CUT HERE

Language Arts and Reading

60 Questions
65 Minutes

1. When a teacher performs a think aloud, he is essentially

    A. asking questions after the reading.
    B. asking questions before the reading.
    C. "talking to the text" during the reading.
    D. None of the above

2. Which of the following would NOT be considered folklore?

    A. nursery rhymes
    B. fairy tales
    C. biographies
    D. myths

3. When an author attempts to convince the reader that a point is valid, the author is using what mode of writing?

    A. descriptive
    B. expository
    C. narrative
    D. persuasive

4. After a kindergarten student named Amy draws a picture in her daily journal, she uses a string of random letters to communicate in writing what she has drawn. One likely next step in her development as a writer might be

    A. labeling her drawing with appropriate initial letters.
    B. writing a paragraph about what she has drawn.
    C. writing a complete sentence.
    D. copying words from around the room that have nothing to do with her drawing.

5. Which of the following would be considered a formal assessment?

    A. anecdotal notes
    B. running record
    C. quiz
    D. criterion-referenced test

6. Classroom news and literature response _____ have become common web-based activities in elementary classrooms.

    A. pdf files
    B. digital stories
    C. blogs
    D. All of the above

GO ON TO THE NEXT PAGE

7. Questioning and retelling are two strategies that enhance _____ skills.

    A. listening and speaking

    B. comprehension

    C. word recognition

    D. A and B only

8. Visual media refers to

    A. any print material including books, journals, and magazines.

    B. anything that is not literally printed: television, video, some radio broadcasts, etc.

    C. illustrations created by an artist.

    D. the newspaper.

9. A group of third-graders is finishing up *All About Me* stories as an introductory assignment at the beginning of the year. To encourage them to revise their work and include appropriate content, the teacher provides each child with a rubric. Which of the following rubrics would assist students in the revision of their content?

    A. a rubric focusing on punctuation and grammar

    B. a rubric focusing on the traits of writing like organization, word choice, and the use of supporting details

    C. a rubric that ensures that each sentence has subject-verb agreement

    D. a rubric that encourages them to check all words for correct spelling

10. During a read aloud, a kindergarten student comments that the teacher is reading the pictures and not the words in the book. This student is demonstrating a lack of understanding in

    A. letter knowledge.

    B. alphabetic principle.

    C. concepts of print.

    D. phonemic awareness.

11. Which of the following is an example of an onset-rime segment?

    A. sh-ut

    B. butter-fly

    C. tell-ing

    D. pre-view

12. Which of the following is NOT a basic concept of print?

    A. directionality

    B. title page

    C. illustrations

    D. captions

13. The knowledge of onset-rime segments in words is a valuable phonological awareness skill. Which of the following is an example of an onset-rime?

    A. blo-w

    B. c-at

    C. cr-eate

    D. digra-ph

14. A grapheme is defined as

   A.   the first consonant or groups of consonants that come before the first vowel in a syllable.

   B.   the first vowel sound and any others that follow it in a syllable.

   C.   a letter or group of letters representing one sound.

   D.   a graphic organizer used for comprehension.

15. The literary device defined as two or more words or syllables near each other with the same beginning consonant is

   A.   hyperbole.

   B.   alliteration.

   C.   satire.

   D.   pun.

16. The teacher has organized her classroom to allow for small groups. Students are listening to books on a digital device, reading poetry, and responding to quality literature in writing. This is an example of what organizational format?

   A.   literature circle

   B.   shared reading

   C.   interactive writing

   D.   reading center/station

17. A second-grade teacher is implementing an interdisciplinary unit about the Native Americans of North America. While reading high-quality children's literature on the topic, the teacher also uses various artifacts like an arrowhead to help teach the students about the culture and ways of life of these peoples. An authentic arrowhead found on a Native American reservation is

   A.   a valuable teaching tool.

   B.   an example of a primary source.

   C.   an artifact.

   D.   All of the above

18. In what grade are students typically taught to write in cursive?

   A.   first

   B.   third

   C.   fourth

   D.   kindergarten

19. The local school board has announced that it plans to do away with music classes in all of the district's elementary schools. The students and teachers at each school are outraged. What would be the best form of written communication to share their feelings and wishes with the school board?

   A.   narrative

   B.   descriptive

   C.   persuasive

   D.   expository

20. The workshop approach to organizing your classroom provides time to

   A.   meet with small groups of students to address individual and small group needs.

   B.   work on your lesson plans.

   C.   offer a great deal of whole group instruction.

   D.   meet briefly with every student in your classroom.

GO ON TO THE NEXT PAGE

21. True literature circles consist of four to six children

    A. all reading the same book they each chose collectively based upon individual interest and then discussing it as a group.
    B. completing worksheets about a book they are reading while sitting at a round table.
    C. all reading a text on the same reading level, with teacher assistance.
    D. reading different books but talking about them in a small group.

22. Ms. Dixon encourages her students to brainstorm ideas about a topic of interest that they might like to write about. Brainstorming takes place during what phase of the writing process?

    A. drafting
    B. revising
    C. editing
    D. prewriting

23. Identify the literary device used in the following example:

    She crawled as slowly as a turtle.
    A. pun
    B. hyperbole
    C. simile
    D. alliteration

24. During the editing phase of writing, the writer should

    A. edit his work for content.
    B. edit his work for mechanical and grammatical errors.
    C. simply read over his work with no intention of making changes.
    D. copy the draft exactly to create a final, published piece.

25. Text-explicit questions are also known as

    A. think and search questions.
    B. inferences.
    C. right-there questions.
    D. reader and author questions.

26. Which of the following instructional methods aids fluency?

    A. repetitive or repeated reading
    B. echo reading
    C. choral reading
    D. All of the above

27. More than 70% of a second-grade class scored at high risk on an oral reading fluency check. The teacher would be wise to incorporate which of the following instructional methods into her daily lesson plans?

    A. daily independent silent reading
    B. round robin reading
    C. popcorn reading
    D. repeated readings of familiar text

28. The element of legible handwriting that refers to consistency of the pencil strokes is

    A. letter alignment.
    B. line quality.
    C. letter formation.
    D. vertical orientation.

29. A student read a 200-word piece in 4 minutes 45 seconds with 6 recorded errors. What would her accuracy rate be for that reading? (WCPM stands for word count per minute.)

    A. 42 WCPM
    B. 40.9 WCPM
    C. 40 WCPM
    D. 41.8 WCPM

30. To summarize either orally or in written form is to

    A. concisely paraphrase what has been read.
    B. expand upon the author's main idea.
    C. infer the author's purpose.
    D. None of the above

31. What are the three cueing systems related to the reading process?

    A. emergent, early, and fluent
    B. word identification, oral language development, and letter identification
    C. graphophonemic, semantic, and syntactic
    D. pre-alphabetic, alphabetic, and conventional

32. Historical fiction is defined as

    A. realistic stories set in the past that usually incorporate significant time periods and/or events in history.
    B. autobiographical text.
    C. informational text usually found in textbooks.
    D. primary source documents used in the social studies classroom.

33. Mr. Lowe's third-grade class has just read an article from a *National Geographic Kids* magazine. Through modeled writing, he is demonstrating how to explain what the whole article is about in five sentences. This is an example of what comprehension skill?

    A. visualizing
    B. making an inference
    C. summarizing
    D. author's purpose

34. Kidspiration is a popular

    A. computer software program used to create assignments.
    B. children's television show.
    C. children's organization.
    D. basal reading series.

GO ON TO THE NEXT PAGE

35. Which of the following is NOT a narrative literary element?

    A. theme

    B. plot

    C. setting

    D. author's purpose

36. There are _____ critical skills needed for reading success.

    A. ten

    B. seven

    C. six

    D. five

37. An example of a primary source document is

    A. a diary entry written by Martin Luther King, Jr.

    B. a biography written about the life of Martin Luther King, Jr.

    C. an illustration of Martin Luther King, Jr., drawn by a child during Black History month.

    D. None of the above

38. All of the following should be included in a classroom library EXCEPT

    A. books from a variety of genres.

    B. a plethora of nonfiction resources.

    C. books that promote stereotypes of various races and ethnicities.

    D. a wide array of multicultural children's literature.

39. A word that is recalled by memory only is known as a(n)

    A. sight word.

    B. high-frequency word.

    C. alliterative phrase.

    D. phonogram.

40. Which of the following words contains a vowel digraph?

    A. car

    B. cause

    C. catch

    D. care

41. In order to foster multiple opportunities for listening and speaking in the classroom, your day should be structured to incorporate

    A. both whole group and small group lessons.

    B. a great deal of independent seatwork.

    C. multiple technology stations.

    D. None of the above

42. Accuracy, rate, prosody, and automaticity are all components of reading

    A. comprehension.

    B. fluency.

    C. speed.

    D. words correct per minute.

43. Which of the following choices are essential elements of reading comprehension?

    A. inferring and questioning
    B. understanding author's purpose and point of view
    C. visualizing the text
    D. All of the above

44. Metonymy is a literary device that refers to

    A. a phrase using *like* or *as*.
    B. substituting a main word or formal word with a word closely related to it.
    C. inanimate objects being endowed with human characteristics.
    D. comparing two completely unlike things.

45. During the graphophonic component of writing, students

    A. write the alphabet legibly.
    B. learn to accurately hear sounds.
    C. learn that letter sounds can be formed in several different ways.
    D. None of the above

46. Graphophonic cues are most evident when reading which of the following literary devices?

    A. onomatopoeia
    B. personification
    C. metaphor
    D. simile

47. A fourth-grade teacher asks her students to meet with their literature circle group to discuss the assigned chapter readings of the Newbery Award–winning book, *Flora & Ulysses* by Kate DiCamillo. While students discuss their reading, the teacher monitors student participation and discussions by walking about the room from group to group. Which of the following forms of assessment is she employing?

    A. formal
    B. standardized
    C. informal
    D. diagnostic

48. _____ writing includes facts and data with the goal of informing the reader.

    A. Persuasive
    B. Expository
    C. Argument
    D. Narrative

49. During a whole group lesson, a first-grade teacher asks her students to do the following task: "I am going to segment a word into parts and pause between each sound. I want you to say the whole word together."

Which progress monitoring assessment is the teacher using?

    A. test of nonsense word fluency
    B. informal reading inventory
    C. test of phonological awareness
    D. test of alphabet knowledge

GO ON TO THE NEXT PAGE

50. Which of the following modes of writing presents the text in a story-like fashion, including the necessary elements of characterization, setting, plot, theme, and style?

    A. Opinion/Argument

    B. Expository

    C. Persuasive

    D. Narrative

51. A kindergarten teacher points to the title of the book, author, and illustrator prior to the read aloud. In this demonstration, he is helping students better understand the

    A. concepts of a book.

    B. vocabulary in the text.

    C. pictures in the book.

    D. comprehension of the text.

52. The best resource for finding words that mean the same thing is a

    A. dictionary.

    B. thesaurus.

    C. atlas.

    D. encyclopedia.

53. A book that contains a collection of maps is an excellent reference to include in your classroom library. The formal name of this kind of book is a(n)

    A. encyclopedia.

    B. dictionary.

    C. thesaurus.

    D. atlas.

54. Which of the following assessment tools best provides the teacher with an idea of students' likes, hobbies, and pastimes that could be used to identify appropriate reading material?

    A. rubric

    B. running record

    C. interest inventory

    D. informal reading inventory

55. The Gates-MacGinitie Reading Tests are an example of what kind of test?

    A. diagnostic

    B. criterion-referenced

    C. norm-referenced

    D. informal reading inventory

56. The purpose of anecdotal notes are

    A. to make note of everything a student is doing wrong.

    B. to observe students while they work and record the observations for later study.

    C. to make notes of student work and stick strictly to your lesson plan regardless of these notes.

    D. None of the above

57. Which of the following cooperative grouping strategies provides the opportunity for a small group to become experts on a given topic and then share it with their peers?

    A. partners
    B. numbered heads together
    C. think-pair-share
    D. jigsaw

58. While reading the *Magic Treehouse* series of books, a third-grader notices that the protagonists in the stories, Jack and Annie, have distinct personality traits: Jack is more serious, while Annie is more impulsive. The teacher, having read the series herself, facilitates the student's understanding of this particular literary element that is present in narrative texts. What literary element is she supporting?

    A. plot
    B. setting
    C. characterization
    D. style

59. Read the following poem written by Edward Lear:

> There was an Old Lady whose folly
> Induced her to sit in a holly;
>   Whereon, by a thorn
>   Her dress being torn,
> She quickly became melancholy.

In what poetic form is this particular poem written?

    A. haiku
    B. clerihew
    C. limerick
    D. ode

60. Knowing that learning goals are meant to align with standards, a level three is considered the target for all students. If this is the case, who fits in level four?

    A. a student working above mastery and extending the learning beyond the required skill(s)
    B. a student working below mastery level
    C. a student who has given up
    D. a student who is on grade level

IF YOU FINISH BEFORE TIME IS CALLED, CHECK YOUR WORK ON THIS SECTION ONLY. DO NOT WORK ON ANY OTHER SECTION IN THE TEST.

Social Science

55 Questions
65 Minutes

1. The two world superpowers that emerged from World War II were

   A. China and Japan.
   B. England and France.
   C. USSR and the USA.
   D. None of the above

2. Prior to Christopher Columbus's arrival, who had discovered the land we once called the New World?

   A. Vasco da Gama
   B. Nicolaus Copernicus
   C. Hernando de Soto
   D. the Vikings and Native Americans

3. What famous Spanish explorer searched the land now known as Florida for the Fountain of Youth?

   A. Juan Ponce de Leon
   B. Hernando Cortes
   C. Francisco Pizarro
   D. Vasco Núñez de Balboa

4. To create interest and motivate students to retain content area information, a variety of instructional methods must be employed. Which of the following instructional methods or strategies would NOT entice learners in the social studies classroom?

   A. use of guest speakers
   B. use of role play and simulation activities
   C. use of learning centers (stations)
   D. sole use of the textbook and chapter tests

5. Human systems refers to what essential element of teaching geography?

   A. location
   B. regions
   C. people
   D. process that shapes the Earth

6. What river did Hernando de Soto discover while exploring the present-day American Southeast?

   A. Missouri River
   B. Nile River
   C. Potomac River
   D. Mississippi River

7. The purpose of the Persian Gulf War was to

   A. liberate Kuwait and expel Iraqi forces.
   B. liberate Iraq.
   C. liberate Kenya.
   D. None of the above

8. Operation Desert Storm was the

    A. name for the United States land and air operations involved in the Gulf War effort.

    B. other name for the Gulf War.

    C. name the media used for the Persian Gulf War.

    D. name for a video game and had nothing to do with the Gulf War effort.

9. Which of the following statements describes the historical figure Thomas Jefferson?

    A. invented bifocals and the Franklin stove

    B. considered one of the founding fathers of our country and the principal author of the Declaration of Independence

    C. implemented and signed the Emancipation Proclamation

    D. led the nursing effort for the North during the Civil War and formed the American Red Cross after the war

10. During the Gilded Age, or the years following the Civil War, the Industrial Revolution made it possible for "robber barons" to accumulate gigantic fortunes. Which of the following people were considered "robber barons" during this time period?

    A. Andrew Carnegie

    B. John D. Rockefeller

    C. Cornelius Vanderbilt

    D. All of the above

11. Which of the following CANNOT be used as an instructional aid and assessment tool in the social studies classroom?

    A. anticipation guide

    B. K-W-H-L chart

    C. Venn diagram

    D. chapter test

12. Which of the following terms means a removal of trees and shrubs that, in mountainous regions, destabilizes the land?

    A. erosion

    B. continental drift

    C. deforestation

    D. None of the above

13. Who was the first astronomer to place the Sun at the center of the universe?

    A. Isaac Newton

    B. Nicolaus Copernicus

    C. Galileo Galilei

    D. John Locke

14. Humans living on Earth seek locations and environments that meet their basic needs. This has been true historically with various original settlers moving from location to location in search of land to farm and waters to fish. Which essential element of geography refers to this vital interaction between people and their surroundings?

    A. Environment and Society

    B. Human Systems

    C. Process that shapes the Earth

    D. World in Spatial terms

GO ON TO THE NEXT PAGE

15. Small representations, usually shapes and pictures, of real things on a map are known as

   A.   a legend.
   B.   cartographers.
   C.   symbols.
   D.   keys.

16. Which of the following is the horizontal, imaginary line that divides the Earth into its northern and southern halves?

   A.   prime meridian
   B.   Tropic of Capricorn
   C.   international date line
   D.   equator

17. What article of the Constitution established the judicial branch of government in the United States of America?

   A.   Article I
   B.   Article III
   C.   Article V
   D.   Article X

18. The Supreme Court is the highest court of appeals in the United States. One of its most important powers is the power of

   A.   legislative review.
   B.   executive review.
   C.   judicial review.
   D.   legal review.

19. On a theme park map, features like bathrooms and restaurants are drawn the right size and distance apart in an effort to accurately represent, in a smaller form, the park's amenities. This map is known as being drawn to

   A.   legend.
   B.   scale.
   C.   coordinates.
   D.   hemispheres.

20. _____ are the people that actually elect the president and vice president.

   A.   Electors
   B.   Voters
   C.   Constituents
   D.   None of the above

21. _____ refer to the physical characteristics of specific places and how they form and change.

   A.   Landmarks and symbols
   B.   Legends and keys
   C.   Places and regions
   D.   Maps and globes

22. In a third-grade classroom, the teacher wants the students to see the most accurate representation of our world, specifically the land masses versus water ratio. Which of the following would best meet this objective?

    A. world relief map

    B. world thematic map

    C. world political map

    D. a globe

23. Policies that stipulate how the United States and its corporations, organizations, and individual citizens interact with other countries is known as

    A. financial policy.

    B. foreign policy.

    C. inflation policy.

    D. trade policy.

24. Which of the following is considered a symbol of American finance and has a physical location in New York City?

    A. federal reserve banks

    B. credit unions

    C. stock market

    D. Wall Street

25. Effective consumer decision making includes all of the following EXCEPT

    A. comparing needs versus wants.

    B. selecting a popular brand.

    C. searching for high-quality products.

    D. making an informed purchase.

26. _____ is/are appointed officials in the judicial branch of government.

    A. Supreme Court justices

    B. The president of the United States

    C. The vice president of the United States

    D. State senators

27. In a market economy, who decides what goods and services will be produced?

    A. consumers

    B. government

    C. private businesses

    D. national organizations

28. The Executive Branch of government contains _____ departments.

    A. 10

    B. 13

    C. 14

    D. 15

GO ON TO THE NEXT PAGE

29. Which level of government has the ability to regulate intrastate trade?

    A. federal

    B. county

    C. local/state

    D. None of the above

30. To allow a student the opportunity to best understand how a witness experienced a historical event, the best resource would be a

    A. secondary source.

    B. primary source.

    C. textbook passage.

    D. WebQuest.

31. Slaves were first brought to the New World in the early _____ by the Spanish to help search for gold.

    A. 1500s

    B. 1600s

    C. 1700s

    D. 1800s

32. After the Industrial Revolution began in this country, _____ became the first major industrial power in the world in the 1700s.

    A. Germany

    B. the United States

    C. England

    D. France

33. If no presidential candidate receives the majority of the electoral votes in a national election, who has the power to choose the president of the United States?

    A. House of Representatives

    B. Senate

    C. Supreme Court

    D. former president may choose his successor

34. When a group of citizens claims that a bill that has gone through the process of becoming federal law is unconstitutional, which governmental body has the power to determine its constitutionality?

    A. Supreme Court

    B. president of the United States

    C. Senate

    D. secretary of state

35. Which historical document includes the right to a trial by a jury of your peers and freedom of religion?

    A. treaty of Paris

    B. Lewis and Clark expedition

    C. Bill of Rights

    D. Emancipation Proclamation

36. What are the three branches of government in the United States of America?

    A.   one, two, and three

    B.   legislative, judicial, and executive

    C.   House of Representatives, Senate, and president

    D.   state, local, and federal

37. Which of the following is NOT a service provided by a local government?

    A.   police and fire protection

    B.   water and sewer utilities

    C.   museums and libraries

    D.   theme parks and restaurants

38. Which of the following is NOT considered a right of a United States citizen?

    A.   right to vote

    B.   right to hold office

    C.   right to avoid paying taxes

    D.   right to serve on juries

39. Which of the following wars led to the start of the American Revolutionary War?

    A.   World War I

    B.   Civil War

    C.   French and Indian War

    D.   Industrial Revolution

40. The Axis Powers were defeated by the Allies in World War II, which led to the emergence of two world superpowers and inevitably the Cold War. Which of the following countries was one of the defeated Axis Powers?

    A.   Germany

    B.   England

    C.   France

    D.   Russia

41. Prince Henry the Navigator of Portugal is well known for pioneering

    A.   sponsored exploration and cartography.

    B.   the first passage to the New World.

    C.   the use of the looking glass.

    D.   None of the above

GO ON TO THE NEXT PAGE

42. There are _____ continents and _____ major oceans on Earth. Refer to the following map to complete this statement.

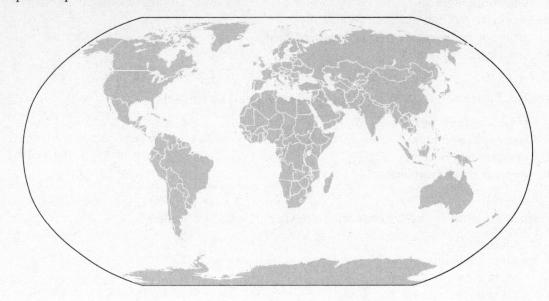

    A. 7, 4
    B. 7, 3
    C. 7, 6
    D. 7, 7

43. _____ assessments measure the products associated with student achievement. While using this form of assessment, the products are considered authentic—in other words, meaningful and significant.

    A. Paper-and-pencil
    B. Performance
    C. Team
    D. Oral

44. Which of the following would be considered an oral assessment task?

    A. cartoon
    B. map
    C. role play
    D. Venn diagram

45. Fourth-grade students are studying how severe weather impacts Florida's coastline. Being a top tourist destination, Florida's beaches significantly impact the state's economy. To effectively assess a student's ability to analyze the effects of severe weather on the economy, the teacher should require the students to

    A. independently read a passage and answer questions.
    B. write a cause-and-effect essay about the topic.
    C. talk about the subject for a few minutes.
    D. None of the above

46. Individuals rely on businesses to provide work as a source of income for themselves and their families. However, businesses also rely on individuals for labor and revenue. This scenario best describes the meaning of

    A. economic interdependence.

    B. fiscal policy.

    C. scarcity.

    D. a recession.

47. During a lesson about the United States government, a third-grade teacher explains that our country's foundation is built upon the Constitution. This important document or a replica of it is considered a(n) _____ source.

    A. excellent

    B. secondary

    C. primary

    D. patriotic

48. The small representations, usually shapes and pictures, of real things shown on a map are known as symbols. In order to understand what these symbols mean, the student must consult the

    A. compass rose

    B. cartographers.

    C. legend or key

    D. scale

49. When referring to geography, the acronym GPS stands for

    A. global press strategies.

    B. global positioning satellites.

    C. global positioning structures.

    D. global positioning system.

50. Understanding academic vocabulary used in a specific text is vital to reading comprehension. Which of the following would be considered an effective method for teaching academic vocabulary words to elementary-age students?

    A. The teacher provides a description and an example of the new word.

    B. The teacher allows her students to discuss the terms in small groups.

    C. The teacher requires the students to write each word five times.

    D. Both A and B

51. The United States and China practice a _____ economy.

    A. traditional

    B. purely command

    C. purely market

    D. mixed

GO ON TO THE NEXT PAGE

52. Teaching students to comprehend discipline specific text can be challenging. _____, where evidence directly from the text is documented on one side of the chart and the student's response to that text is noted on the other, can be a valuable tool for students to utilize when reading content area text.

    A.   Fill-in-the-blank tests

    B.   Double-entry journals

    C.   Semantic feature analysis charts

    D.   Anticipation guides

53. In a traditional economy, _____ influence the production, distribution, and consumption of goods and services.

    A.   cultural traditions

    B.   beliefs

    C.   customs

    D.   All of the above

54. The first ten amendments to the Constitution, known as the _____, were designed to protect individuals rights and limit government power.

    A.   Fundamental Values

    B.   Federalists Papers

    C.   Bill of Rights

    D.   None of the above

55. The NCSS is a specialized organization in this content area. What does NCSS stand for?

    A.   National Council for Safe Start

    B.   National Council for Student Studies

    C.   National Council for the Social Studies

    D.   National Council for the Social Sciences

IF YOU FINISH BEFORE TIME IS CALLED, CHECK YOUR WORK ON THIS SECTION ONLY. DO NOT WORK ON ANY OTHER SECTION IN THE TEST.

Science

55 Questions
70 Minutes

1. Which of the following strategies supports student inquiry in the science classroom?

   A. teacher-led discussion
   B. students designing and conducting an experiment
   C. students reading a textbook
   D. students watching a video of an experiment

2. The part of the Earth's crust that contains the continents is called

   A. the continental crust.
   B. the oceanic crust.
   C. the continental drift.
   D. Pangea.

3. A teacher asked her students to measure the acceleration of toy cars rolling down a ramp. In this experiment, students should use time as what type of variable?

   A. independent
   B. controlled
   C. dependent
   D. observed

4. The process by which a plant converts sunlight into food is called

   A. transpiration.
   B. respiration.
   C. photosynthesis.
   D. fertilization.

5. The necessity of a complete loop utilizing a battery, a small light bulb, and a connecting wire is an example of a(n)

   A. electrical circuit.
   B. mechanical circuit.
   C. kinetic circuit.
   D. application circuit.

6. The three layers of the Earth from inner to outer are

   A. mantle, crust, core.
   B. core, mantle, crust.
   C. crust, core, mantle.
   D. crust, mantle, core.

7. _____ is the classification of living things into categories based on physical characteristics.

   A. Taxidermy
   B. Taxonomy
   C. Topography
   D. Telegraph

GO ON TO THE NEXT PAGE

8. Which of the following is a common misconception in science?

    A. From the Earth, you can only see one side of the Moon.

    B. Seasons are caused by the tilt of the Earth's axis.

    C. Seasons are caused by the Earth's distance from the Sun.

    D. All of the above

9. The _____ is the factor that is changed between the experimental and control groups in an experiment.

    A. observation

    B. variable

    C. question

    D. hypothesis

10. A well-validated and well-supported explanation of some aspect of the natural world is called a

    A. postulate.

    B. hypothesis.

    C. scientific law.

    D. scientific theory.

11. A _____ Moon occurs when the Sun and Moon are on opposite sides of the Earth.

    A. Full

    B. New

    C. First Quarter

    D. Last Quarter

12. Students select a location in Florida, and then search the Internet for monthly temperature data of this location for the most recent El Niño year. Students then compare monthly temperature data for the El Niño year to the average temperature data for the past 25 years in order to assess the impact of El Niño on that particular location.

Which of the following would most likely be the most efficient method for students to use for recording and analyzing this information?

    A. e-mail

    B. spreadsheet

    C. LCD panel

    D. word processor

13. A traffic signal primarily involves which of the following processes?

    A. turns electrical energy into heat energy

    B. turns electrical energy into light energy

    C. turns light energy into electrical energy

    D. turns electrical energy into mechanical energy

14. The term defined as mass per unit of volume is called

    A. buoyancy.

    B. density.

    C. weight.

    D. physical change.

15. Which of the following is NOT a planet?

    A. Mercury

    B. Mars

    C. Pluto

    D. Neptune

16. Which of the following is NOT a kingdom for living things in the Linnaean classification system?

    A. Plants

    B. Animals

    C. Bacteria

    D. Fungi

17. What is defined as a possible answer to a question posed in a scientific experiment?

    A. control

    B. prediction

    C. hypothesis

    D. variable

18. The combustion of gasoline provokes what type of reaction?

    A. mechanical

    B. magnetic

    C. electrical

    D. chemical

19. What type of force always causes a change in motion?

    A. balanced

    B. neutral

    C. unbalanced

    D. motion

20. The theory that attempts to account for changes in species over time is often referred to as

    A. survival of the fittest.

    B. evolution.

    C. adaptation.

    D. heredity.

21. What type of experiment has a control group and an experimental group?

    A. random experiment

    B. quasi-experiment

    C. nested experiment

    D. controlled experiment

22. Alfred Wegener proposed a theory in which all the continents of the Earth were once joined in a supercontinent called

    A. Panacea.

    B. Panorama.

    C. Pangea.

    D. Pacifica.

GO ON TO THE NEXT PAGE

23. A lump of sugar dissolving in water is an example of

    A. physical change.
    B. chemical change.
    C. density change.
    D. volume change.

24. What is the genetic material that contains information needed to make new cells?

    A. RNA
    B. DNA
    C. proteins
    D. amino acids

25. A measurement of the total energy in a substance is called

    A. force.
    B. kinetic.
    C. heat.
    D. temperature.

26. Which of the following will NOT provide the best opportunities for inquiry-based learning?

    A. The teacher asks students to observe the Moon and record their observations. The teacher asks them to develop in small groups a model that will simulate what they have found and how the phases of the Moon change over time. They can also support their ideas with drawings of the model. They will have time to share and compare their findings and make corrections with teacher guidance.
    B. After completing a pre-assessment activity on students' knowledge of Moon phases, a student asks about the correct order of Moon phases. The teacher challenges students to determine the sequence of phases by observing the Moon and recording their observations for one month.
    C. Students complete a Moon phase calendar by cutting out photographs of the Moon in different phases, mounting them on a monthly calendar on the proper date, and appropriately labeling each of the eight major Moon phases.
    D. The teacher begins with the question, "Does the Moon rise and set at the same time every night?" Following a brief discussion of the question, the teacher demonstrates the rising and setting of the Moon for several sequential evenings using a computer simulation. The teacher then facilitates a class discussion.

27. Cells in which a nucleus does NOT exist are called

    A. prokaryotic cells.
    B. eukaryotic cells.
    C. nucleolus.
    D. ribosomes.

28. What causes a tsunami?

    A. volcanoes
    B. earthquakes
    C. continental drift
    D. Richter scale

29. Which of the following is NOT a type of energy?

    A. sound

    B. electric

    C. kinetic

    D. temperature

30. _____ rock is formed when a pre-existing rock changes form into a new rock, often through burial.

    A. Metamorphic

    B. Sedimentary

    C. Igneous

    D. Compressed

31. Bacteria that cause disease are called

    A. pathogens.

    B. infections.

    C. viruses.

    D. symbiotic.

32. Which of the following is NOT an aspect of the scientific method?

    A. predicting

    B. observing

    C. testing

    D. disseminating

33. Which *Apollo* flight took Neil Armstrong and Buzz Aldrin to the surface of the Moon?

    A. *Apollo 7*

    B. *Apollo 8*

    C. *Apollo 11*

    D. *Apollo 13*

34. _____ cells contain chloroplasts.

    A. Animal

    B. Bacteria

    C. Plant

    D. Fungal

35. Which type of electrical circuit uses only one electrical path?

    A. looping circuit

    B. singular circuit

    C. parallel circuit

    D. series circuit

GO ON TO THE NEXT PAGE

36. Convection currents cause

   A. magnetism.
   B. plate tectonics.
   C. electricity.
   D. photosynthesis.

37. Which one of the following terms might NOT be involved when an instrument is reliable?

   A. validity
   B. consistency
   C. repeatability
   D. precision

38. Heat is a measurement of the total energy made up of which of the following two energies of the molecules in a substance?

   A. temperature and potential energies
   B. kinetic and potential energies
   C. static and potential energies
   D. frictional and potential energies

39. Which is NOT a method of heat transfer?

   A. convection
   B. condensation
   C. radiation
   D. conduction

40. An organism that creates its own food is called a(n)

   A. heterotroph.
   B. heterozygote.
   C. autotroph.
   D. parasite.

41. Some students are involved in a scientific experiment. They want to measure the influence of different quantities of fertilizer on plant growth. To start, they consider the type of plant, the type of fertilizer, the amount of sunlight the plant gets, the size of the pots, and other factors that may influence the results. They want to plan ways to keep these factors constant. At this stage of the scientific process, what type of variables are the students dealing with?

   A. extraneous variables
   B. dependent variables
   C. independent variables
   D. controlled variables

42. Which of the following is a conclusion that can be drawn from the following graph?

**Number of Adult
Frogs in Pond**

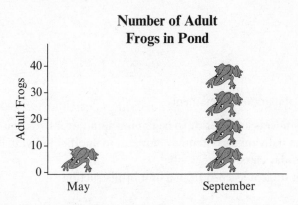

A. Frog eggs hatch between May and September.
B. The number of adult frogs in the south pond decreased between May and September.
C. Adult frogs quadrupled between May and September.
D. Adult frogs died between May and September.

43. Who was the first American to orbit the Earth?

A. John Glenn
B. Neil Armstrong
C. Alan Shepard
D. Yuri Gagarin

44. Which of the following is NOT a type of vertebrate?

A. mammal
B. bird
C. fish
D. worm

45. Which of the following is a good laboratory procedure?

A. sterilizing goggles between uses
B. wearing gowns
C. disposing of chemicals properly
D. All of the above

46. Which of the following do all cells contain?

A. cell membranes
B. cytoplasm
C. DNA
D. All of the above

GO ON TO THE NEXT PAGE

47. Which of the following is an appropriate unit of measure for the weight of a horse?

    A. pounds
    B. ounces
    C. gallons
    D. feet

48. What is the purpose of comparative assessment?

    A. to determine what students know prior to beginning a unit of instruction
    B. to determine how an individual's outcome compares to another individual's outcome
    C. to help guide day-to-day classroom activities
    D. to determine what a student learned from a unit of instruction

49. The type of reproduction in which offspring come from one parent and are an identical copy of the parent is called

    A. sexual reproduction
    B. mitosis
    C. replication
    D. asexual reproduction

50. Which of the following can be used to help students understand the abstract concepts of potential and kinetic energy?

    A. a video about sources of energy
    B. students racing toy cars on an inclined track
    C. a classroom discussion of a teacher demonstration
    D. students creating electrical circuits using light bulbs and batteries

51. Which of the following is NOT a productive disposition for scientific thinking?

    A. closed to new ideas
    B. appropriate skepticism
    C. cooperation
    D. curiosity

52. A well-validated and well-supported explanation of an aspect of the natural world is called a

    A. scientific law.
    B. scientific theory.
    C. hypothesis.
    D. scientific method.

53. Which type of cloud is characterized as wispy and feathery and forms at high altitudes from ice crystals?

    A. stratus
    B. cumulus
    C. cirrus
    D. nimbus

54. Which of the following can help students collect data related to temperature changes throughout an experiment?

    A. database

    B. barometer

    C. spectrometer

    D. temperature probe

55. What does STEM stand for?

    A. Science Teaching of Electricity and Magnetism

    B. Science Teaching with Engineering and Mathematics

    C. Social Technologies for Engineering Mechanics

    D. Science, Technology, Engineering, and Mathematics

IF YOU FINISH BEFORE TIME IS CALLED, CHECK YOUR WORK ON THIS SECTION ONLY. DO NOT WORK ON ANY OTHER SECTION IN THE TEST.

Mathematics

50 Questions
70 Minutes

1. A student wrote $\frac{1}{2}$ as an answer to a fraction computation problem. What type of representation model is the student using?

   A. concrete
   B. pictorial
   C. numeral
   D. number

2. In the following error pattern, which is most likely the weakness this student has?

$$\begin{array}{ccc} \overset{3\,4}{234} & \overset{4\,4}{145} & \overset{4\,4}{244} \\ \times\ 9 & \times\ 9 & \times\ 9 \\ \hline 2110 & 1305 & 2200 \end{array}$$

   A. multiplication concepts
   B. rate
   C. flexibility
   D. accuracy

3. The results of this type of test could help in identifying a student's specific problem areas.

   A. objective test
   B. standardized test
   C. criterion-referenced test
   D. diagnostic test

4. The number 0.77... is equal to

   A. $0.\overline{7}$
   B. 7%
   C. 77%
   D. 0.7

5. Find the next term in the pattern 3, 6, 9, 12, 15, . . .

   A. 17
   B. 18
   C. 19
   D. 20

6. Between which whole numbers could $-6.8 \cdot 10^{-1}$ be on a number line?

   A. -70 and -60
   B. 0 and -1
   C. 0 and 1
   D. 60 and 70

7. The expression $b^3 \cdot b^6$ is equal to

A. b^9
B. $18b$
C. $9b$
D. b^{18}

Use the following data set to answer items 8, 9, 10, and 11.

The students in a class received the following scores in a test worth 25 points:

12, 13, 10, 14, 23, 12, 13, 22, 12, 12, 10, 11, 15, 20, 10, 12, 10, 15, 22, 23

8. What is the mean of the data set?

A. 12
B. 12.5
C. 14.55
D. 291

9. What is the median of the data set?

A. 12
B. 12.5
C. 13
D. 14

10. What is the mode of the data set?

A. 2
B. 10 and 12
C. 10
D. 12

11. What is the range of the data set?

A. 4
B. 12
C. 13
D. 14

12. What is the value of x in the equation $2^{-4} \cdot -1 = x$?

A. -16
B. $\dfrac{-1}{16}$
C. $\dfrac{1}{16}$
D. 16

13. Which expression matches the following description?

Four times a number plus 12

A. $4 + 12n$
B. $4(n + 12)$
C. $4n + 12$
D. $4 + 12 + n$

GO ON TO THE NEXT PAGE

14. Natalie, Paul, Samuel, and Greta were comparing the distances from their houses to school. The distances were Natalie, $2\frac{2}{5}$ miles; Paul, $2\frac{1}{3}$ miles; Samuel, $2\frac{3}{8}$ miles; and Greta, $2\frac{3}{5}$ miles. What is the order of names based on these distances from least to greatest?

    A. Samuel, Paul, Greta, and Natalie
    B. Samuel, Paul, Natalie, and Greta
    C. Greta, Natalie, Samuel, and Paul
    D. Paul, Samuel, Natalie, and Greta

15. What shape could NOT be made by combining a rectangle with a triangle?

    A. pentagon
    B. hexagon
    C. heptagon
    D. octagon

16. A flagpole casts a shadow that is 12 feet long. A man who is 6 feet tall casts a shadow that is 9 feet long. How tall is the flagpole?

    A. 8 feet
    B. 9 feet
    C. 15 feet
    D. 18 feet

17. Which of the following is the same as 6^{-3}?

    A. 216
    B. $\dfrac{1}{216}$
    C. $-\dfrac{1}{216}$
    D. -216

18. A form of assessment that incorporates real-life functions and applications is called

    A. alternative assessment.
    B. authentic assessment.
    C. naturalistic assessment.
    D. diagnostic assessment.

19. The following figure is created through which transformation?

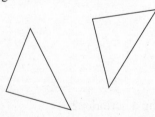

    A. translation
    B. reflection
    C. rotation
    D. dilation

20. Mary has 35 books at her home library, 21 of these books are softcover books, and the rest of the books are hardcover books. What percent of Mary's books are hardcover books?

    A. 60%

    B. 40%

    C. 166%

    D. 250%

21. A zoo sells peanuts and hot dogs. The cost of peanuts is $2 a box. The cost of a hot dog is $3.50. How much will a customer spend to buy p boxes of peanuts and h hot dogs?

    A. $2p + 3.50h$

    B. $2p - 3.50h$

    C. $2p$

    D. $3.50h$

22. The line graph that follows shows the percent of buyers (shoppers who purchased something) at a shopping center from 1988 to 2013. Using this graph, predict the percent of buyers for the year 2018 at this shopping center.

    A. 42%

    B. 46%

    C. 52%

    D. 55%

GO ON TO THE NEXT PAGE

23. Identify the coordinates of point *T* in the figure shown.

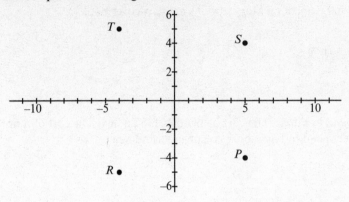

    A. (5, –4)
    B. (–4, 5)
    C. (–4, –5)
    D. (–5, –4)

24. Oranges cost $0.58 for a pound. Laura buys 13 pounds every day from Monday to Friday for her restaurant. How much will she have spent after 4 weeks?

    A. $150.80
    B. $37.70
    C. $30.16
    D. $7.54

25. Nancy made the following picture to show the relationship between products: $(3)(8) = 3(6 + 2) = 18 + 6$.

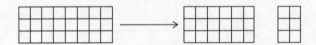

Which of the following multiplication models is most likely involved in this demonstration?

    A. multiplicative comparison
    B. rectangular array or tiling
    C. repeated addition
    D. combination

26. If 4 hands are equivalent to 10 thumbs, how many thumbs are in 12 hands?

    A. 30 thumbs
    B. 20 thumbs
    C. 18 thumbs
    D. 5 thumbs

27. Solve for *x*: $3(2x - 5) \leq 8x - 3$

    A. $x \geq 6$
    B. $x \leq 6$
    C. $x \leq -6$
    D. $x \geq -6$

28. Which one of the following pairs of factors does NOT have a greatest common factor (GCF) equal to 6?

    A.   24, 6

    B.   42, 150

    C.   54, 18

    D.   18, 30

29. Which of the following can NOT be folded to make a rectangular prism?

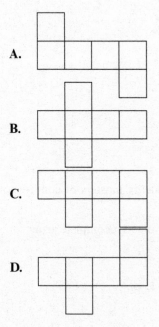

    A.

    B.

    C.

    D.

30. If the radius of a circle is cut in half, what happens to the area of that circle?

    A.   Cut in half

    B.   Cut in fourth

    C.   Doubled

    D.   Tripled

31. Which of the following is NOT an appropriate assessment practice?

    A.   Assessment should be ongoing and summative.

    B.   The best assessment also instructs.

    C.   Best instructional tasks are rich with diagnostic opportunities.

    D.   We should always teach, then assess.

32. Find the greatest common factor (GCF) of the following pair of algebraic expressions: $20x^2y$ and $50xy^2$.

    A. xy

    B.   10

    C. $10xy$

    D. $100x^2y^2$

GO ON TO THE NEXT PAGE

33. What property shows that $3(x - 2) = 3x - 6$?

    A. associative

    B. commutative

    C. distributive

    D. identity

34. Find the area of the trapezoid shown.

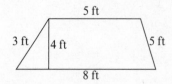

    A. 32 ft²

    B. 26 ft²

    C. 21 ft²

    D. 20 ft²

35. Which of the following is the most appropriate learning progression for students' mastery of concepts of area measurement?

    A. **First:** Draw rows and columns to determine the area of a rectangle, given an incomplete array.

        Second: Form rectangles by tiling with unit squares to make arrays.

        Third: Interpret area models to form rectangular arrays.

        Fourth: Find the area of a rectangle through multiplication of the side lengths.

    B. **First:** Form rectangles by tiling with unit squares to make arrays.

        Second: Interpret area models to form rectangular arrays.

        Third: Draw rows and columns to determine the area of a rectangle, given an incomplete array.

        Fourth: Find the area of a rectangle through multiplication of the side lengths.

    C. **First:** Form rectangles by tiling with unit squares to make arrays.

        Second: Draw rows and columns to determine the area of a rectangle, given an incomplete array.

        Third: Find the area of a rectangle through multiplication of the side lengths.

        Fourth: Interpret area models to form rectangular arrays.

    D. **First:** Form rectangles by tiling with unit squares to make arrays.

        Second: Draw rows and columns to determine the area of a rectangle, given an incomplete array.

        Third: Interpret area models to form rectangular arrays.

        Fourth: Find the area of a rectangle through multiplication of the side lengths.

36. Which of the following exercises best assesses student understanding of the division concepts (for example, sharing division and measurement division)?

    A. Take timed test involving division basic facts.

    B. Solve word problems involving the sharing division concept using cubes to model the solutions.

    C. Write word problems that illustrate division concepts using different types of manipulative materials.

    D. Solve word problems involving division concepts using only paper and pencil.

37. Which of the following is the most appropriate sequence of stages for students' development of basic automaticity?

A. **Stage 1:** Strategies for remembering math facts
Stage 2: Figuring out math facts
Stage 3: Developing speed and accuracy with math facts

B. **Stage 1:** Figuring out math facts
Stage 2: Strategies for remembering math facts
Stage 3: Developing speed and accuracy with math facts

C. **Stage 1:** Developing speed and accuracy with math facts
Stage 2: Figuring out math facts
Stage 3: Strategies for remembering math facts

D. **Stage 1:** Figuring out math facts
Stage 2: Developing speed and accuracy with math facts
Stage 3: Strategies for remembering math facts

38. A teacher asked students to demonstrate the solution process for solving word problems involving two-digit numbers and different operations using base-ten blocks. Which of the following is she most likely assessing?

A. appropriate use of speed accuracy when solving word problems
B. appropriate conceptual knowledge of operations
C. appropriate procedural understanding of computation algorithms
D. appropriate flexibility with computation algorithms

39. Which one of the following is the sum of the prime factors of 120?

A. 14
B. 10
C. 8
D. 7

40. The inputs and outputs of a functional relationship are represented in the table shown. Find the expression that represents the relationship between inputs and outputs, and answer the question that follows.

Input	Output
1	2
2	5
3	8
...	
30	?

Which of the following outputs would be obtained if 30 is the input?

A. 86
B. 89
C. 90
D. 91

GO ON TO THE NEXT PAGE

41. If $y = -3x - 5$, then what is the value of y if x is 2?

   A. 11

   B. 1

   C. −11

   D. −1

42. A survey of 1,188 students at an elementary school was taken to find how they get to school each day. The results are shown in the following table.

**How Students Get to School
Each Day by Grade Level**

	Take a Bus	Walk	Adult Drives	Other	Total
Third grade	139	123	76	85	423
Fourth grade	47	140	113	89	389
Fifth grade	158	143	41	34	376
Total	344	406	230	208	1,188

Which statement can be verified using the information in the table?

   A. At this elementary school, fewer fourth-graders use different forms of transportation than fifth-graders, because fewer students attend fourth grade.

   B. At this elementary school, the number of fourth-graders who take the bus is greater than the number of third-graders who walk to school.

   C. At this elementary school, more students in all grade levels take the bus to get to school than any of the other types of transportation.

   D. At this elementary school, the number of fifth-graders who take the bus is greater than the number of fourth-graders who walk to school.

43. Carla has two jobs. She earns $9 per hour tutoring her neighbor's son, and she earns $12 per hour working at the supermarket. Carla is working 25 hours at the supermarket this week. What is the number of full hours she must work as a tutor to reach a minimum income of $350 for the week?

   A. 5.5 hours

   B. 5 hours

   C. 6 hours

   D. 11 hours

44. Use the following addition exercise to answer this item:

$$32$$
$$48$$
$$12$$
$$+\ 68$$

When a student was solving this exercise, she quickly answered "160." When asked about how she solved the exercise, she indicated that she added 68 and 32 first to get 100, and then she added 48 and 12 to get 60. Finally, she said that she added 100 and 60 to get the final answer, 160. Which of the following combination of addition properties did she use when solving this exercise?

   A. distributive and additive inverse properties

   B. commutative and additive identity properties

   C. commutative and associative properties

   D. associative and additive identity properties

45. Solve for x: $4(2 - x) + 5 = 3(2x - 3) - 8$

    A. $x = 1$

    B. $x = 3$

    C. $x = 8$

    D. $x = 15$

46. Which is the most appropriate sequence for the following learning progression through the levels of geometric thinking?

    A. **First:** Classifying using properties of shapes

        Second: Drawing shapes

        Third: Constructing proofs using postulates or axioms

        Fourth: Determining if a particular shape is included in a given set

    B. **First:** Drawing shapes

        Second: Determining if a particular shape is included in a given set

        Third: Classifying using properties of shapes

        Fourth: Constructing proofs using postulates or axioms

    C. **First:** Drawing shapes

        Second: Classifying using properties of shapes

        Third: Determining if a particular shape is included in a given set

        Fourth: Constructing proofs using postulates or axioms

    D. **First:** Classifying using properties of shapes

        Second: Drawing shapes

        Third: Determining if a particular shape is included in a given set

        Fourth: Constructing proofs using postulates or axioms

47. A student sees the dot arrangement on a domino (four dots on each side) and just knows that the number is eight. Which of the following is most likely represented by this example?

    A. subitizing

    B. iteration

    C. accuracy

    D. automaticity

48. A student provided an alternative computation algorithm for $52 + 38$. He indicated that $52 + 38 = 50 + 40 = 90$. What component of computational fluency is most likely represented by this student's answer?

    A. rate

    B. automaticity

    C. accuracy

    D. flexibility

GO ON TO THE NEXT PAGE

49. Ana needs at least 325 points to break the record for number of points for one regular season in her basketball league. There are 11 games in the regular season. She has scored the following number of points in the last ten games, respectively:

28, 27, 22, 30, 38, 28, 30, 31, 25, 36

How many points does she have to score in the last game of the season to break the record?

  A. 29

  B. 30

  C. 31

  D. 35

50. A 6-ounce can of peaches sells for 89¢. An 8-ounce can of peaches sells for $1.17. Assuming quality is not an issue, which one is the better buy?

  A. They are both good buys, as they both yield the same cost per ounce.

  B. The 6-ounce can of peaches is a better buy.

  C. The 8-ounce can of peaches is a better buy.

  D. I cannot tell from the information provided.

IF YOU FINISH BEFORE TIME IS CALLED, CHECK YOUR WORK ON THIS SECTION ONLY. DO NOT WORK ON ANY OTHER SECTION IN THE TEST.

Answer Key

Language Arts and Reading

1. C	16. D	31. C	46. A
2. C	17. D	32. A	47. C
3. D	18. B	33. C	48. B
4. A	19. C	34. A	49. C
5. D	20. A	35. D	50. D
6. C	21. A	36. D	51. A
7. D	22. D	37. A	52. B
8. B	23. C	38. C	53. D
9. B	24. B	39. A	54. C
10. C	25. C	40. B	55. C
11. A	26. D	41. A	56. B
12. D	27. D	42. B	57. D
13. B	28. B	43. D	58. C
14. C	29. B	44. B	59. C
15. B	30. A	45. C	60. A

Social Science

1. C	15. C	29. C	43. B
2. D	16. D	30. B	44. C
3. A	17. B	31. A	45. B
4. D	18. C	32. C	46. A
5. C	19. B	33. A	47. C
6. D	20. A	34. A	48. C
7. A	21. C	35. C	49. D
8. A	22. D	36. B	50. D
9. B	23. B	37. D	51. D
10. D	24. D	38. C	52. B
11. D	25. B	39. C	53. D
12. C	26. A	40. A	54. C
13. B	27. A	41. A	55. C
14. A	28. D	42. A	

Science

1. B	15. C	29. D	43. A
2. A	16. C	30. A	44. D
3. A	17. C	31. A	45. D
4. C	18. D	32. D	46. D
5. A	19. C	33. C	47. A
6. B	20. B	34. C	48. B
7. B	21. D	35. D	49. D
8. C	22. C	36. B	50. B
9. B	23. A	37. A	51. A
10. D	24. B	38. B	52. B
11. A	25. C	39. B	53. C
12. B	26. C	40. C	54. D
13. B	27. A	41. D	55. D
14. B	28. B	42. C	

Mathematics

1. C	14. D	27. D	40. B
2. D	15. D	28. C	41. C
3. D	16. A	29. C	42. D
4. A	17. B	30. B	43. C
5. B	18. B	31. D	44. C
6. B	19. C	32. C	45. B
7. A	20. B	33. C	46. C
8. C	21. A	34. B	47. A
9. B	22. B	35. D	48. D
10. D	23. B	36. C	49. B
11. C	24. A	37. B	50. C
12. B	25. B	38. C	
13. C	26. A	39. B	

Answer Explanations

Language Arts and Reading

1. **C.** Competency 1. "Talking to the text" or performing a think aloud is a strategy that supports the idea of actively reading a text.

2. **C.** Competency 2. Biography is a literary genre. All other choices are considered subsets of folklore.

3. **D.** Competency 3. Persuasive writing is writing that attempts to convince the reader that a point of view is valid or that the reader should take a specific action. While descriptive, expository, and narrative are all modes of writing, they do not match the description in the question stem.

4. **A.** Competency 3. Amy's use of random strings of letters shows that she knows that print conveys a message; however, her next step would be to convey that she knows that individual letters have a sound symbol relationship.

5. **D.** Competency 4. Criterion-referenced tests are assessment instruments that assess the point at which the student has achieved mastery. These tests enable educators to determine whether or not a student has met a predetermined goal.

6. **C.** Competency 5. Blogs are user-friendly web pages that allow students to post and comment on their work.

7. **D.** Competency 5. Comprehension, listening, and speaking skills are all enhanced by questioning and retelling.

8. **B.** Competency 5. Visual media is nonprint media.

9. **B.** Competency 3. The teacher is truly focusing on the content, is encouraging her students to revise and improve upon what has been written, and is not yet concerned with editing for errors.

10. **C.** Competency 4. Concepts of print include that print conveys meaning, directionality (left to right and top to bottom progression), concept of a word (word boundaries), letter knowledge, phonemic awareness, and literacy language (author, illustrations, title, etc.).

11. **A.** Competency 1. The onset is defined as the first consonant or groups of consonants (*sh*) that come before the first vowel in a syllable. The rime unit is the first vowel sound and any others that follow it in a syllable (*ut*).

12. **D.** Competency 1. Directionality (left to right and top to bottom progression) or reading, the title page, and illustrations are all examples of basic concepts of print. Captions provided to illustrations and photographs are nonfiction text features common in informational text.

13. **B.** Competency 1. An onset rime consists of the phonological unit that precedes the vowel and rime unit or string of letters that usually include a vowel and the final consonants that follow.

14. **C.** Competency 1. A grapheme is a letter or group of letters that represents one sound, like *ough* in *though*. An onset is defined as the first consonant or groups of consonants (*sh*) that come before the first vowel in a syllable. A rime unit is the first vowel sound and any others that follow it in a syllable (*ut*).

15. **B.** Competency 2. Alliteration is defined as two or more words or syllables near each other with the same beginning consonant.

16. **D.** Competency 4. Reading centers/stations allow students to co-construct meaning in a small group setting. For the teacher, this organizational format allows time to meet with guided reading groups and to differentiate instruction to meet the varying needs of students in the classroom.

17. **D.** Competency 5. Primary sources are documents or pieces of work that were written, recorded, or created during a particular time period. They are valuable teaching tools and artifacts.

18. **B.** Competency 5. Students are typically taught cursive in the third grade.

19. C. Competency 3. The students wish to persuade the school board to keep their music classes at each school site.

20. A. Competency 4. The workshop approach is a student-centered approach to teaching where teachers have ample time to meet and confer with small groups and individuals to best meet their academic needs.

21. A. Competency 2. Literature circles (book clubs) are small groups of children reading a chosen text and discussing that text on a routine and regular basis with a group of their peers.

22. D. Competency 3. Prewriting is the phase of the writing process that includes activating prior knowledge, gathering and organizing ideas, and brainstorming. Drafting, editing, and revising are all later phases in the writing process.

23. C. Competency 2. A simile is a literary device that utilizes the words *like* or *as*.

24. B. Competency 3. The editing phase of writing is where teachers encourage students to correct any errors they may see in their writing.

25. C. Competency 1. Right-there or text-explicit questions are literal questions where the answers are found in the text itself.

26. D. Competency 1. In addition to the methods noted, timed reading, readers theater, audio books, poetry readings, independent reading, and paired reading also aid students' reading fluency.

27. D. Competency 4. Oral reading fluency can be enhanced by many instructional methods like repeated reading, choral reading, and readers theater, with the key factor being repetition.

28. B. Competency 5. Line quality is defined in legible handwriting as the consistency of the pencil strokes.

29. B. Competency 4. If a student read a 200-word piece in 4 minutes 45 seconds with 6 recorded errors, her accuracy rate would be as follows: $\frac{(200-6)\cdot 60}{285 \text{ seconds}} = 40.9$ WCPM. Thus, the student reads 40.9 words correct per minute.

30. A. Competency 1. To summarize is to simply and concisely paraphrase the key details of what has been read.

31. C. Competency 1. All of the choices offer terms related to the teaching of the language arts. Graphophonemic, semantic, and syntactic are the three cueing systems in the reading process.

32. A. Competency 2. Historical fiction is a literary genre in which the action takes place in the past. The settings are drawn from history and often contain historical persons and events. Choices B, C, and D are types of nonfiction.

33. C. Competency 1. Summarizing is the ability to simply and concisely paraphrase what has been read.

34. A. Competency 5. Kidspiration is an example of computer software that can be used to create graphic organizers, timelines, etc., that enhance the comprehension of skills taught in the classroom through the use of technology.

35. D. Competency 2. Understanding the author's purpose is critical to comprehension but is not defined as a narrative literary element.

36. D. Competency 1. Phonemic awareness, phonics, fluency, vocabulary, and comprehension are the five critical skills needed for reading success.

37. A. Competency 1. A primary source is a document or piece of work that was actually written, recorded, or created during the specific time under study.

38. C. Competency 2. Classroom libraries should contain a wide variety of multicultural children's literature, nonfiction resources, and various genres.

39. A. Competency 1. A sight word is a word that does not follow the traditional rules of the English language and must be memorized.

40. B. Competency 1. A vowel digraph is defined as two vowels together that make one phoneme or sound, such as the *au* in *cause*.

41. A. Competency 5. The teacher's daily schedule should include opportunities for whole group and small group lessons so students can practice their listening and speaking skills in a supportive environment.

42. B. Competency 1. Accuracy, prosody, rate, and automaticity are all components of reading fluency.

43. D. Competency 1. Understanding the main idea, supporting details and facts, author's purpose, fact and opinion, point of view, making inferences, and visualizing are all critical to making meaning from text, known as comprehension.

44. B. Competency 2. Metonymy is a literary device that refers to substituting a more formal word with a word closely related to it.

45. C. Competency 3. The graphophonic cueing system refers to analyzing letters and phonemes (sounds). In the English language many letters sounds can be formed to sound a variety of ways.

46. A. Competency 3. Graphophonic cues are most evident in onomatopoeia because as you read the word, you also get a clue to its meaning.

47. C. Competency 4. Monitoring student progress by observing and facilitating small group discussions is considered a form of informal assessment.

48. B. Competency 3. The expository mode of writing provides facts and data to inform the reader.

49. C. Competency 4. Segmenting and blending are integral parts of phonological awareness.

50. D. Competency 3. The mode of writing that includes the elements of characterization, setting, plot, theme, and style is narrative.

51. A. Competency 4. During read aloud and shared reading, teachers can model all concepts of a book.

52. B. Competency 5. A thesaurus is the appropriate resource to use when looking for synonyms.

53. D. Competency 5. An atlas is a collection of maps, which is an excellent classroom resource, especially for social studies education.

54. C. Competency 4. Interest inventories provide the teacher with an idea of students' likes, hobbies, and pastimes that could be used to identify appropriate reading material that meet their individual interests.

55. C. Competency 4. The Gates-MacGinitie Reading Tests (K–12) are norm-referenced tests.

56. B. Competency 4. The purpose of anecdotal notes as an informal form of assessment is to document students' strengths and weaknesses to then use this data to inform instruction.

57. D. Competency 4. The cooperative grouping strategy known as a jigsaw provides the opportunity for a small group to become experts on a given topic and then share it with their peers.

58. C. Competency 2. Literary elements in narratives include setting, characterization, plot, and theme. Characterization is the means by which authors demonstrate through their writing style the credibility of their characters.

59. C. Competency 2. A limerick is a five-line poem with the following rhyme scheme: aabba. Haiku poems are usually about nature, and contain 17 syllables and three unrhymed lines (5, 7, 5 syllables in each line). Clerihews possess two rhyming couplets (four lines total) that usually make fun of celebrities. An ode is a poem that celebrates a person, animal, or object.

60. A. Competency 4. A student working above mastery and extending the learning beyond the required skill(s) on a scale would be considered a level four.

Social Science

1. **C.** Competency 2. The attack on Pearl Harbor resulted in the United States involvement in the war. In 1945, the Allies defeated the Axis Powers, with the USSR and the United States emerging as the world's superpowers.

2. **D.** Competency 2. Columbus made four voyages in an effort to find a route to the East. During his expeditions he discovered the Bahamas, Hispaniola, Cuba, Dominica, Guadeloupe, Jamaica, Central America, and South America. As illustrations and historical accounts depict, he was greeted by Native Americans, who had settled the land prior to his arrival; the Vikings had also been known to have explored the area.

3. **A.** Competency 2. All of the listed choices are Spanish explorers; however, Juan Ponce de Leon is known for his search for the Fountain of Youth.

4. **D.** Competency 1. The use of guest speakers, role play/simulation activities, and learning centers are examples of instructional methods that can be used in the social studies classroom to incite interest and comprehension of major concepts being presented.

5. **C.** Competency 3. Human systems refers to people or inhabitants.

6. **D.** Competency 2. Hernando de Soto discovered the Mississippi River.

7. **A.** Competency 2. The purpose of the Persian Gulf War was to liberate Kuwait and expel Iraqi forces.

8. **A.** Competency 2. Operation Desert Storm was the name for the United States land and air operations involved in the Gulf War effort.

9. **B.** Competency 2. Thomas Jefferson is considered one of the founding fathers of our country and is the principal author of the Declaration of Independence. Benjamin Franklin invented bifocals and the Franklin stove. Abraham Lincoln implemented and signed the Emancipation Proclamation. Clara Barton led the nursing effort for the North during the Civil War and formed the American Red Cross once the war was over.

10. **D.** Competency 2. Andrew Carnegie, John D. Rockefeller, and Cornelius Vanderbilt were all considered robber barons and made their fortunes in railroads.

11. **D.** Competency 1. Anticipation guides, K-W-H-L charts, and Venn diagrams are all graphic organizers that can be used for both instructional and assessment purposes. Chapter tests are used as assessment instruments only.

12. **C.** Competency 3. Deforestation is described as a clearing of trees and shrubs that when performed in a mountainous region tends to destabilize the land.

13. **B.** Competency 2. Copernicus placed the Sun at the center of the universe. Newton was an English physicist, mathematician, astronomer, natural philosopher, alchemist, and theologian known for defining gravity and the laws of motion. Galileo Galilei was an Italian physicist, mathematician, astronomer, and philosopher responsible for the birth of modern science. John Locke was a British Enlightenment writer whose ideas influenced the Declaration of Independence and the United States Constitution.

14. **A.** Competency 3. The essential element of geography that refers to the interaction between people and their surroundings is the Environment and Society.

15. **C.** Competency 3. Small representations, usually shapes and pictures, of real things on a map are known as symbols.

16. **D.** Competency 3. The horizontal, imaginary line that divides the Earth into its northern and southern halves is the equator.

17. **B.** Competency 4. Article III established the judicial branch of government.

18. **C.** Competency 4. One of the Supreme Court's most important powers is the power of judicial review.

19. **B.** Competency 3. Scale is when something on a map is drawn to size. In other words, in relation to other items on the map, features are the right size and distance apart; the larger the scale, the more detail shown (for example, a theme park map), the smaller the scale, the more area shown but the less detail (for example, a world map).

20. **A.** Competency 4. After voters express their wishes at the polls, electors are the actual people that elect the president and vice president of the United States of America.

21. **C.** Competency 3. Places and regions refer to the physical characteristics of specific places and how they form and change.

22. **D.** Competency 3. A globe, which is a small scale model, is said to be the most accurate representation of the Earth.

23. **B.** Competency 5. Policies that aid in governing the interactions between United States citizens, corporations, and organizations and other countries around the world is known as foreign policy.

24. **D.** Competency 5. Wall Street is a symbol of American finance and is located in lower Manhattan in New York City.

25. **B.** Competency 5. Consumer decision making entails several steps, including comparing needs versus wants, searching for high-quality products, studying the attributes of those items to ascertain whether or not they meet the need, comparing prices, and eventually making an informed purchase. Selecting a popular brand is not part of effective consumer decision making.

26. **A.** Competency 4. Supreme Court justices are appointed officials in the judicial branch of government. Each of the other choices is an elected official.

27. **A.** Competency 5. According to principles of supply and demand, consumers decide what kinds of goods and services will be produced.

28. **D.** Competency 5. The Executive Branch of the United States government contains 15 departments (i.e., Department of Defense, Department of Justice, Department of Education).

29. **C.** Competency 4. The local and state government have the ability to regulate intrastate (between states) trade.

30. **B.** Competency 1. A primary source document is one that was created during a specific time period and accurately depicts what occurred at that time.

31. **A.** Competency 2. Once Europeans had found the Americas and triangular trade was taking place between Europe, Africa, and North America, Europeans decided they could use Africans as slaves. The Spanish in particular decided to use these African slaves to help search for gold in America.

32. **C.** Competency 2. England became the first major industrial power in the world.

33. **A.** Competency 4. If no presidential candidate receives the majority of the electoral votes in a national election, the House of Representatives has the power to choose the president of the United States.

34. **A.** Competency 4. When a group of citizens claims that a bill that has gone through the process of becoming federal law is unconstitutional, the Supreme Court with its power of judicial review has the power to determine its constitutionality.

35. **C.** Competency 4. The historical document that includes the right to a trial by a jury of your peers and freedom of religion is the Bill of Rights.

36. **B.** Competency 4. The three branches of government are legislative, judicial, and executive.

37. **D.** Competency 4. Theme parks and restaurants are not provided by local governments. Local governments provide many services including but not limited to the following: police and fire protection, water and sewer utilities, education, public housing, transportation and road repair, libraries, museums, and sports facilities.

38. C. Competency 4. An accurate definition of a United States citizen is a person who is legally recognized as a member of this nation with specific inalienable rights and responsibilities, which do not include tax evasion.

39. C. Competency 2. The French and Indian War (1754–1763), which was an extension of the European Seven Years War, was a battle over colonial territory and wealth by the French and the English. This war resulted in effectively ending French cultural and political influence in North America. In their victory, England gained massive amounts of land but also weakened their rapport with the Native Americans. In sum, although the war strengthened England's hold on the colonies, it also worsened their relationship, which inevitably led to the Revolutionary War.

40. A. Competency 2. The Second World War (WWII) was a global military conflict between two opposing forces: the Allies (Leaders)—Great Britain (Churchill), United States (Roosevelt/Truman), Russia (Stalin), Free France (De Gaulle), and China (Chiang Kai-shek), and the Axis Powers (Leaders)—Germany (Hitler), Italy (Mussolini), and Japan (Hirohito).

41. A. Competency 2. Prince Henry the Navigator of Portugal is well known for pioneering sponsored exploration and cartography.

42. A. Competency 3. There are seven continents (North America, South America, Africa, Europe, Antarctica, Asia, and Australia) and four major oceans (Pacific, Atlantic, Indian, and Arctic) on Earth.

43. B. Competency 1. Performance assessments measure real instances of learning (products) that are considered authentic or real-world applications of student learning.

44. C. Competency 1. Role play along with oral reports, skits, discussions, and debates are all oral assessment tasks.

45. B. Competency 1. Writing a cause-and-effect essay allows students the opportunity to analyze multiple sources and synthesize the information into a cohesive expository piece.

46. A. Competency 5. Individuals rely on businesses to provide work as a source of income for themselves and their families. However, businesses also rely on individuals for labor and revenue. This relationship best describes the meaning of economic interdependence.

47. C. Competency 1. A primary source is an original document or object created during the time frame of study.

48. C. Competency 3. The small representations, usually shapes and pictures, of real things on a map are known as symbols. In order to understand what these symbols mean, students must consult the legend or key.

49. D. Competency 3. The acronym GPS stands for global positioning system.

50. D. Competency 1. Discipline-specific or academic vocabulary can be taught directly by the teacher, who provides a description and example of the new terms and then allows the children to discuss the terms in small groups. Using the terms in their oral and written language is the ultimate goal.

51. D. Competency 5. The United States and China practice a mixed economy. This economic system is a mixture of both the market and command economies. Individuals and the government make decisions regarding production, distribution, and consumption of goods and services.

52. B. Competency 1. Double-entry journals, where evidence directly from the text is documented on one side of the chart and the student's response to that text is noted on the other, can be a valuable comprehension tool for students to utilize when reading content area text.

53. D. Competency 5. In a traditional economy, cultural traditions, beliefs, and customs largely affect the production, distribution, and consumption of goods.

54. C. Competency 5. The first ten amendments to the Constitution are known as the Bill of Rights. They were designed to protect individuals rights and limit governmental power.

55. C. Competency 1. Specialized organizations, like the National Council for the Social Studies (NCSS), have a website with multiple links to other reputable websites that assist educators in teaching in this content area.

Science

1. **B.** Competency 1. Students designing and conducting an experiment fosters inquiry in the classroom. Teacher-led discussions, students reading a textbook, and students watching a video are not methods that foster inquiry or student engagement in science.

2. **A.** Competency 4. The crust is divided into two sections—continental crust and oceanic crust. The continental crust contains the continents. The oceanic crust lies under the oceans. Continental drift is the idea that the plates on the Earth's surface are moving. Pangea was a supercontinent.

3. **A.** Competency 2. In this case, time is usually the independent variable, while speed is the dependent variable. This is because when taking measurements, times are usually predetermined, and the resulting speed of the toy cars is recorded at those times. As far as the experiment is concerned, the speed is dependent on the time. Since the decision is made to measure the speed at certain times, time is the independent variable.

4. **C.** Competency 5. Photosynthesis is the process by which a plant converts sunlight into food. Transpiration is the loss of water through the plant's leaves. Respiration is the process by which the cells convert sugar molecules into energy. Fertilization is the process by which the plant reproduces.

5. **A.** Competency 3. An electrical circuit must have a continuous flow of electricity going through a complete loop (circuit), returning to its original position and cycling through again. An example that illustrates the necessity of a complete loop utilizes a battery, a small light bulb, and a connecting wire.

6. **B.** Competency 4. The layers of the Earth are the core, mantle, and crust. The core is the innermost layer. The crust is the outermost layer.

7. **B.** Competency 5. Taxonomy is the classification of living things into categories based on physical characteristics. Topography is the study of land formations. Taxidermy is the art of prepping, stuffing, and mounting skins of animals for display.

8. **C.** Competency 1. Seasons are caused by the tilt of the Earth's axis and revolution of the Earth around the Sun, not its distance from the Sun. We do, in fact, only see one side of the Moon from the Earth. This is related to the rotational speed of the Moon in comparison to the Earth.

9. **B.** Competency 2. In a controlled experiment, the factor that is manipulated between the experimental group and the control group is called the variable.

10. **D.** Competency 1. A well-validated and well-supported explanation of some aspect of the natural world is called a scientific theory. A hypothesis is a tentative and testable insight into the natural world that is not yet verified, but if it were found to be true would explain certain aspects of the natural world and might become a scientific theory. A scientific law is a truthful explanation of different events that happen with uniformity under certain conditions. A postulate is something assumed to be true without testing or verification.

11. **A.** Competency 4. A Full Moon occurs when the Moon and Sun are on opposite sides of the Earth and the entire lit-up surface of the Moon is visible.

12. **B.** Competency 1. Spreadsheets allow tabulation and performance of simple and complicated calculations, mathematical manipulations, and plots and graphs on various types of data, such as numbers, names, alphabetical information, scientific measurements, statistical information, and budget information. A spreadsheet provides a very effective way to organize the data collected by the students.

13. **B.** Competency 3. A traffic signal turns electrical energy into light energy. Notice that there is a heat energy by-product, but this is not the primary purpose of the process.

14. **B.** Competency 3. Density (symbol: ρ, which is the Greek "rho") is defined as mass per unit of volume, or the ratio of total mass (m) to total volume (V): $\rho = \dfrac{m}{V}$ (for example, kilogram per cubic meter or kg/m^3, and grams per cubic centimeter or g/cm^3). In other words, it defines how closely the molecules are packed together.

15. C. Competency 4. The eight planets are Mercury, Venus, Earth, Mars, Jupiter, Saturn, Uranus, and Neptune. Pluto is no longer considered a planet.

16. C. Competency 5. In the Linnaean classification system, the six kingdoms are Archaebacteria, Eubacteria, Fungi, Plants, and Animals (and sometimes Protists). Bacteria is a domain.

17. C. Competency 2. A hypothesis is the possible answer a scientist predicts in a scientific experiment. It is a prediction, but one that is based on research.

18. D. Competency 3. Chemical energy is the energy stored in the chemical bonds of molecules; for example, the combustion (burning) of gasoline provokes a chemical reaction that releases chemical energy. The molecules are broken to produce heat and light.

19. C. Competency 3. Balanced forces do not cause a change in motion. They are opposite in direction and equal in size. In contrast to balanced forces, unbalanced forces always cause a change in motion. They are opposite in direction and not equal in size. Neutral and motion are not terms used to describe forces.

20. B. Competency 5. The theory of evolution attempts to account for changes in species and the creation of new species over time. Survival of the fittest is an aspect of evolution that explains why some adaptations remain and some fall out of the fossil record.

21. D. Competency 2. A controlled experiment is one in which a treatment (experimental) group and a control group exist. The treatment group receives a treatment, while the control group does not. This provides a method for comparison.

22. C. Competency 5. The supercontinent proposed by Wegener was called Pangea.

23. A. Competency 3. A lump of sugar dissolving in water is an example of physical change. Matter is in constant change. A physical change does not produce a new substance (for example, freezing and melting water), but a chemical change or reaction does produce one or more substances.

24. B. Competency 5. DNA contains the genetic material that contains the information to make new cells. Amino acids are the building blocks for proteins. RNA helps in the production of proteins and DNA.

25. C. Competency 3. Heat is a measurement of the total energy in a substance. That total energy is made up of the kinetic and the potential energies of the molecules of the substance. Temperature does not tell you anything about the potential energy. Force is acted upon an object to cause motion.

26. C. Competency 1. In choice C, students completing a Moon phase calendar by cutting out photographs of the Moon in different phases, mounting them on a monthly calendar on the proper date, and appropriately labeling each of the eight major Moon phases does not provide the best opportunities for inquiry-based learning. Choices A, B, and D provide opportunities for both a research question and data analysis, which support inquiry-based learning.

27. A. Competency 5. Prokaryotic cells do not contain a nucleus. Eukaryotic cells contain a nucleus. The nucleolus is inside the nucleus of many cells and creates ribosomes.

28. B. Competency 4. Tsunamis are waves caused by earthquakes that occur under water. Continental drift is the idea that crustal plates are moving on the Earth's surface. The Richter scale measures earthquakes.

29. D. Competency 3. Temperature is not a type of energy; rather, it is a number that relates to the kinetic energy possessed by the molecules of a substance (measured in Kelvin, Fahrenheit, or Celsius degrees).

30. A. Competency 4. Metamorphic rocks are formed when pre-existing rocks change form through changes like burial under intense heat and/or pressure.

31. A. Competency 5. Bacteria that cause disease are called pathogens. Infections are the result of bacteria causing disease. Viruses are a different cause of disease. Symbiotic is the relationship one organism has with another in which both benefit from the relationship.

32. D. Competency 2. The steps of the scientific method include 1) ask a question, 2) make observations, 3) hypothesize, 4) predict, 5) test, and 6) conclude.

33. **C.** Competency 4. *Apollo 11* was the first mission to land on the Moon. *Apollo 7* was the first manned mission. *Apollo 8* was the first manned mission to orbit the Moon. The *Apollo 13* mission was aborted due to the explosion of oxygen tanks and was called a "successful failure" because even though the mission was aborted, all astronauts returned safely to Earth.

34. **C.** Competency 5. Plant cells contain chloroplasts. Chloroplasts allow the plant to harness energy from the Sun. Photosynthesis takes place in the chloroplasts.

35. **D.** Competency 3. Series circuits use only one electrical path. Parallel circuits use several electrical paths. For example, parallel circuits allow the distribution of the electric current throughout a house. Singular and looping are not terms used to describe electrical circuits.

36. **B.** Competency 4. Convection currents move the plates of the Earth's crust. This phenomena is referred to as plate tectonics.

37. **A.** Competencies 1 and 2. An instrument could be reliable but not valid. A reliable instrument might be measuring something consistently, but not necessarily what it is supposed to be measuring validly. Reliability refers to the consistency of the instrument. Validity refers to the degree to which a measure accurately assesses the specific concept it is designed to measure. A good instrument should be both reliable and valid.

38. **B.** Competency 3. Heat is a measurement of the total energy made up of kinetic and potential energies of the molecules in a substance. Temperature is a measure related to the average kinetic energy of the molecules of a substance, and is not a type of energy. Static is a lack of movement, and friction is the force between an object and a surface.

39. **B.** Competency 3. Three methods of heat transfer are convection, radiation, and conduction. Condensation is the change of state from gas to liquid.

40. **C.** Competency 5. An autotroph creates its own food. A heterotroph consumes its food from its environment. Heterozygotes have two different genes for a trait. Parasites feed off of their host.

41. **D.** Competency 2. The students are dealing with controlled variables. This involves the type of plant, the type of fertilizer, the amount of sunlight the plant gets, the size of the pots, and any other variables or factors that need to be controlled. These are variables or factors that would otherwise influence the dependent variable if they were not controlled. The independent variable would be the amount of fertilizer used (the changing factor of the experiment). The dependent variables would be the growth in height and/or mass of the plant (the factors that are influenced in the experiment). Extraneous variables would be those that are unrelated to the experiment at hand.

42. **C.** Competency 2. The graph gives data that supports the number of adult frogs increasing four times between May and September. The cause of the increase is not known from this data.

43. **A.** Competency 4. John Glenn was the first American to orbit the Earth. Neil Armstrong was the first American to walk on the Moon. Alan Shepard was the first American to be launched into space; he completed a suborbital flight of 15 minutes and achieved weightlessness for about 5 minutes. Yuri Gagarin, a Russian, was the first human in space.

44. **D.** Competency 5. Worms are invertebrates (animals without a backbone). The types of vertebrates (animals with a backbone) are fish, amphibians, reptiles, birds, and mammals.

45. **D.** Competencies 1 and 2. All of these are good laboratory procedures. Students should only share goggles if they have been sterilized between uses. All students should wear goggles and gowns, and chemicals should be handled with care and disposed of properly.

46. **D.** Competency 5. All cells contain cell membranes, cytoplasm, organelles, and DNA.

47. **A.** Competency 2. The weight of a horse is best measured in pounds. Ounces is too small a unit of measure for a horse: 16 ounces equal 1 pound. Gallons are a measure of volume, and feet are a measure of length.

48. **B.** Competency 1. A comparative assessment helps a teacher to compare student results of the outcomes of an assessment between students or groups of students. A diagnostic assessment determines knowledge prior to a unit of instruction, while a summative assessment determines what a student learned from a unit of instruction. Formative assessments are used to guide day-to-day activities.

49. **D.** Competency 5. Asexual reproduction occurs when one parent makes an identical copy of itself. Sexual reproduction requires two parents and produces offspring with a combination of each parent's genetic material. Mitosis is normal cell division. Replication is the copying of genetic material.

50. **B.** Competency 1. Manipulatives can be used to help students understand abstract concepts. For the concept of kinetic and potential energy, toy cars on an inclined track can be used to help students understand the concept. The students using the cars is more effective than a teacher demonstration or a video. Students creating electrical circuits using light bulbs and batteries is not related to the concepts of potential and kinetic energy.

51. **A.** Competency 2. Dispositions underlying scientific thinking include being curious, open to new ideas, skeptical in appropriate ways, and cooperative.

52. **B.** Competency 1. A scientific theory is a well-validated and well-supported explanation of an aspect of the natural world (e.g., theory of relativity). A scientific law is a truthful explanation of events that happen with uniformity (e.g., law of gravity). A hypothesis is a testable and tentative belief that has not yet been validated into a theory. Scientific method is a process by which a hypothesis is tested.

53. **C.** Competency 4. Cirrus clouds are wispy and feathery; they form at high altitudes from ice crystals. Stratus clouds are horizontal, layered clouds that blanket the sky. Cumulus clouds are puffy and form with warm, moist air. Nimbus clouds produce precipitation.

54. **D.** Competency 1. A temperature probe collects ongoing data of temperature changes throughout an experiment. A database assembles collections of data. A barometer measures atmospheric pressure. A spectrometer measures absorbance of light.

55. **D.** Competency 2. STEM stands for Science, Technology, Engineering, and Mathematics and is the view that these subject areas are connected in meaningful ways.

Mathematics

1. **C.** Competency 1. The student is using $\frac{1}{2}$ for the answer, which is a numeral or abstract (also known as symbolic) representation. A numeral is a symbolic or written representation of a number. The concrete level would require the use of manipulative materials, like cubes. The pictorial model would need the use of pictures or drawings. Number is the actual cardinality, value, or quantity of the representation, which is understood mentally. It is the idea represented by the abstract (numeral), pictorial, or concrete model. The idea of $\frac{1}{2}$ can be modeled in these ways.

2. **D.** Competency 1. In this error pattern, the student has consistently missed the $9 \cdot 4$ basic fact, by incorrectly answering that $9 \cdot 4$ is equal to 40. This error has caused the student to lack accuracy. We do not have enough information about the student's flexibility with the multiplication algorithm, understanding of the multiplication concepts, or rate of answering multiplication basic facts.

3. **D.** Competency 1. The results of a diagnostic test could help in identifying specific problem areas. Diagnostic tests are used within the diagnostic-prescriptive teaching of mathematics. This process is an instructional model that consists of diagnosis, prescription, instruction, and ongoing assessment.

4. **A.** Competency 3. A non-terminating repeating decimal like 0.77... is equal to $0.\overline{7}$, where the line on top of the 7 indicates that 7 is repeating, which is the same as using "...". The other options are approximations of this number.

5. **B.** Competency 2. The pattern is adding 3 to the previous term. The next term is $15 + 3 = 18$.

6. **B.** Competency 3. In this case, we need to solve $-6.8 \cdot 10^{-1}$, which is equal to $-6.8 \cdot \frac{1}{10}$ or $-6.8 \cdot 0.1 = -0.68$. So, -0.68 is between 0 and -1 on a number line.

   Choice A: -70 and -60: -0.68 is less than -60, and outside this interval.

   Choice B: 0 and -1: -0.68 is between these two whole numbers.

   Choice C: 0 and 1: -0.68 is less than 0, and outside this interval.

   Choice D: 60 and 70: -0.68 is less than 60, and outside this interval.

7. **A.** Competency 2. The expression $b^3 \cdot b^6$ is equal to b^9 (add exponents).

8. **C.** Competency 4. To find the mean of this data set, you need to add the scores and divide by 20 (number of scores): $291 \div 20 = 14.55$.

9. **B.** Competency 4. To find the median, you need to order the data set and find the middle score.

   $$10, 10, 10, 10, 11, 12, 12, 12, 12, \mathbf{12, 13,} 13, 14, 15, 15, 20, 22, 22, 23, 23$$

   Scores 12 and 13 are in the middle because we have an even number of scores or entries in this data set. You need to average these two scores to find the median: $(12 + 13) \div 2 = 25 \div 2 = 12.5$.

10. **D.** Competency 4. The mode is the most frequent score. A frequency table should be used to organize the data.

Scores	Frequency
10	4
11	1
12	5
13	2
14	1
15	2
20	1
22	2
23	2

   The most frequent score for this data set is 12.

11. **C.** Competency 4. The range of the data set is the highest score minus the lowest score: $23 - 10 = 13$.

12. **B.** Competency 3. You need to solve the negative exponent first and then multiply by -1: $2^{-4} = \frac{1}{2^4} = \frac{1}{16}$ and $\frac{1}{16} \cdot -1 = \frac{-1}{16}$.

13. **C.** Competency 2. Four times a number is $4n$. This plus 12 is $4n + 12$.

14. **D.** Competency 4. Start by ordering the fractions from least to greatest. One way to do this ordering is by changing all the possible answers to decimal form, comparing to each other, and ordering them accordingly from least to greatest: $2\frac{1}{3} = 2.333...$, $2\frac{3}{8} = 2.375$, $2\frac{2}{5} \approx 2.4$, $2\frac{3}{5} = 2.6$. Another way is to convert the fractions to their lowest common denominator and then compare them and order them accordingly. Finally, look at the names and decide who lives closer and who lives the farthest. In this case, the order would be Paul $\left(2\frac{1}{3}\right)$, Samuel $\left(2\frac{3}{8}\right)$, Natalie $\left(2\frac{2}{5}\right)$, and Greta $\left(2\frac{3}{5}\right)$.

15. D. Competency 5. A pentagon is a five-sided figure. If one side of the triangle matches one side of the rectangle, the figure has five sides. If one side of the triangle does not match one side of the rectangle and it is matched to the end (at the very edge) of one side, the figure would have six sides, making it a hexagon. If one side of the triangle does not match one side of the rectangle, and the triangle was placed in the middle of a side, the final figure would have seven sides, making it a heptagon. See figure below for possible results. An octagon is not possible.

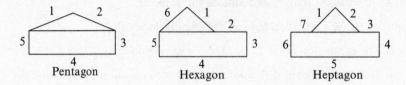

Pentagon   Hexagon   Heptagon

16. A. Competency 3. Set up a proportion: $\dfrac{x \text{ feet}}{12 \text{ feet}} = \dfrac{6 \text{ feet}}{9 \text{ feet}}$. Solve this proportion by cross multiplication:

$9x = 12(6)$. So $9x = 72$. Therefore, $x = 8$ feet.

17. B. Competency 3. $6^{-3} = \dfrac{1}{6^3} = \dfrac{1}{(6 \cdot 6 \cdot 6)} = \dfrac{1}{216}$.

18. B. Competency 1. Authentic assessment is a form of alternative assessment that incorporates real-life functions and applications. Alternative assessment refers to other (non-traditional) options used to assess students' learning, which are not necessarily a form of authentic assessment. However, authentic assessments are usually based on alternative forms of assessment. Naturalistic assessment involves evaluation that is based on the natural setting of the classroom. It involves the observation of students' performance and behavior in an informal context. Naturalistic assessments are also are not necessarily a form of authentic assessment.

19. C. Competency 5. A rotation is a turn. A translation is a slide. A reflection is a flip. A dilation is making smaller or larger.

20. B. Competency 3. First, we need to find the number of hardcover books by subtracting 21 from 35, which results in 14 hardcover books. Then, divide 14 by 35 to calculate the percent of hardcover books: 40%.

21. A. Competency 2. The cost of peanuts is $2 a box; therefore, p boxes of peanuts would cost $2p$ dollars. Hot dogs cost $3.50 each; therefore, h hot dogs would cost $3.50h$ dollars. The total of these is $2p + 3.50h$.

22. B. Competency 4. There seems to be a pattern of increasing the number of buyers (shoppers who purchased something) every 5 years: approximately 4% to 5%. The percent for 2013 seems to be about 42% at the end of the year. The year 2018 is included in the next 5-year cycle. Therefore, 46% seems to be the best prediction. In this manner, 42% seems to be to low, and 52% and 55% seem to be too high.

23. B. Competency 5. Point T is to the left and above the origin $(0, 0)$. To get from $(0, 0)$ to point T, you move left 4 and up 5. This gives the coordinates of $(-4, 5)$.

24. A. Competency 4. You need to translate the word problem into a mathematical sentence. You have 13 pounds of oranges for $0.58 times 5 days for 4 weeks:

$$4\big(5(13 \cdot \$0.58)\big) = 4\big(5(\$7.54)\big)$$
$$= 4(\$37.70)$$
$$= \$150.80$$

25. B. Competency 1. In this case, the representation is using rectangular array or tiling to demonstrate the distributive property, which is the same as the area model: Nancy has a room that is 5 yards by 13 yards. What is the area of this room?

The following is an example of the multiplicative comparison: Nancy has 3 apples and Tom has 5 times as many apples as Nancy does. How many apples does Tom have?

The following is an example of the repeated addition model: Nancy has 5 bags of apples with 3 apples in each bag. How many apples does Nancy have altogether?

The following is an example of the combination model: How many combinations of shirts and pants can Nancy make out of 5 shirts and 3 pants?

26. **A.** Competency 3. $12 \text{ hands} \times \dfrac{10 \text{ thumbs}}{4 \text{ hands}} = 30 \text{ thumbs}$

27. **D.** Competency 2. First distribute across the parentheses. This gives $6x - 15 \leq 8x - 3$. Then isolate the variable on one side of the inequality by subtracting $8x$ from both sides and adding 15 to both sides. This gives $-2x \leq 12$. Divide both sides by -2, which reverses the inequality. This gives $x \geq -6$.

28. **C.** Competency 2. One way to solve this problem is to find the factors of each pair of numbers and then use these factors to find the GCF. Look for the GCF within each pair (shown in **bold text** for each pair below).

Choice A : $24 : 1, 2, 3, 4, \mathbf{6}, 8, 12, 24$ and $6 : 1, 2, 3, \mathbf{6}$ GCF $= 6$ Yes, they have 6 as the GCF.

Choice B : $42 : 1, 2, 3, \mathbf{6}, 7, 14, 21, 42$ and $150 : 1, 2, 3,$ GCF $= 6$ Yes, they have 6 as the GCF.
                                                          $5, \mathbf{6}, 10, 15, 25,$
                                                          $30, 50, 75, 150$

Choice C : $54 : 1, 2, 3, 6, 9, \mathbf{18}, 27, 54$ and $18 : 1, 2, 3,$ GCF $= 18$ No, they don't have 6 as GCF.
                                                          $6, 9, \mathbf{18}$

Choice D : $18 : 1, 2, 3, \mathbf{6}, 9, 18$ and $30 : 1, 2, 3, 5, \mathbf{6}$ GCF $= 6$ Yes, they have 6 as the GCF.

Another way to solve this problem is by using prime factorization. Find the prime factorization of each pair of numbers and then use these prime factorizations to find the GCF. Look at the common prime factors within each pair (shown in **bold text** for each pair below).

Choice A: $24 = \mathbf{2} \cdot 2 \cdot 2 \cdot \mathbf{3}$,   and $6 = \mathbf{2} \cdot \mathbf{3}$ GCF $= 2 \cdot 3 = 6$ Yes, they have 6 as GCF.
Choice B: $42 = \mathbf{2} \cdot \mathbf{3} \cdot 7$,   and $150 = \mathbf{2} \cdot \mathbf{3} \cdot 5 \cdot 5$ GCF $= 2 \cdot 3 = 6$ Yes, they have 6 as GCF.
Choice C: $54 = \mathbf{2} \cdot \mathbf{3} \cdot \mathbf{3} \cdot 3$,   and $18 = \mathbf{2} \cdot \mathbf{3} \cdot \mathbf{3}$ GCF $= 2 \cdot 3 \cdot 3 = 18$ No, they don't have 6 as GCF.
Choice D: $18 = \mathbf{2} \cdot \mathbf{3}$,   and $30 = \mathbf{2} \cdot \mathbf{3} \cdot 5$ GCF $= 2 \cdot 3 = 6$ Yes, they have 6 as GCF.

29. **C.** Competency 5. In choice C, the front and back squares will overlap, and a face is missing. All other choices give each face.

30. **B.** Competency 5. The radius is squared to find the area of the circle. If the radius is cut in half, the area would be divided by 2^2 or cut in fourth. For example, if the radius of the circle was 4 inches, the area would be $A = \pi(4)^2 = 16\pi$. If the radius were cut in half, the new radius would be 2 inches. The area would then be $A = \pi(2)^2 = 4\pi$. Since 4 is one-fourth of 16, the new area is one-fourth of the old area.

31. **D.** Competency 1. We should not teach, then assess. Assessment should be ongoing and summative. The best assessment also instructs, and the best instructional tasks are rich with diagnostic opportunities.

32. **C.** Competency 2. Look at the common factors within this pair of expressions (shown in **bold text** below).

$$20x^2 y = \mathbf{2} \cdot 2 \cdot \mathbf{5} \cdot \mathbf{x} \cdot x \cdot \mathbf{y}$$
$$50xy^2 = \mathbf{2} \cdot 5 \cdot \mathbf{5} \cdot \mathbf{x} \cdot \mathbf{y} \cdot y$$
$$\text{GCF} = 2 \cdot 5 \cdot x \cdot y = 10xy$$

33. **C.** Competency 2. The associative property says you can multiply or add three numbers together in any order. The commutative property says you can add or multiply two numbers in either order. The distributive property allows for multiplication across parentheses with addition or subtraction. Under a particular operation, a set has the identity property if there is an element of the set that leaves every other element of the set unchanged as a result. Zero is the identity element for addition, and 1 is the identity element for multiplication. In this item, $3(x-2) = 3x - 6$ shows the distributive property.

34. **B.** Competency 5. The formula for the area of a trapezoid is $A = \frac{1}{2}(b_1 + b_2)h$. Base 1 is 5 feet; base 2 is 8 feet; height is 4 feet. Therefore, the area is $A = \frac{1}{2}(5+8)(4) = 26$ ft².

35. **D.** Competency 1. This is the most appropriate learning progression for students' mastery of concepts of area measurement because of the cognitive and complexity levels involved in it:

Concrete level: **First:** Form rectangles by tiling with unit squares to make arrays.

Pictorial level: **Second:** Draw rows and columns to determine the area of a rectangle.

Pictorial level at a higher complexity level: **Third:** Given an incomplete array, interpret area models to form rectangular arrays.

Abstract and pictorial levels: **Fourth:** Find the area of a rectangle through multiplication of the side lengths.

36. **C.** Competency 1. In this case, you need a more conceptually based activity that will provide a good idea of students' understanding of the different division concepts. An example of sharing or partitive division is the following: Mary has 10 apples, and she wants to divide them into 5 bags of apples. How many apples will she have in each bag after dividing them equally? An example of measurement or subtractive division is the following: Mary has 10 apples, and she wants to make bags of 2 apples each. How many bags of apples can she make?

Choice A: Asks students to solve exercises in a timed test involving division basic facts. This activity only involves the abstract level for memorization skills and speed and accuracy skills. It is more procedural in nature. Choice A is therefore an incorrect assessment activity for this situation.

Choice B: Asks students to solve word problems involving the sharing division concept using cubes to model the solutions. You want to assess understanding of different division concepts, but this exercise provides for assessing only one of the division concepts. Choice B is therefore an incorrect assessment activity for this situation.

Choice C: Asks students to write word problems that illustrate division concepts using different types of manipulative materials. This alternative has the best potential for providing evidence of students' conceptual understanding of the different division concepts or models. Choice C is therefore the correct assessment activity for this situation.

Choice D: Asks students to solve word problems involving division concepts using only paper and pencil. Choice D is therefore an incorrect assessment activity for this situation.

37. **B.** Competency 1. This is the most appropriate sequence of stages because of the cognitive and complexity levels involved in it. The students need to learn how to figure out math facts before they work with memorization strategies and eventually develop speed and accuracy.

38. **C.** Competency 1. Even though appropriate speed and accuracy, conceptual knowledge of operations, and flexibility with computation algorithms are involved in the solution of the word problems that have two-digit numbers, the teacher is most likely concerned with their appropriate procedural understanding of the computation algorithms. In other words, procedural knowledge requires proper conceptual understanding of operations and mastery of basic facts for speed and accuracy.

39. B. Competency 2. The prime factors of 120 are 2, 3, and 5. The sum of these prime factors is $2 + 3 + 5 = 10$. There are several ways to find the prime factors of 120. One of them is to use the divisibility rules, when possible, using prime numbers less than 11 (the square root of 120 is approximately less than 11) or 2, 3, 5, and 7:

Since 120 is an even number, then it is divisible by 2.

Since the sum of the digits of 120 ($1 + 2 + 0 = 3$) is divisible by 3, then 120 is also divisible by 3.

Since the last digit of 120 is 0, then 120 is divisible by 5.

There is no divisibility rule for 7, but we know that 120 is not divisible by 7.

40. B. Competency 2. The output is represented by $3n - 1$. Then, if $n = 30$, you have $3(30) - 1 = 90 - 1 = 89$.

41. C. Competency 2. If $y = -3x - 5$, then the value of y if x is 2 is calculated by substituting for x: $y = -3(2) - 5$ $= -6 - 5 = -11$. Notice that you can also solve $-6 - 5$ by changing it to addition: $-6 - 5 = -6 + -5 = -11$.

42. D. Competency 4. The best way to find the best choice for this item is by analyzing each alternative. Choice A indicates that there are more fifth-graders than fourth-graders attending this elementary school, but this is not true. There are more fourth-graders (389) than fifth-graders (376). Choice B indicates that more fourth-graders take the bus than third-graders who walk to school, but this is not true. The number of fourth-graders who take the bus is 47, and the number of third-graders who walk to school is 123, which indicates that there are more third-graders walking than fourth-graders taking the bus. Choice C indicates that more students take the bus than students who use any of the other types of transportation. This is not true, because fewer students (344) take the bus than students who walk to school (406). More students walk to school than any of the other types of transportation. Choice D for this item indicates that more fifth-graders (158) take the bus than fourth-graders who walk to school (140). This is true, and is the only answer choice that can be verified by the information provided in the table.

43. C. Competency 2. Write an inequality to represent the number of hours (t) tutoring and the number of hours (s) working at the supermarket that Carla will need to work to earn a minimum of $350 this week.

$$9t + 12s \geq 350$$
$$9t + 12(25) \geq 350$$
$$9t + 300 - 300 \geq 350 - 300$$
$$\frac{9t}{9} \geq \frac{50}{9}$$
$$t \geq 5.\overline{5}$$

Since she wants to work full hours, you need to round up to 6 hours.

You can check your answer by substituting the values for t and s in the inequality. Notice that working 5 full hours tutoring will not be enough to earn $350.

$$9t + 12s \underline{\quad} 350$$
$$9(5) + 12(25) \underline{\quad} 350$$
$$45 + 300 \underline{\quad} 350$$
$$345 \leq 350$$

By substituting t for 6, you can get to over $350, which is the minimum amount she wants to earn at the end.

$$9t + 12s \underline{\quad} 350$$
$$9(6) + 12(25) \underline{\quad} 350$$
$$54 + 300 \underline{\quad} 350$$
$$354 \geq 350$$

44. **C.** Competency 2. The student used the following addition properties for each step of the calculation:

$$32 + 48 + 12 + 68 = 32 + 68 + 48 + 12 \qquad \text{Commutative Property}$$
$$= (32 + 68) + (48 + 12) \quad \text{Associative Property}$$
$$= 100 + 60$$
$$= 160$$

45. **B.** Competency 2. First distribute through the parentheses: $8 - 4x + 5 = 6x - 9 - 8$. Then combine like terms: $13 - 4x = 6x - 17$. Isolate the x variable on one side of the equation by adding 17 to both sides and adding $4x$ to both sides: $30 = 10x$. Divide both sides by 10: $x = 3$.

46. **C.** Competency 1. In this case, the progression starts with the most basic level involved with drawing shapes. The next one would be determining if a particular shape is included in a given set, which involves a higher level of complexity, followed by classifying using properties of shapes. Constructing proofs using postulates and axioms represents the highest level of complexity among these geometric tasks.

47. **A.** Competency 1. There are two types of subitizing abilities: perceptual and conceptual. Perceptual subitizing is instantly recognizing a number without using other mathematical processes. For example, a child might recognize three as she sees three dots on a die without using any mathematical knowledge, or might perceive that three dots are more than two dots. This usually limited to two or three dots. Conceptual subitizing is a bit more complicated. It is ability to see sets of numbers with larger sets, which is the case in this example. For example, a child might know that four dots and two more dots make six dots.

48. **D.** Competency 1. The student is showing flexibility in solving the exercise. This is because an alternative algorithm was used to solve the problem.

49. **B.** Competency 3. First, add the scores for the first 10 games of the regular season: $28 + 27 + 22 + 30 + 38 + 28 + 30 + 31 + 25 + 36 = 295$ total points so far. Next, subtract 295 from 325, which is the target score to break the regular season record: $325 - 295 = 30$ points. Ana needs to score at least 30 points in the last game of the regular season in order to break the record for number of points for one regular season in her basketball league.

50. **C.** Competency 3. Calculate the cost per ounces for each one of the products. In other words, divide the total of cost by the number of ounces.

Cost per ounce for the 6-ounce can is 89¢ ÷ 6 ounces ≈ 14.83 cents per ounce.

Cost per ounce for the 8-ounce can is 117¢ ÷ 8 ounces ≈ 14.625 cents per ounce.

The cost per ounce is called the unit cost. The 8-ounce can has a slightly lower unit cost than the 6-ounce can. So, the 8-ounce can is a better buy.

Chapter 7

Practice Test 2

Answer Sheet

Language Arts and Reading

1 Ⓐ Ⓑ Ⓒ Ⓓ	31 Ⓐ Ⓑ Ⓒ Ⓓ
2 Ⓐ Ⓑ Ⓒ Ⓓ	32 Ⓐ Ⓑ Ⓒ Ⓓ
3 Ⓐ Ⓑ Ⓒ Ⓓ	33 Ⓐ Ⓑ Ⓒ Ⓓ
4 Ⓐ Ⓑ Ⓒ Ⓓ	34 Ⓐ Ⓑ Ⓒ Ⓓ
5 Ⓐ Ⓑ Ⓒ Ⓓ	35 Ⓐ Ⓑ Ⓒ Ⓓ
6 Ⓐ Ⓑ Ⓒ Ⓓ	36 Ⓐ Ⓑ Ⓒ Ⓓ
7 Ⓐ Ⓑ Ⓒ Ⓓ	37 Ⓐ Ⓑ Ⓒ Ⓓ
8 Ⓐ Ⓑ Ⓒ Ⓓ	38 Ⓐ Ⓑ Ⓒ Ⓓ
9 Ⓐ Ⓑ Ⓒ Ⓓ	39 Ⓐ Ⓑ Ⓒ Ⓓ
10 Ⓐ Ⓑ Ⓒ Ⓓ	40 Ⓐ Ⓑ Ⓒ Ⓓ
11 Ⓐ Ⓑ Ⓒ Ⓓ	41 Ⓐ Ⓑ Ⓒ Ⓓ
12 Ⓐ Ⓑ Ⓒ Ⓓ	42 Ⓐ Ⓑ Ⓒ Ⓓ
13 Ⓐ Ⓑ Ⓒ Ⓓ	43 Ⓐ Ⓑ Ⓒ Ⓓ
14 Ⓐ Ⓑ Ⓒ Ⓓ	44 Ⓐ Ⓑ Ⓒ Ⓓ
15 Ⓐ Ⓑ Ⓒ Ⓓ	45 Ⓐ Ⓑ Ⓒ Ⓓ
16 Ⓐ Ⓑ Ⓒ Ⓓ	46 Ⓐ Ⓑ Ⓒ Ⓓ
17 Ⓐ Ⓑ Ⓒ Ⓓ	47 Ⓐ Ⓑ Ⓒ Ⓓ
18 Ⓐ Ⓑ Ⓒ Ⓓ	48 Ⓐ Ⓑ Ⓒ Ⓓ
19 Ⓐ Ⓑ Ⓒ Ⓓ	49 Ⓐ Ⓑ Ⓒ Ⓓ
20 Ⓐ Ⓑ Ⓒ Ⓓ	50 Ⓐ Ⓑ Ⓒ Ⓓ
21 Ⓐ Ⓑ Ⓒ Ⓓ	51 Ⓐ Ⓑ Ⓒ Ⓓ
22 Ⓐ Ⓑ Ⓒ Ⓓ	52 Ⓐ Ⓑ Ⓒ Ⓓ
23 Ⓐ Ⓑ Ⓒ Ⓓ	53 Ⓐ Ⓑ Ⓒ Ⓓ
24 Ⓐ Ⓑ Ⓒ Ⓓ	54 Ⓐ Ⓑ Ⓒ Ⓓ
25 Ⓐ Ⓑ Ⓒ Ⓓ	55 Ⓐ Ⓑ Ⓒ Ⓓ
26 Ⓐ Ⓑ Ⓒ Ⓓ	56 Ⓐ Ⓑ Ⓒ Ⓓ
27 Ⓐ Ⓑ Ⓒ Ⓓ	57 Ⓐ Ⓑ Ⓒ Ⓓ
28 Ⓐ Ⓑ Ⓒ Ⓓ	58 Ⓐ Ⓑ Ⓒ Ⓓ
29 Ⓐ Ⓑ Ⓒ Ⓓ	59 Ⓐ Ⓑ Ⓒ Ⓓ
30 Ⓐ Ⓑ Ⓒ Ⓓ	60 Ⓐ Ⓑ Ⓒ Ⓓ

Social Science

1 Ⓐ Ⓑ Ⓒ Ⓓ	31 Ⓐ Ⓑ Ⓒ Ⓓ
2 Ⓐ Ⓑ Ⓒ Ⓓ	32 Ⓐ Ⓑ Ⓒ Ⓓ
3 Ⓐ Ⓑ Ⓒ Ⓓ	33 Ⓐ Ⓑ Ⓒ Ⓓ
4 Ⓐ Ⓑ Ⓒ Ⓓ	34 Ⓐ Ⓑ Ⓒ Ⓓ
5 Ⓐ Ⓑ Ⓒ Ⓓ	35 Ⓐ Ⓑ Ⓒ Ⓓ
6 Ⓐ Ⓑ Ⓒ Ⓓ	36 Ⓐ Ⓑ Ⓒ Ⓓ
7 Ⓐ Ⓑ Ⓒ Ⓓ	37 Ⓐ Ⓑ Ⓒ Ⓓ
8 Ⓐ Ⓑ Ⓒ Ⓓ	38 Ⓐ Ⓑ Ⓒ Ⓓ
9 Ⓐ Ⓑ Ⓒ Ⓓ	39 Ⓐ Ⓑ Ⓒ Ⓓ
10 Ⓐ Ⓑ Ⓒ Ⓓ	40 Ⓐ Ⓑ Ⓒ Ⓓ
11 Ⓐ Ⓑ Ⓒ Ⓓ	41 Ⓐ Ⓑ Ⓒ Ⓓ
12 Ⓐ Ⓑ Ⓒ Ⓓ	42 Ⓐ Ⓑ Ⓒ Ⓓ
13 Ⓐ Ⓑ Ⓒ Ⓓ	43 Ⓐ Ⓑ Ⓒ Ⓓ
14 Ⓐ Ⓑ Ⓒ Ⓓ	44 Ⓐ Ⓑ Ⓒ Ⓓ
15 Ⓐ Ⓑ Ⓒ Ⓓ	45 Ⓐ Ⓑ Ⓒ Ⓓ
16 Ⓐ Ⓑ Ⓒ Ⓓ	46 Ⓐ Ⓑ Ⓒ Ⓓ
17 Ⓐ Ⓑ Ⓒ Ⓓ	47 Ⓐ Ⓑ Ⓒ Ⓓ
18 Ⓐ Ⓑ Ⓒ Ⓓ	48 Ⓐ Ⓑ Ⓒ Ⓓ
19 Ⓐ Ⓑ Ⓒ Ⓓ	49 Ⓐ Ⓑ Ⓒ Ⓓ
20 Ⓐ Ⓑ Ⓒ Ⓓ	50 Ⓐ Ⓑ Ⓒ Ⓓ
21 Ⓐ Ⓑ Ⓒ Ⓓ	51 Ⓐ Ⓑ Ⓒ Ⓓ
22 Ⓐ Ⓑ Ⓒ Ⓓ	52 Ⓐ Ⓑ Ⓒ Ⓓ
23 Ⓐ Ⓑ Ⓒ Ⓓ	53 Ⓐ Ⓑ Ⓒ Ⓓ
24 Ⓐ Ⓑ Ⓒ Ⓓ	54 Ⓐ Ⓑ Ⓒ Ⓓ
25 Ⓐ Ⓑ Ⓒ Ⓓ	55 Ⓐ Ⓑ Ⓒ Ⓓ
26 Ⓐ Ⓑ Ⓒ Ⓓ	
27 Ⓐ Ⓑ Ⓒ Ⓓ	
28 Ⓐ Ⓑ Ⓒ Ⓓ	
29 Ⓐ Ⓑ Ⓒ Ⓓ	
30 Ⓐ Ⓑ Ⓒ Ⓓ	

CUT HERE

Tip: For the Mathematics section, you may consult the Mathematics Reference Sheet in Appendix C (pages 343–344) for common formulas.

Science

1 Ⓐ Ⓑ Ⓒ Ⓓ	31 Ⓐ Ⓑ Ⓒ Ⓓ
2 Ⓐ Ⓑ Ⓒ Ⓓ	32 Ⓐ Ⓑ Ⓒ Ⓓ
3 Ⓐ Ⓑ Ⓒ Ⓓ	33 Ⓐ Ⓑ Ⓒ Ⓓ
4 Ⓐ Ⓑ Ⓒ Ⓓ	34 Ⓐ Ⓑ Ⓒ Ⓓ
5 Ⓐ Ⓑ Ⓒ Ⓓ	35 Ⓐ Ⓑ Ⓒ Ⓓ
6 Ⓐ Ⓑ Ⓒ Ⓓ	36 Ⓐ Ⓑ Ⓒ Ⓓ
7 Ⓐ Ⓑ Ⓒ Ⓓ	37 Ⓐ Ⓑ Ⓒ Ⓓ
8 Ⓐ Ⓑ Ⓒ Ⓓ	38 Ⓐ Ⓑ Ⓒ Ⓓ
9 Ⓐ Ⓑ Ⓒ Ⓓ	39 Ⓐ Ⓑ Ⓒ Ⓓ
10 Ⓐ Ⓑ Ⓒ Ⓓ	40 Ⓐ Ⓑ Ⓒ Ⓓ
11 Ⓐ Ⓑ Ⓒ Ⓓ	41 Ⓐ Ⓑ Ⓒ Ⓓ
12 Ⓐ Ⓑ Ⓒ Ⓓ	42 Ⓐ Ⓑ Ⓒ Ⓓ
13 Ⓐ Ⓑ Ⓒ Ⓓ	43 Ⓐ Ⓑ Ⓒ Ⓓ
14 Ⓐ Ⓑ Ⓒ Ⓓ	44 Ⓐ Ⓑ Ⓒ Ⓓ
15 Ⓐ Ⓑ Ⓒ Ⓓ	45 Ⓐ Ⓑ Ⓒ Ⓓ
16 Ⓐ Ⓑ Ⓒ Ⓓ	46 Ⓐ Ⓑ Ⓒ Ⓓ
17 Ⓐ Ⓑ Ⓒ Ⓓ	47 Ⓐ Ⓑ Ⓒ Ⓓ
18 Ⓐ Ⓑ Ⓒ Ⓓ	48 Ⓐ Ⓑ Ⓒ Ⓓ
19 Ⓐ Ⓑ Ⓒ Ⓓ	49 Ⓐ Ⓑ Ⓒ Ⓓ
20 Ⓐ Ⓑ Ⓒ Ⓓ	50 Ⓐ Ⓑ Ⓒ Ⓓ
21 Ⓐ Ⓑ Ⓒ Ⓓ	51 Ⓐ Ⓑ Ⓒ Ⓓ
22 Ⓐ Ⓑ Ⓒ Ⓓ	52 Ⓐ Ⓑ Ⓒ Ⓓ
23 Ⓐ Ⓑ Ⓒ Ⓓ	53 Ⓐ Ⓑ Ⓒ Ⓓ
24 Ⓐ Ⓑ Ⓒ Ⓓ	54 Ⓐ Ⓑ Ⓒ Ⓓ
25 Ⓐ Ⓑ Ⓒ Ⓓ	55 Ⓐ Ⓑ Ⓒ Ⓓ
26 Ⓐ Ⓑ Ⓒ Ⓓ	
27 Ⓐ Ⓑ Ⓒ Ⓓ	
28 Ⓐ Ⓑ Ⓒ Ⓓ	
29 Ⓐ Ⓑ Ⓒ Ⓓ	
30 Ⓐ Ⓑ Ⓒ Ⓓ	

Mathematics

1 Ⓐ Ⓑ Ⓒ Ⓓ	26 Ⓐ Ⓑ Ⓒ Ⓓ
2 Ⓐ Ⓑ Ⓒ Ⓓ	27 Ⓐ Ⓑ Ⓒ Ⓓ
3 Ⓐ Ⓑ Ⓒ Ⓓ	28 Ⓐ Ⓑ Ⓒ Ⓓ
4 Ⓐ Ⓑ Ⓒ Ⓓ	29 Ⓐ Ⓑ Ⓒ Ⓓ
5 Ⓐ Ⓑ Ⓒ Ⓓ	30 Ⓐ Ⓑ Ⓒ Ⓓ
6 Ⓐ Ⓑ Ⓒ Ⓓ	31 Ⓐ Ⓑ Ⓒ Ⓓ
7 Ⓐ Ⓑ Ⓒ Ⓓ	32 Ⓐ Ⓑ Ⓒ Ⓓ
8 Ⓐ Ⓑ Ⓒ Ⓓ	33 Ⓐ Ⓑ Ⓒ Ⓓ
9 Ⓐ Ⓑ Ⓒ Ⓓ	34 Ⓐ Ⓑ Ⓒ Ⓓ
10 Ⓐ Ⓑ Ⓒ Ⓓ	35 Ⓐ Ⓑ Ⓒ Ⓓ
11 Ⓐ Ⓑ Ⓒ Ⓓ	36 Ⓐ Ⓑ Ⓒ Ⓓ
12 Ⓐ Ⓑ Ⓒ Ⓓ	37 Ⓐ Ⓑ Ⓒ Ⓓ
13 Ⓐ Ⓑ Ⓒ Ⓓ	38 Ⓐ Ⓑ Ⓒ Ⓓ
14 Ⓐ Ⓑ Ⓒ Ⓓ	39 Ⓐ Ⓑ Ⓒ Ⓓ
15 Ⓐ Ⓑ Ⓒ Ⓓ	40 Ⓐ Ⓑ Ⓒ Ⓓ
16 Ⓐ Ⓑ Ⓒ Ⓓ	41 Ⓐ Ⓑ Ⓒ Ⓓ
17 Ⓐ Ⓑ Ⓒ Ⓓ	42 Ⓐ Ⓑ Ⓒ Ⓓ
18 Ⓐ Ⓑ Ⓒ Ⓓ	43 Ⓐ Ⓑ Ⓒ Ⓓ
19 Ⓐ Ⓑ Ⓒ Ⓓ	44 Ⓐ Ⓑ Ⓒ Ⓓ
20 Ⓐ Ⓑ Ⓒ Ⓓ	45 Ⓐ Ⓑ Ⓒ Ⓓ
21 Ⓐ Ⓑ Ⓒ Ⓓ	46 Ⓐ Ⓑ Ⓒ Ⓓ
22 Ⓐ Ⓑ Ⓒ Ⓓ	47 Ⓐ Ⓑ Ⓒ Ⓓ
23 Ⓐ Ⓑ Ⓒ Ⓓ	48 Ⓐ Ⓑ Ⓒ Ⓓ
24 Ⓐ Ⓑ Ⓒ Ⓓ	49 Ⓐ Ⓑ Ⓒ Ⓓ
25 Ⓐ Ⓑ Ⓒ Ⓓ	50 Ⓐ Ⓑ Ⓒ Ⓓ

CUT HERE

Language Arts and Reading

60 Questions
65 Minutes

1. Which of the following would be most likely NOT be considered a biography?

   A. *Martin's (Luther King, Jr.) Big Words*
   B. *The Picture Book of Sacagawea*
   C. *Helen Keller*
   D. *The Best Baseball Game Ever*

2. When an author attempts to explain something to the reader, he or she is using what mode of writing?

   A. descriptive
   B. expository
   C. narrative
   D. persuasive

3. The Florida Comprehensive Assessment Test (FCAT) is a(n)

   A. norm-referenced test.
   B. informal reading inventory.
   C. criterion-referenced test.
   D. performance-based assessment

4. In order to communicate in writing, penmanship must be legible. Which of the following contributes to legible handwriting?

   A. spacing
   B. letter formation
   C. letter alignment
   D. All of the above

5. _____ groups are small groups charged with the task of becoming experts on one aspect of a topic who then share their piece of expertise with the entire class.

   A. Ad hoc
   B. Jigsaw
   C. Guided reading
   D. Shared reading

6. Jade is experiencing reading difficulties as noted on her recent timed fluency check. Rather than quickly identifying high-frequency words, it takes her an extended amount of time to say these words presented on the page. This shows a weakness in which area of fluency?

   A. prosody
   B. accuracy
   C. automaticity
   D. rate

GO ON TO THE NEXT PAGE

7. When an author presents his thoughts in his writing in the form of a story, what mode of writing is he using?

    A. descriptive

    B. expository

    C. narrative

    D. persuasive

8. Which of the following is considered a phonological awareness skill?

    A. knowledge of the letter-sound relationship

    B. knowledge of onset-rime segments

    C. knowledge of alphabet letter identification

    D. None of the above

9. Mrs. Engel asks her second-graders to use *text-based* evidence to support their answers to comprehension questions in their adopted reading text. In the context of this scenario, what does *text-based* mean?

    A. evidence that is vaguely implied by the author

    B. evidence that is not stated in the text

    C. evidence that is presented in the text

    D. evidence that requires the reader to seek out additional resources

10. Literacy centers or stations allow students time to practice and apply what they are learning in a small group setting. Which of the following could be examples of literacy centers?

    A. poetry

    B. literature response

    C. word work

    D. All of the above

11. Which of the following is NOT a critical element of narrative writing?

    A. plot structure

    B. setting

    C. fluency

    D. characterization

12. Identify the literary device used in the following example:

The teenager stole some soap from the grocery store. The police said he made a clean getaway.

    A. pun

    B. hyperbole

    C. simile

    D. alliteration

13. A classroom library should include which of the following components?

    A. books from a variety of genres

    B. a plethora of nonfiction resources

    C. a wide array of multicultural children's literature

    D. All of the above

14. _____ reading takes place between two students of differing grade levels, usually primary and intermediate students/classes. The pair of students usually has a copy of the same text and read chorally or take turns reading to each other.

    A. Guided
    B. Shared
    C. Paired
    D. Buddy

15. A kindergarten teacher pulls a small group of students to test their knowledge of individual phonemes. Which progress monitoring assessment is the teacher using?

    A. test of nonsense word fluency
    B. informal reading inventory
    C. test of phonological awareness
    D. test of alphabet knowledge

16. The teacher has organized her classroom to allow for small group instruction. The teacher acts as a facilitator while students discuss important aspects of a common text. This is an example of what organizational format?

    A. literature circles
    B. shared reading
    C. interactive writing
    D. reading centers/stations

17. The original Declaration of Independence is

    A. a valuable teaching tool.
    B. an example of a primary source.
    C. an artifact.
    D. All of the above

18. In what grade are students typically taught to hold their pencil and perform the basic strokes of traditional manuscript?

    A. first
    B. kindergarten
    C. fourth
    D. third

19. The local fire department has announced that it plans to do away with the volunteer firefighter program in all of the county's fire stations. The students and teachers at Red Bug Elementary School learn of this on their field trip during Fire Prevention month. In support of the volunteer firefighters, the students wish to express their views on keeping the program. What would be the best form of written communication?

    A. narrative
    B. descriptive
    C. expository
    D. opinion/argument

GO ON TO THE NEXT PAGE

20. There are many ways for a teacher to organize the instructional time in her classroom. While many organizational structures are considered effective, a workshop approach to organizing your classroom provides time to

   A. work on your lesson plans.
   B. offer a great deal of whole group instruction.
   C. differentiate instruction to meet the needs of individual students.
   D. meet briefly with every student in your classroom.

21. With prior knowledge of their specific deficiencies, Mrs. Hynes pulls a small group of students to work specifically on sight word identification. This is an example of a(n) _____ group.

   A. homogeneous
   B. heterogeneous
   C. impromptu
   D. None of the above

22. Mr. Duffy encourages his students to reread and improve upon their journal writings from the previous school day. What phase of the writing process is being described?

   A. drafting
   B. revising
   C. editing
   D. prewriting

23. Which of the following is an example of onset-rime segments?

   A. c-at
   B. home-run
   C. hold-ing
   D. pre-view

24. Johnny, a first-grader, reads a passage that contains 120 words. While reading, he makes six errors. What would his error rate be for this reading passage?

   A. 10
   B. 20
   C. 30
   D. 40

25. A cloze test offers the student the opportunity to _____ and _____.

   A. read; illustrate
   B. record feelings; retell
   C. visualize the text; draw
   D. predict; use context clues

26. Gavin, a kindergarten student, made approximations while reading at the beginning and middle of the school year. However, by the end of the year, he was pointing to each word on the page as he read his guide reading books. What concept of print is Gavin exhibiting?

   A. directionality
   B. voice-to-print match
   C. return sweep
   D. sight word recognition

27. A group of third-graders is finishing up *narrative biographies* about a historical figure of their choosing that they had learned about during a social studies thematic unit. To help them with their sentence structure skills, the teacher provides each student with a rubric. Which of the following rubrics would assist students in the revision of their content?

    A. a rubric focusing on punctuation and grammar
    B. a rubric that ensures that each sentence has subject-verb agreement
    C. a rubric that encourages them to check all words for correct spelling
    D. Both A and B

28. During a read aloud of an alphabet book, a first-grade student named Emily comments that the word the teacher is reading, *elephant,* has the same initial letter as her name. This child is demonstrating an understanding of

    A. letter knowledge.
    B. vocabulary.
    C. syllables.
    D. phonological awareness.

29. Which of the following choices would be considered a consonant blend?

    A. ch
    B. th
    C. wh
    D. bl

30. John is experiencing reading difficulties as noted on his recent timed fluency check. His reading speed is slow and halted. This shows a weakness in which area of fluency?

    A. prosody
    B. accuracy
    C. automaticity
    D. rate

31. Making predictions about what a particular text is going to be about aids student

    A. automaticity.
    B. sight word recognition.
    C. analysis of cause and effect.
    D. comprehension.

32. A hyperbole is an exaggerated statement used for effect and is not meant to be taken literally. Which of the following is a hyperbole?

    A. The elephant was enormous!
    B. She ran very fast.
    C. Her nose was red like a strawberry.
    D. She must have weighed 1,000 pounds!

GO ON TO THE NEXT PAGE

33. Carmen Agra Deedy is a *New York Times* best-selling author. As a Cuban immigrant, she has inherent knowledge of Cuban culture and traditions. Many of her books include aspects of the Cuban culture. These texts are examples of _____ children's literature.

   A.   multicultural

   B.   hybrid

   C.   fantasy

   D.   science fiction

34. Anecdotal notes are a way of _____ the progress of your students in an informal way.

   A.   assigning

   B.   monitoring

   C.   illustrating

   D.   None of the above

35. _____ is the phase prior to conventional spelling.

   A.   Temporary

   B.   Invented

   C.   Phonetic

   D.   All of the above

36. During what stage of reading have students mastered basic concepts of print and are beginning to use various strategies for problem solving in reading?

   A.   early

   B.   pre-reading

   C.   fluent

   D.   emergent

37. What cueing system focuses on meaning that is associated with language through prior knowledge and experience?

   A.   graphophonemic

   B.   semantic

   C.   visual

   D.   auditory

38. An example of visual media is

   A.   an online game.

   B.   a journal.

   C.   the newspaper.

   D.   an atlas.

39. Questioning and retelling enhance communication skills among students in the classroom. What critical reading skill is most enhanced by these strategies?

   A.   fluency

   B.   word recognition

   C.   phonics

   D.   comprehension

40. Which of the following is a web-based activity that could take place in the elementary classroom?

    A. blog
    B. online newsletter
    C. Wiki page
    D. All of the above

41. Working and/or growth _____ can be used to collect work samples over time to gain true insight into how students' skills have progressed.

    A. portfolios
    B. chapter tests
    C. benchmark tests
    D. rubrics

42. Prior to a read aloud, setting a purpose aids what specific language art that is often neglected?

    A. reading
    B. writing
    C. speaking
    D. listening

43. A first-grade teacher performs a shared reading of a big book about butterflies during a science lesson. She identifies the way the words are read from left to right while reading with her pointer. She is modeling _____ for her students.

    A. the use of captions
    B. directionality
    C. alphabetic principle
    D. letter identification

44. Information and media literacy would be enhanced by which of the following instructional aids?

    A. primary sources
    B. printed material (magazines, textbooks, etc.)
    C. the Internet
    D. All of the above

45. Which of the following statements best describes how an educator should use the Internet in her primary (K–2) classroom?

    A. Students should be provided preselected sites to choose from in order to avoid exposure to inappropriate web content.
    B. Students can be provided preselected sites but should be taught advanced search skills to collect information helpful to their learning.
    C. Students should be taught to critically question and evaluate the site based on its content and their needs.
    D. Students should be left to surf the Web as they desire.

46. Games, rubrics, checklists, and portfolios are all forms of

    A. informal assessments.
    B. formal assessments.
    C. comprehension aids.
    D. None of the above

GO ON TO THE NEXT PAGE

47. Mr. Wells decides to assess his students' knowledge of the Revolutionary War by having them reenact a key battle, including historical individuals, proper language, and props to show what they truly know about this time period in American history. Which of the following types of assessment is Mr. Wells utilizing in his classroom?

    A. standardized

    B. diagnostic

    C. performance-based

    D. formal

48. *She sells seashells by the seashore* is considered a(n)

    A. alliterative phrase.

    B. high-frequency word.

    C. sight word.

    D. phonogram.

49. An English Learner (EL) is having difficulty reading in English; however, the teacher wants him to hear the content that is required for his grade level. Which of the following is an effective option for the EL student?

    A. independent reading

    B. using an audio book on a digital device

    C. SSR

    D. short readings assigned for homework

50. Which of the following questions should be asked of the reader during close readings of a text?

    A. What does the text say?

    B. How does the text work?

    C. What does the text mean?

    D. All of the above

51. In the classic story *The Giving Tree* by Shel Silverstein, the main character evolves throughout the text from an innocent boy to a selfish young adult and eventually to a wise older man. Citing text-based evidence, what type of young adult was the male character?

    A. innocent

    B. wise

    C. selfish

    D. unruly

52. Ms. Brumer, a first-grade teacher, requires her students to orally retell the classic folktale *Little Red Riding Hood,* reciting key details of the text. Which of the following would be considered a key plot detail that should be included in the retelling?

    A. Little Red Riding Hood wore a red hoodie.

    B. Little Red Riding Hood walked down a concrete sidewalk.

    C. Little Red Riding Hood came across a wolf on her way to Grandmother's house.

    D. Little Red Riding Hood said, "Wee, wee, wee, wee" all the way home.

53. Which of the following sets of terms related to language conventions and clarity are placed in the correct order from simple, to moderate, to complex?

    A. literal, figurative, literary
    B. literary, figurative, literal
    C. simple, mediocre, challenging
    D. None of the above

54. Assessment is a vital component used to identify when it is appropriate to increase the complexity of a student's reading. Which of the following is NOT an appropriate assessment tool to use for this purpose?

    A. IRI (informal reading inventory)
    B. running record
    C. anecdotal notes
    D. diagnostic assessment

55. Which of the following would be considered an idiom?

    A. Grayson's jokes were flat, like warm soda pop.
    B. America is a melting pot.
    C. His heart was beating out of his chest.
    D. The camera loves me.

56. An episodic biography is one in which only a portion of the significant individual's life during a particular time and place is portrayed in the text. Which of the following best exemplifies the characteristics of an episodic biography?

    A. Abraham Lincoln's experiences during the time of the Civil War
    B. Barack Obama's life as the 44th President of the United States
    C. Sandra Day O'Connor's life during the period she was the first female Supreme Court Justice of the United States of America
    D. All of the above

57. Near the end of the school year, a kindergarten teacher asks her students to write about their favorite color and why that color is the best color in the world. This form of writing is considered a(n)

    A. opinion-argument.
    B. expository.
    C. narrative.
    D. informational.

58. In Mo Willem's *Piggy and Elephant* books, the author uses speech bubbles rather than quotation marks to show _____ between the two main characters.

    A. literary devices
    B. dialogue
    C. temporal words
    D. linking words

GO ON TO THE NEXT PAGE

59. A second-grade teacher is performing an author study on Tomie dePaola. This particular author writes multicultural children's literature and lives in the northeastern United States. Providing him with the funds to travel and stay to visit your classroom is not in the budget. Which of the following technological tools would best aid in visually bringing this author to your classroom?

    A. blogs
    B. glogs
    C. videoconferencing
    D. podcasts

60. _____ is the first developmental phase of writing.

    A. Scribbling
    B. Drafting
    C. Letter strands
    D. Invented spelling

IF YOU FINISH BEFORE TIME IS CALLED, CHECK YOUR WORK ON THIS SECTION ONLY. DO NOT WORK ON ANY OTHER SECTION IN THE TEST.

Social Science

55 Questions

65 Minutes

1. Japanese forces launched an attack on the United States naval base at Pearl Harbor in Oahu, Hawaii, on what date?

    A. December 7, 1991
    B. December 7, 1492
    C. December 7, 1941
    D. December 7, 1931

2. The Gulf War was a conflict in the early 1990s authorized by the

    A. United Nations.
    B. United Arab Emirates.
    C. Secretary of the Treasury.
    D. Federal Bureau of Investigation.

3. Who was the writer during the British Enlightenment period that greatly influenced the authors of the Declaration of Independence?

    A. Isaac Newton
    B. Nicolaus Copernicus
    C. Debra Sampson
    D. John Locke

4. In the years following the Civil War, the Industrial Revolution made it possible for "robber barons" like _____to accumulate gigantic fortunes.

    A. Henry Ford
    B. John D. Rockefeller
    C. Clara Barton
    D. Abraham Lincoln

5. _____ refers to the physical characteristics of specific places and how they form and change.

    A. Places and Regions
    B. Human Systems
    C. Process that Shape the Earth
    D. World in Spatial Terms

6. Along with maps, what other educational tools provide valuable geographical information?

    A. graphs
    B. photographs
    C. satellite images
    D. All of the above

GO ON TO THE NEXT PAGE

7. According to the Library of Congress, it is important for students to do which of the following when analyzing primary sources?

    A. investigate, search, and inquire

    B. analyze, examine, and explore

    C. I do, you do, and we do

    D. observe, reflect, and question

8. Which of the following is a primary responsibility of the United States government?

    A. administering justice

    B. maintaining statistics about society

    C. overseeing the national defense

    D. All of the above

9. The legislative branch of government is comprised of what two governing bodies?

    A. The President and Vice President

    B. The Secretary of State and the Secretary of Foreign Policy

    C. The Senate and the House of Representatives

    D. None of the above

10. On a map of downtown Orlando, structures like the Orlando Arena, Bob Carr Auditorium, and the Creative Village are drawn the correct size and distance apart in an effort to represent, in a smaller form, the city's amenities accurately. This map is known as being drawn to

    A. legend.

    B. hemispheres.

    C. coordinates.

    D. scale.

11. Prior to Columbus's arrival in the New World, native populations had settled the land. What happened to the native populations as a result of his discovery?

    A. They were decimated by disease and warfare.

    B. They flourished under the European influence.

    C. They warmly welcomed all assistance provided by the Europeans.

    D. They fought for their land and were victorious in their efforts.

12. The concept that events in history are linked to one another through a series of cause-and-effect occurrences is known as historic causation. Which of the following events would NOT be considered to possess historic causation?

    A. Columbus's discovery of the New World

    B. Industrial Revolution

    C. Japanese attack on Pearl Harbor

    D. Signing any bill into law

13. The ancient civilization of the Sumerians invented

    A. the wheel.

    B. cuneiform writing.

    C. initial forms of irrigation.

    D. All of the above

14. _____ is just one of many reputable websites that can be used to enhance your students' knowledge of subject matter for social studies topics required to be taught to your grade level.

    A. Pinterest
    B. The Library of Congress
    C. Henry's site for all things history
    D. None of the above

15. The _____ is the indicator on a map of the directions: north, south, east, west, northeast, northwest, southeast, and southwest.

    A. key
    B. scale
    C. grid
    D. compass rose

16. The _____ is the form of currency used in much of Europe, including Spain, Portugal, the Netherlands, and Germany.

    A. yen
    B. dollar
    C. peso
    D. euro

17. Which of the following are powers of the local and state governments *and* the federal government?

    A. ability to tax
    B. ability to establish a postal service
    C. regulate foreign commerce
    D. oversee national defense

18. Why was the Electoral College included in Article II as one of the checks and balances in the U.S. system of government?

    A. to give more equal weight to states with small populations.
    B. to assist voters in making an informed decision regarding our highest elected officials.
    C. to give the Electoral college a greater amount of power to override the citizen vote
    D. Both A and B

19. Which of the following is defined as a high rate of inflation accompanied by rising unemployment?

    A. inflation
    B. stagflation
    C. recession
    D. depression

20. What article of the Constitution established the legislative branch of government in the United States of America?

    A. Article I
    B. Article II
    C. Article III
    D. Article IV

GO ON TO THE NEXT PAGE

21. Which of the following people advises the President on matters of foreign policy?

    A. Secretary of State

    B. Secretary of the Treasury

    C. Press Secretary

    D. First Lady

22. The Supreme Court is the highest court of appeals in the United States. Who is responsible for appointing Supreme Court justices?

    A. the Senate

    B. the President

    C. the House of Representatives

    D. the public

23. Which of the following is an economic principle that citizens should understand for overall economic prosperity?

    A. People's choices involve costs.

    B. People create economic systems that influence individual choices and incentives.

    C. People's choices have future consequences.

    D. All of the above

24. Ancient Egyptians made many contributions to the world, including

    A. cuneiform writing.

    B. the division of time.

    C. preservation of bodies after death.

    D. devising the famous Code of Hammurabi.

25. In the event of an assassination, the _____ takes on the position of President of the United States.

    A. Vice President

    B. people's choice of a replacement

    C. Secretary of State

    D. Speaker of the House

26. Which of the following government officials or groups has the sole power to conduct impeachment trials?

    A. President of the United States

    B. Supreme Court

    C. Senate

    D. Secretary of State

27. Which of the following patriots designed and carried out the famous Boston Tea Party incident?

    A. George Washington

    B. Thomas Jefferson

    C. Patrick Henry

    D. Samuel Adams

28. Which of the following countries was a part of the Allies in WWII that defeated the Axis Powers?

    A. United States
    B. Japan
    C. Italy
    D. Germany

29. The ancient Phoenicians were well known for

    A. their manufacturing of glass.
    B. their manufacturing of metals.
    C. the development of their famous purple dye.
    D. All of the above

30. Which of the following is the vertical, imaginary line that divides the Earth into its eastern and western halves?

    A. prime meridian
    B. Tropic of Capricorn
    C. International Date Line
    D. equator

31. In the United States, we operate in a _____ economy, or one in which the government and private businesses both play vital roles. The majority of goods and services are produced by the private sector.

    A. traditional
    B. command
    C. market
    D. mixed

32. Recently, fancy athletic socks with a variety of patterns and colors were sought after by elementary- and middle school-age boys. When a population demands more of something like these socks, the _____ is (are) increased and so is the price.

    A. demand
    B. interest
    C. supply
    D. taxes

33. Societies like _____ have educational divisions and publish valuable social studies resources for students.

    A. Association of Childhood Education International
    B. National Council for the Teaching of Mathematics
    C. National Geographic
    D. None of the above

GO ON TO THE NEXT PAGE

34. The belief that the United States should control all of North America was known as _____. This idea fueled much of the warfare that took place against the Native Americans.

   A.   Manifest Destiny
   B.   the Louisiana Purchase
   C.   Westward Expansion
   D.   the arrival of the *Mayflower*

35. What element on the map shows the viewer the map's orientation in terms of cardinal directions?

   A.   legend
   B.   scale
   C.   compass rose
   D.   key

36. The Magna Carta of 1215 (England) is

   A.   considered the very first modern European document that sought to limit the powers of the governing body.
   B.   an English legal charter.
   C.   the most significant early influence on the extensive historical process that led to the rule of constitutional law today.
   D.   All of the above

37. Who is considered the leader of the local government?

   A.   city council
   B.   mayor
   C.   governor
   D.   president

38. What are the three levels of government in the United States?

   A.   local, state, and federal
   B.   legislative, judicial, and executive
   C.   domestic, national, and international
   D.   local, federal, and abroad

39. What famous American gave a speech that so eloquently began with the following phrase?

Four score and seven years ago, our fathers brought forth on this continent, a new nation, conceived in liberty and dedicated to the proposition that all men are created equal.

   A.   Martin Luther King, Jr.
   B.   John F. Kennedy, Jr.
   C.   Abraham Lincoln
   D.   Susan B. Anthony

40. The following image identifies what imaginary line that designates the official change of each day?

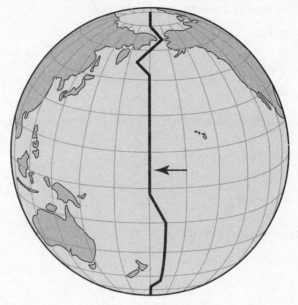

    A. International Date Line
    B. prime meridian
    C. equator
    D. Tropic of Cancer

41. The President's Cabinet includes many important departments. In these departments, which secretary of that division is responsible for collecting taxes, printing money, and overseeing the finances of the nation?

    A. Secretary of Energy
    B. Secretary of the Treasury
    C. Secretary of Labor
    D. Secretary of Transportation

42. Which of the following methods can be used in isolation or in collaboration to effectively teach social studies concepts?

    A. cooperative learning
    B. role play
    C. simulation
    D. All of the above

43. Mrs. Johnson poses an issue to her fifth-grade class regarding the limited funds for new playground equipment at Spalding Street Elementary. She asks them to discuss the issue and to collectively work on possible solutions. Which of the following instructional methods is Mrs. Johnson using in her classroom?

    A. expository teaching
    B. problem-based learning
    C. role play
    D. simulation

GO ON TO THE NEXT PAGE

44. Role play is considered a method of orally assessing student content knowledge. Which of the following depicts a topic that could be used in a role play in the classroom?

    A. the Egyptian hieroglyphics
    B. the constitution
    C. the Battle of Bunker Hill
    D. None of the above

45. Which of Earth's seven continents is considered the largest in terms of size or area?

    A. Asia
    B. Africa
    C. Antarctica
    D. North America

46. Which of the following is the largest of Earth's oceans?

    A. Caribbean
    B. Atlantic
    C. Pacific
    D. Artic

47. The majority of goods and services are produced by the

    A. private sector.
    B. consumers.
    C. public sector.
    D. national organizations.

48. _____ is defined as the science that deals with the production, consumption, and distribution of goods and services.

    A. Civics
    B. History
    C. Economics
    D. Democracy

49. Which of the following continents is located entirely in Earth's Southern hemisphere?

    A. South America
    B. Antarctica
    C. North America
    D. Greenland

50. In 2014, a severe drought in California affected avocado and citrus trees in that region of the United States. These trees are considered important and nutritious _____ resources.

    A. natural
    B. human
    C. political
    D. capital

51. In the late 1980s, what country fell due to the collapse of their command economy?

    A. Soviet Union
    B. England
    C. France
    D. Germany

52. Mr. Castle, a third-grade teacher, is planning an interdisciplinary unit on the regions of the United States. Knowing how vital it is to incorporate the English language arts in the content area of social studies, specifically reading and writing, he gathers appropriate resources that will allow his students to interact with the content. Which of the following resources will help Mr. Castle accomplish his goals?

    A. artifacts
    B. quality nonfiction children's literature
    C. maps
    D. All of the above

53. While learning about Nelson Mandela, students are instructed to read his biography and create a _____ containing two columns. In the first column, they are to note text-based evidence; in the second column, they are to make personal connections to the content to aid comprehension.

    A. worksheet
    B. double-entry journal
    C. semantic web
    D. None of the above

54. Knowing that social studies is a subject that is difficult for many students to relate to, the highly effective teacher should display enthusiasm for the content and provide students with a(n) _____ and _____ learning environment.

    A. boring; silent
    B. collaborative; authoritative
    C. supportive; engaging
    D. unstructured; loud

55. Using the interactive whiteboard, Ms. Gaffney, a third-grade teacher, displays her digital copy of *Scholastic News* magazine for all of her students to see. The current event articles are read aloud together by her and the students. What instructional strategy is Ms. Gaffney using to teach the social studies content?

    A. shared reading
    B. round robin reading
    C. independent reading
    D. silent reading

IF YOU FINISH BEFORE TIME IS CALLED, CHECK YOUR WORK ON THIS SECTION ONLY. DO NOT WORK ON ANY OTHER SECTION IN THE TEST.

Science

55 Questions
70 Minutes

1. What is the name for the amount of cubic space that an object occupies?

    A. volume
    B. mass
    C. density
    D. weight

2. What creates Earth's magnetism?

    A. the rotation of Earth around the Moon
    B. the rotation of the Moon around Earth
    C. the rotation of the outer core around the inner core
    D. the rotation of the Solar System

3. Which of the following tools would be suitable for collecting experimental data related to temperature?

    A. thermometer
    B. barometer
    C. seismograph
    D. calculator

4. Which is NOT a property of a living thing?

    A. grows and develops
    B. reproduces
    C. has a skeleton
    D. made up of cells

5. What causes the seasons?

    A. the tilt of the Earth
    B. the distance of Earth from the Sun
    C. the rotation of the Moon around Earth
    D. the gravitational pull of the Moon

6. Which of the following instructional activities provides the best opportunity for inquiry-based learning?

    A. Students define and describe the El Niño effect by using text and images they find on the Internet.
    B. Students select a location in the U.S. and then search the Internet for monthly temperature data of this location for the most recent El Niño year. Students then compare monthly temperature data for the El Niño year to the average temperature data for the past 50 years in order to assess the impact of El Niño on that particular location.
    C. Students read an article about El Niño provided in their textbook and complete a test based on their reading.
    D. Students go to the library to find newspaper accounts describing the impact of El Niño on the California coast. They then summarize what they find in a two-page written report.

7. Which is the LEAST specific level of taxonomy?

   A. species

   B. genus

   C. domain

   D. kingdom

8. Which of the following strategies could be used to differentiate instruction in the science classroom?

   A. video-based instruction

   B. group project

   C. stations

   D. web-based instruction

9. The _____ makes up the majority of Earth's volume.

   A. crust

   B. core

   C. Moon

   D. mantle

10. A truthful explanation of different events that happen with uniformity under certain conditions is called a

   A. law.

   B. theory.

   C. hypothesis.

   D. postulate.

11. Ms. Andrew's fifth-grade class is planting a garden and measuring the amount of water given to different plants on each day. The class has made a guess that the more water a plant receives, the larger the plant will become. This class has created which of the following?

   A. laboratory

   B. hypothesis

   C. controlled experiment

   D. prediction

12. A _____ Moon occurs when the Sun and Moon are on the same side of Earth.

   A. Full

   B. New

   C. First Quarter

   D. Last Quarter

13. What type of energy does the Sun provide?

   A. magnetic energy

   B. radiant energy

   C. nuclear energy

   D. acoustic energy

GO ON TO THE NEXT PAGE

14. Which *Apollo* flight was considered a "successful failure" when its mission had to be aborted due to the explosion of oxygen tanks, but the crew returned to Earth safely?

- **A.** *Apollo 7*
- **B.** *Apollo 8*
- **C.** *Apollo 11*
- **D.** *Apollo 13*

15. The iron in an iron bar combining with oxygen in the air to produce rust is an example of

- **A.** volume change.
- **B.** density change.
- **C.** chemical change.
- **D.** physical change.

16. What is the second step in the scientific method?

- **A.** ask a question
- **B.** predict
- **C.** make observations
- **D.** conclude

17. Which of the following is NOT a domain for living things?

- **A.** Archaea
- **B.** Fungi
- **C.** Eukarya
- **D.** Bacteria

18. Which of the following is NOT a continent?

- **A.** South America
- **B.** Antarctica
- **C.** Arctic Circle
- **D.** Australia

19. What type of energy travels in a straight line?

- **A.** magnetic energy
- **B.** acoustic energy
- **C.** light energy
- **D.** nuclear energy

20. Which of the following is NOT a stage in the water cycle?

- **A.** evaporation
- **B.** perspiration
- **C.** condensation
- **D.** collection

21. All cells contain the following parts EXCEPT

    A. DNA.
    B. cell walls.
    C. organelles.
    D. cell membranes.

22. Which of the following occurs when light passes through a transparent material like water at a slant angle?

    A. refraction
    B. diffraction
    C. transformation
    D. dislocation

23. What part of the cell breaks down sugar to create energy?

    A. endoplasmic reticulum
    B. ribosomes
    C. Golgi complex
    D. mitochondrion

24. In an experiment, students have not yet determined exactly what data will be collected. The perspective and objective of the study determine which data are important. The students are most likely involved in

    A. planning a controlled experiment.
    B. identifying a research question.
    C. formulating a hypothesis.
    D. revisiting the hypothesis to answer a question.

25. A class is conducting an experiment in which liquids of different colors are exposed to sunlight and are left in the dark. The temperature of each liquid is measured. These students are engaged in which type of experiment?

    A. random experiment
    B. quasi-experiment
    C. nested experiment
    D. controlled experiment

26. Optics is a branch of physics that studies the physical properties of

    A. sound.
    B. eyes.
    C. vision.
    D. light.

27. Who proposed the theory that the continents were once joined in a supercontinent called Pangea?

    A. Alfred Wegener
    B. Albert Einstein
    C. Benjamin Franklin
    D. Neil Armstrong

GO ON TO THE NEXT PAGE

28. Which of the following is NOT a shape of bacteria?

    A. rods

    B. cones

    C. spheres

    D. spirals

29. A transparent object with flat polished surfaces that refract or diffuse light is called a

    A. prism.

    B. diamond.

    C. pyramid.

    D. plastic.

30. _____ rocks are formed when debris is compressed and fused together.

    A. Metamorphic

    B. Sedimentary

    C. Igneous

    D. Compressed

31. _____ reproduction requires two parents.

    A. Asexual

    B. Nonsexual

    C. Binary fission

    D. Sexual

32. Which of the following may be best explained through a computer simulation?

    A. growth of a plant over time

    B. temperature change on the playground over time

    C. height compared to shoe size for a group of students

    D. the relationship between predator and prey populations

33. Which of the following is NOT considered an electromagnetic wave?

    A. ultraviolet waves

    B. X-rays

    C. radio waves

    D. sound waves

34. Which of the following is the fifth step of the scientific method?

    A. predicting

    B. observing

    C. testing

    D. concluding

35. Which is NOT a group of fungi?

  A. perfect fungi
  B. club fungi
  C. imperfect fungi
  D. threadlike fungi

36. Does an instrument that is considered valid also have to be reliable?

  A. No, it is valid so it does not need to be reliable.
  B. No, they are two separate issues.
  C. Yes, you need it to be valid as well as reliable. You cannot have a valid instrument without reliability.
  D. Yes, if the instrument is valid we can assume it is also reliable.

37. A physical occurrence related to stationary and moving electrons and protons is called

  A. vibration.
  B. electricity.
  C. light.
  D. sound.

38. An organism that consumes food from its environment is called a(n)

  A. heterotroph.
  B. heterozygote.
  C. autotroph.
  D. parasite.

39. Which of the following forms when two plates slide against each other in opposite directions?

  A. earthquake
  B. canyon
  C. mountain
  D. volcano

40. Students are exploring the relationship between two variables and will either manually enter the data for each variable into a table of values or import the data using a link cable. In this experiment, the students are most likely using

  A. word processors.
  B. spreadsheets.
  C. online databases.
  D. graphing calculators.

41. Which of the following is NOT an example of a conductor?

  A. aluminum
  B. copper
  C. rubber
  D. graphite

GO ON TO THE NEXT PAGE

42. A third-grade teacher is administering a unit test to assess student learning from a unit on electricity. This teacher is using which type of assessment?

    A. formative assessment

    B. summative assessment

    C. standardized assessment

    D. alternative assessment

43. In an investigation activity, students generate questions about a topic they are following. They identify the questions they can answer themselves. Which of the following sources should the students use to answer the questions they cannot answer themselves?

    A. Visit online science videos through YouTube

    B. Visit science-related Ask the Expert websites

    C. Visit social network websites

    D. Visit online science databases

44. Which of the following is NOT a type of rock?

    A. metamorphic

    B. sedimentary

    C. hard

    D. igneous

45. The process by which a plant converts glucose into energy is called

    A. transpiration.

    B. respiration.

    C. photosynthesis.

    D. fertilization.

46. Which form of assessment gives day-to-day data related to ongoing student learning for classroom use?

    A. formative

    B. diagnostic

    C. summative

    D. standardized

47. Which of the following do plant cells contain, but animal cells do not?

    A. organelles

    B. cell membranes

    C. chloroplasts

    D. cytoplasm

48. All of the following are methods of heat transfer through Earth's system EXCEPT

    A. radiation.

    B. conduction.

    C. filtration.

    D. convection.

49. Which equipment should be present in a classroom laboratory?

   A. microscopes
   B. aprons
   C. eyewash stations
   D. All of the above

50. Which of the following is an appropriate safety procedure for a laboratory?

   A. washing hands frequently
   B. wearing glasses
   C. using chemicals in an open space
   D. opening windows

51. Which of the following statements is FALSE?

   A. The phases of the Moon are a result of the Sun reflecting off the Moon's surface.
   B. Gravitational force increases with height above the Earth's surface.
   C. Earth revolves around the Sun.
   D. Seasons are due to the tilt of the Earth.

52. A fifth-grade teacher takes her class of students on a mud walk to gather specimens from the water. This teacher is using which of the following strategies?

   A. experiential learning
   B. differentiated instruction
   C. formative assessment
   D. diagnostic assessment

53. Which must be present for an experiment to be considered a controlled experiment?

   A. observational data
   B. hypothesis
   C. technology
   D. control group and experimental group

54. Which instructional strategy involves basing instruction on student needs using data from assessments so all students' needs are met?

   A. student inquiry
   B. student-centered instruction
   C. informal science instruction
   D. differentiated instruction

55. The process by which species survive based upon genetic traits providing the best fit for survival is known as

   A. natural selection.
   B. evolution.
   C. adaptation.
   D. fossils.

IF YOU FINISH BEFORE TIME IS CALLED, CHECK YOUR WORK ON THIS SECTION ONLY. DO NOT WORK ON ANY OTHER SECTION IN THE TEST.

Mathematics

50 Questions
70 Minutes

1. What operation concept is most likely represented by the following problem?

   A student is solving the following word problem: Alberto has n apples. He arranges the apples into groups of g apples each. How many groups of apples did he make?

   A. measurement or subtractive division concept
   B. sharing or partition division concept
   C. array or area multiplication concept
   D. repeated addition multiplication concept

2. Find the next term in the pattern 1, 3, 4, 7, 11, 18, 29, . . .

   A. 36
   B. 40
   C. 47
   D. 50

3. Sara is completing a test involving skills and concepts related to two-digit addition computation algorithm, such as place value, addition concept, addition facts memorization, among others. Which one of the following testing practices could most likely be represented by this testing process?

   A. alternative assessment
   B. standardized test
   C. diagnostic assessment
   D. authentic assessment

4. A bedroom is rectangular and has dimensions of 12 feet and 10 feet. If one dimension is doubled and the other dimension is tripled, the area of the bedroom floor has increased by how many times?

   A. 2 times
   B. 3 times
   C. 5 times
   D. 6 times

5. Sue found the following set of measures for a project she was doing: $\frac{1}{4}, \frac{3}{8}, \frac{3}{16}, \frac{5}{8}$. Which one of these sets of fractions is arranged in ascending order (from least to greatest)?

   A. $\frac{3}{16}, \frac{3}{8}, \frac{5}{8}, \frac{1}{4}$

   B. $\frac{5}{8}, \frac{3}{8}, \frac{1}{4}, \frac{3}{16}$

   C. $\frac{3}{16}, \frac{1}{4}, \frac{3}{8}, \frac{5}{8}$

   D. $\frac{1}{4}, \frac{5}{8}, \frac{3}{8}, \frac{3}{16}$

6. What is the value of $4.1 \cdot 10^{-2}$?

    A. 0.041

    B. 0.41

    C. 41

    D. 410

7. A teacher is conducting frequent assessments of students, which are designed to estimate rates of their improvement. Which one of the following best describes this teacher's procedures?

    A. diagnostic assessment

    B. progress monitoring

    C. formative assessment

    D. authentic assessment

8. A tree that is 8 feet tall casts a shadow that is 4 feet long. A girl casts a shadow that is 2.5 feet long. How tall is the girl?

    A. 1.25 feet

    B. 4 feet

    C. 5 feet

    D. 6.5 feet

9. Which equation matches the following description?

        The difference of a number and 4 is two times the number.

    A. $N - 4 = 2N$

    B. $4 - N = 2N$

    C. $N + 4 = 2N$

    D. $N - 4 = 2 - N$

Use the following figure for items 10, 11, and 12.

This is a line plot representing students' scores on an exam with 35 items.

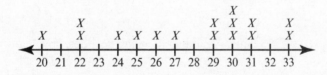

10. What is the mean of the data set? Round your answer to the nearest ones.

    A. 28

    B. 30

    C. 31

    D. 442

11. What is the mode of the data set?

    A. 29

    B. 30

    C. 31

    D. 33

GO ON TO THE NEXT PAGE

12. What is the median of the data set?

    A. 26.5
    B. 29
    C. 29.5
    D. 30

13. Which of the following is NOT an example of alternative assessment?

    A. multiple-choice assessment item
    B. portfolio assessment task
    C. rubric
    D. performance assessment task

14. Select the unit of measure that is most appropriate for the length of time it may take to run a mile.

    A. seconds
    B. minutes
    C. hours
    D. days

15. Which of the following arithmetic sentences best describes the following problem?

Carl has 85 apples. Carl has 56 more apples than Frank. How many apples does Frank have?

    A. Smaller number unknown: $56 + \underline{\quad} = 85$, or $85 - 56 = \underline{\quad}$
    B. Larger number unknown: $29 + 56 = \underline{\quad}$, or $\underline{\quad} - 56 = 29$
    C. Difference unknown: $29 + \underline{\quad} = 85$, or $85 - 29 = \underline{\quad}$
    D. None of the above

16. Select the number that will result in a smaller number after it is squared.

    A. −0.03
    B. 0.3
    C. 1.3
    D. 3

17. A train takes 3 hours to travel 225 miles. Assuming there are no stops, how many miles will this train travel in 12 hours?

    A. 56.25 miles
    B. 825 miles
    C. 900 miles
    D. 1,125 miles

18. Which expression can be used for the table below?

x	y
1	5
2	7
3	9
4	11

A. $y = 2x - 3$
B. $y = x + 4$
C. $y = 2x + 3$
D. $y = 3x + 2$

19. Identify the coordinates of point S in the figure shown.

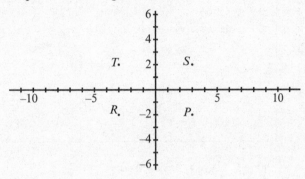

A. $(3, 2)$
B. $(2, 3)$
C. $(-3, -2)$
D. $(-2, -3)$

20. The box-and-whisker plot below displays the list of Peter's test scores this semester in a math class. What is the median of Peter's test scores?

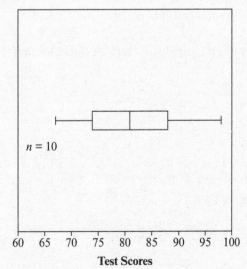

A. 67
B. 72
C. 81
D. 87

GO ON TO THE NEXT PAGE

21. How many meters are in 120 centimeters?

   A.   1.2 meters
   B.   12 meters
   C.   120 meters
   D.   1200 meters

Use the figure for items 22 and 23.

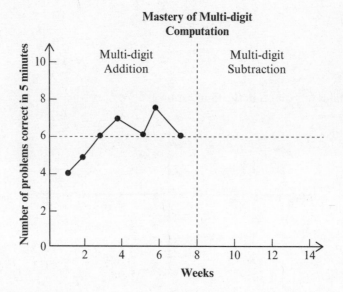

22. Every week, Mrs. Smith is having Robert complete a series of probes. He has to solve as many multi-digit addition computation exercises as possible in 5 minutes. She then graphs the results (see figure above). Which of the following best describes what Mrs. Smith is most likely concerned with?

   A.   providing the student with testing experiences similar to the ones from the county that require speed
   B.   making sure the student receives enough practice and masters multi-digit computation
   C.   assigning the student a grade at end of 14 weeks
   D.   estimating rate of student improvement over time

23. The previous graph is most likely an example of which of the following?

   A.   progress monitoring
   B.   diagnostic assessment
   C.   standardized test
   D.   formative assessment

24. A car dealer offered Frank a used car at a 10 percent discount off of the original price. If Frank paid $9,000 for this car, what was the original price of the car? This problem does not include taxes and other fees.

   A. $900
   B. $8,100
   C. $10,000
   D. $90,000

25. Find the area of the figure shown.

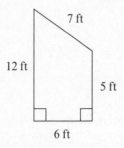

A. 30 ft^2
B. 51 ft^2
C. 55 ft^2
D. 102 ft^2

26. Which one of the following ideas related to mathematics teaching is true?

A. Mastery of skills is the key for teaching mathematics, and problem solving is not appropriate for elementary school level.
B. Problem solving should come before mastery of skills.
C. Problem solving does not come after mastery of skills.
D. Problem solving should come after mastery of skills.

27. Which of the following is a unit of area?

A. ft^3
B. in^2
C. m^3
D. cm

28. Simplify the following expression: $300 - 40 \div 5 \cdot (2^3 - 2) \cdot 3 + 8$

A. 148
B. 164
C. 308.44
D. 944

29. Which one of the following algebraic expressions is equivalent to $x^2 - x - 42$?

A. $(x + 6)(x + 7)$
B. $(x - 6)(x + 7)$
C. $(x + 6)(x - 7)$
D. None of the above

30. At a supermarket, Samuel needs to arrange cans of food (all the same size) on seven shelves. He estimates that he could fit about 45 cans of food on half a shelf. The cans of food come in boxes of 30 cans each. Approximately how many boxes will Samuel need to fill the seven shelves?

A. 3 boxes
B. 10.5 boxes
C. 21 boxes
D. 630 cans

GO ON TO THE NEXT PAGE

31. Five times a number plus nine is forty-five. If *n* stands for the unknown number, what is the algebraic equation that represents this situation?

    A. $5n - 45 = 9$
    B. $5n - 9 = 45$
    C. $5n + 45 = 9$
    D. $5n + 9 = 45$

32. Which of the following proportions best represents the relationship stated in the following word problem?

The unit of currency in Jordan is called the dinar. If the exchange rate is $3 to 2 dinars, how many dollars would you receive if you exchanged 22 dinars?

    A. $\dfrac{2}{3} = \dfrac{x}{22}$

    B. $\dfrac{3}{2} = \dfrac{22}{x}$

    C. $\dfrac{3}{2} = \dfrac{x}{22}$

    D. $\dfrac{2}{22} = \dfrac{x}{3}$

33. At a local school, Carlos decided to develop and administer a survey for a school project. He wanted to know whether the students in the school county were in favor of a new rule mandated by the school board. At the end of the school day, he stood outside the school exit and asked a few students to complete the survey as they went out. Some students participated, and others did not. He gathered and analyzed the data and concluded that the students in the school county were not in favor of the new rule mandated by the school board. Did Carlos interpret the results of the survey correctly?

    A. The procedures used by Carlos to develop the survey were valid, but the interpretation of the survey's results is not correct.
    B. The procedures used by Carlos to develop the survey were sufficiently systematic and valid, and the interpretation of the survey's results is basically correct. Asking students in one school is enough of a sample to make some generalizations about a whole school county.
    C. The procedures used by Carlos to develop the survey were not systematic and valid, and the interpretation of the survey's results is not correct.
    D. The procedures used by Carlos to develop the survey were not systematic and valid, but the interpretation of the survey's results is probably correct.

34. Which one of the following algebraic expressions is equivalent to $-x + 3 + 8 + 6x - 12$?

    A. $-9 + 3x + 8 - 6x - 8x$
    B. $-9 - 3x + 8 - 6x + 8x$
    C. $9 + 3x + 8 - 6x + 8x$
    D. $-9 + 3x + 8 - 6x + 8x$

35. Tom was asked to identify each of the following numbers as prime number, composite number, or neither one: 1, 3, 6, 17, and 89. Which of the following is correct?

    A. 1 is prime, 3 is prime, 6 is composite, 17 is prime, and 89 is prime
    B. 1 is neither, 3 is prime, 6 is composite, 17 is prime, and 89 is prime
    C. 1 is neither, 3 is prime, 6 is composite, 17 is prime, and 89 is composite
    D. 1 is prime, 3 is prime, 6 is composite, 17 is prime, and 89 is composite

36. A parallelogram must have which of the following properties?

    A.   all equal sides
    B.   two sets of parallel sides
    C.   all right angles
    D.   five sides

37. What is the **smallest** 4-digit number that is divisible by 2, 3, 4, 5, 6, 8, 9, and 10?

    A.   1,080
    B.   1,260
    C.   1,170
    D.   1,008

Use the following table to answer items 38 and 39.

Number of Hours	Frequency
1	21
2	15
3	2
4	7

38. Find the median for the data set given in the table above. Round your answer to the nearest tenth.

    A.   1 hour
    B.   1.9 hours
    C.   2 hours
    D.   2.5 hours

39. Find the range of the data set given in the table.

    A.   2
    B.   3
    C.   14
    D.   Not possible

40. When solving a subtraction computation exercise, Natalie uses the following strategy to find the difference: $376 - 59$, add 1 to each, $377 - 60 = 317$. Which of the following strategies is she most likely using?

    A.   compensation strategy
    B.   decomposition strategy
    C.   make a ten strategy
    D.   composition strategy

41. If a swimming pool is 60 meters long, and each day Pedro swims a total of 45 lengths of the pool for practice, then how many kilometers did he swim over a 10-day period?

    A.   27 kilometers
    B.   270 kilometers
    C.   2,700 kilometers
    D.   27,000 kilometers

GO ON TO THE NEXT PAGE

42. Which of the following demonstrates the commutative property of multiplication?

    A. $(3 \times 4) \times 6 = 3 \times (4 \times 6)$
    B. $3 \times 4 \times 6 = 4 \times 3 \times 6$
    C. $3 \times 4 \times 6 \times 1 = 3 \times 4 \times 6$
    D. $0 \times 3 \times 4 \times 6 = 0$

43. Which of the following is NOT a necessary skill or concept for the effective learning of addition computation involving two- and three-digit whole numbers?

    A. addition concept with cubes
    B. addition facts memorization
    C. place value up to hundreds with base-ten blocks
    D. All of the above skills and concepts are necessary.

44. The figure shown can be called which of the following names?

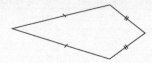

    A. rhombus
    B. kite
    C. trapezoid
    D. rectangle

45. Given that m and n are elements of the set of integers, Felix was asked to find out if the possible resulting integers from the following two expressions had the same parity:

First expression: $[(2m + 1) + 2n] \cdot [(2n + 1) + (2m + 1)]$

Second expression: $[2m + (2n + 1)] \cdot [2n + (2m - 1)]$

He said that the parity of the possible integers resulting from these expressions would be different. Was Felix correct in his assertion?

    A. No, the parity of the possible integer resulting from the first expression is odd, and the parity for the possible integer resulting from the second expression is odd. So, they have the same parity.
    B. Yes, the parity of the possible integer resulting from the first expression is even, and the parity for the possible integer resulting from the second expression is odd. So, they have opposite parity.
    C. Yes, the parity of the possible integer resulting from the first expression is odd, and the parity for the possible integer resulting from the second expression is even. So, they have opposite parity.
    D. No, the parity of the possible integer resulting from the first expression is even, and the parity for the possible integer resulting from the second expression is even. So, they have the same parity.

46. What mathematical property does the following situation represent?

Martin said that if the length of the desk, A, *is greater than the length of the chair,* B, *and the length of the chair is greater than the length of cabinet,* C, *then the length of the desk,* A, *is greater than the length of the cabinet,* C.

    A. reflexivity
    B. symmetry
    C. iteration
    D. transitivity

47. Mrs. Taylor has been working with four students on fraction computation (addition). She decided to monitor their progress using a measure of fraction addition fluency. She measures their performance initially (shown in the Initial Scores column) and then twice per week over the 3-week review period. The 3-week goal is 12 correct problems out of 14 for fraction addition. The results for the students are shown below:

| Student | Initial Scores | Test Scores Twice Per Week | | | | | |
| | | Week 1 | | Week 2 | | Week 3 | |
		1	2	3	4	5	6
Allan	2	3	4	5	7	9	10
Nicosha	2	2	1	3	2	2	3
Sabrina	2	4	6	9	9	10	11
Daniel	2	2	7	6	8	10	11

Based on this information, which of the following best describes how students are responding to the instruction?

A. Generally, it appears that Allan, Sabrina, and Daniel are responding to the instruction. Their scores show progress toward the goal of 12 correct problems at the conclusion of the 3-week review period. They then should remain in the whole class environment. Nicosha is not showing improvement. Her scores have remained stagnant over the 3-week review period. Nicosha is in need of further intervention.

B. Generally, it appears that Sabrina, Allan, Nicosha, and Daniel are not responding to the instruction. Their scores show no progress toward the goal of 12 correct problems at the conclusion of the 3-week review period. They are in need of further intervention.

C. Generally, it appears that Allan, Nicosha, Sabrina, and Daniel are responding to the instruction. Their scores show enough progress toward the goal of 12 correct problems at the conclusion of the 3-week review period. They then should remain in the whole class environment.

D. Generally, it appears that Sabrina and Daniel are responding to the instruction. Their scores show progress toward the goal of 12 correct problems at the conclusion of the 3-week review period. They then should remain in the whole class environment. Allan and Nicosha are not showing improvement. Their scores have not improved enough over the 3-week review period. They are in need of further intervention.

48. Which of the following is equivalent to 9^{-3}?

A. 9^3

B. $\dfrac{1}{9^{-3}}$

C. $\dfrac{1}{9^3}$

D. $\dfrac{1}{-9^{-3}}$

49. Carlos was asked to find out if 1,234 is divisible by 9. How do you think he should solve this? Select the most appropriate answer.

A. He should use a paper-and-pencil computation algorithm and check if 9 divides 1,234 evenly.

B. He should use a divisibility rule involving 9 as a divisor and check if 9 divides the sum of the digits 1,234 evenly.

C. He should use base-ten blocks and check if 9 divides 1,234 evenly.

D. He should use a calculator to divide 1,234 by 9 and check if 9 divides 1,234 evenly.

GO ON TO THE NEXT PAGE

50. When solving exercises involving two-digit whole number subtraction computation, a student invented the following algorithm for $37 - 19 = \underline{\ \ }$.

$$
\begin{array}{r}
37 \\
-\ 19 \\
\hline
-2 \\
20 \\
\hline
18
\end{array}
$$

Which of the following is the most appropriate teacher's response to this student's invented algorithm?

A. This is a correct computation algorithm, and students should be allowed to invent, explain, and share their own operational procedures. This practice has positive benefits on their motivation to solve problems as they come up with their own strategy instead of just following a rote procedure.

B. This is an incorrect algorithm, which will work some of the time, but not always. It should be avoided.

C. This is a correct computation algorithm, but students should be using manipulative materials, such as base-ten blocks, to solve computation problems.

D. This is a correct computation algorithm, but students should be corrected and only learn the standard computation algorithm to avoid further confusion.

IF YOU FINISH BEFORE TIME IS CALLED, CHECK YOUR WORK ON THIS SECTION ONLY. DO NOT WORK ON ANY OTHER SECTION IN THE TEST.

Answer Key

Language Arts and Reading

1.	D	16.	A	31.	D	46.	A
2.	B	17.	D	32.	D	47.	C
3.	C	18.	B	33.	A	48.	A
4.	D	19.	D	34.	B	49.	B
5.	B	20.	C	35.	D	50.	D
6.	C	21.	A	36.	A	51.	C
7.	C	22.	B	37.	B	52.	C
8.	B	23.	A	38.	A	53.	A
9.	C	24.	B	39.	D	54.	D
10.	D	25.	D	40.	D	55.	C
11.	C	26.	B	41.	A	56.	D
12.	A	27.	D	42.	D	57.	A
13.	D	28.	A	43.	B	58.	B
14.	D	29.	D	44.	D	59.	C
15.	C	30.	D	45.	A	60.	A

Social Science

1.	C	15.	D	29.	D	43.	B
2.	A	16.	D	30.	A	44.	C
3.	D	17.	A	31.	D	45.	A
4.	B	18.	D	32.	C	46.	C
5.	A	19.	B	33.	C	47.	A
6.	D	20.	A	34.	A	48.	C
7.	D	21.	A	35.	C	49.	B
8.	D	22.	B	36.	D	50.	A
9.	C	23.	D	37.	B	51.	A
10.	D	24.	C	38.	A	52.	D
11.	A	25.	A	39.	C	53.	B
12.	D	26.	C	40.	A	54.	C
13.	D	27.	D	41.	B	55.	A
14.	B	28.	A	42.	D		

Science

1. A	15. C	29. A	43. B
2. C	16. C	30. B	44. C
3. A	17. B	31. D	45. B
4. C	18. C	32. D	46. A
5. A	19. C	33. D	47. C
6. B	20. B	34. C	48. C
7. C	21. B	35. A	49. D
8. C	22. A	36. C	50. A
9. D	23. D	37. B	51. B
10. A	24. A	38. A	52. A
11. B	25. D	39. A	53. D
12. B	26. D	40. D	54. D
13. B	27. A	41. C	55. A
14. D	28. B	42. B	

Mathematics

1. A	14. B	27. B	40. A
2. C	15. A	28. B	41. A
3. C	16. B	29. C	42. B
4. D	17. C	30. C	43. D
5. C	18. C	31. D	44. B
6. A	19. A	32. C	45. B
7. B	20. C	33. C	46. D
8. C	21. A	34. D	47. A
9. A	22. D	35. B	48. C
10. A	23. A	36. B	49. B
11. B	24. C	37. A	50. A
12. B	25. B	38. C	
13. A	26. C	39. B	

Answer Explanations

Language Arts and Reading

1. **D.** Competency 2. Biographies are books written about important, famous, or infamous people.

2. **B.** Competency 3. Expository writing is writing that attempts to explain or inform. Descriptive, persuasive, and narrative are all modes of writing as well.

3. **C.** Competency 4. FCAT is a criterion-referenced test. These types of tests are assessment instruments that assess the point at which the student has achieved mastery.

4. **D.** Competency 5. Letter formation, spacing, letter size and alignment, along with line quality all contribute to legible handwriting or penmanship.

5. **B.** Competency 4. Jigsaw groups are small groups charged with the task of becoming experts on one aspect of a topic; they then share their knowledge with the whole class.

6. **C.** Competency 1. Automaticity is the ability to say the words quickly and easily. Accuracy, prosody, and rate are also crucial elements of fluency.

7. **C.** Competency 3. Narrative writing is writing that tells a story.

8. **B.** Competency 1. Knowledge of onset-rime segments, individual words in sentences, syllables, and the awareness of individual phonemes in words is known as phonological awareness.

9. **C.** Competency 1. *Text-based* evidence is evidence stated in the text that is used by students to support their answers to comprehension questions in their readings.

10. **D.** Competency 4. Literacy centers or stations include, but are not limited to, any of the following: poetry, literature response, word work, listening, writing, spelling, comprehension, vocabulary, art, and independent reading.

11. **C.** Competency 3. Narrative writing should include the following elements: plot structure, conflict, characterization, setting, theme, point of view, sequencing, and transitions. Fluency is a critical skill in reading.

12. **A.** Competency 2. A pun is defined as a play on words.

13. **D.** Competency 2. Classroom libraries should contain various genres, nonfiction resources, and a wide variety of multicultural children's literature.

14. **D.** Competency 4. Buddy reading takes place between two students of differing grade levels, usually primary and intermediate students/classes.

15. **C.** Competency 1. Phoneme identification is a critical element of phonological awareness.

16. **A.** Competency 4. The teacher acts as a facilitator during literature circle discussion groups while students discuss important aspects of a common text.

17. **D.** Competency 5. Primary sources are documents or pieces of work that were written, recorded, or created during a particular time period. They are valuable teaching tools and artifacts. The Declaration of Independence is just one example of a primary source that can be used to educate students.

18. **B.** Competency 5. Kindergarten students are taught to hold their pencil and perform the basic strokes of traditional manuscript. These skills are built upon in subsequent grade levels.

19. **D.** Competency 3. The students wish to convince others to keep the volunteer firefighter program. The most appropriate mode of writing would be the opinion/argument.

20. **C.** Competency 4. The workshop approach is a student-centered approach to teaching, in which teachers have ample time to differentiate instruction and confer with small groups and individuals to best meet their academic needs.

21. **A.** Competency 4. Homogeneous groups consist of students with similar needs, while heterogeneous groups mix students of varying needs.

22. **B.** Competency 3. Prewriting, drafting, editing, and revising are all phases in the writing process. During the revising phase, students are encouraged to reread and improve their writing.

23. **A.** Competency 1. The onset is defined as the first consonant or groups of consonants that come before the first vowel in a syllable (*c*). The rime unit is the first vowel sound and any others that follow it in a syllable (*at*).

24. **B.** Competency 1. The error rate is the total number of words divided by the total errors. In this case, the answer is 20: $120 \div 6 = 20$.

25. **D.** Competency 1. A cloze procedure intentionally omits words from a passage and offers students the opportunity to predict and use context clues to fill in the correct answers.

26. **B.** Competency 1. Voice-to-print match, also known as one-to-one correspondence, shows that Gavin now understands the concept of a word and word boundaries.

27. **D.** Competency 3. If the teacher is encouraging her students to concentrate on sentence structure in this assignment, then a rubric focusing on punctuation and grammar or on subject-verb agreement would assist the students in the revision of their content.

28. **A.** Competency 1. This child is demonstrating an of understanding of letter knowledge, which is one concept of print.

29. **D.** Competency 1. The first three choices are digraphs (two consonants that together represent one sound). A consonant blend is two consonants that together keep their individual sounds.

30. **D.** Competency 1. Rate is defined as the speed of reading and greatly influences whether or not a student can comprehend the text. Accuracy, prosody, and automaticity are also crucial elements of fluency.

31. **D.** Competency 1. Along with accessing prior knowledge, making predictions about what is about to be read is a common strategy used to enhance comprehension.

32. **D.** Competency 2. A hyperbole is an exaggerated statement used for effect and is not meant to be taken literally. A person weighing 1,000 pounds would be an example of a hyperbole.

33. **A.** Competency 2. Multicultural children's literature includes information from multiple cultures, ethnicities, traditions, and locations around the world.

34. **B.** Competency 4. The purpose of using anecdotal notes is to observe students while they work and record the observations for later study.

35. **D.** Competency 3. The spelling phase prior to conventional spelling is called temporary, invented, or phonetic—all three terms are used interchangeably.

36. **A.** Competency 1. During pre-reading/emergent reading phases, young children are exposed to basic concepts of print and may approximate the text. During the early phase of reading, children have mastered basic concepts of print and are attempting to apply reading strategies that they have been taught in the classroom. Fluent readers are proficient readers and employ the necessary reading strategies when needed to gain meaning from text.

37. **B.** Competency 1. Of the three cueing systems (graphophonemic, syntactic, semantic), semantic refers to the meaning of the text.

38. **A.** Competency 5. Visual media is nonprint media.

39. **D.** Competency 1. The critical reading skill most enhanced by questioning and retelling is comprehension.

40. **D.** Competency 5. Blogs, online newsletters, Wiki pages, online book clubs, WebQuests, etc. are all examples of web-based activities that could take place in the elementary classroom.

41. A. Competency 2. All are considered assessment options; however, portfolios are the only option that shows growth over time through a collection of student samples.

42. D. Competency 1. Listening is the language art used most often, yet it is also the one most often neglected. Listening requires the student to take in or receive what has been heard and seen, attend to what is most important, and then comprehend the message. Setting a purpose for listening ensures that students understand the objective of the lesson.

43. B. Competency 1. Directionality is how the words are read from left to right and top to bottom.

44. D. Competency 5. Information and media literacy are aided by the use of artifacts, primary sources, the Internet, printed material, and visual media.

45. A. Competency 5. Primary students should be provided preselected sites to choose from in order to avoid exposure to inappropriate web content.

46. A. Competency 1. Games, rubrics, checklists, and portfolios are all forms of informal assessments tools that teachers can use to gauge student learning in the classroom.

47. C. Competency 4. A dramatic reenactment of a key battle in the Revolutionary War is considered a performance-based assessment.

48. A. Competency 1. An alliterative phrase is one in which the beginning sound of each word is the same.

49. B. Competency 2. Using an audio book on a digital device would help an English Learner (EL) who is having difficulty reading in English so that he can still hear the content that is required for his grade level.

50. D. Competency 1. An effective teacher should ask the following questions during a close reading of a text: What does the text say? How does the text work? What does the text mean?

51. C. Competency 1. In order to cite text-based evidence, the reader must refer back to the text and pull the information directly from the source. In this case, the young adult is described as selfish.

52. C. Competency 4. "Little Red Riding Hood came across a wolf on her way to Grandmother's house" would be considered a key detail that should be included in the story retelling.

53. A. Competency 2. Literal, figurative, literary are terms (placed in order from simple, to moderate, to complex) related to language conventions and clarity.

54. D. Competency 4. Assessment is a vital component used to identify when it is appropriate to increase a student's reading of more complex text. IRIs, running records, and anecdotal notes all provide specific data. While diagnostic assessment is important, it is not appropriate for this purpose.

55. C. Competency 2. An idiom is an expression or phrase whose meaning cannot be deciphered or inferred from the meanings of the words used. An example of an idiom is: *His heart was beating out of his chest.*

56. D. Competency 2. Abraham Lincoln's experiences during the time of the Civil War; Barack Obama's life as the 44th President of the United States; and Sandra Day O'Connor's life during the period she was the first female Supreme Court Justice of the United States of America would all exemplify the characteristics of an episodic biography in which only a portion of their lives during a particular time and place is portrayed in the text.

57. A. Competency 3. The kindergarten teacher is encouraging her students to write an opinion-argument piece about their favorite color and why that color is the best color in the world.

58. B. Competency 3. In Mo Willem's *Piggy and Elephant* books the author uses speech bubbles rather than quotation marks to show dialogue between the two main characters.

59. C. Competency 5. Videoconferencing is an option to utilize when funds for bringing in a guest speaker (travel and food/hotel) are not available.

60. A. Competency 3. Scribbling is the first developmental phase of writing.

Social Science

1. **C.** Competency 2. Japanese forces launched an attack on the United States naval base at Pearl Harbor in Hawaii on December 7, 1941. This event prompted the United States involvement in World War II and undoubtedly contributed to the victory of the Allied forces.

2. **A.** Competency 2. The Gulf War was a conflict in the early 1990s authorized by the United Nations.

3. **D.** Competency 2. John Locke was the writer from the British Enlightenment period that greatly influenced the authors of the Declaration of Independence.

4. **B.** Competency 2. Andrew Carnegie, John D. Rockefeller, and Cornelius Vanderbilt were all considered robber barons and made their fortunes in railroads.

5. **A.** Competency 3. Places and Regions refers to the physical characteristics of specific places and how they form and change.

6. **D.** Competency 3. Along with maps, graphs, photographs, satellite images, and diagrams provide valuable geographical information.

7. **D.** Competency 1. According to the Library of Congress, it is important for students to observe, reflect, and question primary sources.

8. **D.** Competency 4. The government is primarily responsible for administering justice, maintaining statistics about society, overseeing the national defense, the education system, and maintaining roads.

9. **C.** Competency 4. The legislative branch of government is comprised of the Senate and the House of Representatives.

10. **D.** Competency 3. Scale is when something on a map is drawn to size. In other words, compared to other items on the map, items are the correct size and distance apart; the larger the scale, the more detail shown (i.e., city map), the smaller the scale, the more area shown but less detail (i.e., world map).

11. **A.** Competency 2. Prior to Christopher Columbus's arrival in the New World, native populations had settled the land. As a result of his "discovery," these native populations were decimated by disease and warfare.

12. **D.** Competency 2. Signing a bill into law is not an example of historic causation. The other choices are: Columbus's discovery of the New World opened up the Western hemisphere to economic and political development. The Industrial Revolution was a technological development that led to the use of machinery over manual labor. The Japanese attack on Pearl Harbor forced the United States to become involved in WWII.

13. **D.** Competency 2. The ancient civilization of the Sumerians invented the wheel, cuneiform writing, and initial forms of irrigation by using dikes and canals.

14. **B.** Competency 1. The Library of Congress is one of many reputable websites that can be used to enhance your students' knowledge of subject matter for topics required to be taught to your grade level.

15. **D.** Competency 3. The compass rose is the indicator on a map of the directions: north, south, east, west, northeast, northwest, southeast, and southwest.

16. **D.** Competency 5. The euro is the form of currency used in much of Europe, including Spain, Portugal, the Netherlands, and Germany.

17. **A.** Competency 4. The ability to tax are powers of the local and state governments *and* the federal government. The ability to establish a postal service, regulate foreign commerce, and oversee national defense are all powers of the federal government alone.

18. **D.** Competency 4. The Electoral College was included in Article II as one of the checks and balances in the system of government for two reasons: to give more equal weight to states with small populations and to assist voters in making an informed decision regarding our highest elected officials.

19. **B.** Competency 5. Stagflation is defined as a high rate of inflation accompanied by rising unemployment. Inflation is a persistent, general increase in prices over a period of time. A recession is a painful slowing of the economy, while a depression is a long-lasting painful slowing of the economy.

20. **A.** Competency 4. Articles I, II, and III of the Constitution established the legislative, executive, and judicial branches of the U.S. government, respectively. Article IV established the relationship between the states.

21. **A.** Competency 4. The Secretary of State advises the President on matters of foreign policy.

22. **B.** Competency 4. The President appoints Supreme Court justices.

23. **D.** Competency 5. The following are all economic principles that citizens should understand: people choose, people's choices involve costs, people respond to incentives in predictable ways, people create economic systems that influence individual choices and incentives, people gain when they trade voluntarily, and people's choices have future consequences.

24. **C.** Competency 2. Ancient Egyptians made many contributions to the world, including the construction of the great pyramids, hieroglyphic writing, preservation of bodies after death, and completion of the solar calendar.

25. **A.** Competency 4. In the event of an assassination, the Vice President takes on the position of President of the United States.

26. **C.** Competency 4. The Senate has the sole power to conduct impeachment trials. Since 1789, the Senate has exercised this right 17 times.

27. **D.** Competency 2. Samuel Adams of Boston designed and carried out the famous Boston Tea Party incident.

28. **A.** Competency 2. The Second World War (WWII) was a global military conflict between two opposing forces: The Allies (Leaders) – Great Britain (Churchill), United States (Roosevelt/Truman), Russia (Stalin), Free France (De Gaulle), China (Chiang Kai-shek) and the Axis Powers (Leaders) – Germany (Hitler), Italy (Mussolini), Japan (Hirohito).

29. **D.** Competency 2. The ancient Phoenicians were sea traders who were proficient in sailing at night using the stars as their guide. They were also well known for their manufacturing of glass, metals, and the development of their famous purple dye.

30. **A.** Competency 3. The vertical, imaginary line that divides the Earth into its eastern and western halves is the prime meridian.

31. **D.** Competency 5. In the United States, we operate in a mixed (market/command) economy, or one in which the government and private businesses both play vital roles. The majority of goods and services are produced by the private sector.

32. **C.** Competency 5. When a population demands more of something, the supply is increased, as is the price.

33. **C.** Competency 1. The Association of Childhood Education International and the National Council for the Teaching of Mathematics are valuable associations, but they do not specifically offer social studies resources like that of the National Geographic Society.

34. **A.** Competency 2. The belief that the United States should control all of North America fueled much of the warfare that took place against the Native Americans. This belief was called Manifest Destiny.

35. **C.** Competency 3. The compass rose identifies the cardinal directions on the map.

36. **D.** Competency 2. The Magna Carta of 1215 (England) is considered the very first modern European document that sought to limit the powers of the governing body, an English legal charter, and the most significant early influence on the extensive historical process that led to the rule of constitutional law today.

37. **B.** Competency 4. The leader of the local government is the mayor.

38. **A.** Competency 4. The three levels of government in the United States are local, state, and federal.

39. **C.** Competency 2. Abraham Lincoln gave the Gettysburg Address on November 19, 1863, at the dedication of the Soldiers' National Cemetery in Gettysburg, Pennsylvania.

40. **A.** Competency 3. The date officially changes according to the International Date Line. The line follows 180° longitude, except where it crosses land, so there are some departures from the meridian.

41. **B.** Competency 4. The President's Cabinet includes many important departments. The Secretary of the Treasury collects taxes, prints money, and handles the nation's finances. The Secretary of Energy researches fuel sources and electricity for our nation. The Secretary of Labor ensures that workers earn fair wages in acceptable working conditions. The Secretary of Transportation oversees highway safety and air, train, and sea travel.

42. **D.** Competency 1. The following methods can be used in isolation or in collaboration, depending on the specific subject matter, and are often employed while teaching social studies concepts: expository teaching, problem-based learning, inductive thinking, cooperative learning, role play, and simulation.

43. **B.** Competency 1. Problem-based learning provides to students the opportunity to analyze a real-world problem and in small groups, develop plausible solutions.

44. **C.** Competency 1. Role play, along with oral reports, skits, discussions, and debates, are all oral assessment tasks. The Battle of Bunker Hill could be assessed orally through a role play activity in the classroom.

45. **A.** Competency 3. There are seven continents: North America, South America, Africa, Europe, Antarctica, Asia, and Australia. Asia is the largest continent in terms of area.

46. **C.** Competency 3. The Pacific Ocean is the largest ocean in terms of area.

47. **A.** Competency 5. The majority of goods and services are produced by the private sector.

48. **C.** Competency 5. Economics is defined as the science that deals with the production, consumption, and distribution of goods and services.

49. **B.** Competency 3. Antarctica is located entirely in the Southern hemisphere.

50. **A.** Competency 5. The avocado and citrus trees in California are considered important and nutritious natural resources.

51. **A.** Competency 5. In the late 1980s, the Soviet Union fell due to the collapse of their command economy.

52. **D.** Competency 1. Interdisciplinary units require a variety of resources to meet the needs of diverse students in the classroom. Some of these resources include artifacts, quality nonfiction texts, and maps when preparing a geography unit related to the regions of our country.

53. **B.** Competency 1. A double-entry journal has two columns. The first column notes text-based evidence, while the second column allows the student to make personal connections to the content to aid comprehension.

54. **C.** Competency 1. The social studies teacher should display enthusiasm for the content and provide students with a supportive and engaging learning environment so they can better relate to the content.

55. **A.** Competency 1. Ms. Gaffney is using the instructional strategy of shared reading on the interactive whiteboard, encouraging her students to read along with her as she reads the enlarged, digital text.

Science

1. **A.** Competency 3. Volume and mass are both properties of matter. The amount of cubic space that an object occupies is called volume.

2. **C.** Competency 4. The rotation of the Earth causes the iron outer core to rotate around the inner core, creating the Earth's magnetism.

3. **A.** Competency 1. Temperature data is best collected using a thermometer. A barometer measures air pressure. A seismograph measures earthquakes.

4. **C.** Competency 5. Not all living things have a skeleton. There are six properties of living things: They are made up of cells, obtain and use energy, grow and develop, reproduce, respond to stimuli in environment, and adapt to environment.

5. **A.** Competency 4. The seasons are caused by the tilt and revolution of the Earth, which allows the Sun's vertical rays to migrate between the Tropic of Cancer and the Tropic of Capricorn over the course of a year.

6. **B.** Competency 1. In choice B, the students are challenged to answer the question, "What is El Niño's impact on the climate at a given locality?" Students answer that question based on analysis of data collected on the Internet. This activity provides the best opportunity for inquiry-based learning.

7. **C.** Competency 5. The levels of taxonomy from broadest to most specific are as follows: domain, kingdom, phylum, class, order, family, genus, and species.

8. **C.** Competency 1. Stations are an effective strategy for differentiating instruction. Stations allow students to learn using various approaches and allow the teacher to meet the needs of all students. The other choices are less structured and are limited in scope.

9. **D.** Competency 4. The mantle is the largest layer of the Earth and makes up the majority of Earth's volume. The crust is the Earth's thin outer layer, and the core is the innermost layer, consisting of the outer core and the inner core.

10. **A.** Competency 2. A law is a truthful explanation of different events that happen with uniformity under certain conditions; for example, laws of nature or laws of gravitation.

11. **B.** Competency 2. A hypothesis is a possible answer to a scientific question. Ms. Andrew's class has made a hypothesis about the relationship between the amount of water and the growth of a plant.

12. **B.** Competency 4. A New Moon occurs when the Moon and Sun are on the same side of Earth and no reflection of the Sun off the Moon's surface is visible. The dark side of the Moon faces Earth at this time.

13. **B.** Competency 3. The Sun provides radiant or light energy. Magnetic energy is the force (pull or push) of a magnet. Nuclear energy is present in the nucleus of atoms. Dividing, combining, or colliding of nuclei can result in the release of nuclear energy. Acoustic energy is energy in the form of mechanical waves that are transmitted through materials like plastic or air. These waves can be an audible or inaudible.

14. **D.** Competency 4. *Apollo 7* was the first manned mission. *Apollo 8* was the first manned mission to orbit the Moon. *Apollo 11* was the first mission to land on the Moon. *Apollo 13's* mission was aborted due to the explosion of oxygen tanks and was called a "successful failure" because even though they didn't land on the Moon as planned, all astronauts returned safely to Earth.

15. **C.** Competency 3. The iron in an iron bar combining with oxygen in the air to produce rust is an example of chemical change. The chemical properties of a substance indicate the ability of a substance to be altered into a new substance or substances. The molecular structure of the substance or object is changed. These chemical changes may include burning, rusting, and digestion. Under some conditions, a chemical reaction may involve breaking apart, combining, recombining, or decomposing substances.

16. **C.** Competency 2. The steps of the scientific method include 1) ask a question, 2) make observations, 3) hypothesize, 4) predict, 5) test, and 6) conclude. The second step is to make observations.

17. **B.** Competency 5. The three domains are Archaea, Bacteria, and Eukarya. Fungi is a kingdom, not a domain.

18. **C.** Competency 4. The seven continents are Europe, Asia, North America, South America, Africa, Australia, and Antarctica. The Arctic Circle is not a continent.

19. **C.** Competency 3. Light travels in a straight line. It can change direction, but still keeps traveling in a straight line; for example, when a light ray strikes a mirror, it changes direction, but continues traveling in a straight line. In this case, the mirror *reflects* light.

20. **B.** Competency 5. The stages in the water cycle are evaporation, condensation, precipitation, and collection. Perspiration is the "sweating" of an animal to cool off or maintain proper body temperature.

21. B. Competency 5. All cells contain DNA, organelles, cell membranes, and cytoplasm. Only eukaryotic cells contain cell walls.

22. A. Competency 3. Refraction occurs when light passes through a transparent material like water at a slant angle; the ray of light appears to bend as it changes speed. Diffraction occurs when a ray of light bends around the edges of an object; the ray of light has been diffracted.

23. D. Competency 5. The mitochondrion breaks down sugar to create energy. The endoplasmic reticulum creates proteins, lipids, and other materials. Ribosomes build proteins. The Golgi complex packages and distributes proteins.

24. A. Competency 2. The students are most likely involved in planning a controlled experiment since they have not identified the data to be collected.

25. D. Competency 2. A controlled experiment is one in which a treatment (experimental) group and a control group exist. The treatment group receives a treatment; the control group does not. This provides a method for comparison. In this case, the liquids exposed to sunlight are the treatment group, and the liquids kept in the dark are the control group.

26. D. Competency 3. Optics is a branch of physics that studies the physical properties of light. It provides information about the behavior and properties of light and its interaction with matter.

27. A. Competency 4. Alfred Wegener proposed the concept of Pangea.

28. B. Competency 5. The three shapes of bacteria are rods, spheres, and spirals. Bacteria are not cone shaped.

29. A. Competency 3. A transparent object with flat polished surfaces that refract or diffuse (break apart) light is called a prism. The amount of refraction that occurs depends upon the angle between the surfaces.

30. B. Competency 4. Sedimentary rocks are formed when debris settles and is compressed and fused together.

31. D. Competency 5. Sexual reproduction requires two parents. Asexual reproduction, of which binary fission is one type, requires only one parent.

32. D. Competency 1. The relationship between predator and prey populations is best demonstrated with a computer simulation. Plant growth, temperature change, and height vs. shoe size are data that can be collected in the classroom.

33. D. Competency 3. Light is considered an electromagnetic radiation that has a wavelength (electromagnetic waves); for example, radiant waves, X-rays, radio waves, and ultraviolet waves. A sound wave is produced by vibration and is not considered an electromagnetic wave.

34. C. Competency 2. The steps of the scientific method include 1) ask a question, 2) make observations, 3) hypothesize, 4) predict, 5) test, and 6) conclude. The fifth step is testing.

35. A. Competency 5. The four groups of fungi are club, imperfect, threadlike, and sac fungi. Perfect fungi is not a group of fungi.

36. C. Competency 2. Yes, you need it to be valid as well as reliable. You cannot have a valid instrument without reliability. You cannot assume that an instrument is reliable if it is considered valid.

37. B. Competency 3. A physical occurrence related to stationary and moving electrons and protons is called electricity. Vibrations of molecules can cause sound. The movement of electrons between energy levels can create light.

38. A. Competency 5. A heterotroph consumes its food from its environment. Heterozygotes have two different genes for one trait. An autotroph creates its own food. A parasite takes energy from its host.

39. A. Competency 4. Earthquakes are formed when plates intersect and slide against each other in opposite directions. Canyons, mountains, and volcanoes are geologic features on Earth.

40. D. Competency 2. In this experiment, because of the use of the link cable, the students are most likely using graphing calculators.

41. **C.** Competency 3. Electric current is the flow of electricity through a conductor. Electrical cables are usually made of conductors (for example, copper) and insulation (for example, rubber on the outside part). An electrical circuit is a path or combination of paths that allow the flow of the electrical current from one place to another. Most familiar conductors are metallic: copper (the most common material used for electrical wiring), silver (the best conductor, but expensive), and gold (used for high-quality surface-to-surface contacts). There are also many non-metallic conductors, including graphite, solutions of salts, and all plasmas.

42. **B.** Competency 1. This teacher is giving a summative assessment. The unit of instruction is completed and she is assessing what her students learned.

43. **B.** Competency 1. Out of the choices provided, students should use science-related Ask-the-Expert websites to answer the questions they cannot answer themselves. On these websites, students can ask questions on any topic and have them answered for free by science experts or scientists. The other choices are not as appropriate or effective for this purpose, as they are not consistently reliable sources of data (YouTube or social media) or are not appropriate for elementary school investigation (science databases).

44. **C.** Competency 3. The three types of rock are igneous, sedimentary, and metamorphic. Rocks are classified based on their origin.

45. **B.** Competency 5. Respiration is the process by which the cells convert sugar molecules into energy. Transpiration is the loss of water through the plant's leaves. Photosynthesis is the process by which a plant makes food. Fertilization is the process by which the plant reproduces.

46. **A.** Competency 1. Formative assessment provides day-to-day data for classroom use. Diagnostic assessment provides pre-assessment data to determine student misconceptions and knowledge prior to a unit. Summative assessment provides a summary of learning, and standardized assessment provides data relative to other students or a set standard.

47. **C.** Competency 5. All cells contain organelles, cell membranes, cytoplasm, and DNA. Plant cells contain chloroplasts, but animal cells do not.

48. **C.** Competency 4. Radiation, conduction, and convection are three forms of energy transfer through Earth's system. Filtration is the removal of particles.

49. **D.** Competency 2. Laboratory equipment should include science equipment like microscopes, graduated cylinders, thermometers, and hot plates, as well as safety equipment like safety goggles, aprons or gowns, eyewash stations, and ventilation.

50. **A.** Competency 1. Washing hands frequently is a good safety procedure for a laboratory. Wearing glasses is not necessarily a safety procedure; students should wear goggles. Chemicals should be used under a fume hood, and opening windows does not enhance safety in the laboratory.

51. **B.** Competency 1. Gravitational force decreases, not increases, with height above the Earth's surface. The remaining statements are correct.

52. **A.** Competency 1. This teacher is involving her students in experiential learning. Differentiated instruction, formative assessment, and diagnostic assessment are strategies within the classroom. Experiential learning can go outside the classroom, allowing students to put science learning into action.

53. **D.** Competency 2. In order to be a controlled experiment, there must be a control group and an experimental group. All scientific inquiry contains observations and hypotheses. Technology may or may not be present.

54. **D.** Competency 1. Differentiated instruction involves teachers assessing student needs and basing instruction on assessment results so that all students' needs are met. The other strategies listed are methods of instruction, but they don't ensure that all students' needs are met.

55. **A.** Competency 5. Natural selection is the process by which nature selects species best adapted to survive. Evolution is the process by which one species changes into a new species over time through adaptations. Fossils are used as evidence for evolution and natural selection.

Mathematics

1. A. Competency 1. The problem involves the measurement or subtractive division concept because it requires finding the number of equal groups (g) that can be subtracted or measured from the initial number of apples (n):

$$n \div g = ? \text{ or } n - n - n - \ldots - n = g$$

This is different from the sharing or partition division concept, which requires finding how many apples will go into each group.

2. C. Competency 2. In this pattern, the sum of the previous two terms makes the next term. The previous two terms are 18 and 29. Their sum is 47.

3. C. Competency 1. Diagnostic assessment is most likely represented by the task completed by Sara. It involves trying to find possible weaknesses and strengths Sara might have related to the two-digit addition computation. Standardized tests are least likely to provide information to help in identifying a student's specific problem areas. Their validity and reliability depends on three basic assumptions: Students have been equally exposed to the test content in an instructional program, students know the language of the test directions and the test responses, and students just like those taking the test have been included in the standardization samples to establish norms and make inferences. These assumptions are better for making programmatic decisions. Alternative assessment refers to other (non-traditional) options used to assess students' learning. When using alternative assessment, the teacher is not basing student progress only on the results of a single test or set of evidence. Some forms of alternative assessment include portfolios, journals, notebooks, projects, and presentations. Authentic assessment is a form of alternative assessment that incorporates real-life functions and applications.

4. D. Competency 5. The area of a rectangle is length times width. If the length is doubled and the width is tripled, the area is now $(2 \times \text{length})(3 \times \text{width}) = 6 \times \text{length} \times \text{width}$. Alternatively, the original area of the bedroom would be $12 \times 10 = 120 \text{ ft}^2$. If one dimension is doubled and the other is tripled, the dimensions become either 24 ft × 30 ft or 36 ft × 20 ft. Either way, the new area is 720 ft², which is six times the original area of 120 ft².

5. C. Competency 3. One way to solve this problem is by changing all the fractions to common denominators and arranging them from there. The denominators involved in this case are 4, 8, and 16. The least common multiple (LCM) or least common denominator (LCD) is 16 (indicated in bold type below). You can find this by finding the nonzero multiples of these denominators and selecting the LCM:

4: 4, 8, 12, **16**, 20, 24, 28, 32, 36, 40, 44, 48, . . .

8: 8, **16**, 24, 32, 40, 48, . . .

16: **16**, 32, 48, . . .

Notice that there are other common multiples, but you want to select the least common multiple (or denominator). Another way to find the least common multiple is by using prime factorization: $4 = 2^2$, $8 = 2^3$, and $16 = 2^4$. You select the common and noncommon multiples out of the prime factorizations. In this case, $2^4 = 16$ is the least common multiple (denominator).

You still need to use this denominator to change each fraction to its equivalent fraction (whenever needed) and then arrange them in order from least to greatest: $\frac{5}{8} = \frac{10}{16}$, $\frac{3}{8} = \frac{6}{16}$, $\frac{1}{4} = \frac{4}{16}$, and $\frac{3}{16}$. The correct order is the following: $\frac{3}{16}, \frac{4}{16}, \frac{6}{16}, \frac{10}{16}$ or $\frac{3}{16}, \frac{1}{4}, \frac{3}{8}, \frac{5}{8}$.

You can also change all the fractions to their equivalent decimal form and arrange them from least to greatest using this information: $\frac{5}{8} = 0.625$, $\frac{3}{8} = 0.375$, $\frac{1}{4} = 0.25$, and $\frac{3}{16} = 0.1875$. Order these decimal numbers from least to greatest and then convert back to the reduced fractions. The order of the fractions is still the same.

6. **A.** Competency 3. You have that $4.1 \cdot 10^{-2} = 4.1 \cdot \dfrac{1}{100} = 0.041$ (move the decimal point twice to the left as a result of multiplying by $\dfrac{1}{100}$ or 0.01).

7. **B.** Competency 1. Progress monitoring is designed to estimate rates of students' improvement over time, identify students who are not demonstrating adequate progress, compare the efficacy of different forms of instruction, and design more effective and individualized interventions to help students learn.

8. **C.** Competency 3. Set up a proportion: $\dfrac{8 \text{ feet}}{4 \text{ feet}} = \dfrac{x}{2.5 \text{ feet}}$. Since $\dfrac{8}{4}$ is 2, then $x = (2.5)(2) = 5$ feet.

9. **A.** Competency 2. The difference of a number and 4 is $N - 4$. Two times the number is $2N$. These expressions are equal, so the equation is $N - 4 = 2N$.

10. **A.** Competency 4. The mean of this data set is 27.625, which is approximately 28 (to the nearest ones). This is the sum of all the measures divided by the total number of measures: $442 \div 16$.

11. **B.** Competency 4. The mode of this data set is 30, which is the most frequent measure with three scores.

12. **B.** Competency 4. The median is the middle of the data set. Since we have 16 measures, the middle is the 8th measure. You need to count 8 from left to right and 8 from right to left. The middle measure is 29.

13. **A.** Competency 1. Multiple-choice assessment item is not an example of alternative assessment. It is an example of traditional assessment.

14. **B.** Competency 4. Running a mile generally take less than 1 hour. Seconds are too small a unit to use. Minutes is the most appropriate unit.

15. **A.** Competency 1. In this case, the best arithmetic sentence for the problem is "smaller number unknown."

Choice A: Smaller number unknown: Carl has 85 apples. Carl has 56 more apples than Frank. How many apples does Frank have? $56 + \_\_\_ = 85$, or $85 - 56 = \_\_\_$

Choice B: Larger number unknown: Frank has 29 apples, and Carl has 56 more apples than Frank. How many apples does Carl have? $29 + 56 = \_\_\_$, or $\_\_\_ - 56 = 29$

Choice C: Difference unknown: Carl has 85 apples and Frank has 29 apples. How many more apples does Carl have than Frank? $29 + \_\_\_ = 85$, or $85 - 29 = \_\_\_$

16. **B.** Competency 3. You need to examine each of the alternatives:

Choice A. -0.03: $(-0.03)^2 = 0.0009$ (negative $\cdot$ negative = positive), and $0.0009 > -0.03$; a positive number is greater than a negative number.

Choice B. 0.3: $(0.3)^2 = 0.09$, and $0.09 < 0.3$

Choice C. 1.3: $(1.3)^2 = 1.69$, and $1.69 > 1.3$

Choice D. 3: $3^2 = 9$, and $9 > 3$

17. **C.** Competency 4. You might notice that 12 hours is four times as long as a 3-hour trip. Then you have that $225 \cdot 4 = 900$, meaning the train will travel 900 miles in 12 hours.

Another way to solve this problem is by establishing a proportion: 225 miles to 3 hours = x to 12 hours. By cross-multiplying and solving for x, you have $225 \cdot 12 = 3x$; $2,700 \div 3 = x$; and $900 = x$.

You can also notice the ratio for miles per hour is 75 miles/1 hour. For 12 hours, you have $75 \cdot 12 = 900$.

18. **C.** Competency 2. Each term in the "y" column increases by 2. This is the slope. If you subtract 2 from 5, you will get the value of the expression when x is 0. This value is 3. When x is 0, y will be 3. This is the y-intercept. The expression is then $y = 2x + 3$.

19. **A.** Competency 5. Point S is 3 points to the right and 2 points up from the origin. This makes the coordinates (3, 2).

20. **C.** Competency 4. In a box-and-whisker plot, the median is the middle line of the box, which divides the data set in half. In this case, the median is 81.

The following figure illustrates the different parts of a box-and-whisker plot:

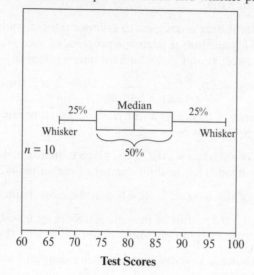

The lowest number is the left whisker. The highest number is the right whisker. The median is in the middle of the box. In this case, the median is 81, lowest score is 67, highest score is 98, lower quartile is 73, and upper quartile is 88. The lower quartile is the middle of the lower half of the numbers. The upper quartile is the middle of the upper half of the numbers. Joining the lower quartile, upper quartile, and median forms the box. Joining the box to the high number on the right and the low number on the left forms the whiskers.

21. **A.** Competency 3. There are 100 centimeters in a meter. $120 \text{ centimeters} \times \left(\dfrac{1 \text{ meter}}{100 \text{ centimeters}} \right) = 1.2 \text{ meters}.$

22. **D.** Competency 1. Mrs. Smith is most likely concerned with estimating the rate of student improvement over time. The graph illustrates the rate of a student's development of multi-digit addition and subtraction computation over time. Graphing student scores is a vital part of the progress-monitoring process. Graphing provides a straightforward way to review a student's progress, monitor the appropriateness of student goals, judge the adequacy of student progress, and compare and contrast successful and unsuccessful intervention aspects provided as part of a student's program.

23. **A.** Competency 1. The graph is an example of progress monitoring.

24. **C.** Competency 3. There are several ways to solve this problem. One way is by noticing that if Frank received a 10 percent discount off of the original price, then the new price is 90 percent of the original price (100% – 10% = 90%). This implies that 90 percent · original price = new discount price, or 90 percent · original price = $9,000. You can find the original price by dividing $9,000 by 90 percent or 0.90 or 0.9. This will give you the original price: $10,000.

25. **B.** Competency 5. The figure can be viewed two main ways—as a trapezoid or as a rectangle with a triangle on top. If you view it as a trapezoid, the bases are 12 and 5 and the height is 6. The area, then, is $A = \dfrac{1}{2}(12+5)(6) = \dfrac{1}{2}(17)(6) = (17)(3) = 51 \text{ ft}^2.$

26. **C.** Competency 1. Problem solving does not come after mastery of skills. You do not need to wait until skills or concepts are mastered or formalized in order to present problem-solving tasks. In many cases, problem solving and application of mathematics should be used as a context for presenting ideas, and skills and concepts are learned as means for solving a problem. According to the National Council of Teachers of Mathematics (NCTM), problem solving should be the key for teaching mathematics.

27. **B.** Competency 5. Area is a square unit. The only unit that is squared is choice B.

28. B. Competency 2. You need to use the correct order of operations for this expression:

$300 - 40 \div 5 \cdot (2^3 - 2) \cdot 3 + 8$ First, calculate exponentials: $2^3 = 8$.

$300 - 40 \div 5 \cdot (8 - 2) \cdot 3 + 8$ Second, solve parentheses: $(8 - 2) = (6)$.

$300 - 40 \div 5 \cdot (6) \cdot 3 + 8$ Third, calculate multiplication and division, from left to right:

                            $40 \div 5 \cdot (6) \cdot 3 = 144$.

$300 - 144 + 8 = 156 + 8 = 164$ Fourth, calculate addition and subtraction as they appear from left to right.

29. C. Competency 2. In this case, the expression $x^2 - x - 42$ is equivalent to $(x + 6)(x - 7)$ by factorization.

You should check your answer:

$$(x + 6)(x - 7) = (x \cdot x) + (6 \cdot x + -7 \cdot x) + (6 \cdot -7)$$
$$= x^2 + 6x + -7x - 42$$
$$= x^2 - x - 42$$

30. C. Competency 2. Samuel could fit 45 cans of food on half a shelf, which means that he can fit about 90 cans on a full shelf (45 cans of food × 2). He has seven shelves, which means he could fit up to 630 cans of food all together (7 shelves × 90 cans of food per shelf). Each box contains 30 cans. You need to divide total number of cans that can fit on the seven shelves by 30 to find the number of boxes needed: 630 ÷ 30 = 21 boxes. This means that he needs 21 boxes to fill the seven shelves.

31. D. Competency 2. If n stands for the unknown number, the equation five times a number plus nine is forty-five is represented by the algebraic equation $5n + 9 = 45$.

32. C. Competency 3. Choice C, $\dfrac{3}{2} = \dfrac{x}{22}$, correctly represents the relationship established in the word problem:

3 dollars to 2 dinars = x dollars to 22 dinars. Remember that a proportion is composed of two rates, but the rates must have the same relationship between the attributes involved in the problem. The other alternatives represent incorrect relationships: Choice A, $\dfrac{2}{3} = \dfrac{x}{22}$, is 2 dinars to 3 dollars and x dollars to 22 dinars;

Choice B is 3 dollars to 2 dinars and 22 dinars to x dollars, and Choice D is 2 dinars to 22 dinars and x dinars to 3 dollars.

There are other correct proportions that correctly represent the relationship in this problem:

$\dfrac{22}{2} = \dfrac{x}{3}$ or 22 dinars to 2 dinars = x dollars to 3 dollars

$\dfrac{2}{3} = \dfrac{22}{x}$ or 2 dinars to 3 dollars = 22 dinars to x dollars

33. C. Competency 1. The procedures used by Carlos to develop the survey were not systematic and valid, and the interpretation of the survey's results is not correct. Asking a few students in one school is not enough of a sample to make generalizations about a whole school county. This is not representative of the whole intended population.

34. D. Competency 2. Start by simplifying $-x + 3 + 8 + 6x - 12$, which is $-x + 6x + 3 + 8 - 12 = 5x - 1$. Evaluate each expression to find out which one is equivalent to $5x - 1$:

Choice A. $-9 + 3x + 8 - 6x - 8x = 3x - 6x - 8x - 9 + 8 = -11x - 1$ It is not equivalent to $5x - 1$.

Choice B. $-9 - 3x + 8 - 6x + 8x = -3x - 6x + 8x + 8 - 9 = -x - 1$ It is not equivalent to $5x - 1$.

Choice C. $9 + 3x + 8 - 6x + 8x = 3x - 6x + 8x + 8 + 9 = 5x + 17$ It is not equivalent to $5x - 1$.

Choice D. $-9 + 3x + 8 - 6x + 8x = 3x - 6x + 8x + 8 - 9 = 5x - 1$ It is equivalent to $5x - 1$.

35. B. Competency 2. By definition 1 is neither prime nor composite; 3 is prime because it is only divisible by 1 and itself; 6 is composite because it is divisible by 1, 2, 3, and itself; 17 is prime because it is only divisible by 1 and itself; and 89 is prime because it is only divisible by 1 and itself.

36. B. Competency 5. A parallelogram is a quadrilateral (four-sided figure) with two sets of parallel sides. It could have all equal sides and/or right (90 degree) angles, but it is not required in order to be a parallelogram.

37. A. Competency 2. We are trying to find the smallest four-digit number that is divisible by 2, 3, 4, 5, 6, 8, 9, and 10. A possible reasoning to find the solution involves divisibility rules. These are some rules you can use:

- A number is divisible by 2 if it is even (or if the ones digit is 0, 2, 4, 6, or 8).
- A number is divisible by 3 if the sum of its digits is divisible by 3 (e.g., 27 is divisible by 3 because 2 + 7 = 9, and 9 is divisible by 3).
- A number is divisible by 4 if the number formed by the last two digits is divisible by 4.
- A number is divisible by 5 if the ones digit is 0 or 5.
- A number is divisible by 6 if it is divisible by 2 and 3 (e.g., 36 is divisible by 2 and 3, so it is also divisible by 6).
- A number is divisible by 8 if the number formed by the last 3 digits is divisible by 8 (e.g., 1,240 is divisible by 8 because 240 is divisible by 8).
- A number is divisible by 9 if the sum of the digits is divisible by 9 (e.g., 927 is divisible by 9 because 9 + 2 + 7 = 18, and 18 is divisible by 9). Notice that if it is divisible by 9 it is also divisible by 3.
- A number is divisible by 10 if the ones digit is a 0.

Using the divisibility rules, we know the four-digit number must end in zero to be divisible by 10; eliminate choice D. Next, move to the divisibility rule for 9. Since the digits must add up to 9 in order to also be divisible by 9, the middle two digits must add up to 8 (0 + 8, 1 + 7, 2 + 6, 3 + 5, or 4 + 4); choices A, B, and C all qualify. Now test the divisibility rule for 8. The last three digits must form a number that is divisible by 8; eliminate choice C since 170 is not divisible by 8. The two remaining choices are divisible by 2, 3, 4, 5, and 6. Since 1,080 is the smaller of the two, it is the smallest four-digit integer divisible by 2, 3, 4, 5, 6, 8, 9, and 10.

38. C. Competency 4. The median is a measure of central tendency. You need to have the data in order from least to greatest or from greatest to least. The median is the number that falls in the middle of the ordered data set. In this case, you have 45 numbers, and the middle of the data set is the 23rd number. The median is 2 hours.

39. B. Competency 4. The range of the data set is the highest number minus the lowest value: 4 − 1 = 3.

40. A. Competency 2. Natalie is using the compensation strategy to solve this subtraction computation exercise.

There are several strategies to solve computation problems, such as the following:

- Algorithm (a step-by-step procedure to solve a particular type of problem)
- Compensation (a simplifying strategy where students add or subtract the same amount to or from both numbers to create an equivalent but easier problem; for example, 234 − 28 = 238 − 32 = 206)
- Compose (for example, to make 1 larger unit from 10 smaller units: 8 tens + 2 tens = 10 tens = 1 hundred)
- Decompose (for example, to break 1 larger unit into 10 smaller units: 1 hundred = 20 tens = 19 tens + 1 ten = 18 tens + 2 tens)
- New groups below (show newly composed units on the line below the appropriate place in the addition algorithm)
- Simplifying strategy (for example, to solve 299 + 6, think 299 + 1 + 5 = 300 + 5 = 305)

41. A. Competency 3. First, you need to calculate the total number of meters swam each day: 45 repetitions per day · 60 meters = 2,700 meters, which is the total number of meters swam each day.

Next, calculate the total number of meters swam in a 10-day period: 10 days' meters · 2,700 = 27,000 meters, which is the total number of meters swam over the 10-day period.

Finally, you need to convert from a small unit (meter) to a large unit (kilometer), so you need to divide. In this case, the conversion factor is 1 kilometer = 1,000 meters, then the number of kilometers in 10 days is equal to 27,000 meters divided by 1,000 (number of meters per kilometer). This gives you 27 kilometers (you can simply move the decimal point three places to the left since you are dividing by 1,000). Pedro swam 27 kilometers over a 10-day period.

42. B. Competency 2. The commutative property of multiplication states that the order of multiplication can be reversed, so $ab = ba$. This is demonstrated by choice B. Choice A is the associative property of multiplication, choice C is the identity property of multiplication, and choice D is the zero property of multiplication.

43. D. Competency 1. All of the skills and concepts included in this item are necessary for effective learning of addition computation involving two- and three-digit whole numbers. The addition concept with cubes provides the basic model for demonstrating and development of the proper computation algorithm (step-by-step systematic process to attain a goal, which is usually memorized and carried out using paper-and-pencil procedures). Memorizing addition facts helps with speed and accuracy. Place value up to hundreds with base-ten blocks is a very important concept. Place value is considered the key for understanding computation.

44. B. Competency 5. The figure shown is a kite: a four-sided figure with adjacent sides of equal length, but opposite sides of unequal length.

45. B. Competency 2. The parity of an integer could be even or odd. For example, we can say that 8 and 26 have the same parity because both are even, but 5 and 26 have opposite parity because 5 is odd and 26 is even. Given that n is an integer, we can represent an even integer as $2n$ (a multiple of 2), and an odd integer as $2n + 1$ (a multiple of 2 plus 1).

The following are the resulting parity for addition and subtraction of even and odd integers:

- even + even = even
- even + odd = odd
- odd + odd = even

- even − even = even
- even − odd = odd
- odd − odd = even

The following are the resulting parity for multiplication of even and odd integers:

- even × even = even
- even × odd = even
- odd × odd = odd

In this problem, we have the following for the first expression: $[(2m + 1) + 2n] \cdot [(2n + 1) + (2m + 1)]$:

$$[(2m+1)+2n]=2m+2n+1 \qquad \text{This will result in an odd number.}$$
$$[(2n+1)+(2m+1)]=2n+2m+1+1=2n+2m+2 \quad \text{This will result in an even number.}$$

This means that we have an odd number times an even number, which will result in an even number. We have the following for the second expression: $[2m + (2n + 1)] \cdot [2n + (2m − 1)]$:

$$[2m+(2n+1)]=2m+2n+1 \quad \text{This will result in an odd number.}$$
$$[2n+(2m-1)]=2n+2m-1 \quad \text{This will result in an odd number.}$$

This means that we have an odd number times an odd number, which will result in an odd number. Therefore, Felix was correct—the parity of the possible integer resulting from the two expressions was different.

46. D. Competency 1. This situation represents the transitivity property: If the length of an object is greater than the length of another object, and the length of this second object is greater than the length of a third object, then the length of the first object is greater than the length of the third object.

47. A. Competency 1. Based on the information provided in the table, Allan, Sabrina, and Daniel are responding to the instruction. Their scores show progress toward the goal of 12 correct problems at the conclusion of the 3-week review period, and they should remain in the whole class environment. On the other hand, Nicosha is not showing improvement. Her scores have remained stagnant over the 3-week review period, and she is in need of further intervention.

48. C. Competency 3. A negative exponent can be written as a positive exponent under a numerator of 1: $a^{-n} = \dfrac{1}{a^n}$. There is a negative exponent, $^{-3}$, in the expression 9^{-3}. You can rewrite the expression with an exponent of 3 instead, with 1 as the numerator: $\dfrac{1}{9^3}$.

49. B. Competency 2. Carlos should use a divisibility rule involving 9 as a divisor and check if 9 divides 1,234 evenly. The divisibility rule states that if the sum of the digits involved in a number is divisible by 9, then the number is also divisible by 9. In this case, we have $1 + 2 + 3 + 4 = 10$. This sum is not divisible by 9; therefore, 1,234 is not divisible by 9.

50. A. Competency 1. This is the appropriate answer because the student's invented algorithm is a correct computation algorithm, and students should be allowed to invent, explain, and share their own operational procedures. This practice has positive benefits on their motivation to solve problems, as they come up with their own strategy instead of just following a rote procedure. The student should be able to see why it works and find out if it always works.

Resources and References

Resources

Books

The Arizona Board of Regents (2007). Progressions Documents for the Common Core Math Standards. Retrieved from ime.math.arizona.edu/progressions.

Bass, J. E., Carin, A. A., and Contant, T. L. (2004). *Teaching Science as Inquiry*. Upper Saddle River, NJ: Prentice Hall.

Bear, D. R., Ivernizzi, M. A., Templeton, S. R., and Johnston, F. R. (2011). *Words Their Way,* 5th ed. Upper Saddle River, NJ: Prentice Hall.

Beck, I. L., McKeown, M. G., and Kucan, L. (2002). *Bringing Words to Life*. New York: Guilford Press.

Billstein, R., Libeskind, S., and Lott, J. W. (2012). *A Problem Solving Approach to Mathematics for Elementary School Teachers,* 11th ed. Boston, MA: Addison-Wesley.

Blair, T. R. (2013). *Teaching Children to Read in Diverse Communities*. Solon, OH: YOLO Learning Solutions. Also available at www.textbookmedia.com.

Buxton, C. A., and Provenzo, E. F. (2007). *Teaching Science in Elementary & Middle School: A Cognitive and Cultural Approach*. Thousand Oaks, CA: Sage Publications.

Bybee, R.W. (1997). *Achieving Scientific Literacy: From Purposes to Practices.* Portsmouth, NH: Heinemann.

Calkins, L., Ehrenworth, M., and Lehman, C. (2012). *Pathways to the Common Core: Accelerating Achievement.* Portsmouth, NH: Heinemann.

Carpenter, T. P., Fennema, E., Franke, M. L., Levi, L., and Empson, S. (1999). *Children's Mathematics: Cognitively Guided Instruction.* Portsmouth, NH: Heinemann.

Carpenter, T. P., and Moser, J. M. (1982). The development of addition and subtraction problem-solving skills. In T. P. Carpenter, J. M. Moser, and T. A. Romberg (eds.), *Addition and Subtraction: A Cognitive Perspective,* pp. 9–24. Hillsdale, NJ: Erlbaum.

Cathcart, W. G., Pothier, Y. M., Vance, J. H., and Bezuk, N. S. (2010). *Learning Mathematics in Elementary and Middle Schools: A Learner-Centered Approach,* 5th ed. Upper Saddle River, NJ: Prentice Hall.

Chapin, J. R. (2012). *Elementary Social Studies: A Practical Guide,* 8th ed. Boston, MA: Allyn and Bacon.

Cunningham, P. M. (2004). *Phonics They Use.* Boston, MA: Allyn and Bacon.

DeVries, B. A. (2011). *Literacy Assessment & Intervention for Classroom Teachers,* 3rd ed. Scottsdale, AZ: Holcomb Hathaway Publishers.

Dorn, L. J., and Soffos, C. (2001). *Scaffolding Young Writers: A Writers' Workshop Approach*. Portland, MI: Stenhouse Publishers.

Fountas, I., and Pinnell, G. S. (2006). *Teaching for Comprehending and Fluency*. Portsmouth, NH: Heinemann.

Fountas, I., and Pinnell, G. S. (2000). *Guiding Readers and Writers*. NH: Portsmouth, NH: Heinemann.

Freeman, D. E., and Freeman, Y. (2004). *Essential Linguistics*. Portsmouth, NH: Heinemann.

Fritzer, P. J., and Brewer, E. A. (2010). *Social Studies Content for Elementary and Middle School Teachers*. Boston, MA: Allyn and Bacon.

Galda, L., Sipe, L. R., Liang, L.A., and Cullinan, B. E. (2013). *Literature and the Child*, 8th ed. Independence, KY: Cengage Learning.

Greer, B. (1992). Multiplication and division as models of situations. In D. A. Grouws (ed.), *Handbook of Research on Mathematics Teaching and Learning*, pp. 276–299. New York: Macmillan.

Harvey, S. and Daniels, H. (2009). *Inquiry Circles in Action*. Portsmouth, NH: Heinemann.

Harvey, S. and Goudvis, A. (2007). *Strategies that Work*, 2nd ed. ME: Portland, MI: Stenhouse Publishers.

Heddens, J. W., Speer, W. R., and Brahier, D. J. (2009). *Today's Mathematics, Concepts and Classroom Methods, and Instructional Activities*, 12th ed. Hoboken, NJ: John Wiley and Sons, Inc.

Heilman, A. W. (2005). *Phonics in Proper Perspective*, 10th ed. Upper Saddle River, NJ: Prentice Hall.

Heilman, A. W., Blair, T. R., and Rupley, W. H. (2002). *Principles and Practices of Teaching Reading*, 10th ed. Upper Saddle River, NJ: Prentice Hall.

Leu, D. J., and Kinzer, C. K. (2011). *Phonics, Phonemic Awareness, and Word Analysis for Teachers: An Interactive Tutorial*, 9th ed. New York: Pearson.

Lindquist, T. (2002). *Seeing the Whole Through Social Studies*, 2nd ed. Portsmouth, NH: Heinemann.

Ma, L. (2010). *Knowing and Teaching Elementary Mathematics: Teachers' Understanding of Fundamental Mathematics in China and the United States*, 2nd ed. New York: Routledge, Taylor & Francis Group.

Martin, R., Sexton, C., and Franklin, T. (2008). *Teaching Science for All Children: An Inquiry Approach*. Boston, MA: Allyn and Bacon.

Mayesky, M. (2005). *Creative Activities for Young Children*. Independence, KY: Cengage Learning.

National Science Education Standards. (1996). Washington, DC: National Academy Press.

Norton, D. E. (2012). *Multicultural Children's Literature: Through the Eyes of Many Children*, 4th ed. New York: Pearson.

Opitz, M. F., and Rasinski, T. (1998). *Good-bye Round Robin*. Portsmouth, NH: Heinemann.

Payne, R. K. (2005). *A Framework for Understanding Poverty*, 4th ed. Highlands, TX: Aha! Process, Inc.

Prescott-Griffin, M. L., and Witherell, N. L. (2004). *Fluency in Focus*. Portsmouth, NJ: Heinemann.

Rasinski, T. V. (2003). *The Fluent Reader*. New York: Scholastic.

Rasinski, T. V., and Padak, N. D. (2012). *From Phonics to Fluency: Effective Teaching of Decoding and Reading Fluency in the Elementary School*. Upper Saddle River, NJ: Prentice Hall.

Reys, R. E., Lindquist, M., Lambdin, D. V., and Smith, N. L. (2012). *Helping Children Learn Mathematics*, 12th ed. Hoboken, NJ: John Wiley and Sons, Inc.

Taberski, S. (2000). *On Solid Ground: Strategies for Teaching Reading K-3*. Portsmouth, NJ: Heinemann.

Tipps, S., Johnson, A., and Kennedy, L. M. (2010). *Guiding Children's Learning of Mathematics*, 12th ed. Independence, KY: Cengage Learning.

Tompkins, G. E. (2013). *Literacy for the 21st Century: A Balanced Approach,* 6th ed. Upper Saddle River, NJ: Prentice Hall.

Tompkins, G. E. (2006). *Language Arts Essentials.* Upper Saddle River, NJ: Prentice Hall.

Vacca, J. L., Vacca, R. T., Gove, M. K., Burkey, L. C., Lenhart, L. C., and McKeon, C. A. (2011). *Reading and Learning to Read,* 8th ed. Boston, MA: Allyn and Bacon.

Van de Walle, J. A., Karp, K. S., and Bay-Williams, J. M. (2012). *Elementary and Middle School Mathematics: Teaching Developmentally,* 8th ed. Upper Saddle River, NJ: Prentice Hall.

Wasylyk, T. M. (2006). *Handwriting Manuscript Writing Book C,* 2nd ed. Honesdale, PA: Universal Publishing.

Weaver, C. (2002). *Word Perception and Reading Process.* In *Reading Process and Practice,* 3rd ed. Portsmouth, NJ: Heinemann.

Helpful Websites

achievethecore.org Achieve the Core (Common Core State Standards)
www.acei.org Association for Childhood Education International
www.corestandards.org Common Core State Standards
www.cpalms.org CPALMS, Florida's official source for standards information and course descriptions
www.definingthecore.com Defining the Core (Common Core State Standards)
www.fldoe.org Florida Department of Education
www.flreads.org Florida Reading Association
www.loc.gov Library of Congress
www.marzanoresearch.com Marzano Research Laboratory
www.ncte.org National Council of Teachers of English
www.nctm.org National Council of Teachers of Mathematics
www.nlvm.usu.edu National Library of Virtual Manipulatives
www.nsta.org National Science Teachers Association
www.parcconline.org Partnership for Assessment of Readiness for College and Careers
www.reading.org International Reading Association
www.readingandwritingproject.com Teachers College Reading and Writing Project, Columbia University
www.readworks.org Read Works
www.socialstudies.org National Council for the Social Studies

References

The Arizona Board of Regents (2007). Progressions Documents for the Common Core Math Standards. Retrieved from ime.math.arizona.edu/progressions.

CDC. (n.d.). Centers for Disease Control and Prevention. Retrieved May 26, 2009, from www.cdc.gov/nccdphp/dnpa/obesity/index.htm.

Chapin, J. R. (2012). *Elementary Social Studies: A Practical Guide,* 8th ed. Boston, MA: Allyn and Bacon.

CPALMS (2013). Retrieved from www.cpalms.org//page23.aspx.

DeVries, B. A. (2011). *Literacy Assessment & Intervention for the Elementary School Classroom,* 3rd ed. Scottsdale, AZ: Holcomb Hathaway Publishers.

Dorn, L. J., and Soffos, C. (2001). *Scaffolding Young Writers: A Writers' Workshop Approach.* Portland, MI: Stenhouse Publishers.

Fritzer, P. J., and Brewer, E. A. (2010). *Social Studies Content for Elementary and Middle School Teachers.* Boston, MA: Allyn and Bacon.

Galda, L., Sipe, L. R., Liang, L. A., and Cullinan, B. E. (2013). *Literature and the Child,* 8th ed. Independence, KY: Cengage Learning.

Geometry. (n.d.). In *Dictionary.com* online. Retrieved May 13, 2009, from dictionary.reference.com/browse/Geometry.

Harvey, S., and Daniels, H. (2009). *Inquiry Circles in Action.* Portsmouth, NH: Heinemann.

National Council of Teachers of Mathematics (1995). *Assessment Standards for School Mathematics.* Reston, VA: NCTM.

National Governors Association Center for Best Practices and Council of Chief State School Officers (2010). *Common Core State Standards for English Language Arts and Literacy in History/Social Studies, Science, and Technical Subjects.* Washington, DC: Authors. Retrieved from www.corestandards.org/assets/CCSSI_ELA%20Standards.pdf.

National Governors Association Center for Best Practices and Council of Chief State School Officers (2010). *Common Core State Standards for English Language Arts and Literacy in History/Social Studies, Science, and Technical Subjects: Appendix A: Research Supporting Key Elements of the Standards and Glossary of Key Terms.* Washington, DC: Authors. Retrieved from www.corestandards.org/assets/Appendix_A.pdf.

National Governors Association Center for Best Practices and Council of Chief State School Officers (2010). *Common Core State Standards for English Language Arts and Literacy in History/Social Studies, Science, and Technical Subjects: Appendix B: Text Exemplars and Sample Performance Tasks.* Washington, DC: Authors. Retrieved from www.corestandards.org/assets/Appendix_B.pdf.

National Governors Association Center for Best Practices and Council of Chief State School Officers (2010). *Common Core State Standards for Mathematics.* Washington, DC: Authors. Retrieved from www.corestandards.org/Math.

National Governors Association Center for Best Practices and Council of Chief State School Officers. (2010). *Common Core State Standards for Mathematics: Mathematics Glossary.* Washington, DC: Authors. Retrieved from www.corestandards.org/Math/Content/mathematics-glossary/glossary.

Norton, D. E. (2009). *Multicultural Children's Literature: Through the Eyes of Many Children.* Boston, MA: Allyn and Bacon.

Polya, G. (1957). *How to Solve It.* Garden City, NY: Doubleday.

Tomlinson, C. A. (1999). *The Differentiated Classroom: Responding to the Needs of All Learners.* Upper Saddle River, NJ: Prentice Hall.

Tompkins, G. E. (2006). *Language Arts Essentials.* Upper Saddle River, NJ: Prentice Hall.

Wasylyk, T. M. (2006). *Handwriting Manuscript Writing Book C,* 2nd ed. Honesdale, PA: Universal Publishing.

Webb, N. L., et al. (2005). Web Alignment Tool. Wisconsin Center of Educational Research. University of Wisconsin-Madison. Retrieved from www.wcer.wisc.edu/WAT/index.aspx (Depth of Knowledge Levels chart).

Glossary

General Terminology

abstract level: *See* symbolic level (Mathematics).

argumentation: The student's ability to listen or read the arguments of others, decide whether or not they make sense, and ask useful questions to clarify or improve the arguments (National Governors Association Center for Best Practices & Council of Chief State School Officers, 2014; see www.corestandards.org/Math/Practice for more information).

cognitive complexity of a task: A structure for identifying the alignment of the cognitive demands that standards and corresponding assessments place on learners. See www.cpalms.org//page23.aspx (CPALMS, 2013) and www.wcer.wisc.edu/WAT/index.aspx (Webb, N. L., et al., n.d.) for more information.

cognitive levels: There are three cognitive levels: concrete, pictorial (also known as *representational*), and symbolic (also known as *abstract*). *See individual definition of each level for more details.*

collaborative learning: *See* cooperative learning.

concrete level: Cognitive level that involves the use of manipulative materials or other real-life objects to represent ideas; for example, in mathematics, a student uses five cubes to represent the numerical value of number five; or in science, experiments with real-life leaves from a tree.

cooperative learning: A way of organizing the classroom to support and facilitate students' development. In this approach, the classroom is organized in small groups of two, three, four, or five students each. The students are also assigned roles or duties to perform during activities.

depth of knowledge rating: *See* cognitive complexity of a task.

diagnostic assessment: An assessment of a student's strengths and weaknesses and of conceptual understanding, misunderstanding, and misconceptions when learning a concept or skill. This process includes three parts: deciding what to diagnose, utilizing diagnostic techniques to gather required data, and analyzing the data.

differentiated instruction: A way to meet the needs of students with different learning styles, different abilities, and different methods of interpreting and expressing what they have learned. Tomlinson (1999) indicated that differentiation means giving students multiple options for taking in information. It requires that the teacher observes and understands the differences and similarities among students, and uses this information to plan effective instruction.

educational coaching: *See* scaffolding.

formative assessment: Provides information needed to adjust teaching and learning while they are still occurring. It also provides practice for the student and assessment of understanding during the learning process. This process guides teachers in making decisions about future instruction.

graphic organizers: Synthesizing and summarizing tools that aid comprehension.

heterogeneous: Differing in kind.

learner-centered instruction: A learning approach that is being advocated and supported by the constructivist learning approach to teaching. This is based on the premise that the student actively, not passively, constructs knowledge.

multicultural: Related to or representative of diverse cultures.

multimedia: Media that is composed of more than one form of communication.

peer tutoring: In peer tutoring, students work together on a subject that is giving them trouble. They help and support each other as they learn. One student can be the tutor and assist another student in learning a subject. The students benefit from the shared insights and individual attention they get in this environment.

pictorial representation: This cognitive level involves the use of pictures or drawings to represent ideas; for example, using the drawings of five cubes to represent the numerical value of number five.

progress monitoring: A systematic and scientifically based assessment practice that involves students' academic performance and evaluates the effectiveness of instruction. It can be implemented with individual students, small groups, or an entire class. The student's current levels of performance are determined on regular bases (weekly or monthly), goals are identified for learning that will take place over time, and progress toward meeting those goals is measured by comparing expected and actual rates of learning. Based on findings from the collected data and student's needs, instruction is adjusted if necessary.

representational: *See* pictorial representation.

scaffolding: An instructional technique in which the teacher provides guidance and support to a student as he or she learns, without limiting the student's investigation abilities. Scaffolding provides the basic support and accommodations to facilitate a student's social, academic, emotional, and mental development.

summative assessment: Assessment based on achievement; evaluates what a student has learned at a particular point in time; typically a formal test.

WebQuest: Web-based learning experience.

Wiki: Collaboratively authored searchable documents linked internally and externally, like mini web pages.

Language Arts and Reading

alliteration: Two or more words or syllables, near each other, with the same beginning consonant sound.

analogy: A detailed and sometimes lengthy comparison of two ideas or events.

antonym: A word that means the opposite of the given word.

argument: Writing that usually includes a claim or thesis statement backed up by evidence that supports the idea.

automaticity: The ability to recognize a large bank of words by sight; ability to decode unfamiliar words quickly; includes the ability to comprehend the words.

blending: Mixing sounds in words smoothly while reading.

buddy reading: Partner reading that includes students of different grade levels reading the same text together.

chunking: Breaking down words or content into digestible bites.

clerihew: A humorous verse consisting of two rhyming couplets, one of which includes a person's name.

climax: The point of highest dramatic interest or a turning point in the story.

comprehension: The ability to understand what one has read.

concepts of print: Print concepts that include book orientation knowledge, directional arrangement of print on the page, understanding of simple punctuation, and understanding that print contains the story.

consonant blend: Two consonants that when placed together keep their individual sounds.

creative writing: Uses the writer's imagination.

decode: To sound out words; segmenting and blending phonemes.

descriptive writing: Writing that describes a person, place, thing, or idea.

digraph: Two consonants that when placed together lose their individual sounds and combine to represent one sound.

diamante: A seven-line poem that forms a diamond shape.

emergent literacy: The reading and writing behaviors that come before conventional literacy; earliest phase of literacy development.

encode: The process of changing oral language into writing.

evaluation: A judgment of the significance, worth, or value of a student's work.

expository writing: Writing that gives information, explains why or how, clarifies a process, or defines a concept. Also known as *explanatory writing*.

fable: Folklore that includes a moral to the story or the teaching of a lesson.

figurative language: Language that utilizes figures of speech, especially metaphors.

fluency: In reading, the ability to read quickly, accurately, and with proper expression.

genre: A set of principles or conditions and styles within a particular media. In music, genres are categories for established forms of compositions, like classical music. In cinema, western, horror, and romantic comedy are recognized genres. In painting, genres include still life and pastoral landscape; a particular artwork may combine genres, but each genre has a recognizable group of principles. In literature, a category of composition with defining characteristics and overall form, such as traditional literature/folklore, poetry, nonfiction, fantasy, realistic fiction, science fiction, and historical fiction.

haiku: A poetic form that includes three lines with 5-7-5 syllables in each line, respectively.

high-frequency words: Words that are used often in print.

hyperbole: An obvious and intentional exaggeration used in writing.

idiom: An expression that is peculiar and cannot be understood by the literal meaning of its elements; *my heart's beating out of my chest.*

informative writing: Informs the reader in an attempt to create newfound knowledge.

interactive writing: Students and teachers collaborate on constructing a written work and write it together.

irony: Using words or situations that mean the opposite of what the author intends.

legend: A story passed down over time that is believed to be true but cannot be proven.

limerick: A five-line poetic form that is humorous and utilizes an aabba rhyme scheme.

literal language: Obvious or non-figurative language used in many forms of writing.

literary element: Essential parts of narratives; setting, character, plot, theme, and style.

literary language: A dialect of language used in literary writing.

literature circles: Small, temporary, and heterogeneous groups of students that gather together to discuss a common book that each of them is reading with the goal of enhancing comprehension.

metonym: A word or phrase used in metonymy, such as *the wagon* being used instead of *sobriety.*

metaphor: A figure of speech where something is described as though it were something else.

myth: A story often describing the adventures of superhuman beings in order to describe a people's customs or beliefs.

narrative writing: Writing that recounts a personal or fictional experience or tells a story based on a real or imagined event.

nonfiction: Informational text about real people, places, events, and things.

ode: A lyrical and expressive poem.

onomatopoeia: The use of words that imitate sounds, such as "buzz."

opinion/argument writing: Writing that attempts to convince the reader that a point of view is valid or that the reader should take a specific action.

partner reading: *See* buddy reading.

penmanship: The quality or style of one's handwriting.

personification: A type of figurative language in which an inanimate object or nonhuman subject is given human characteristics.

phonemic awareness: Ability to hear and manipulate the sounds of spoken language; includes noticing rhyme and recognizing the separate, small sounds in words (phonemes).

phonics: The understanding of the relationships between the written letters of the alphabet and the sounds of spoken language.

plagiarism: The use of another author's work as one's own without consent or the provision of credit.

prosody: Ability to read with appropriate rhythm, intonation, and expression.

pun: A humorous play on words.

rate: The speed of reading.

readers theater: Script reading that focuses the reader on the key elements of fluency, accuracy, rate, and prosody.

simile: Comparison of two unlike things or ideas using *like* or *as* (e.g., *good as gold*).

summarize: To restate in a concise form.

synonym: A word that means the same as or similar to a given word.

syntax: Rules for the formation of grammatical sentences in a language.

synthesis: The combination of ideas into a complex whole.

think aloud: An instructional method that involves the teacher modeling her thoughts *aloud* while reading text (fiction and informational) aloud to her students. Teachers often incorporate vocabulary into their think alouds to pre-teach new words and their meaning. Once modeled by the teacher, think alouds can be practiced by students with partners.

vocabulary: Includes all the words one can understand and use. The more words a student knows, the better the student will understand what is read. Knowing how words relate to each other is a building block that leads to comprehension.

voice-to-print matching: Voice-to-print matching is essentially reading aloud and matching the voice to the print. This technique is often used with beginning readers in the primary grades.

Social Science

absolute location: Formal geographic location; street names or coordinates are used to describe location.

Bill of Rights: Formal statement of the rights belonging to people of the United States; amendments 1 through 10 of the United States Constitution; added in 1791 to protect the rights of citizens.

capital resource: Any asset used in the production of goods and services.

cartographer: Mapmaker.

city council: Group of people elected to serve as part of the city government.

Congress: National, legislative body of the United States; consists of the Senate and the House of Representatives.

consumption: The using or intake of goods and services.

currency: Something that is used as a medium of exchange, such as money.

democracy: Government by the people.

depository: A firm entrusted with the safekeeping of valuable assets like funds (money).

depression: Long-lasting and painful recession or slowing of economic activity.

distribution: The dissemination or dispersing of goods and services.

economic reasoning: Problem solving and strategic thinking skills.

economics: The science that deals with the production, consumption, and distribution of goods and services.

electoral college: A body of electors chosen by the voters in each state to elect the President and Vice President of the United States.

geography: The study of Earth's surface, atmosphere, and people.

governor: Leader of the state government.

GPS: This acronym stands for Global Positioning System. These systems involve multiple satellites and computers working together to compute locations on Earth.

Gross Domestic Product (GDP): Formerly known as the "gross national product"; total monetary value of all goods and services produced in a nation during a specific time frame (for example, 1 year).

House of Representatives: Lower house of the United States Congress; sometimes known as the most representative body in the federal government.

human resource: A person used to accomplish a goal.

immigration: The act of moving to another country, usually for permanent residence.

inflation: A persistent, general increase in prices over a period of time.

judicial review: Includes the power of the courts to declare laws invalid if they violate the Constitution, supremacy of federal laws or treaties when they differ from state/local laws, and the role of the Supreme Court as the final authority on the meaning of the Constitution.

limited resource: An item that is in short supply.

mayor: Elected official; leader of the local government.

Middle East: The area from Libya to Afghanistan, usually including Egypt, Sudan, Jordan, Lebanon, Syria, Turkey, Iraq, Iran, Saudi Arabia, and several other countries of the Arabian peninsula.

monopoly: One company or institution that has exclusive control of a particular good or service in a market.

natural resource: An available supply of something occurring in nature (e.g., water, oil, and trees).

preamble: The introductory statement of the United States Constitution.

primary source: An original record created at the time a historical event occurred, or well after an event in the form of a memoir and oral history.

production: The creation of goods and services.

recession: A slowing of economic activity.

relative location: Informal geographic location; local landmarks are used to identify location (e.g., near schools and shopping malls).

scarcity: Insufficient supply or shortage of goods and services.

Senate: Upper house of the United States Congress.

stagflation: High rate of inflation accompanied by rising unemployment.

timeline: A linear representation of historical events shown in the order in which they occurred.

Trade: The exchange of goods and services.

United States Constitution: Fundamental law of the United States; effective date March 4, 1789, when the U.S. Senate first convened.

Science

acoustic energy: *See* sound energy.

adaptation: A trait that is advantageous to a species.

algae: One category of plantlike protists.

allele: A form that a gene can take; received from parents in sexual reproduction.

amino acids: Building blocks of proteins.

amniotic eggs: Eggs of reptiles; hold a fluid that protects the embryo.

amphibian: A type of vertebrate that lives part of life in water and part of life on land.

angiosperms: Another name for flowering seed plants.

animals: Eukaryotic, multicellular heterotrophs.

anther: In plants, the part of the stamen that makes pollen.

applied force: A force that is applied to an object by a person or another a object.

aquifer: A formation that transmits water under the surface of the Earth.

Archaea: One of three domains of taxonomy; single-celled organisms.

archaeabacteria: Single-celled microorganisms.

arthropods: The largest group of animals; invertebrates that have a segmented body with specialized parts, jointed limbs, an exoskeleton, and a well-developed nervous system; examples include centipedes, lobsters, spiders, and insects.

asexual reproduction: Reproduction that depends on one parent; a duplicate copy of the parent is made.

asteroids: Made up of rock, metal, or ice and are like planets in that they orbit the Sun. A belt of asteroids exists between Mars and Jupiter and separates the planets.

at-a-distance forces: Forces that result when the interacting objects are not in physical contact, but still exert a push or pull despite the physical separation; for example, gravitational, electrical, and magnetic forces.

atom: The smallest particle of the element, which retains the properties of that element.

atmosphere: The layers of gas that surround the Earth; the air.

ATP: Made by mitochondrion; form of energy that cells can use.

autotroph: An organism that creates its own food.

bacilli: Rod-shaped bacteria.

Bacteria: One of three domains of taxonomy; single-celled organisms.

balanced forces: Forces that do not cause a change in motion; they are in opposite directions and equal in size.

biosphere: The portion of the Earth's crust, water, and air that supports life; the ecosystem of the Earth.

birds: Vertebrates that are generally fliers; have feathers and wings.

birds of prey: Birds that hunt and eat other animals; have sharp claws and a sharp beak; examples include eagles, hawks, and owls.

bladder: Organ that holds urine until it can be removed from the body.

boiling: Having reached the temperature in which a liquid bubbles.

bones: Part of the skeletal system.

burning: The act of using heat to impact an object.

canyon: Geologic formation that occurs when erosion changes the face of the Earth's surface.

cardiac muscle: The heart.

cardiovascular (circulatory) system: Transports materials in the blood throughout the body.

carnivore: Meat eater.

cartilage: Part of the skeletal system; between bones.

cell: The smallest unit of a living thing; all cells contain cell membranes, cytoplasm, organelles, and DNA.

cell membrane: Surrounds the cell and provides a protective layer that covers the surface of the cell and acts as a barrier to its environment.

cell theory: The theory that cells are the basic unit of structure in all living organisms.

cell walls: Rigid structures that give support to cells.

cellular respiration: The process by which plants convert the energy that is stored in glucose molecules into energy that cells can use; occurs in the mitochondrion.

cellulose: A complex sugar that animals cannot digest without help.

central nervous system: Brain and spinal cord.

centripetal force: Involved when an object moves in a circular path and force is directed toward the center of the circle in order to keep the motion going; for example, gravitational force keeping a satellite circling Earth.

chemical change: Produces one or more substances (for example, burning); also called a chemical reaction.

chemical energy: The energy created by a chemical reaction.

chemical reaction: *See* chemical change.

chemical rocks: Sedimentary rocks that form when standing water evaporates and leaves dissolved minerals behind.

chemical weathering: A component of the weathering process in which rocks are decomposed chemically; changes the chemical composition of the rock.

chlorophyll: Green pigment found inside the inner membrane of a chloroplast.

chloroplasts: Organelles present in plant and algae cells that allow the plant to harness energy from the Sun.

cilia: Hairlike structures that beat back and forth, causing the ciliate to move.

ciliates: Complex protists that have hundreds of tiny, hairlike structures called cilia that beat back and forth, causing the ciliate to move.

cirrus clouds: Clouds that are wispy and feathery.

classifying: Categorizing based on observable traits.

clastic rocks: Basic sedimentary rocks that are accumulations of broken pieces of rocks.

climate: The weather conditions of a region, including temperature, air pressure, humidity, precipitation, and winds, throughout a year or series of years.

cnidarians: Invertebrates that have stinging cells; more complex than sponges; examples include jellyfish, sea anemone, and coral.

cocci: Spherical-shaped bacteria.

collection: Part of the water cycle that occurs when the water returns to the surface of the Earth and falls back into water sources like oceans, lakes, or rivers.

comets: Bodies in space made of rocks, frozen water, frozen gases, and dust. Comets orbit the Sun and contain a tail that follows the comet. The most famous comet is Halley's Comet.

compound: Matter that combines atoms chemically in definite weight proportions. Water is an example of a compound of oxygen and hydrogen.

condensation: Part of the water cycle in which water vapor in the air cools and changes back into liquid, forming clouds.

conduction: When heat transfers through molecular movement. For example, when you pick up a metal bar, it is cold. As you hold it, the warmth of your body conducts heat to the metal bar.

conductor: Allows electricity to flow freely through it; for example, copper is a good conductor of electricity.

contact force: The result of the physical interaction between objects; for example, frictional forces, tensional forces, normal forces, air resistance forces, and applied forces.

continental crust: The part of the crust that is not under the oceans; the part of the crust that forms the continents.

control group: The group in an experiment on which no treatment is conducted; the comparison group in an experiment.

controlled experiment: Experiment in which there is a treatment group and a control group.

convection: Occurs through the movement of masses, either air or water. Convection occurs when hot air rises, cools, and then falls.

convection current: The transfer of heat by movement of heated particles into an area of cooler fluid.

core: Innermost layer of the Earth; made up of two sections: the inner core and the outer core.

crust: The top layer of the Earth.

cryosphere: The portion of the Earth's surface that is frozen water or ground; includes polar ice caps and glaciers.

cumulus clouds: Clouds that are puffy and look like cotton balls; produce heavy thunderstorms.

cuticle: A waxy layer that coats the surfaces of plants that are exposed to air.

cytoplasm: Fluid found inside a cell.

cytoskeleton: Web of proteins inside the cytoplasm.

Darwin, Charles: Father of evolution; developed the theory of natural selection.

deciduous trees: Trees that lose most or all of their leaves, typically in the fall.

density: Mass per unit of volume, or the ratio of total mass (m) to total volume (V): $\rho = \dfrac{m}{V}$ (for example, kilogram per cubic meter or kg/m^3). In other words, it defines how closely the molecules are packed together.

deposition: Material that is collected, typically in rock formation in waterways.

dermis: Bottom layer of the skin.

diffraction: Occurs when a ray of light bends around the edges of an object.

diffusion: Method by which nonvascular plants move materials from one part of the plant to another.

digestive system: Digests food into small particles so that nutrients can be absorbed.

DNA: Genetic material that contains information needed to make new cells; passed from parent cells to new cells; determines the function of a cell.

doldrums: Low-pressure regions of little steady air movement.

dominant traits: Traits that appear more frequently in a population.

dynamics: The branch of mechanics that studies the relationship between motion and the forces affecting motion of bodies.

Earth: Third planet from the Sun; the planet on which we live.

earthquake: Shaking of the Earth's crust; occurs when two continental plates slide against each other in opposite directions; the earthquake occurs when there is a large slippage that shakes the continental plates at their border or fault line.

echinoderms: Spiny-skinned invertebrates; examples include sea stars, sea urchins, and sand dollars.

ecosystem: The system that is formed by the interaction of organisms and their environment.

ectotherms: Cold-blooded animals; animals that are unable to regulate their own body temperature.

electric current: The flow of electricity through a conductor.

electrical circuit: A path or combination of paths that allow the flow of electrical current from one place to another; an electrical circuit must have a continuous flow of electricity going through a complete loop (circuit), returning to the original position and cycling through again.

electrical energy: Energy stored in electric fields that results from the presence of electric charges; produced by moving electrons; made available by the flow of electrical charge through a conductor.

electricity: A physical occurrence related to stationary and moving electrons and protons.

electrons: Part of an atom located in the outer part of the atom.

electrostatic force: The force between electrically charged particles; also called Coulomb's Law.

element: Consists of only one type of atom; for example, iron or carbon.

embryos: Fertilized eggs.

endocrine system: Controls glands that send out hormones.

endoplasmic reticulum: A system of folded membranes in which proteins, lipids, and other materials are made.

endotherms: Warm-blooded animals; animals that are able to regulate their own body temperature.

energy: The ability to move other matter or provoke a chemical change in other matter; for example, heat energy, mechanical energy, electrical energy, wave energy, chemical energy, and nuclear energy; also the ability to do work.

energy transformation: The process of converting one form of energy to another.

epicenter: The point on a fault line in which slippage of tectonic plates occurs, causing an earthquake.

epidermis: Top layer of the skin.

erosion: The movement of earth due to water movement.

eubacteria: Large groups of single-celled organisms; bacteria.

Eukarya: One of three domains of taxonomy.

eukaryotes: Organisms whose cells contain complex structures, including membrane-bound organelles and a nucleus containing DNA; most are multicellular.

eukaryotic cells: Cells in which a nucleus exists.

evaporation: Part of the water cycle in which the Sun heats up water on the surface of the Earth, turning it into steam that goes into the air.

evergreen trees: Trees that lose some leaves year-round but keep most of them.

evolution: Change over time; the process of species adapting and creating new species.

experiment: A scientific study in which a treatment group is compared to a control group to determine the impact of specific intervention.

experimental group: The group in an experiment that undergoes the experimental treatment.

exoskeleton: A hard outer skeleton.

fertilization: When a sperm fuses with an egg.

filament: In plants, the part of the stamen that holds up the anther.

fins: Fan-shaped structures that help fish steer, stop, and balance in the water.

fish: One type of vertebrate; live in water; contain gills that allow fish to breathe under water.

flagella: Whiplike strands extending out from a cell that move back and forth to move the cell.

flatworms: Invertebrates; simplest kind of worms; have bilateral symmetry.

flightless birds: Birds that cannot fly; examples include penguins, kiwi, and ostriches.

flowering seed plant: Type of vascular plant; also called angiosperm.

focus: The point where pressure from sliding plates is released, causing an earthquake to occur.

food web: The connection of organisms interrelated by food chains; predator-prey and consumer-producer relationships and interactions.

force: A pull or a push; necessary to make a machine work.

fossil record: The timeline of life gathered from examining fossils.

fossils: Imprints of once-living organisms found in rock layers.

freezing: Having reached the temperature at which a substance changes from liquid to solid.

friction: Happens when surfaces that touch each other have a certain resistance to motion.

fungi: Eukaryotic heterotrophs that have rigid cell walls and no chlorophyll.

gametes: Egg and sperm.

gametophyte stage: Stage of plant's life cycle in which male and female parts make gametes.

gas: One of the three main states of matter that is distinguished from liquid and solid by its relatively low density and viscosity, relatively great expansion and contraction with changes in pressure and temperature, ability to diffuse easily, and spontaneous tendency to distribute uniformly throughout space. It has no definite volume or shape; for example, water vapor or steam.

genes: Factors that determine genetic traits.

geological formations: Features of the Earth that are formed by geological processes.

geology: The study of the Earth; science that deals with the physical history of the Earth.

geosphere: The solid portion of the Earth's surface; the crust.

germination: When the seed is dropped or planted in a suitable environment and the seed sprouts and forms a new plant.

gills: Organs that remove oxygen from the water, allowing fish to breathe underwater.

Golgi complex: Organelle that packages and distributes proteins.

gravitational force: The force on an object created by the pull of gravity.

gravity: An attractive force that draws objects toward the center of the Earth.

gymnosperms: Another name for nonflowering seed plants.

hardness: A measure of how resistant a solid object is to change when force is applied.

heat: A measurement of the total energy in a substance. That total energy is made up of the kinetic and the potential energies of the molecules of the substance.

heat transfer: The process of transferring heat from one object to another; uses radiation, conduction, convection, or a combination of these.

herbivore: Plant eater.

heredity: Passing of traits from parents to their offspring.

heterogeneous: Differing in kind.

heterogeneous mixture: A mixture of distinct substances with different properties; does not have uniform composition.

heterotrophs: Organisms that consume food from their environment.

homogeneous mixture: A mixture that is uniform throughout. *See also* solution.

hydrosphere: The portion of the Earth's surface that is covered by water; the oceans and water in the atmosphere.

hyphae: Chains of cells that make up multicellular fungi.

hypothesis: A tentative and testable insight into the natural world that is not yet verified; if it were found to be true, it would explain certain aspects of the natural world and might become a scientific theory.

igneous rocks: Rocks that are formed by the cooling of magma.

inner core: The innermost part of the core; solid and thick.

insulator: A material that does not allow the electrons to flow freely; for example, glass, rubber, and air.

integumentary system: Skin, hair, and nails.

invertebrates: Animals that do not have a backbone.

Jupiter: Fifth planet from the Sun; known for its large red spot; largest planet.

kidneys: Pair of organs that filter waste from the blood and regulate the body's water balance.

kinetic energy: Energy of motion of a mechanical system. For example, a moving car has mechanical energy because of its motion (kinetic energy), and a moving baseball has mechanical energy because of both its high speed (kinetic energy) and its vertical position above the ground (gravitational potential energy).

lava: Magma that has reached Earth's surface.

leaching: The process by which materials in the soil are transferred into the water.

lens: A piece of transparent curved material; light bends when it passes through a lens.

ligaments: Part of the skeletal system; connect bones to other bones.

light: A type of energy with a comparatively low level of physical weight or density; considered an electromagnetic radiation that has a wavelength (electromagnetic waves). Also known as *radiant energy.*

Linnaean system: A classification system for living organisms developed by Carl Linnaeas.

lipids: Along with proteins, they control the movement of larger materials into and out of the cell.

liquid: One of the three main states of matter that is distinguished from gas and solid by its readiness to flow and little or no tendency to disperse; has a definite volume, but no shape; for example, water.

living things: Organisms that are capable of self-organizing and self-producing; biology is the study of living things.

lungs: Pair of organs that removes oxygen from the air and delivers it to the blood.

lymph: Fluid that moves through the lymphatic system.

lymph nodes: Small bean-shaped masses of tissue that remove pathogens from the lymph.

lymphatic system: Removes excess fluid from around cells; eliminates bacteria and waste.

lysosomes: Vesicles responsible for digestion inside a cell.

magma: Hot material that forms below Earth's surface.

magma chamber: The accumulation of magma in one location under Earth's surface.

magnetic energy: The force (push or pull) of a magnet; stored in magnetic fields that are produced by moving electric charges.

mammal: Type of vertebrate; all mammals have hair and mammary glands.

mammary glands: Glands in the body that make milk.

manipulating variables: Causing a change in one variable to determine effect.

mantle: The layer of Earth that is above the core; makes up the majority of Earth's volume.

Mars: Fourth planet from the Sun; the red planet; second smallest planet.

marsupials: Mammals that carry their young in a pouch.

mass: A measure of the amount of matter in a substance or object; different than weight; also a measure of an object's resistance to acceleration.

matter: Makes up everything in our world—rocks, people, chairs, buildings, animals, and chemical substances, among others. It takes up space and has mass.

measurement: The act of measuring; using a standard or nonstandard unit to describe an aspect of a shape.

mechanical energy: Energy that is associated with motion and position of an object; the sum of potential energy and kinetic energy.

mechanical force: The application of force to bend, dent, scratch, compress, or break something; for example, machines in general multiply force or change the direction of force.

meiosis: In sexual reproduction, the process that creates gametes; cells are produced that contain half the genetic material of the parent sex cells.

Mendel, Gregor: Discovered the principles of heredity.

Mercury: The closest planet to the Sun; smallest planet.

metamorphic rocks: Rocks that form when a pre-existing rock is moved into an environment in which the minerals that make up the rock become unstable, often burial.

metamorphosis: A transformation in which an animal changes form; examples include a tadpole becoming a frog or toad or a caterpillar becoming a butterfly.

meteoroids: Objects that rotate around the Sun but are too small to be called asteroids or comets; made from bits and pieces of the Solar System; called meteors when they fall through the Earth's atmosphere.

Milky Way: Our Solar System.

minerals: A group of substances made up of inorganic materials; examples include quartz and feldspar.

mitochondrion: Power source of the cell; the organelle in which sugar is broken down to produce energy.

mitosis: A sexual reproduction in which structures of the cell are copied identically.

mixture: Refers to any combination of two or more substances; the substances keep their own chemical properties. *See* homogeneous mixture and heterogeneous mixture.

molecules: The smallest particle of substance that may exist independently and maintain all the properties of the substance. Molecules of most elements are made of one atom, but the molecules of oxygen, hydrogen, nitrogen, and chlorine are made of two atoms each.

mollusks: Invertebrates that usually, but not always, have a shell; examples include snails, squids, and octopi.

molten: Melted.

monotremes: Mammals that lay eggs.

moons: Satellites of planets. They generally orbit around a planet.

mountain: Geologic formation that occurs when plates collide and push each other upward.

multiple trial: An experiment that is conducted over many groups or sites.

muscular system: System of muscles in the body.

mycelium: Twisted mass of hyphae.

natural selection: Theory that explains how evolution occurs over time to create new species from existing species.

Neptune: Eighth planet from the Sun; fourth largest planet.

nervous system: Senses the environment and controls the body; receives and sends electrical signals throughout the body.

neurons: Used to send and receive electrical signals throughout the body.

neutrons: Part of an atom located in the nucleus (or solid center) of an atom, together with protons.

nimbus clouds: Clouds that produce precipitation. They appear darker than other clouds and are formed at lower altitudes.

nonflowering seed plant: One type of vascular plant; also called a gymnosperm.

nonliving things: Organisms that are not capable of self-organizing and self-producing.

nonrenewable resources: Materials that, when consumed, are no longer available; resources that are not reproduced at an efficient rate to be sustainable. Fossil fuels are nonrenewable resources.

nonvascular plants: Plants that do not have specialized tissues to move water and nutrients through the plant.

Northern hemisphere: The half of Earth that is north of the equator.

nuclear energy: The energy present in the nucleus of atoms; released by fission, fusion, or radioactive decay.

nucleolus: A dark area in which the cell begins to make ribosomes.

nucleus: Organelle that contains DNA.

oceanic crust: The part of the crust that is under the oceans.

omnivore: Meat or plant eater. Also may eat fungi and bacteria.

optics: A branch of physics that studies the physical properties of light; provides information about the behavior and properties of light and its interaction with matter.

organ: Two or more tissues working together to carry out a specific function.

organ system: Organs working together.

organelles: "Little organs" that carry out the life processes within the cell.

organic rocks: Sedimentary rocks that are formed by organic material, such as calcium from shells, bones, and teeth.

outer core: The outermost part of the core; molten material.

ovary: In plants, part of the pistil.

ovule: Inside the ovary; contains an egg.

Pangea: Supercontinent believed to have once existed and to have included all the continental crust in one region.

parallel circuits: Electrical circuits that use several electrical paths.

parasite: Organisms that invade other organisms (hosts) to obtain the nutrients they need.

perching birds: Birds that have adaptations for landing on branches; examples include songbirds like robins and sparrows.

percolation: The downward movement of water through the soil and rock in the ground.

peripheral nervous system: Nerves of the body that connect all parts of the body to the central nervous system.

phase change: Matter can undergo a phase change through heating and cooling, shifting from one form to another; for example, melting (changing from a solid to a liquid); freezing (changing from a liquid to a solid); evaporation (changing from a liquid to a gas); boiling (past the boiling point, which is the temperature at which a liquid boils at a fixed pressure; for example, boiling water to form steam); and condensation (changing from a gas to a liquid).

phases of the Moon: The portion of the Moon visible by an observer, typically from Earth, at different points in time; includes Full Moon, waxing Moon, waning Moon, First Quarter Moon, Third Quarter Moon, crescent Moon, gibbous Moon, and New Moon.

phloem: Type of vascular tissue.

phospholipids: A group of fatty compounds found in living cells.

photosynthesis: Process that allows plants and algae to use sunlight, carbon dioxide, and water to make sugar and oxygen.

physical change: A change that keeps the characteristics of the original substance. A physical change does not produce a new substance (for example, freezing and melting water).

physical weathering: Weathering processes that cause physical changes to a rock without altering chemical composition.

phytoplankton: Free-floating single-celled protists; microscopic and usually float near the water's surface.

pistil: Female part of the plant.

placental mammals: Mammals whose embryos develop inside the mother's body and are attached to the mother through a placenta.

planets: Heavenly bodies that rotate around the Sun. The Milky Way is made up of eight planets: Mercury, Venus, Earth, Mars, Jupiter, Saturn, Uranus, and Neptune.

plantlets: A type of asexual reproduction in plants in which tiny plants grow along the edges of a plant's leaves.

plants: Eukaryotic, multicellular autotrophs.

plate tectonics: The movement of the plates of the Earth's crust.

Pluto: Celestial body, which was once considered a planet; now is considered a dwarf planet.

pollution: The incorporation of harmful substances into the environment.

potential energy: Stored energy of position; for example, a moving baseball has mechanical energy because of both its high speed (kinetic energy) and its vertical position above the ground (gravitational potential energy).

precipitation: Part of the water cycle that occurs when the amount of water that has condensed in the air is too much for the air to hold. The clouds that hold the water become heavy and the water falls back to the Earth's surface in the form of rain, hail, sleet, or snow.

prevailing westerlies: Winds that come out of the west and move toward the poles, appearing to curve to the east.

prism: A transparent object with flat polished surfaces that refract or diffuse (break apart) light.

prokaryotes: Single-celled organisms; divided between two domains—Archae and Bacteria.

prokaryotic cells: Cells in which a nucleus does not exist.

proteins: With lipids, control the movement of larger materials into and out of the cell.

protists: One of the kingdoms; organisms that are similar to plants, fungi, and animals, but do not fit neatly into those kingdoms.

protons: Part of an atom located in the nucleus (or solid center) of an atom, together with neutrons.

protozoans: Animal-like protists.

pseudopodia: A component of cell known as false feet. Used for movement and capturing prey.

pull: A force that moves an object toward another object.

push: A force that moves an object away from another object.

radiant energy: *See* light.

radiation: When heat is transferred through electromagnetic waves. Examples of radiation are the heating of the skin by the Sun and the heat of a bonfire. The heat is transferred through the movement of electromagnetic waves.

recessive traits: Traits that appear less frequently in a population.

refraction: Occurs when light passes through a transparent material such as water at a slant angle; the ray of light bends or changes speed.

reliability: The consistency of a set of measurements or a measuring instrument.

reliance on evidence: Making a scientific decision based upon evidence or data.

renewable resources: Resources that replenish themselves over time quickly enough to be sustainable; examples include wood and solar energy.

reproductive system: Provides the components for making new life.

reptiles: Vertebrates that live primarily on land, have lungs, and thick, dry skin.

reservoir: A lake-like area where water is kept until needed.

respiration: The process by which oxygen is provided to tissues and cells, and carbon dioxide and water are removed.

respiratory system: Transports oxygen to the blood and removes carbon dioxide from the blood.

ribosomes: The smallest of all organelles; protein builders.

Richter scale: A scale that indicates the intensity of an earthquake's magnitude.

rough ER: Endoplasmic reticulum that is covered in ribosomes and is usually found near the nucleus.

roundworms: Invertebrate worms with bodies that are long, slim, and round; have bilateral symmetry and a simple nervous system.

runners: Above-ground stems that form new plants.

runoff: Occurs when rainwater falls to land and moves across the land to rivers, streams, or other water sites.

rusting: The physical process that occurs when metal such as iron is exposed to air and moisture.

Saturn: Sixth planet from the Sun; known for its rings; second largest planet.

scientific inquiry: Process of developing and answering scientific questions.

scientific law: A truthful explanation of different events that happen with uniformity under certain conditions; describes how things behave, but does not necessarily explain why the behavior occurs.

scientific method: The systematic way in which scientists answer questions and solve problems; includes the following steps, in order: 1) ask a question, 2) make observations, 3) hypothesize, 4) predict, 5) test, and 6) conclude.

scientific theory: A well-validated and well-supported explanation of some aspect of the natural world.

seasons: One of four periods of the year that are defined by specific characteristics of the climate; spring, summer, autumn (fall), and winter; produced by Earth's rotation around the Sun, along with the tilt of the Earth on its axis.

sedimentary rocks: Rocks that are created when layers of debris, or sediment, are compacted and fuse together.

seedless plant: Type of vascular plant; examples include ferns and horsetails.

segmented worms: Invertebrates; have bilateral symmetry but are more complex than flatworms and roundworms; have a closed circulatory system and a complex nervous system.

seismometer: Instrument that measures the magnitude or strength of an earthquake.

senses: Structures that allow the brain to collect information; include sight, sound, taste, touch, and smell.

series circuits: Electrical circuits that use only one path.

sexual reproduction: Reproduction that requires two parents; offspring contain a combination of DNA from both parents.

sinkhole: Occurs when cavities form under the Earth's surface. These cavities are formed when water filling the space is removed through evaporation or absorption. The weight of the soil or other material above the cavity collapses it, forming a sinkhole.

skeletal muscle: Attaches to bones with tendons for body movement.

skeletal system: Provides the frame for the body and protects body parts.

smooth ER: Endoplasmic reticulum that does not contain ribosomes; makes lipids and breaks down toxic material that could damage the cell.

smooth muscle: Moves food through digestive system.

soil: The ground or the earth; formed by the physical weathering of rocks and minerals.

solar energy: The energy from the Sun that can be converted into thermal electrical energy.

solid: One of the three main states of matter that is different from gas and liquid in that it has definite volume and shape; for example, ice.

solution: Mixture that is homogeneous—uniform and consistent throughout. For example, seawater is a solution containing water and salt, which could be separated through the evaporation process.

sound energy: Energy in the form of mechanical waves transmitted through materials, such as plastic or air; the waves can be audible or inaudible; also known as *acoustic energy.*

Southern hemisphere: The half of Earth that is south of the equator.

spirilla: Spiral-shaped bacteria.

sponges: The simplest invertebrates; asymmetrical and have no tissues; marine animals.

sporangia: Spore cases that are used when threadlike fungi reproduce asexually.

spores: A means of asexual reproduction in which a fungi breaks apart, forming new fungi.

sporophyte stage: Stage of plant's life cycle in which plants make spores, which then can grow in a suitable environment.

stamen: Male part of the plant.

star: Made up entirely of gases and are mostly made of hydrogen. Stars are born in hot gas and dust. Color, temperature, and size depend on the star's mass. Star colors can vary from slightly reddish, orange, and yellow to white and blue.

static electricity: The accumulation of excess electric charge in a region that has poor electrical conductivity; the build-up of electric charge on the surface of objects.

stigma: In plants, a part of the pistil.

stomata (stoma): Openings in the leaf's surface that can open and close, allowing carbon dioxide to enter the plant's leaves.

stratus clouds: Clouds that are horizontal, layered clouds that appear to blanket the sky.

style: In plants, a part of the pistil.

Sun: The star that is the central body of the Solar System, around which objects including planets revolve.

survival of the fittest: Those with the most advantageous adaptations survive.

tadpole: An early stage of a frog or toad; must live in water; has gills and a tail; develops lungs and limbs, which allow the frog or toad to live in water and on land.

taxonomy: Classification of living things based on physical characteristics.

temperature: Measure related to the average kinetic energy of the molecules of a substance. For example, in Kelvin degrees, this measure is directly proportional to the average kinetic energy of the molecules.

texture: Visual and tactile quality of a surface; characterized by size, shape, arrangement, and proportions of parts.

thermal energy: The most internal energy of objects created by vibration and movement; a form of kinetic energy; transferred as heat.

tides: The rise and fall of the oceans produced by the attraction of the Moon and Sun.

trachea: Top of the respiratory system; air enters the body through the trachea.

trade winds: Warm, steady breezes that blow continuously; act as the steering force for tropical storms.

transpiration: Loss of water through leaves.

tsunami: A tidal wave that occurs as a result of an underwater earthquake.

tubers: Underground stems that can produce new plants.

unbalanced forces: Forces that always cause a change in motion, are in opposite direction to each other, and are not equal in size. When two unbalanced forces are exerted in opposite directions, their combined force is equal to the difference between the two forces and exerted in the direction of the larger force.

Uranus: Seventh planet from the Sun; third largest planet.

urinary system: Removes waste from the body.

vacuoles: Large vesicles.

validity: The degree to which a measure accurately assesses the specific concept it is designed to measure.

variable: Something that is manipulated through experimentation.

vascular plants: Plants that have tissues, called vascular tissues, which move water and nutrients from one part of the plant to another.

vascular tissues: Tissues that move water and nutrients from one part of a plant to another.

Venus: Second planet from the Sun.

vertebrates: Animals that have a backbone.

vesicle: Piece of the Golgi complex's membrane that pinches off in a small bubble that transports the lipids and proteins to other parts of the cell or outside the cell.

virus: An infectious agent that replicates within living hosts.

volcano: Geologic formation that occurs when magma erupts from below the Earth's surface.

volume: Another property of matter; the amount of cubic space that an object occupies.

water birds: Birds that live in the water, have webbed feet for swimming, or long legs for wading; examples include cranes, ducks, and loons.

water cycle: The cycle of the Earth's water between the oceans and atmosphere; includes evaporation, condensation, and precipitation.

weather: The state of the atmosphere, including wind, temperature, moisture, and precipitation.

weight: The measure of Earth's pull of gravity on an object. It is measured in pounds (English or traditional system) or grams (metric system). An object's weight on Earth is the force that Earth's gravity exerts on an object with a specific mass.

wind: Horizontal movement of air.

xylem: Type of vascular tissue.

zooflagellate: Protozoan that moves with flagella.

Mathematics

acute triangle: A triangle in which all three angles measure less than 90 degrees.

area: The amount of surface that a shape covers; measured in square units.

associative property: When more than two terms are added together or multiplied together, the order in which the terms are paired does not affect the sum or product. In addition, the sum of three or more addends can be found in any order: $a + (b + c) = (a + b) + c$. In multiplication, the product of three or more factors can be found in any order: $a \cdot (b \cdot c) = (a \cdot b) \cdot c$.

attributes: Aspects of a shape that are particular to a specific shape.

automaticity: Instant recall of a math fact without having to think about it.

average: The sum of a set of quantities divided by the total number of quantities; also known as *mean*.

bar graph: A statistical graph used to compare quantities; may be made up of all vertical bars or all horizontal bars; used mainly for purposes of comparison.

base: Side of a polygon in relation to a height; side of a polygon that forms a 90-degree angle with the height.

circumference: The distance around a circle.

classifications: Those names given to shapes that use properties to classify but also take into account the relationships between different classifications of shapes. Classifications use the properties of shapes to lead to a hierarchical structure.

commutative property: The order in which you add two terms together or multiply two terms together does not affect the sum or product. In addition, the order of addition can be reversed: $a + b = b + a$. In multiplication, the order of multiplication can be reversed: $a \cdot b = b \cdot a$.

composite numbers: Numbers composed of several whole-number factors. For example, 30 is a composite number because it is composed of several whole-number factors other than 1 and itself, like 2, 3, 5, 6, 10, and 15.

computation algorithm: A set of predefined steps applicable to a class of problems that gives the correct result in every case when the steps are carried out correctly. *See also* computation strategy (National Governors Association Center for Best Practices & Council of Chief State School Officers, 2014). This may include invented or standard algorithms or strategies.

computation strategy: Purposeful manipulations that may be chosen for specific problems, may not have a fixed order, and may be aimed at converting one problem into another. *See also* computation algorithm (National Governors Association Center for Best Practices & Council of Chief State School Officers, 2014).

cone: A three-dimensional figure that has one circular base and a separate face that comes to a vertex point; similar to a pyramid, but with a circular base.

congruent: Exactly the same; congruent figures are the same shape and same size.

coordinate system: A system of two or three dimensions that allows for the positioning of points, lines, and shapes in space.

cylinder: A three-dimensional figure that has two circular bases and a curved rectangular face between them; similar to a prism.

decagon: Ten-sided polygon.

decimals: A set of numbers based on powers of ten. They are fractions expressed in a decimal notation. The denominators of these fractions are powers of 10 (like 10, 100, or 1,000). For example, 0.6 (read six-tenths) is equivalent to $\frac{6}{10}$ (dividing the numerator by the denominator).

denominator: In a fraction of the form $\frac{a}{b}$, where a is any integer and b is any integer except zero, b represents the denominator of the fraction. It expresses the number of equal parts by which the whole is divided. For example, in the fraction $\frac{4}{8}$, the 8 indicates that the whole was divided into eight equal parts.

dilation: A shrinking or expanding of a figure.

distributive property: When a sum or difference is multiplied by a common term, each part of the sum or difference can be multiplied by the common term and then added or subtracted. A number multiplied by a sum/difference can be found by multiplying each term of the sum/difference by the multiplier: $a \cdot (b + c) = a \cdot b + a \cdot c$.

dodecagon: Twelve-sided polygon.

edges: Intersection of two faces of a polyhedron.

equilateral triangle: A triangle in which all three sides are the same length.

exponent: A number or symbol (like a letter), placed above and to the right of the expression, which is called the base of the expression to which the exponent applies. The exponent indicates the number of times the base is used as a factor multiplied by itself. For example, the exponent 3 in the expression 8^3 indicates the 8 is multiplied by itself three times: $8 \times 8 \times 8$. The exponent x in the expression $(a + b)^x$ indicates $(a + b)$ is multiplied by itself x times.

exponential notation: A way to represent repeated multiplication in a simpler manner. For example, 3 multiplied by itself four times or $3 \times 3 \times 3 \times 3$ can be represented as 3^4, which is equal to 81. Remember that 3^4 is _not_ equivalent to 3×4 or 4×3.

faces: Surfaces of a polyhedron.

factors: Any of the numbers or symbols that you multiply together to get another number or product. For example, 5 and 6 are factors of 30 because $5 \times 6 = 30$; similarly, 1 and 30 are factors of 30 because $1 \times 30 = 30$.

fluency: In mathematics, it is the ability to recall facts with speed, accuracy, and automaticity. Fluency requires time to develop with proper understanding of the operations involved. Sufficient practice, conceptual building blocks, and extra support should be provided at each grade level.

fractions: Can be expressed as a ratio of two whole numbers, $\frac{a}{b}$, where $b > 0$; for example, $\frac{1}{2}$, $\frac{2}{3}$, and $\frac{12}{4}$.

frequency: For a collection of data, the number of items in a given category.

frequency table: A table for organizing a set of data that shows the number of pieces of data that fall within given intervals or categories.

geometry: The branch of mathematics that deals with the deduction of the properties, measurement, and relationships of points, lines, angles, and figures in space from their defining conditions by means of certain assumed properties of space.

graph: A representation of data that compares two variables or displays information in a pictorial or graphical form.

greatest common factor (GFC): In a set of numbers, the largest whole number that is a factor of all the given numbers. For example, the GCF of 30 and 20 is 10, which is the largest whole-number common factor that divides both numbers evenly.

height: Minimum distance between two bases; perpendicular distance from one base to another; perpendicular distance from a vertex to a base.

heptagon: Seven-sided polygon.

hexagon: Six-sided polygon.

integers: Integers represent whole numbers that can be positive, negative, or zero. For example, 23, –23, and 0 are all integers. On a number line, negative numbers are on the left side of zero and positive numbers on the right. An integer without a sign is assumed to be a positive number. All integers can be expressed as fractions, but not all fractions can be expressed as integers ($\frac{-25}{5}$ is a fraction that can be expressed as the integer –5).

irrational numbers: This set of numbers includes real numbers that cannot be written as the ratio of two integers. This includes infinite and non-repeating decimals. For example, the square root of $2 = \sqrt{2} = 1.414213...$ and pi = $\pi = 3.141592....$

isosceles triangle: A triangle in which at least two sides are the same length.

iteration: This process is used to express the length of an object as a whole number of length units, by laying multiple copies of a shorter object (the length unit) end to end. The student also needs to understand that the length measurement of an object is the number of same-size length units that span it with no gaps or overlaps (National Governors Association Center for Best Practices & Council of Chief State School Officers, 2014).

kite: A quadrilateral with adjacent sides of equal length and opposite sides of different lengths.

learning progressions: Involve narrative documents describing the progression of a topic across a number of grade levels, which are informed by research on students' cognitive development and logical structure of mathematics. Also, they can be used to explain why standards are sequenced in a given manner, point out cognitive difficulties and pedagogical solutions, and give more detail on particularly challenging areas of mathematics (The Arizona Board of Regents, 2007, ime.math.arizona.edu/progressions).

least common multiple (LCM): In a set of numbers, the smallest non-zero number that all of the given numbers divide into. For example, the LCM of 30 and 20 is 60.

line graph: Statistical graph that uses lines to show how values change over time.

manipulatives: Small objects that can be touched and moved about by students in ways that enable descriptions and learning to come alive. They are used to help students internalize mathematics concepts and work with abstract ideas at a concrete level; for example, base-ten blocks are used to help students understand place value ideas.

mean: The sum of a set of quantities divided by the total number of quantities; also known as *average*.

median: The middle quantity of a set of data when arranged according to size (or numerical order); for an even number of quantities, the median is the average of the middle two quantities.

mode: The number that occurs with the greatest frequency in a set of data. There may be one or more modes or no mode for a set of data.

modeling: The process of choosing and using appropriate mathematics and statistics to analyze empirical situations, to understand them better, and to improve decisions. Modeling links classroom mathematics and statistics to everyday life, work, and decision-making (National Governors Association Center for Best Practices & Council of Chief State School Officers, 2014; see www.corestandards.org/Math/Practice for more information).

multiples: The products of any numbers or symbols that you multiply together; for example, 30 is a multiple of 5 and 6 because $5 \times 6 = 30$; similarly, 30 is a multiple of 1 and 30 because $1 \times 30 = 30$.

natural numbers: They are the counting numbers (1, 2, 3, 4, 5, …).

nonagon: Nine-sided polygon.

number: A number represents the cardinality or the idea of how many objects are contained in a set.

numeral: A numeral is the symbolic representation of a numerical quantity; for example, the numeral written as "5" represents symbolically how many objects are contained in a set—in this case, five objects.

numerator: In a fraction of the form $\frac{a}{b}$, where a is any integer and b is any integer except zero, a represents the numerator of the fraction. The numerator expresses the number of equal parts taken from the whole after the whole is divided into equal parts. For example, in the fraction $\frac{4}{8}$, the 4 indicates the number of equal parts that were taken from a whole that was divided into 8 equal parts.

obtuse triangle: A triangle in which one angle measures more than 90 degrees.

octagon: Eight-sided polygon.

operations: The operations indicate what is to be done with the numbers involved in a given mathematical situation. The main four operations are addition, subtraction, multiplication, and division.

parallelogram: A quadrilateral with exactly two pairs of parallel sides.

pentagon: Five-sided polygon.

percent: Refers to the number of parts out of 100 parts; for example, 76 percent (written 76%) indicates that you have 76 parts out of 100 parts.

perimeter: The distance around a polygon.

pictograph: Diagram or graph using pictured objects, icons, or symbols to convey ideas or information.

polygon: Two-dimensional figure that is closed and contains at least three straight sides that meet only at corners.

polyhedron: Three-dimensional figure in which all faces are polygons.

prime number: A number with exactly two whole-number factors (1 and the number itself). The first several prime numbers are 1, 2, 3, 5, 7, 11, 13, and 17.

prism: A polyhedron that has two congruent and parallel faces, with all other faces being parallelograms.

properties: Aspects of a shape that define the shape.

proportion: A statement indicating that two ratios are equal; for example, at the market today, if four apples cost $1.20, then eight apples should cost $2.40.

pyramid: A polyhedron with one base; all other faces are triangles that intersect at a common point called a vertex.

quadrilateral: Four-sided polygon.

range: The difference between the largest quantity and smallest quantity in a data set.

rate: A ratio in which the measuring units describing two quantities being compared are different. For example, Gill drove the car at 65 miles per hour, or you can get 12 cans for $3. *See also* unit rate.

ratio: The comparison of two numbers or quantities; another use of fractions.

rational numbers: A set of numbers that contains integers and positive and negative fractions; expressed as the ratio of two integers, $\frac{a}{b}$, where $b > 0$; for example, $\frac{2}{5}$, $-\frac{3}{8}$, or $\frac{7}{1} = 7$.

real numbers: Include both rational numbers (such as 42, –42, $\frac{1}{2}$, and 0.25) and irrational numbers (such as pi, π, or the square root of 2, $\sqrt{2}$). Real numbers can be thought of as points on an infinite number line.

rectangle: A parallelogram with four right angles.

reflection: Mirror image.

rhombus: A parallelogram with all equal sides; opposite sides are parallel and opposite angles are equal.

right triangle: A triangle in which one angle measures exactly 90 degrees.

rotation: Moving a figure by turning it around a given point; a turn.

scalene triangle: A triangle in which all three sides are different lengths.

similar: Figures of the same shape, but a different size.

slope: Rate of change of one variable in relation to a second variable.

sphere: A three-dimensional figure in which all points on the surface are the same distance from the center of the sphere; a ball.

square: A parallelogram with all equal sides and four right angles.

subitize: The ability to look at a number pattern and instantly recognize the quantity in the arrangement without counting. For example, the student is able to instantly recognize the quantities on the faces of a die represented by dot patterns. It is also considered an important component of number sense.

symbolic level: A cognitive level that involves the use of symbols to represent mathematical ideas. In this case, you either read or say the words representing the mathematical idea. For example, using the numeral "5" or the number name "five" to represent the numerical value of number five.

transitivity principle for indirect measurement: If the length of object A is greater than the length of object B, and the length of object B is greater than the length of object C, then the length of object A is greater than the length of object C. This principle applies to measurement of other quantities as well (National Governors Association Center for Best Practices & Council of Chief State School Officers, 2014).

translation: Moving a figure along a straight line from one location to another; a slide.

trapezoid: A quadrilateral with exactly one pair of parallel sides.

triangle: Three-sided polygon.

unit rate: When the second term in the rate is 1, the rate is referred to as unit rate. For example, Natalie types 36 words per minute, or Samuel earns $14 per hour.

variable: A quantity that may assume any numerical value or set of numerical values.

vertex: Intersection of two edges of a polyhedron.

volume: The amount of space a shape contains. It is measured in cubic units.

whole numbers: Whole numbers are natural numbers and zero. Natural numbers are the counting numbers (1, 2, 3, 4, 5, . . .).

Mathematics Reference Sheet

Area

Triangle		$A = \dfrac{1}{2}bh$
Rectangle		$A = lw$
Trapezoid		$A = \dfrac{1}{2}h(b_1 + b_2)$
Parallelogram		$A = bh$
Circle		$A = \pi r^2$ $C = \pi d = 2\pi r$

Key	
b = base	d = diameter
h = height	r = radius
l = length	A = area
w = width	C = circumference
$S.A.$ = surface area	V = volume
	B = area of base

Use $\pi = 3.14$ or $\dfrac{22}{7}$.

Surface Area

1. Surface area of a prism or pyramid = the sum of the areas of all faces of the figure
2. Surface area of a cylinder = the sum of the areas of the two bases + the area of its rectangular wrap

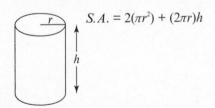

$S.A. = 2(\pi r^2) + (2\pi r)h$

3. Surface area of a sphere: $S.A. = 4\pi r^2$

Volume

1. Volume of a prism or cylinder equals (area of base) times (height): $V = Bh$
2. Volume of a pyramid or cone equals $\dfrac{1}{3}$ times (area of base) times (height): $V = \dfrac{1}{3}Bh$
3. Volume of a sphere: $V = \dfrac{4}{3}\pi r^3$

Pythagorean Theorem: $a^2 + b^2 = c^2$

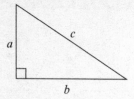

Simple Interest Formula: $I = prt$

I = simple interest, p = principal, r = rate, t = time

Distance Formula: $d = rt$

d = distance, r = rate, t = time

Given a line containing points (x_1, y_1) and (x_2, y_2),

■ Slope of line $= \dfrac{y_2 - y_1}{x_2 - x_1}$

■ Distance between two points

$$= \sqrt{(x_2 - x_1)^2 + (y_2 - y_1)^2}$$

■ Midpoint between two points $= \left(\dfrac{x_2 + x_1}{2}, \dfrac{y_2 + y_1}{2} \right)$

Conversions	
1 yard = 3 feet = 36 inches	1 cup = 8 fluid ounces
1 mile = 1,760 yards = 5,280 feet	1 pint = 2 cups
1 acre = 43,560 square feet	1 quart = 2 pints
1 hour = 60 minutes	1 gallon = 4 quarts
1 minute = 60 seconds	
	1 pound = 16 ounces
1 liter = 1000 milliliters = 1000 cubic centimeters	1 ton = 2,000 pounds
1 meter = 100 centimeters = 1000 millimeters	
1 kilometer = 1000 meters	
1 gram = 1000 milligrams	
1 kilogram = 1000 grams	

Note: Metric numbers with four digits are written without a comma (e.g., 2543 grams). For metric numbers with more than four digits, a space is used instead of a comma (e.g., 24 300 liters).